Cooperation in Economy and Society

SOCIETY FOR ECONOMIC
ANTHROPOLOGY (SEA) MONOGRAPHS

Dolores Koenig, American University
General Editor, Society for Economic Anthropology

Monographs for the Society for Economic Anthropology contain original essays that explore the connections between economics and social life. Each year's volume focuses on a different theme in economic anthropology. Earlier volumes were published with the University Press of America, Inc. (#1–15, 17) and Rowman & Littlefield Publishers, Inc. (#16). The monographs are now published jointly by AltaMira Press and the Society for Economic Anthropology (https://seawiki.wikidot.com).

No. 18 Jean Ensminger, ed., *Theory in Economic Anthropology*
No. 19 Jeffrey H. Cohen and Norbert Dannhaeuser, eds., *Economic Development: An Anthropological Approach*
No. 20 Gracia Clark, ed., *Gender at Work in Economic Life*
No. 21 Cynthia Werner and Duran Bell, eds., *Values and Valuables: From the Sacred to the Symbolic*
No. 22 Lillian Trager, ed., *Migration and Economy: Global and Local Dynamics*
No. 23 E. Paul Durrenberger and Judith Martí, eds., *Labor in Cross-Cultural Perspective*
No. 24 Richard Wilk, ed., *Fast Food/Slow Food*
No. 25 Lisa Cliggett and Christopher A. Pool, eds., *Economies and the Transformation of Landscape*
No. 26 Katherine E. Browne and B. Lynne Milgram, eds., *Economics and Morality: Anthropological Approaches*
No. 27 Eric C. Jones and Arthur D. Murphy, eds., *The Political Economy of Hazards and Disasters*
No. 28 Robert C. Marshall, ed., *Cooperation in Economy and Society*

To find more books in this series, go to www.altamirapress.com/series.

Cooperation in Economy and Society

Edited by
Robert C. Marshall

ALTAMIRA
PRESS

A division of
ROWMAN & LITTLEFIELD PUBLISHERS, INC.
Lanham • New York • Toronto • Plymouth, UK

Published by AltaMira Press
A division of Rowman & Littlefield Publishers, Inc.
A wholly owned subsidiary of The Rowman & Littlefield Publishing Group, Inc.
4501 Forbes Boulevard, Suite 200, Lanham, Maryland 20706
http://www.altamirapress.com

Estover Road, Plymouth PL6 7PY, United Kingdom

British Library Cataloguing in Publication Information Available

Library of Congress Cataloging-in-Publication Data

Cooperation in economy and society / edited by Robert C. Marshall.
p. cm. — (Society for economic anthropology monograph series ; v.28)
Includes bibliographical references and index.
ISBN 978-0-7591-1981-9 (hardcover : alk. paper) — ISBN 978-0-7591-1983-3 (ebook)
1. Cooperation. 2. Cooperative societies. 3. Institutional cooperation. 4. Economic anthropology. I. Marshall, Robert C., 1948–.
GN448.8.C66 2011
306.3—dc22 2010018147

∞™ The paper used in this publication meets the minimum requirements of American National Standard for Information Sciences—Permanence of Paper for Printed Library Materials, ANSI/NISO Z39.48-1992.

Printed in the United States of America

Contents

Introduction vii
Robert C. Marshall

Part I: Cooperation and Competition

1 From Reciprocity to Trade: How Cooperative Infrastructures Form the Basis of Human Socioeconomic Evolution 3
Rahul Oka and Agustín Fuentes

2 Market Integration and Prosocial Behavior: Evidence from the Standard Cross-Cultural Sample 29
E. Anthon Eff and Malcolm McLaren Dow

3 Critique of Reciprocity: Shifting Uses and Meanings of *Ayni* among Andean Groups 55
Matthew Bird

4 Commerce and Cooperation among the Classic Maya: The Chunchucmil Case 81
Scott R. Hutson, Bruce H. Dahlin, and Daniel Mazeau

Part II: Cooperation and Hierarchy

5 Cooperation in Conflict: Negotiating Inequality in Midwestern U.S. Hog Contracting 107
Ronald Rich

6 Cooperation, Equality, and Difference: Loyalty and Accountability in Ghana's Marketplace Commodity Groups 129
Gracia Clark

7 Testing the Limits of Nonzero: Cooperation, Conflict, and Hierarchy in Ancient Near Eastern Marginal Environments 149
Benjamin W. Porter

Part III: Cooperation and Cooperatives

8 Cooperation in the Informal Economy: The Case of Recyclers at a Brazilian Garbage Dump 175
Kathleen Millar

9 Is It Possible to Overcome the "Tragedy of *Ubuntu*"? The Journey of a Black Women's Economic Empowerment Group in South Africa 195
Katrina T. Greene

10 The Normative Construction of U.S. Agricultural Cooperatives, 1900–2008 215
Julie Hogeland

Part IV: Cooperation Rising

11 Creating Common Grazing Rights on Private Parcels: How New Rules Produce Incentives for Cooperative Land Management 239
Carolyn K. Lesorogol

12 Cooperation and the Development of Conservation Laws: The Case of the Maine Lobster Industry 259
James M. Acheson

Index 279

About the Editor and Contributors 291

Introduction

Robert C. Marshall

Among anthropologists, political scientists, economists, evolutionary psychologists, and biologists, interest in human cooperation has recently taken off. This strong interdisciplinary effort now focuses on how our capacity to learn and our capacity to make choices together influence the range of possibilities for cooperative human interaction and relationships. The chapters of this volume each take up a thread leading to this central question, searching for answers that explain enduring and emerging patterns of cooperation. And as these chapters show, we cooperate with one another widely, in relations of exchange and reciprocity, in hierarchies and as equals, in relations of production as well as distribution, in experiments on sharing, monitoring, and punishing as well as in daily life, and in institutions that intentionally foster cooperative behaviors.

This renewal of interest in human cooperation held the spotlight with the awarding of the 2009 Bank of Sweden Nobel Prize in Economics to Elinor Ostrom and Oliver Williamson, whose work offers alternatives to the now-orthodox assertion that cooperative participation is generally unwise, if not impossible, for rational well-informed egoists. But how can it not be rational for us to vote, make decisions together, cooperate at work, punish defectors from social norms, monitor one another's performance, provide ourselves with public goods, share common property, and indeed, join together in collective action at all? When cooperation is such a universally observed feature of human culture in all the world's societies, how can it be less rational for us to cooperate than to compete, or obey orders?

Some conventional economists have concluded that we cannot serve ourselves effectively or efficiently through cooperation; others suggest that working together cannot be in our self-interest. This is nonsense; in many cases cooperation clearly is in our self-interest. The deep problem we face is that *Homo economicus*, an abstraction, cannot do these things real people actually do and still act as theory requires, in a way that allows markets to reach a competitive equilibrium, without which they cannot provide stable prices.

Yet even as early as the 18th century, economists recognized the limits of the invisible hand of self-interest. Adam Smith acknowledged that markets required Thomas Hobbes's Leviathan—a state strong enough to ensure "the certainty of being able to exchange all that surplus part of the produce of his own labor" (Smith 1937:15 [1776]). *Homo economicus* could not act effectively without Leviathan's support from the start. When he bargains with another like himself to reach a mutually agreeable price, he cannot then carry out his exchange at this price without the assistance of Leviathan's conspicuously visible hand. And now we see that transactions themselves are costly; this was the pathbreaking insight of the New Institutional Economics (NIE).

Transaction cost analysis examines "the comparative costs of planning, adapting and monitoring task completion under alternative governance structures" (Williamson 1985:2). We can try different ways to keep ourselves honest, but none of them are free. Ronald Coase (1937) argues that firms, organizations that rely on authority to reduce competition, emerge historically from market failure to economize on transaction costs. Foremost among these are efforts such as monitoring to ensure compliance with agreements. Nor does Leviathan keep us from temptation cheap: Coase estimates transaction costs, the single greatest expense of institutions and individuals, at a stunning "50 percent of the gross national product" for the United States (Coase 1993:63). For insights such as these, he won the 1991 Nobel Prize in Economics.

Douglass North developed the NIE concept of transaction costs further, in the direction of economic growth and development. Nowhere can the necessary costs of contract enforcement be taken for granted. For North, the absence of a reliable means to enforce contracts emerged as "the most important source of both historical stagnation and contemporary underdevelopment in the Third World" (1990:54). This broad and fruitful line of inquiry into relations between markets and institutions focused on the connection between two processes: how prices are reached in markets and how transfers are subsequently effected. It is the relation between these two matters, the agreement and its performance, that is so deeply vexed. The source of "friction" in transactions is called "moral hazard," which means simply that people might be tempted not to do what they have said they will. For his analysis, Douglass North too won the Nobel Prize in Economics, in 1993.

The depth of the problem of living up to our explicit agreements is clear, but the source of this problem has been less so. Hobbes offered the specious explanation that we are betrayed not by our rationality, but by our baser selves, our emotionality: "He that performeth first, has no assurance that the other will perform after; because the bonds of words are too weak to bridle men's ambition, avarice, anger and other Passions, without the fear of some coercive Power" (1955:89–90 [1651]).

As human beings, we are both rational and emotional, but it cannot make sense to simply blame our emotional nature for our failures to be more cooperative. Acting less emotionally will not make us more cooperative or less conniving. Anthropology reveals why we end up paying half our GNP to keep ourselves honest: ironically enough, our immensely social intelligence makes it all too easy put ourselves in one another's shoes as we examine the possible consequences of our actions. For the purposes of fostering sociality and prosocial behavior, this predisposition might be thought a good thing. Certainly we encourage it in each other as much as we can. But such propensities do not make markets work.

Anthropology constantly reaffirms our knowledge that we were never "solitary," however "poore, nasty, brutish and short" was the life Hobbes imagined we lived before we surrendered our liberty to Leviathan. It is not the shortcomings of our brute nature, then, but the profound connection between two of our most evolved features, empathy and foresight, which leads to what Henrich and Henrich (2007:43) call the "Core Dilemma" for human cooperation, the difficulties we face in sustaining "the conditions that allow cooperators to benefit other cooperators."

Game theory, emerging in the mid-20th century, offers an in-depth analytic understanding of this dilemma. Specifically, the game known as the "prisoner's dilemma" identifies the foundation of Hobbes's and the NIE's insight that promises are made to be broken. This game has two basic properties germane to the problem at hand. First, what both of two players get as an outcome of their interaction is a result not only of what ego decides to do but also what alter decides to do, even though both decide and act independently of each other. Second, they cannot take turns exploiting each other. The situation is such that each player has the same two courses open: to cooperate or cheat. This yields an outcome payoff matrix with four possibilities: (1) the players might both cooperate with each other, (2) they might both cheat each other, or (3) and (4) either might choose to cooperate while the other cheats.

What makes this dilemma so devilish is that the possible payoffs for these choices have the following order of value. The temptation to defect from the agreement (T) is greater than the reward for cooperation (R), which in turn is greater than the punishment for mutual defection (P), in its turn more valuable than the sucker's payoff (S). In brief, $T > R > P > S$. Nor can players get rich taking in each other's laundry, such that $R > (T + S)/2$. Now we can understand why Smith requires Leviathan both in theory and in history. Enforcement mechanisms remain necessary even while markets work so much less effectively than their theoretical optimum predicted under the assumption of cost-free transactions. If it is in our basic nature "to truck and barter," it can be no real surprise when the *Oxford English Dictionary* tells us that the modern English word *barter* has arisen from the Old French *barater*, "to deceive, to cheat."

A pair of rational egoists able to put themselves in each other's shoes and imagine the consequences of each other's actions, therefore, find themselves prisoners of a dilemma. If they have been able to agree on a rate of exchange, they have also learned that each would keep what he or she could if the other would hand it over first. The process of bargaining has required and revealed that each would prefer to have all that is available, keeping his or her own property and gaining all the other would have given for it. Each has learned one cannot transfer property to another unilaterally without additional material assurances that the other will do the same. We can assign the following plausible values to T, R, P, and S to illustrate exchange at an agreed-on price as one more expression of the prisoner's dilemma:

T = 6 (the value of what alter has to ego, and vice versa)
R = 1 (the value of what ego has to alter, and vice versa, minus the value of what ego has to ego, alter to alter)
P = −1 (the transaction cost of learning that neither can release what he has to the other first)
S = −5 (the loss of what one has at stake in the exchange)

This set of values satisfies the second requirement ($R > (T + S)/2$) as well: $1 > 0.5$.

To the extent players are rational and self-interested, they see the dilemma facing them clearly. If only human beings were not so deeply rational and so thoroughly social, so empathetic, so imaginative, so easily able and willing and so often encouraged to see the world through alter's eyes, perhaps market exchange by and of itself could truly be a perpetual motion machine producing endless, cost-free human value. Instead, we find ourselves in the nonviolent "warre of every man against every man" that characterizes a fully competitive marketplace.

If as Hayek has it then, that "markets are marvels," they are expensive marvels. What additional possibilities beyond reliance on markets or bureaucracies have there been and are there now for humans to increase value in their lives through interaction with one another? This volume approaches that question through four separate sections. The first section explores the different human relationships and social institutions that encourage cooperation where competition reigns. The second section focuses on hierarchies to understand better when cooperation does not mean mere obedience. The third section looks specifically at cooperatives, specialized institutions designed to enhance cooperation, and the extent to which they realize their own promises. The last section, "Cooperation Rising," looks closely at attempts to regulate access to common property resources.

COOPERATION AND COMPETITION

"At the request of the Subcommittee on Competitive Cooperative [*sic*] Habits of the Committee on Personality and Culture of the Social Science Research Council," Margaret Mead (1937:v) undertook a review of the ethnography on the topic at that time. Her introduction to the studies in the volume insisted that researchers of all disciplines must take into account "the way in which a given type of culture is laid down in the human organism" (Mead 1937:2). Her work built on an anthropology that connected conceptions of both evolution and culture to the assertion that, unlike goods produced for markets, people are not fungible. Human beings come with as well as develop those qualities and identities that fit them to diverse specific relationships. The first section of this volume identifies some of those qualities and identities.

Oka and Fuentes show the possibilities for collective survival in hostile social environments that also offer substantial opportunities. They compare vastly different societies: early hominid populations in East Africa and premodern networks of commercial ethnic traders around the Indian Ocean. Their model offers important potential for understanding "bushy" hominid competition on the one hand, and widespread long-term ethnic trading networks on the other. In both situations, internal cooperation could tip the scale toward survival in ecologies that separate related species from direct competition. Their argument treats closely related species as a form of ethnicity; this is a novel way to examine the possibilities for the evolution of clustered identities that Henrich and Henrich (2007) call "ethnicity." They suggest that these identities can foster the growth of a diversity of adaptive strategies, including prosocial norms that favor cooperation within groups whose members can identify one another easily.

Dow and Eff challenge the findings of Henrich et al. (2004) that markets foster other forms of prosocial behavior to the extent that they integrate a society's economic activity. Using available cross-cultural data, Dow and Eff are unable to validate this assertion. Instead, they conclude that markets by themselves are not a sufficient condition for broader prosocial behavior.

Perhaps the foremost relationship available to those who would exchange with one another away from the anonymity of the market, before or beyond the reach of Leviathan, is that of reciprocity, that each will do what the other has done, by turns. In a world of relationships, there is no initiating exchange, only returning what one has received; each return provokes another one, and the circle never closes.

The analysis of reciprocity that Bird develops takes up a theme that Henrich and Henrich (2007:51–52) left undeveloped, that the concept of reciprocity hides within itself two quite different characterizations of cooperative relationships. The first meaning is linked to the connection ascribed to "the gift." In this case, reciprocity is used outside market contexts as a means through which two partners to a prolonged exchange may use the future to replace the effects of Leviathan in the market. If people exchanging at a mutually agreed-on price in markets learn that they are the sort of people who would take what they can get and give nothing in return, then the gift allows both participants to believe themselves to be generous in giving. Mauss (1967 [1925]), however, pointed out many years ago that the "precommodity" *they* are in fact no better than the *we* whose lives are lived among markets. *They* find keeping one another honest no easier than we do. There is no escape from the strategic nature of our sociality that what we get from interaction is a result not only of what we do but what our alter does as well.

The second aspect of reciprocity is its use to explain the origin and functions of institutions needed to lower transaction costs and foster market exchange; here the concept is linked directly to the existence of markets. However, Henrich and Henrich (2007:51) identify a core problem: how to handle such institutions as warfare, voting, recycling, or even food sharing in small-scale societies. Their answer is the firm assertion that "direct reciprocity cannot be used to explain cooperation in large groups." If a duo may imagine that together they have the key to the cornucopia and act on this basis until they discover they are wrong, what hope do "*n*-persons" engaged in collective action have? Bird's detailed analysis of secular economic trends and sequential modes of exchange in the Andes generally favors North's explanation. Insofar as "extra-legal solutions in places like Gamarra fail to achieve economies of scale," Bird offers in turn a serious critique of exchange models alone. This is because the reciprocity of "then" is not the reciprocity of "now." Rather, "we must understand the concept by interpreting it within the context of how societies organize to produce sustenance."

Whether market relations, trade, or reciprocal exchange might foster cooperation, they are not the only sorts of relations that do so. While it is true that we lack the mathematical sophistication to model cooperative relations involving more than two people at once, it is easy enough in principle to see that the very problem that Smith addresses, the division of labor, might be a source of organized cooperation. Hutson and his coauthors look at cooperation as a set of processes within local relationships that integrate exchange and production. They show in turn how these can lead to unexpected levels of complexity. This chapter reverses Smith's and Hobbes's historical sequence; in Chunchcumil, local cooperation in production and distribution led to the certainty of being able to exchange surplus over great distances. While trade and distribution were located in the hands of elites elsewhere on the Yucatán Peninsula, artifact-rich and population-dense sites on its northwest tip developed as long-distance trade centers with more egalitarian production strategies. Although poor in rainfall and soil quality, elites cooperated with one another in the absence of a strong central state to maintain local markets, especially for the obsidian trade that made subsistence possible.

COOPERATION AND HIERARCHY

Today, although we may take for granted the notion that organizations can offer solutions to problems of cooperation and market exchange, we know little about how organizations actually operate to solve such problems. Hobbes would say that we can agree on nothing else except willingly to shed our independence to Leviathan, but today, this is naturalized by the fact that we *do* live in states and we *do* function in many instances in hierarchical organizations. To say that fear of the violence of the state keeps us honest tells us nothing about why states act as they do. The very counterposition of market and hierarchy requires at least some nonmarket processes within hierarchies. March (1966) and Latour (1986) have both argued that our current conception of "power" as the ability to get one's way socially leads ultimately to paradox and contradiction. In this section, the chapters all cast doubt on the standard notion that relations of hierarchy in economic settings operate directly through obedience, devotion, or threat. Cooperation inside hierarchical relations is not simpler than outside them, nor can it be reduced to pair-wise interactions.

Rich offers a view of hierarchical relations among midwestern pork producers that draws us into the complexity of such relationships. He also offers a fundamental paradox of exchange within hierarchy. If two people in a long-term relationship agree to exchange again and again, does the hierarchy within their relationship give one an advantage over the other? Within the notion of exchange, can we usefully develop a concept of advantage?

Here, farmers who agree to raise another owner's pigs for market have a relatively free hand in their treatment of the animals, but the pigs' owners, each of whose operations span multiple sites and pig-raising contracts, have unilateral control over scheduling, many inputs, and fee payment when the pigs are marketed. Rich notes that the parties to this contract consciously use an emic understanding of "trust and honesty" as the basis for cooperation in resolving conflicts that may arise. In the same way that distortions in global maps are accumulated and displaced outside the immediate field of view so that Greenland comes to look larger than Africa when three dimensions are expressed in two, this form of personalism allows contracting to endure by serving the interests of economies of scale that in turn reproduce the hierarchical, integrated, and industrialized commodity/supply chains that capture, control, and exploit family farms.

On the other side of the world, in informal-sector Ghanaian produce markets operated and dominated by Asante women traders, we get a look at cooperative hierarchical relations in commodity production and marketing within the broader system. Clark notes that it is common for vulnerable traders to attach themselves to patrons who can shield them from uncertainty, but these relationships of dependency are not created through the extension of credit. Rather, the direction of credit reverses direction seasonally. Wholesalers in the Kumasi Central Market are not Renaissance princes who can demand support for "loans" that they and their creditors know will never be repaid. Market leaders do not fight their way to the top through financial manipulation; rather, they are chosen by a council of others like them heading the several different commodity markets.

Leaders' willingness to support regular business procedures and settle disputes quickly in these informal markets draws traders' voluntary compliance with the leaders' decisions. This leads in turn to the paradox that a trader who would take a dispute outside the market to a genuine court of law becomes herself an outlaw in the eyes of the market, a person with whom others will not want to do business. The converse of this internalization of dispute resolution points to the other major source of support for leadership. A market *ohemma* will use her skill, experience, and status to negotiate for her followers with people outside the market, that is, government officials, the military, chiefs, drivers, porters, and others. For their pains, these women have long been a target of government hostility and are regarded as a "nuisance" by city officials even in the current era of neoliberal reform.

While Clark and Rich offer us an opportunity to see the processes of cooperative interaction among actors within contemporary hierarchical structures, Porter portrays a long sequence of alternating competition and cooperation, community and hierarchy, among household-based organizations in the more marginal environment of the ancient Near East. Using the sensitive tool of the prisoner's dilemma, he examines decision-points within communities in sequential shifting conditions. Some conditions favor cooperation among strategic agents, while others favor competition. At the same time, there are always efforts to displace the resolution of the dilemma from the current transaction into the future, onto authority structures, symbol systems, technologies, and externalities. Porter notes that in the harsh circumstance of increasing aridity, flexibility in community form can be a functional alternative to increasing political complexity and consolidation among marginal agriculturalists.

COOPERATION AND COOPERATIVES

It is not possible in principle to identify those conditions in the world around us that favor either cooperation or competition, two strategies available in non-zero-sum games. When times get tough, do we come together, or is it every woman for herself? Even at the level of the transaction, we still cannot necessarily identify the conditions that favor one strategy over another. Integral to our environment is the field of possible strategies others too may choose. We are left to identify spheres of action in which one or another pattern of competition, cooperation, and authority might maintain a momentary hegemony against a shifting background.

When, in 1977, I first saw the effort people in Nakahara hamlet were putting into their spring festival, I was impressed. I said so to an elderly farmer of the hamlet. He responded, "Yes, this is a really good group of household heads. They are determined to make this a strong community. Nothing like their fathers, who were a stiff-necked lot, and couldn't get anything done, couldn't get along with each other at all." This did seem to be the case. As I began to analyze hamlet heads' decision and finance records and household budget records, from the 1930s into the 1970s, it became clear that I was witnessing the local expression of a phenomenon common at that time throughout Japan: the revival of community on the basis of a deliberate reinvigoration of traditions through a mix of invention, imagination, and increasing interest. The growing postwar prosperity of this community allowed all families to participate more and more fully in its affairs, and yet, as I looked deeper, I found at the root of this steadily growing wave of increased participation and cooperation the nourishing spring of status competition among the hamlet's leading families (Marshall 1985).

During this period, a process usually labeled "modernization" was predicted to spell the end for continued commitment to traditional forms of rural solidarity. Instead, competition, cooperation, and authority all worked together to create a rising sense of community and increasing community participation. "Before," the farmer told me, "people were so poor they could hardly manage anything at all. Now that they are prosperous, they all want to do things for the hamlet." Indeed, at the same time, new national governments began to encourage cooperative efforts, often through the creation of formal structures, as a way to encourage participation in local development. This section of this volume offers several chapters that look at formal and informal cooperatives. It asks the following questions: How do people go about creating institutions? What can they expect from their efforts? What would disappoint or satisfy them in their results? What would allow and encourage them to continue?

It is clear that the utmost degree of economic difficulty will not necessarily produce cooperation, nor does it raise a barrier to it. Millar documents the active organizational capacity of the poor and their capacity to fashion cooperative responses to the demands of their situation. At the same time, she shows that a government-sponsored cooperative is not necessarily cooperative in practice. She finds great solidarity and willingness to act together among the most independent of the dump workers who work together to pursue a variety of economic and political ends. In contrast, members of a formal sorter cooperative are cooperative in name only, and the organization is dominated by an undemocratic leadership with close ties to dump managers. The members show very little willingness to participate in collective action. In this instance, where everyone is poor and life is precarious, those with the greatest autonomy seek cooperation. For those who work in the formal cooperative, their actual relations of production appear to be typical of wage employment, and they act in terms of this constraint.

Greene introduces us to a group of women who are not poor and would like to do better yet. They are determined to cooperate with one another in an investment pool, but find themselves in a particularly unpleasant bind, a situation in which their own best motivation militates against their success in transforming themselves from employees with stable incomes on which they can live to businesswomen contributing as entrepreneurs and investors to a growing, and now free, South African economy. Rather than abandon community and seek personal success through a local adaptation of "acquisitive individualism," these women band together to pool their resources to increase their collective strength. Yet even while their ideological commitment to community values would appear to strengthen the possibilities available to them, they find themselves less and less able to take collective advantage of investment opportunities for a number of reasons, which Greene analyzes with great care.

Two mottoes kicked off Deng Xiaoping's economic reforms in China. The one everyone recalls now is "It is glorious to be rich." The second is less commonly recalled: "Some people will become prosperous first." If anyone in South Africa now might embrace the euphoria of the first slogan, many still find it difficult to understand whether the second slogan is the necessary means to that end, a description of history, or even a causal analysis: is there any sense in which this largely forgotten second slogan must or even can be necessarily true? The sort of acquisitive individualism capitalism seems to insist on contrasts strongly with the popular African proverb "When the people cross the river together, the crocodiles stay on the banks." And yet these particular participants in the Women's Economic Empowerment groups examined here continue to have "difficulty operating in a capitalist environment that states that those who can progress economically should do so even if that means leaving others behind." (See chapter 9 in this book, page 211.)

America's farmer cooperatives—businesses owned by farmers to market their products to manufacturers and final consumers—emerged to manage both risk and competition that farmers encountered in markets. One might have imagined that these institutions would then have enabled farmers to maintain family farming as a way of life in the face of industrialization. Hogeland argues compellingly that this was probably never the case. As the fundamental principles through which farmers engaged with markets continued to change through the 20th century, farmers' marketing cooperatives began to face intense pressures from large, global retailers to reduce costs, even as they themselves struggled to become global suppliers. It is an open question whether cooperative marketing arrangements originally undertaken by farmers in order to remain family farmers can even transform themselves successfully into components of that same industrialized agriculture they originally feared. Will they become part of the "value-added" chain, or will they fail? Even if they succeed, is there any prospect that the occupation of successful owners will still be farming, the life Wendell Berry (2009) lives and portrays?

COOPERATION RISING

The fourth and final section of this volume looks at the regulation of access to common property resources. Lesorogol takes up the issue of evolving norms and the emergence of cooperative behaviors in new contexts. In contrast to the problem facing Greene's women investors, the norms of community among northern Kenyan pastoralists made the transformation needed for reliable investment decisions difficult to achieve. The impetus for change came from outside, through imposed programs of land privatization. Communal sanctions now are used to enforce cooperation in maintaining shared grazing rights on parcels of land newly created through privatization. The willingness of the community to monitor and police these new norms has let them work in surprisingly effective ways. The new norms governing access to grazing lands have even proven adequate to the needs of those with large herds and those with more land than their herds can use.

The problem of how to handle communal property does not necessarily require the transformation of every aspect of community into products that can be marketed in formal markets with even partially enforceable contracts and laws. Distant authority often tends to make matters worse for local users. Ostrom (1992, 2005) demonstrated that local users can manage collective property not just adequately, but better than markets or hierarchies, with a few simple rules and a willingness to enforce violations. As Acheson shows so clearly in the Maine lobster industry, this approach can work well. Taking it a long way toward making this industry sustainable, a system of laws governing the conservation of lobsters has evolved within the political process throughout the 20th century. Here Acheson takes up the conundrum of one common practice that lies outside the system of ordinances.

Gravid lobsters cannot be taken legally. Lobstermen voluntarily mark the tails of "berried lobsters" by cutting a notch that lasts through several years' molts. If they catch a lobster with a notched tail that is not gravid and of a good size, they can legally take it. But they do not. Effectively, a lobsterman does not keep a lobster with a notched tail. For the entire industry, it might make sense to return proven reproductives to the pool, even at the expense of permanently losing those animals to the catch. But why would any individual fisherman throw a valuable animal back? And why would any rational, self-interested, well-informed lobsterman notch a lobster tail at all? What sort of answer might we expect to satisfy us? Schelling (1978) gives us the means to distinguish individual and system rationality, to see *that*, but not *how*, irrational individuals might fashion a rational system. Is there any way we can understand that even though these fishermen individually keep and sell the lobsters they catch, Maine lobster fishing is a social process that could be modeled as an *n*-person, non-zero-sum game? Lobstermen themselves apparently interpret their own behavior as a variety of parental investment.

CREATIVITY AND COOPERATION

As we add value to the world through our creativity, how shall we understand the relationship between who does what and who gets what? That organizations might offer alternatives to markets makes substantial sense, but this observation does not tell us how organizations—bundles of relationships—function. Nor does it tell us what sorts of functions provide the context for the enforceable contracts that markets require. It is clear only that they must be at least as complicated as dyads, and probably more so.

Individuals can and do cooperate as well as compete. The discovery that analyses of cooperation, competition, and hierarchy among rational egoists all lead to paradox requires us to bear simultaneously in mind two difficult points. First, we cannot suppose that more rationality among actors is what the world needs to make it better under all conditions. To say that someone is not acting rationally is to not say much of anything at all. Rather, we must recognize that paradox is an artifact of our analysis, not a property of the world. Second, we cannot lose sight of the major contribution of game theory to human science: that our sociality is fundamentally strategic, that what we get from social action depends not only on what we do but also on what others do in response. This reaction is not "equal and opposite"; it is creative, innovative, and often unpredictable.

What then might be the tools available to us for analysis? Equilibrium thinking has brought us a long way. More recently, game theory and within it, the prisoner's dilemma, have opened up a variety of fruitful lines of inquiry. Researchers have developed additional games that can be carried out as experiments to help us understand the practices of people in different cultures and in a variety of situations. It is also possible to specify what sort of tool the next phase requires, by the situations we cannot yet figure out at all: *n*-person, non-zero-sum games. The problem we face and do not know how to solve yet is that it is difficult analytically to tell the difference between exchange and production. Several of the authors in this volume make this point in different ways. This new tool could possibly help address this problem.

Nevertheless, how to handle this problem within the parameters of agency and rationality remains elusive. The first game-theory approach to production that I read with interest was Davenport's (1960) analysis of Jamaican lobster fishermen's decisions on the placement of pots inside or outside the reef. The analysis got a fine result by imagining the fishermen and nature to be playing a zero-sum game. The fishermen wanted lobsters and risked pots, while nature wanted pots and risked lobsters. But the lobstermen were just fishing, and nature is an imaginary being. And just recently Lansing's (2006) examination of Balinese rice production has drawn my perplexed attention. He uses the prisoner's dilemma in such a way that the upstream farmers appear to be releasing water to the downstream farmers under the threat that the downstream farmers will release pests upstream if they do not get the water they need. But again, they are all only raising rice the Balinese way, and of course downstream farmers have no control over pests apart from the standard techniques of Balinese ancient agricultural practice. We will have a clear understanding of cooperation either in production or in exchange when we no longer need to reduce the patterns of social relations to two-person, zero-sum, *or* non-zero-sum games. Without this, we will not clearly know which interactions are better understood as two-person games and which as *n*-person games. We cannot yet understand the relationship between what more than two people do and what they get in strategic relations, and thus why they cooperate or why they do something else.

In the end this volume does not show that cooperation demonstrates the limitations of either hierarchies or markets. The theme that runs through the chapters is the fundamental creativity of cooperation, that we are a social species that has no choice but to live together, despite the fact that we have to make up the rules we live by as we go along. It now appears that our cooperation is contingent; perhaps we might do better to think of cooperation and competition as offering alternative possibilities under varying circumstances rather than imagining one as the default in light of the other's failure to offer universal solutions. It is now entirely certain, however, that we do not require Leviathan to punish failure to adhere to norms. As a social species, we seem perhaps all too willing to punish those who violate our sense of what is fair. We live and work socially and depend on the actions of others, for the results of our effort. We have no choice in this matter, but many of the chapters in this volume show how cooperation does work to our mutual satisfaction.

REFERENCES

Berry, Wendell. 2009. *Bringing it to the table: On farming and food*. Berkeley, CA: Counterpoint.

Coase, Ronald. 1937. "The nature of the firm." *Economica* 4:386–405.

———. 1993. "The nature of the firm: Influence." In *The nature of the firm: Origins, evolution and development*, ed. Oliver E. Williamson and Sidney G. Winter. New York: Oxford University Press.

Davenport, William. 1960. *Jamaican fishing: A game theory analysis*. Yale Univ. Pubs. in Anthro., No. 59, New Haven.

Henrich, Joseph, Robert Boyd, Samuel Bowles, Colin Camerer, Ernst Fehr, and Herbert Gintis et al. 2004. *Foundations of human sociality: Economic experiments and ethnographic evidence from fifteen small-scale societies*. Oxford: Oxford University Press.

Henrich, Natalie, and Joseph Henrich. 2007. *Why humans cooperate: A cultural and evolutionary explanation*. Oxford: Oxford University Press.

Hobbes, Thomas. 1955 [1651]. *Leviathan*. Oxford: Blackwell.

Lansing, J. Stephen. 2006. *Perfect order: Recognizing complexity in Bali*. Princeton, NJ: Princeton University Press.

Latour, Bruno. 1986. "The powers of association." In *Power, action and belief*, ed. John Law, 264–280. London: Routledge, Kegan Paul.

March, James G. 1966. “The power of power.” In *Varieties of political theory*, ed. David Easton, 39–70. Englewood Cliffs, NJ: Prentice Hall.

Marshall, Robert C. 1985. “Giving a gift to the hamlet: Rank, solidarity and productive exchange in rural Japan.” *Ethnology* 24 (3): 167–182.

Mauss, Marcel. 1967 [1925]. *The gift*. New York: W. W. Norton.

Mead, Margaret. 1937. *Cooperation and competition among primitive peoples*. New York: McGraw-Hill.

North, Douglass. 1990. *Institutions, institutional change and economic performance*. New York: Cambridge University Press.

Ostrom, Elinor. 1992. *Crafting institutions for self-governing irrigation systems*. San Francisco: Institute for Contemporary Studies.

———. 2005. Policies that crowd out reciprocity and collective action. In *Moral sentiments and material interests: The foundations of cooperation in economic life*, ed. Herbert Gintis, Samuel Bowles, Robert Boyd, and Ernst Fehr. Cambridge, MA: MIT Press.

Schelling, Thomas. 1978. *Micromotives and macrobehavior*. New York: W. W. Norton.

Smith, Adam. 1937 [1776]. *The wealth of nations*. New York: Random House.

Williamson, Oliver E. 1985. *The economic institutions of capitalism*. New York: Free Press.

I

COOPERATION AND COMPETITION

1

From Reciprocity to Trade

How Cooperative Infrastructures Form the Basis of Human Socioeconomic Evolution

Rahul Oka and Agustín Fuentes, University of Notre Dame

INTRODUCTION

"The reason why minority groups do not perform well and advance in mainstream economic processes is because they rely too much on social cooperative networks. Their dependence upon these networks, whether religious or kin-based, acts as a limiting factor for their ability to compete with the larger world and hence they will remain at a socio-economic disadvantage." These were the words of a colleague remarking on a seminal paper by Azzi and Ehrenberg (1975) correlating ethnicity, class, and income with church attendance. This above interpretation of Azzi and Ehrenberg's paper fits neoclassical economic theory and efficiently "explains" why minorities suffer from economic stasis and marginalization: the lack of competition, the inability to compete, and collusion that lead to limited opportunity. However, this explanation conflates correlation with causation as it ignores the counterexplanation that church attendance and hence access to the social networks therein might well be a strategic alternative to socioeconomic marginalization. Despite seeing the strong correlation between ethnicity (nonwhites) and church attendance, the authors themselves suggested that racial discrimination may limit "market consumption alternatives of nonwhites relative to whites and thus lead to higher nonwhite religious participation" (Azzi and Ehrenberg 1975:38).

Hence, social cooperative networks might "emerge" precisely because various forms of discrimination keep "nonwhites" out of participation in mainstream economic processes and hence create the demand for and a continual investment in the church social networks. Though neoclassical interpretations that focus on competition have been critiqued before (e.g., Acheson 1994;

Granovetter 1985; Yoffee and McAnany 2006), we chose to start this chapter with this anecdote not only to underscore the debate between cooperation and competition but because it illustrates our two key points, that

- groups under predatory stress (e.g., racial discrimination) will invest in cooperative social networks to ensure greater survival than would be possible outside the networks, and
- there is a deep-set antipathy toward considering cooperation as a core behavioral strategy in the evolution of human behavior, specifically in modern economic behavior.

The reliance on a rational, maximizing, and self-interested actor that fuels the intellectual development of this antipathy raises many questions about the patterns in the human evolutionary (hominin) past. Why do substantial cooperative infrastructures endure throughout history (both social and evolutionary)? In trade and commerce, where competition is key, why does cooperation emerge as a structuring mechanism? Why do groups that could gain "more" through contest choose instead to gain "less but sufficient" through cooperation? We argue that the key benefits of cooperation, those of sustainability and adaptive resilience, are powerful forces that cause the "selection" of cooperative behaviors to mitigate against external attritional pressures, namely, predation.

We present our approach not as a one-size-fits-all solution to understanding socioeconomic behavior but as an additive-alternative to the dominant paradigm of the competing maximizing rational actor-driven evolution. Our approach argues for multistrategy synergies and the effects of feedback from cooperation on incipient socioeconomies: from the baseline of reciprocal social relations in early *Homo*, to the division of labor and long-distance trade in later *Homo sapiens*, and to the transcontinental commerce of modern ethnic trading diasporas.

MODELING HUMAN BEHAVIORAL EVOLUTION AND SOCIOECONOMIC EVOLUTION

Human behavioral patterns are structured by evolutionary histories, biocultural development, and social context and histories. We have very limited material evidence of behavior prior to the last few hundred thousand years and extremely limited, but growing, evidence of the range of morphological and material variation at any given time period in our past (prior to ~100,000 years ago). This forces a heavy reliance on reconstruction scenarios using various assumptions from the comparative primate record and modern human forager groups. It is quite common for theorists reconstructing the behavior and evolution of humans to use patterns of behavior exhibited by modern human forager groups as a baseline for our ancestral behavior (Boehm 1999; Cronk 1999; Lee and DeVore 1968). This reliance of data sets from Amazonian, Australian, Papuan (New Guinean), and South African forager and horticultural societies has structured the kinds of questions we ask (see S. Kusimba 2003 and Terrell et al. 2003). Commonalities and differences between them such as group sizes, marriage practices, and foraging patterns form many of the assumptions we have about past human behavior (Bailey 1988). This is a cultural phylogenetic analogy approach that assumes that the similarities or patterns across groups may be homologies for humans (same due to similar ancestral state). However, there are a number of dangers inherent in this approach (Headland 1997). We do not know the range of successful "ways" to be a human forager, and how many of these may not be represented in modern groups. Nor do we know how past action by humans has changed the structure of selection pressures and the resultant ecological and behavioral inheritance patterns.

More common in the past two decades has been the assessment of societies as they transition to global trading systems and cash economies, and are integrated into broader national identities (Headland 1997; Kent 2002; Morrison and Junker 2002). The focus then is on the patterns of behavior and exchange related to trading, conflict resolution, and marriage, and how they change relative to earlier patterns and what impacts that has on the physiology and behavior of such peoples. Understanding these patterns of interaction can also provide insight into the range of human response and possibly trajectories of response that occurred in the human past. It is difficult to use modern peoples and their ecologies as mirrors for the past, but there may be factors in overarching behavioral repertoires and patterns whose structure and outcomes are related socially and evolutionarily across broad stretches of time. However, we must be very cognizant of social, political, and economic factors that manipulate behavior at rapid rates, potentially producing results that are fully modern but cloaked with a few trappings of possibly historically relevant behavioral and/or ecological features (Wilmsen 1989; Fuentes 2009).

COOPERATION IN HUMAN EVOLUTION

Here we use the term *cooperation* to mean the process in which relationships, resources, information, and activities are *shared* within and between social groups. There is widespread evidence that the human niche is characterized by a good deal of social coordination (Ingold 2001; Richerson and Boyd 1998; Wilson and Sober 1994). Given our neurological complexity, individual biobehavioral diversity, and ability to convey extremely large and temporally disparate amounts of information behaviorally as humans, it appears that cooperation and shared information exchange, combined with socially negotiated distribution of labor, seems to effectively coordinate large groups of people (Fuentes 2004, 2009). Indeed, human cooperative social interactions form the backbone of human societies.

How might we envision the role of such cooperative interaction in our hominin past? Intergroup interactions—including the transport and trade of raw materials, coordinated use of the landscape and resources therein, and other associated interactions—alter the selective landscape. Engaging in these behaviors can increase the threat of predation as well as increase travel costs and other potential fitness costs to individuals; however, the impact of many individuals within a population, across groups, engaging in these cooperative behaviors may alter the patterns and contexts of environmental pressures such that they result in long-term benefits to offset short-term costs.

As a caveat, we state that though we have referred to cooperation through the lens of "social group" interactions, we prefer to think of cooperation as part of a social network linking members of con-specific yet (potentially) ethnically/geographically disparate groups. We distinguish "social networks" from "social groups" specifically to enable dealing with patterns of persisting social relationships that are ego focused rather than being bounded by ethnicity, geography, or purpose, and that allow cooperation between such bounded groups. There is increasing evidence for differential development of ethnicity seen through differences in material culture (subsistence, technology, aesthetics) across Afro-Eurasia since 300,000 B.P. that is paralleled by evidence of material exchange within and between these groups. Economist Haim Ofek (2001) argues that the constant interaction and cooperative exchange between geographically separated and/or culturally distinct groups enabled by trade and the concurrent flow of genetic materials might have led to increased "species stability." Archaeologist Clive Gamble uses the network intimacy/proximity approach to argue the enduring structuring role of non-kin conspecific cooperative networks linking premodern *Homo* sp. groups further into the Paleolithic past (1998).

COOPERATION AND ITS LINKS TO EXCHANGE, RECIPROCITY, AND TRADE

Based on our definition, cooperation is inextricably linked to exchange; in other words, networks of individuals within groups that cooperate are by default "exchange networks." Simulation studies on small-group colonization show that sets of migrating groups linked by exchange networks have significantly greater reproductive success (176 percent) than do sets of isolated groups (112 percent) (Moore 2001). Goods, services, favors, ideas, innovations, and so forth, flow between members of a social network. The multidirectional flow of resources within the exchange network, or obligatory reciprocity, is managed and enforced by the members of the networks. Specifically, we stress that a majority of the members within a network must agree on cooperative reciprocity, so that the few who do not or "whose needs are more so they give less," are tolerated and the risk of their nonparticipation is distributed across the network. Reciprocity hence is a primary structuring mechanism of cooperative networks and the basis of functional relationships. From reciprocity and exchange we get trade: the material component of exchange within and between networks, and a central focus in the evolution of hominin sociality (Oka and Kusimba 2008).

Pleistocene *Homo* sp. is differentiated from other extant hominin groups such as the Australopithecines and Paranthropids not just by specific factors in their anatomy, but also by the emergence of a distinct material culture with serious implications for differential cognitive development. The production-distribution of tools and the intergenerational transmission of this knowledge involves more than serendipity or simple observational learning. We suggest that the production of these tools also led to coevolution of social embedding mechanisms. These mechanisms would necessarily involve cooperation within and between groups to manage the access to raw materials, to create conditions for specialization beyond expedient tools, to distribute products across the network, and eventually lead to the social division of labor and skills within and between groups. By the time *Homo ergaster* / *Homo erectus* appears on the African scene ca. 2.0–1.6 million years ago, substantial and complex intragroup cooperation had developed. This type of cooperation existed in early *Homo* sp. and has been maintained through today. How exactly did it shape social evolution? We suggest that the intertwined concepts of niche construction and feedback offer a viable explanation for understanding the structuring role played by cooperation in determining species/group success and survival.

COOPERATION AND PREDATION PRESSURE IN NICHE CONSTRUCTION

Niche construction is defined as the process in which groups or populations modify the functional relationship between themselves and their environment by actively changing one or more factors in their environment, thus altering structural pressures on themselves and their descendants. A niche is the totality of the relationship between an organism and its ecology. "All living creatures, though their metabolism, their activities, and their choices, partly create and partly destroy their own niches, on scales ranging from the extremely local to the global" (Odling-Smee et al. 2003). Niche construction impacts or alters energy flows in ecosystems through ecosystem engineering, thus creating an ecological inheritance. Organisms inherit more than just genes; they inherit the ecologies they are born into. Niche construction is a process, in addition to natural selection, that contributes to changes over time in the dynamic relationship between organisms and environments (Odling-Smee et al. 2003).

Humans are the "ultimate niche constructors, [and] much of human niche construction is guided by socially learned knowledge and cultural inheritance, but the transmission of this knowledge is itself dependent on preexisting information acquired through genetic evolution, complex ontogenetic processes, or prior social learning" (Odling-Smee et al. 2003:260–261). If selection pressures are seen as restricting and constricting factors for reproduction of genes, behaviors, and ideas, then external pressures such as predation would count as one of the most significant selection forces in evolution (Hart and Sussman 2005). Here we define *predatory pressure* as an external force that causes the attrition of individuals, resources, and labor within a group. In keeping with this definition, three types of predatory pressure are identified:

Type 1: Active biological predation by one species over another: African Pleistocene hominin species were prey for wide array of large mammalian predators such as lions, leopards, saber-toothed cats, and hyenids, and hence both *Homo* sp. and *Paranthropus* sp. would have to deal with predatory pressure that routinely deprived the group of individuals and their contributions.

Type 2: "Predatory competition" between groups: This is the situation when two or more species and/or social groups occupy the same niche and hence indirectly compete with each other over resources, services, or labor. We stress here that this is competition through scramble (think of three people trying to get through a narrow doorway) rather than direct contest (altercation, warfare). Hence *Homo sapiens* and Neanderthals would compete over foraging land, raw materials, access to water, and trade routes; small traders operating within family groups or trading networks compete with politically connected "portfolio capitalists" over access to commodities and markets. Either way, the competition might lead to predatory attrition of resources from the group.

Type 3: "Predatory" sociopolitical regulation and coercive control over commercial activities: This happens when political elites or other social groups try to control commercial activities through forcible embedding of the economy through taxation, levies, duties or fines, and/or punitive measures such as scapegoating and targeted violence (or the threat thereof) against economic specialists.

We suggest that these three types of predatory pressures have had major influences on hominin evolution and human behavior.

WHAT HAPPENED IN HUMAN EVOLUTION: AN ULTRABRIEF PRIMER

The earliest human ancestors lived in multiadult groups and were at least as socially complex as living ape and monkey societies. Between ~2 million years to 1 million years ago early *Homo* sp. coexisted with other hominins, namely, members of the genus *Paranthropus*. Early in this time period predators remained a significant selective pressure on all hominins (Berger and Clarke 1995; Hart and Sussman 2005; Lockwood et al. 2007). As ancestral humans moved around and out of Africa they encountered diverse ecologies and novel environments leading to an expansion of the kind and complexity of behavior they displayed. The transition from early *Homo* through *Homo erectus/ergaster* was marked by increased energetic and child-rearing costs. Cooperative food collection (in scavenging, hunting, and exploitation of roots and tubers, for example), substantial food sharing, and cooperative/multiple caretakers of young also likely appeared during this period. Active biological predation (Type 1), a major selective force earlier in human evolution, was lessened during this time but this must have led to the rise of Type 2 predation, that of "predatory competition." During the time period of ~1.5–0.5 million years ago we see innovation in tool creation and use and an overall increased manipulation of the environment resulting in niche construction by *Homo* sp. During this period, the other living hominin group, the genus *Paranthropus*, became extinct and *Homo* sp. continued as the dominant species. Colonization of new territories and niche construction resulted in local variations of the *Homo* lineage (Flores hominins, Neanderthals, archaic *Homo sapiens*), some of which were contemporaries of anatomically modern *Homo sapiens* until 30,000–15,000 years ago (Fuentes 2009).

By 50,000 B.P. *Homo sapiens sapiens* was nearly globally distributed with increased rates of intergroup and interpopulation encounters. *Homo sapiens* exploited a wide variety of resources and began to increase both their geographic range (into higher stress/more seasonal climates/ecotypes) and their pattern of energy acquisition (expanding the types and intensity of hunting and gathering). The human tool kit expanded into more fine-tuned tools of diverse types and uses, resulting in the emergence of aesthetic traditions in some groups and populations. Language of some form probably emerged at this time. Role differentiation along age, sex, and some social lines became more commonplace in human groups and populations. Symbolic representation (painting, figurines) became common, indicating the integration of symbol into everyday life. From 45,000 years ago through today, human language and material culture are full blown. The precursors of sedentism and agriculture influenced the initiation of regional, socioreligious groups. Conflict between groups becomes more common as such units invest more and more in local material and mythical stakes. A complex division of labor, gender stratification, material wealth stratification, social restrictions on mating, and the creation of socioeconomic unions of marriage all become standard (but not necessarily universal) components of human societies (Fuentes 2009).

For the sake of space, we jump here from the evolution of complex "hunter-gatherers" ca. 12,000–10,000 B.P. to the emergence of agriculturally based urban hierarchical polities in Mesopotamia and then North Africa and South Asia between 7000 and 5000 B.P., where trade played a significant role in the distribution of resources between the core areas in Mesopotamia to the Anatolia or highland Iran, from the Indus Valley to western India (Stein 1999). From the Bronze Age onward, human history is shaped by cooperative interactions summed under the rubric of trade and carried out by specialized commercial groups that operated in systems of interconnected networks (Dercksen 1999). By 2000 B.P., these networks connected the landmasses of Afro-Eurasia. Roman wine and its imitations were being sold to South Asians. African gold and ivory were pouring into Eurasia, and the demands for South Asian pepper and East Asian silks were draining Rome of its resources (Parkins and Smith 1998; Ray 2003). Similar networks emerged in the Americas and Oceania (Oka and Kusimba 2008). Throughout the last two millennia, traders have crossed oceans and helped structure cooperative relationships between political elites, craftsmen, and producers to enable the building of colonies and fuel the rise of the empires, the modern world, and the industrial age (Smith 2004 [1759]:181; Webb 1975:155).

The rise of trade was accompanied by a near-universal rise in the political and social attempts to embed, control, and regulate trading behaviors and agents (Type 3 predation pressure). Also, as we will suggest in this chapter, the rise of "portfolio capitalists" or politically connected economic specialists gave rise to predatory competition within trading groups (Type 2 predation pressure). Throughout history, the rise and fall of empires, natural and anthropogenic disasters, and various predation forces, trader networks have endured and even thrived when other institutions or socioeconomic behaviors have collapsed. This denotes an adaptive resilience that spans over 10,000 years, from the postulated pastoral traders of the prepottery Neolithic to the known contemporary trading communities of Asia, Africa, and Europe.

BEGINNING WITH RECIPROCITY: EMERGENT EFFECTS OF COOPERATION IN HOMININ SOCIAL EVOLUTION

Our first case study focuses on hominin species' interactions by looking at the evolutionary success of Early *Homo* sp. over *Paranthropus* sp. and the purported success of modern *Homo sapiens* over Neanderthals. Early *Homo* and *Paranthropus* both experienced predation pressure (Hart and Sussman 2005). Borrowing from Fuentes et al. (forthcoming), we outline a potential model for this relationship using a nonlinear dynamics scenario involving increased reliance on complex cooperation as an antipredator strategy. We model the proposed selective pressures of predation on early humans to suggest that increasingly complex sociality, patterns of cooperation, and niche construction laid the foundation for the successful emergence and spread of the species *Homo* and potentially a concomitant decline for the genus *Paranthropus*. In the case of modern humans and Neanderthals, archaeological data from studies on Upper Paleolithic Eurasia shows marked differences in the level and intensity of intra- and intergroup cooperative interaction between these groups indicated by a gender-based division of labor, and the movement and distance-transport of materials. This differentiation may have impacted modern human success and Neanderthal extinctions and/or replacement.

Homo sp. and *Paranthropus*: Type 1: Predation Pressure

Between 2.5 and 1 million years ago members of the genera *Homo* (the human lineage) and *Paranthropus* (another hominin lineage) were sympatric and likely overlapped in morphological, locomotory, dietary, and some behavioral facets (Ciochon and Fleagle 2006; Conroy 2004; Wood and Strait 2004). Therefore we (following others, see Hart and Sussman 2005 for a review) suggest that both may have been under pressure from similar predators. Consideration of shifting social behavior within a niche construction perspective melded with standard models of population growth and the impact of predation can facilitate an understanding of this relationship between *Homo*, *Paranthropus*, predation, and its outcomes as an example of the proposed approach.

A modified niche-construction mathematical model (Fuentes et al. forthcoming) examining population growth, predation, and carrying capacities suggests that as effectiveness of cooperation increases the impact of factors such as predation and carrying capacity shift and diminish. This suggests that human ancestors' social cooperation, including information transfer and its concomitant alteration of local ecologies, may have been a major factor in human evolutionary success. While acknowledging that such a simple system will not offer a truly accurate model of human evolution, we hold that it might produce alternative perspectives that help explain the patterns in the fossil record and simultaneously demonstrate how relatively small changes in social (cultural?) behavior resulting in niche construction can radically alter relationships between species or human groups in shared environments (see Table 1.1).

There are a few specific assumptions core to this model. Ecological pressures include initially roughly equivalent predation pressure on *Homo* and *Paranthropus* and increasing physiological (energetic) and child-rearing (increased dependency period) costs for the genus *Homo*. The hypothesized responses to these pressures by members of the genus *Homo* include: increased cooperative interactions between group members associated with changes in foraging and child-rearing behavior (associated with an increase in communicative complexity); increased effectiveness at avoiding preda-

Table 1.1. Models for Impact of Cooperation

Model Name	*#*	*Equation*
Exponential	1	$dH/dt = rH$
Logistic	1	$dH/dt = r\ (1 - H/K)\ H$
Cooperation	1	$dH/dt = r\ (1 - H/K + SH^2)\ H$
Two-species cooperation **Hominin**	2	$dH/dt = r_H\ (1 - H/K_H - S_P P^2 + S_H H^2)\ H$ $dP/dt = r_P\ (1 - P/K_P - S_H H^2 + S_P P^2)\ P$
Two-species cooperation **Trade**	2	$dNBT/dt = r_{NBT}\ (1 - NBT/K_{NBT} - S_{IT} IT^2 + (S_{NBT})^2 NBT) NBT$ $dIT/dt = r_{IT}\ (1 - IT/K_{IT} - (S_{NBT})^2 NBT + S_{IT} IT^2) IT$
Three Species cooperation **Trade and Commerce**	3	$dPC/dt = r_{PC}\ (1 - PC/K_{PC} - (S_{NBT})^2 NBT - S_{IT} IT^2 + S_{PC} PC_2) PC$ $dNBT/dt = r_{NBT}\ (1 - NBT/K_{NBT} - S_{PC} PC^2 - S_{IT} IT^2 + (S_{NBT})^2 NBT) NBT$ $dIT/dt = r_{IT}\ (1 - IT/K_{IT} - S_{PC} PC^2 - S_{NBT} NBT + S_{IT} IT^2) IT$

ParamNBTers

r	intrinsic growth rate
K	nominal carrying capacity
S	Cooperation
H	*Homo habilis/ergaster, Homo sapiens*
P	*Paranthropus* sp. or Neanderthals
NBT	Ethnic Trader Succes
IT	Individual Trader Success
PC	Portfolio Capitalist Success

tion (including active antipredator strategy, possibly including tools, projectiles, other extrasomatic manipulation and multi-individual coordination of antipredator behavior); and an expansion of types and patterns of habitat exploitation (niche expansion). This pattern of intracommunity interactions combined with complex information exchange requires substantial learning, instruction, and coordination—all elements that are constructed over time in the individual and the group (creating complex social networks).

These responses result in niche construction that alters the patterns of selection pressures on both *Homo* and *Paranthropus*. As *Homo* becomes more costly for predators (due to the above responses), the predators shift emphasis to more accessible prey items of similar size in roughly the same environments, most likely both baboons (*Theropithecus*) and *Paranthropus*. As predation pressures wane (relatively) on *Homo*, there is increased opportunity for social interactions involving enhanced information transfer and social learning, and range exploration involving testing a variety of novel foraging opportunities and targets and the communication of those efforts across (local) space and across time. With increased cooperative interactions between members of *Homo* groups (and potentially across social networks in local areas), foraging efficiency, predator avoidance, and care for offspring further increase in effectiveness (positive feedback) facilitating the observed range and habitat expansion in the period 1.8–1.0 million years ago (as seen in the fossil record).

This combination of elements can lead to specific patterns of niche construction wherein by establishing these cooperative relationships and networks, members of the genus *Homo* not only influence the nature of their social and ecological world, but also in part affect the selection pressures and social milieu to which they and their descendants are exposed, and they do so in a nonrandom manner (Day et al. 2003). This can alter the relationship between other organisms in the shared environment, such as *Paranthropus* and predators. The positive feedback in populations that construct their niches can only be modeled by nonlinear mathematical terms, such as those introduced in cooperation population models (Fuentes et al. forthcoming).

A two-species cooperation model (see Figure 1.1) allows for a compelling description of an extinction event. *Homo* and *Paranthropus* existed at equilibrium for an evolutionarily long period of time (as evidenced by the fossil record). As *Homo* acquired enhanced cognitive abilities and material manipulation of the environment, and increasingly sophisticated social structure (social networks), cooperation in (and possibly between) groups increased. Small changes in such a system typically yield small changes in population size and structure. There are critical regions, however, where small changes yield disproportionate changes to the system as a whole: equilibriums disappear and

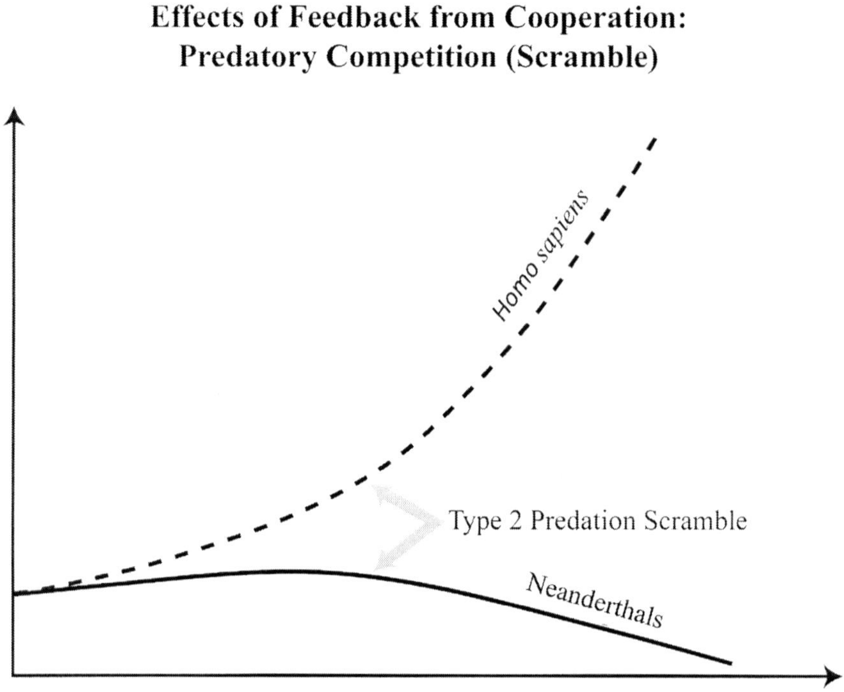

Figure 1.1. Effects of feedback from cooperation: predatory competition (scramble)

populations crash or explode, in the model (Figure 1.1). These small changes arise, more or less, from behavioral patterns and social innovation. While simplistic and obviously nowhere near a full representation of the complex ecological and social landscapes for the genus *Homo* in the Terminal Pliocene / Early Pleistocene, the model does suggest that social interactions and the creation of social networks, via cooperation, and the resultant niche construction can be important aspects of evolutionary processes.

The trends for the two species seen in the figure above apply also to other hominin interactions. We can see the possible ratcheting effects of feedback from cooperation in the differential success of *Homo sapiens* and Neanderthals as they coexisted between 50,000 and 28,000 years ago in Europe and Southwest Asia (also modeled in Figure 1.1). We classify this as Type 2 predation pressure in which *Homo sapiens* and Neanderthals competed over food, water, raw materials, and use of overlapping areas.

Horan, Bulte, and Shogren (2005) argue that the differentiation between *Homo sapiens* and Neanderthals was due not to contest competition but to scramble competition. They argue that because both humans and Neanderthals were adept at hunting the megafauna, there is little evidence of direct conflict between them, and that although Neanderthal tools were less innovative than those of *Homo sapiens*, they were fully functional and sufficient. Therefore, Neanderthals should have successfully survived even in face of the environmental and Type 2 predatory challenges. But when one factors in trade and exchange, things change. Neanderthals probably exchanged goods, resources, and ideas across regions, but the volume of this exchange as shown in the archaeological record is miniscule compared to that for modern humans (Horan, Bulte, and Shogren 2005). While Neanderthal material culture might have occasionally traveled over 150 km, the bulk was confined to 20 km between source and use/residence (Milisauskas 2002). *Homo sapiens* groups in the Upper Paleolithic, however, show regular exchange of commodities over 200 km. Shell and lithic material were exchanged over distances of 1,000 km in the Ukraine, northern Europe, and Africa (Oka and Kusimba 2008; Soffer 1985).

These trading networks may have been established and negotiated during seasonal aggregational events when social relationships were cemented by goods exchange or by itinerant traders traveling between groups. Such networks are based primarily on reciprocity (hence cooperation), as the key element therein is sharing of resources. As Horan, Bulte, and Shogren (2005) suggest, it was this factor that allowed the mobilization of resources from a wider area, a broader "spectrum" of resources, technologies, and the exchange of peoples themselves, that created a ratcheting effect in terms of *Homo sapiens* social evolution. The constant flow of resources would create an interdependency of people on the networks and the resources. This would spur increased production of commodities and a constant need to reinvest in cooperative relationships. The continual movement of ideas, genes, and materials across Afro-Eurasia between *Homo sapiens* groups would lead to increased species stability within humans even as Neanderthals and other hominins experienced isolation events (Ofek 2001). The feedback from cooperation would depend on the network scale as well as the flow volume within these networks, and would lead to greater overall reproductive success of *Homo sapiens* over their contemporaries, the Neanderthals.

COOPERATION, RECIPROCITY, AND THE TRADER NETWORK

In our second case study, the role of cooperation in the construction and maintenance of traders' networks, we counter the argument that cooperation is just a general result of species' responses to adversity. Networks of trading communities show tremendous endurance and high levels of adaptability and resilience to social, economic, and environmental stress. Our data are drawn from Oka's ethnographic research on contemporary ethnic trading diasporas in South Asia and East Africa and archival research on business practices utilized in the Indian Ocean trade over the past six centuries. Our findings show that most ethnic traders emphasize "intentional" cooperation as a primary strategy to counter predatory political elites and institutions (Type 3) and/or competition from other economic organizations (Type 2).

Though our data draw from ethnographic and oral historical research on contemporary trading groups, evidence from other epigraphic, archaeological, and cliometric research suggests dramatic similarities in the strategies used by contemporary or historically proximate traders and those active in the Bronze Age (Dercksen 1999), the early Common Era (Ray 2003; Parkins and Smith 1998), and the medieval period (Hunt and Murray 1999) through the modern day (Oka 2008; Oka and Kusimba 2008). The conservatism of these strategies follows from the same reason as the centrality of cooperation in trading behavior: externally imposed predatory pressure. This includes both Types 2 (predatory competition within trading groups) and 3 (predatory regulation, control and/or forcible embedding of trading activities by social groups or political elites), as seen in Figure 1.2.

As seen in Figure 1.2, Type 3 predation has shaped official fiscal policies and social attitudes regarding traders leading to a universal metanarrative of scapegoating of traders (Farber 2006; Moore Jr. 2000; Milne and Goodburn 1990). One of the primary functions of this narrative is to "name" and supply the culprits causing problems and deflect blame and social censure away from the ruling elite. The blame is usually assigned to extant marginalized groups who are easily categorized. Specifically, in the case of trade specialists who are (a) members of diasporas, (b) ethnically "other," (c) easily identified as a group, (d) seen as wealthy, and (e) do not do any "proper" work, these narratives suggest that wealth is extracted from the common people by the foreign merchants creating an irreversible outflow of resources (Igue 1976; Oka 2008). These narratives help sustain a general distrust of trader diasporas within the larger populace. During crises or calamities, it is universally observed that the first groups of foreign traders as well other transient network-centric groups such as gypsies, tinkers, and peddlers are targeted with violence and/or expulsion by people and political elites alike (Gmelch 1986).

Scapegoating theory explains this tension arising as a result of *mimetic desire* followed by *mimetic crisis* (Girard 1996). Mimetic desire here suggests that political groups wish to procure the economic groups' abilities and skills through imitation. Hence political elites desire the wealth, wealth-creating ability, access to the fluid transregional networks, and above all, the ability to distribute products with minimal problems. Their inability to imitate then leads the move from desire to crisis through the generation of the scapegoating narratives (Girard 1996). When attempts to control the distributive

Effects of Trader Cooperation in Networks:
Predatory Competition and Political and Social Regulation

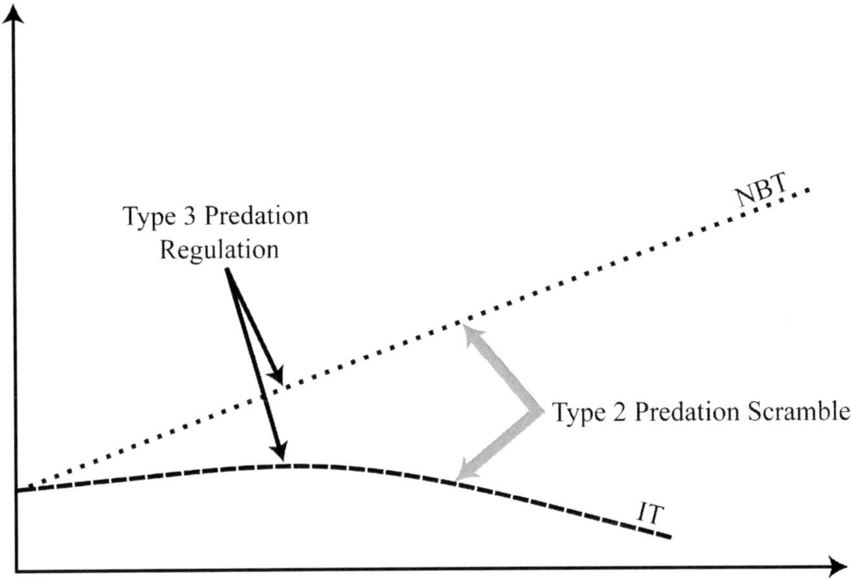

··· NBT: Network-Based Trader

— IT: Individual Trader

Figure 1.2. Effects of trader cooperation in networks: predatory competition and political and social regulation (tracking network-based and individual traders)

economy fail, they explode into socially justified violence aimed at traders. Historical and contemporary examples include violence against the Chinese in Indonesia; Indians in Fiji, Trinidad, Kenya, Uganda, and Mozambique; the Jews in Europe; the Marwari, Sindhi, and Gujarati in India; the Lebanese in North and West Africa and Latin America; the Ibo in west Africa; and the Yao and Nyamwezi in East and central Africa (Abdullah 2001; Alexander and Alexander 1991; Hunt and Murray 1999; Lindh de Montoya 1999; Lombard and Aubin 2000; Markovits 2000; Meneses 1987; Nwabughuogu 1981; Seidenberg 1996).

This dynamic and antagonistic interaction among traders, political elites, and the populace results in constant need for negotiation and renegotiation of alliances. In the words of an informant, this means continuously "looking over your back to watch for a [predator] elite who is eyeing your wealth or the clients that will turn on you even when (and probably because) they need you." Subsequently, traders trust only "known" entities (other members of their networks) and remain wary of their sociopolitical sponsors, patrons, or partners (Landa 1994). Furthermore, as sociopolitical conditions are beyond their control and often at odds with their aims, traders "know" that they "will be" targeted at any time for their economic ability, their adaptive resilience, and their "otherness." To protect themselves, trade specialists develop various strategies that minimize wealth concentration and ostentatious displays/consumption.

Traders reduce their visibility by distributing wealth across the trader network and across geographic and intergenerational boundaries, relying on cooperation between multiple "trusted" individuals or groups (Oka 2008). This cooperation is based on reciprocity; services, goods, favors, ideas, information, credit, and capital have to be exchanged in a network by all members. People who do not cooperate or otherwise diverge from the self-limiting strategies are rebuked and punished through social means: ostracism, withholding of favors, and sometimes expulsion from the personalized networks of influence. One informant stated:

> We all invest in the network and help each other because who knows when the leaders or the people will lose their minds and attack us. [A] is attacked today in this city, [B] might be attacked tomorrow in that. We are the only ones who will help each other. Things are always changing in politics and our [political] friends today might not be able to protect us tomorrow. [. . .] so our relationships are the only way we can be sure of keeping our business safe, [. . .] in good times we can work with the politicians but in bad times, we can generate opportunities, credit, and capitalization through olakh [personalized networks of influence].

As evidenced by the ubiquity of trader networks across space and time, it is the self-limiting strategies and primarily that of cooperation that have given the networks maximum adaptive resilience for maintaining business over distances and over generations. We can see that network organization is a path-dependent (interdependency + feedback) process in which the tensions and scapegoating relations between traders and predatory elites determine the traders' network-centric responses that in turn fuel the policies and narratives of the populace and political actors, and ad infinitum.

Hence the emphasis on network endurance through conservatism, self-restraint, and cooperation is a desired outcome of network-based traders leading to a situation wherein networks that undergo consistent shocks (or predatory pressure) also develop the highest resilience, and those networks that have the least restrictions on the flow of resources and information have the highest adaptability (Holling 2004; Redman and Kinzig 2003). This creates constant incentive to remain within the network, leading to emergence of network-based traders (NBT). The NBTs encountered in our research stressed the paramount importance of cooperative relationships for sustainable commerce. One informant summed it up thus: "We don't need to teach our children how to do business; making money is in their blood. What we have to teach them is how to make and keep relationships."

There are three levels of cooperative relationships used to structure these networks: ties with other trade specialists, with consumers and clients, and with political elites. These relationships structure the network and are managed through gifts, favors, and services. The "knowledge" of someone or something is usually passed from individual/family to other individuals/families as a quid pro quo. Past interactions are also passed within the network as stories, myths, and legends about the doings of the traders and their families/clans and political elites. Most important, these narratives contain historicized information about an individual, family, or group that can or cannot be trusted, and their reputed abilities and ethics.

The constant tension among political elites, social groups, and traders can be seen as a structuring predatory force to which traders respond by investing in cooperative networks. The success of the network leads to selection of cooperative behaviors generation after generation (Lomnitz 1988, 2002). This feedback from cooperation through narrative, teaching, and censure can be considered a form of social niche construction. Based on the modeling approach shown in Table 1.1 and Figure 1.1 for *Homo* sp. versus *Paranthropus* sp. or Neanderthals, we postulate a similar divergence between IT (individual traders) and NBT (network-based traders).

As seen in Equation 2 (Table 1.1) and Figure 1.2, due to their emphasis on self-limiting strategies, the trajectory for NBTs is linear and not exponential. We also hold that some ITs will learn by association and practice similar self-restraining strategies. But what happens when conditions of political stability lead to sustained epochs of trade-friendliness? Would cooperation continue to structure trader networks? Our informants stated that it would but other studies have noted that in times of stability, some NBTs and many ITs will choose to invest within the political infrastructure, turning to their political allies for protection (Oka 2008; Oka in review). These individuals, referred to as *portfolio capitalists*, are usually found in large states and empires. They actively control production centers and/or handle large volumes of goods, commodities, and capital. Along with diverse production/distribution activities, they control large amounts of cash and credit and hence have close relationships with political elites (Morrison 1997). They have significant effect on commercial economies and also influence economic policies by managing state finance, public banking, and political investments (Calmard 2000; Leonard 1998; Subramanian 1996). To include these components we have developed a three-competition model (Equation 3, Table 1.1) and the postulated results are shown in Figure 1.3.

As seen in Figure 1.3, after the decline of Type 3 predatory pressure due to stability and trade-friendliness, the emergence of Type 2 predation will again have an adverse effect on ITs but not on NBTs who will continue, albeit in

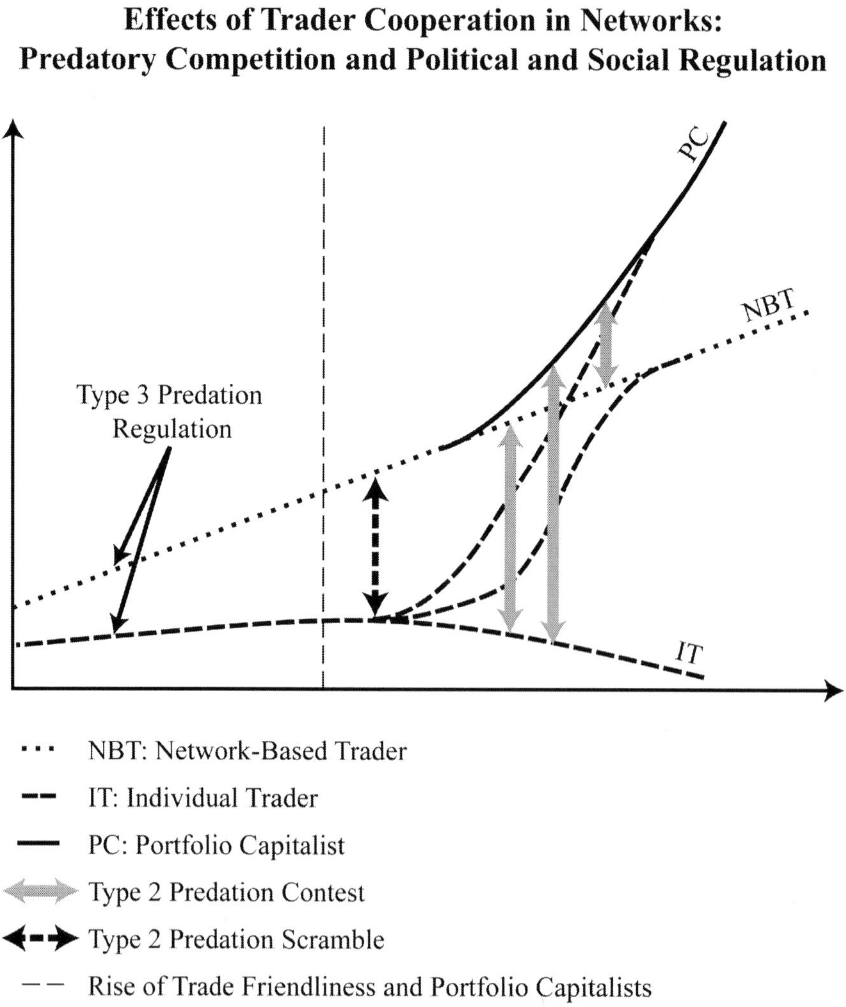

Figure 1.3. Effects of trader cooperation in networks: predatory competition and political and social regulation (tracking network-based traders, individual traders, and portfolio capitalists)

their self-limiting fashion. As we stated before, the emergence of portfolio capitalists can happen from the ranks of both ITs and NBTs. The prevailing trade-friendly conditions make it feasible for these individuals within both groups to maximize their profits, but even that takes place as a result of cooperation and collaboration with political elites and extant groups of portfolio capitalists. We would also venture here a caveat that with the return of political instability, the predatory pressure would affect both the portfolio capitalists who may choose to return to their networks and/or give up an interest in the business (Nwabughuogu 1981). This is modeled in Figure 1.4.

As seen in Figure 1.4, the reemergence of Type 3 predatory pressure (political and social regulation or political instability) would actually cause a return to the conditions and trajectories seen in Figure 1.2 where the groups that cooperated have a distinct selective advantage and ability to manage stress and predation pressure over those that do not. We suggest that it is precisely

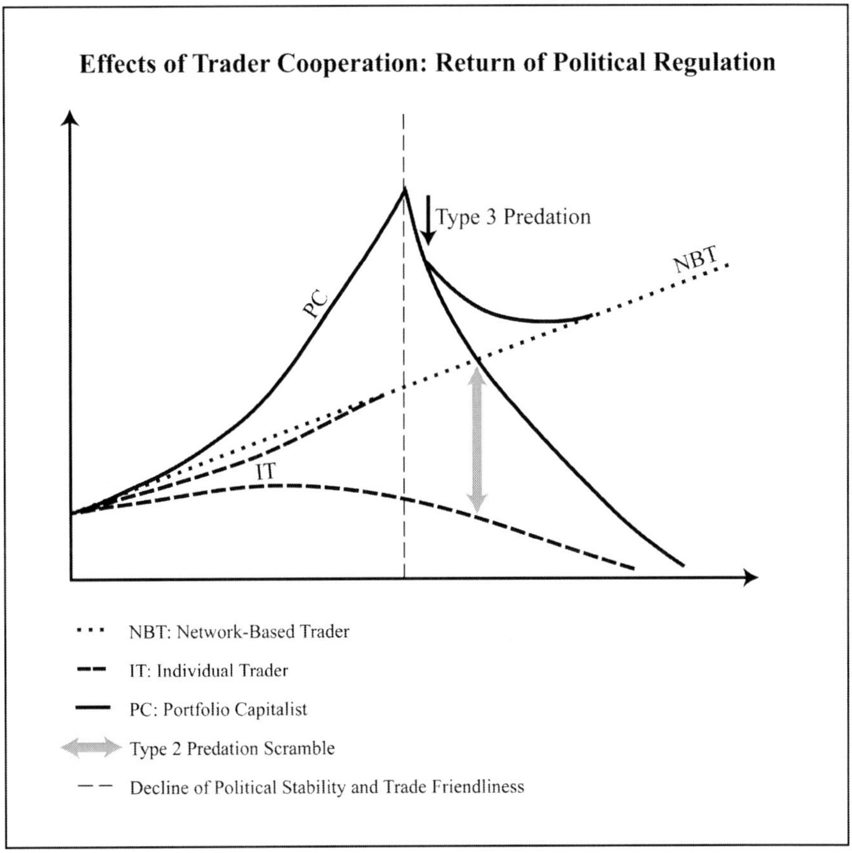

Figure 1.4. Effects of trader cooperation: return of political regulation

the ability to cooperate that has given trader networks and their members the ability to take advantage of good times and bad, to thrive in conditions under which most other socioeconomic institutions would collapse, to sustain activities and reestablish presence in areas where they have been targeted and scapegoated.

CONCLUSION: CONNECTING TRADE, COOPERATION, AND QUESTIONS ABOUT HUMAN BEHAVIOR

We began this chapter asking, why do cooperative infrastructures endure throughout history? We answered that it is due to the key benefits of cooperation: sustainability and adaptive resilience. These are powerful forces playing central roles in the development of human behavior, in both evolutionary and economic senses. We are not arguing one can easily or always apply this same tool kit to ask about human evolution and market economies, but we are suggesting that a focus on cooperation as a driving force as opposed to (or in addition to) competition might offer insight in each of these cases. Using cooperation and its potential niche-constructing impacts can add to our understanding of human behavioral patterns. The resiliency of cooperation as a central facet of human behavioral strategies across diverse contexts and time frames suggests that it must be a core factor in structuring our methodological and theoretical approaches to questions about why humans do what they do.

By understanding the effects of feedback from cooperation in niche construction, we can better model the outcomes of evolutionary processes affecting ancestral humans and their contemporaries. At the same time we can see that modern human NBTs imposing self-limiting strategies are engaged in a complex type of cooperation that, while restricting their individual ability to expand, imparts a sustainable and continuous growth to the trader network. Hence, for these traders, cooperating across social networks provides greater chances of success under various kinds of predatory pressure (via a form of social/economic niche construction).

In general when economists and many anthropologists speak about the struggle for existence (biological or economic), they use rhetoric about "out-competing" others in a directed rational-actor maximizing/optimizing manner. With this chapter we would like to suggest that at least for species or institutions that organize themselves in complex social networks, success is not only, or necessarily, about out-competing your neighbors, but about "out-cooperating" them and the niche-construction impacts. The resultant species/economic niche/landscape reflects benefits not necessarily for the winners of a direct free-market competition but rather for those individuals and networks that are the beneficiaries of, and participants in, cooperation. This is the way in which we envision cooperation as a central tool for anthropology, and recommend its inclusion as a driving force when studying both modern economic behavior and human evolutionary patterns.

REFERENCES

Abdullah, Thabit A. J. 2001. *Merchants, Mamluks and Murder: The Political Economy of Trade in Eighteenth-Century Basra*. State University of New York Press, Albany.

Acheson, J. M. 1994. *Anthropology and Institutional Economics*. University Press of America, Lanham, Maryland.

Alexander, Jennifer, and Paul Alexander. 1991. Protecting Peasants from Capitalism: The Subordination of Javanese Traders by the Colonial State. *Comparative Studies in Society and History* 33:370–394.

Allouche, Adel. 1994. *Mamluk Economics: A Study and Translation of Al-Maqrîzî's Ighãthah*. University of Utah Press, Salt Lake City.

Ambrose, Stanley H. 1998. Late Pleistocene Human Population, Bottlenecks, Volcanic Winter, and Differentiation of Modern Humans. *Journal of Human Evolution* 34:623–651.

Azzi, Corry, and Ronald Ehrenberg. 1975. Household Allocation of Time and Church Attendance. *Journal of Political Economy* 83(1):27–56.

Bailey, Robert C. 1988. The Significance of Hypergyny for Understanding the Subsistence Behavior of Contemporary Hunters and Gatherers. In *Diet and Subsistence: Current Archaeological Perspectives*, edited by B. V. Kennedy and G. M. LeMoine, pp. 56–67. University of Calgary Press, Calgary.

Berger, L. R., and R. J. Clarke. 1995. Eagle Involvement in Accumulation of the Taung Child Fauna. *Journal of Human Evolution* 29:275–299.

Boehm, C. 1999. *Hierarchy in the Forest: The Evolution of Egalitarian Behavior*. Harvard University Press, Cambridge, Massachusetts.

Boesche, Roger. 2005. Han Feizi's Legalism versus Kautilya's Arthashastra. *Asian Philosophy* 15:157–172.

Bowen, Huw V. 2006. *The Business of Empire: The East India Company and Imperial Britain, 1756–1833*. Cambridge University Press, Cambridge.

Calmard, Jean. 2000. The Iranian Merchants: The Formation and Rise of a Pressure Group between the Sixteenth and Nineteenth Centuries. In *Asian Merchants and Businessmen in the Indian Ocean and the China Sea*, edited by Denys Lombard and Jean Aubin, pp. 87–104. Oxford University Press, New Delhi.

Ciochon, R. L., and J. G. Fleagle. 2006. *The Human Evolution Source Book*. 2nd ed. Advances in Human Evolution Series. Pearson Prentice Hall, Upper Saddle River, New Jersey.

Conroy, G. C. 2004. *Reconstructing Human Origins: A Modern Synthesis*. 2nd ed. W. W. Norton, New York.

Cronk, L. 1999. *That Complex Whole: Culture and the Evolution of Human Behavior*. Westview Press, Boulder, Colorado.

Day, R. L., K. N. Laland, and J. Odling-Smee. 2003. Rethinking Adaptation: The Niche-Construction Perspective. *Perspectives in Biology and Medicine* 46(1):80–95.

Dercksen, J. G. (editor). 1999. *Trade and Finance in Ancient Mesopotamia: Proceedings of the First MOS Symposium (Leiden 1997)*. Nederlands Historisch-Archaeologisch Institut te Istanbul, Istanbul.

Farber, Lianna. 2006. *An Anatomy of Trade in Medieval Writing: Value, Consent, and Community*. Cornell University Press, Ithaca, New York.

Fuentes, A. 2004. It's Not All Sex and Violence: Integrated Anthropology and the Role of Cooperation and Social Complexity in Human Evolution. *American Anthropologist* 106(4):710–718.

———. 2009. *Evolution of Human Behavior*. Oxford University Press, New York.

Fuentes, A., M. Wyczalkowski, and K. C. MacKinnon. 2010. Niche Construction through Cooperation: A Nonlinear Dynamics Contribution to Modeling the Evolutionary History in the Genus Homo. *Current Anthropology* 51(3):435–444.

Gamble, Clive. 1998. Palaeolithic Society and the Release from Proximity: A Network Approach to Intimate Relations. *World Archaeology* 29(3):426–449.

Girard, René. 1996. *The Girard Reader*, edited by J. G. Williams. Crossroad, New York.

Gmelch, S. B. 1986. Groups That Don't Want In: Gypsies and Other Artisan, Trader, and Entertainer Minorities. *Annual Review of Anthropology* 15:307–330.

Granovetter, Mark. 1985. Economic Action and Social Structure: The Problem of Embeddedness. *American Journal of Sociology* 91:481–510.

Hart, D., and R. W. Sussman. 2005. *Man the Hunted: Primates, Predators and Human Evolution*. Westview Press, New York.

Headland, Thomas. 1997. Revisionism in Ecological Anthropology. *Current Anthropology* 38:605–630.

de Heinzelien, Jean, J. Desmond Clark, Tim White, William Hart, Paul Renne, Gidaywolde Gabriel, Yonas Beyene, and Elisabeth Vrba. 1999. Environment and Behavior of 2.5 Million Year Old Bouri Hominids. *Science* 284(5414):625–629.

Holling, C. S. 2004. From Complex Regions to Complex Worlds. *Ecology and Society* 9(1):11. Electronic document, http://www.ecologyandsociety.org/vol9/iss1/art11.

Horan, Richard D., Erwin Bulte, and Jason F. Shogren. 2005. How Trade Saved Humanity from Biological Exclusion: An Economic Theory of Neanderthal Extinction. *Journal of Economic Behavior and Organization* 58:1–29.

Hunt, Edwin S., and James M. Murray. 1999. *History of Business in Medieval Europe, 1200–1550*. Cambridge University Press, Cambridge.

Ibrahim, M. 1990. *Merchant Capital and Islam*. University of Texas Press, Austin.

Igue, Ogunsola John. 1976. Evolution of Illicit Trade between Dahomey and Nigeria since the War of "Biafra." *Canadian Journal of African Studies* 10:235–257.

Ingold, Tim. 2001. From Complementarity of Obviation: On Dissolving the Boundaries between Social and Biological Anthropology, Archeology and Psychology.

In *Cycles of Contingency: Developmental Systems and Evolution*, edited by S. Oyama, P. E. Griffiths, and R. D. Gray, pp. 255–280. MIT Press, Cambridge, Massachusetts.

Kent, Susan (editor). 2002. *Ethnicity, Hunter-Gatherers, and the Other: Association or Assimilation in Africa*. Smithsonian Institution Press, Washington, D.C.

Kusimba, Sibel Barut. 2003. *African Foragers: Environment, Technology, Interactions*. AltaMira Press, Walnut Creek, California.

Landa, Janet T. (editor). 1994. *Trust, Ethnicity, and Identity: Beyond the New Institutional Economics of Ethnic Trading Networks, Contract Law, and Gift-Exchange*. University of Michigan Press, Ann Arbor.

Lee, Richard B., and I. DeVore (editors). 1968. *Man the Hunter*. Aldine, Chicago.

Leonard, Karen. 1998. The "Great Firm" Theory of the Decline of the Mughal Empire. In *The Mughal State, 1526–1750*, edited by Muzaffar Alam and Sanjay Subrahmanyam, pp. 398–419. Oxford University Press, New Delhi.

Lindh De Montoya, M. 1999. Markets As Mirror or Model: How Traders Reconfigure Economic and Social Transactions in Rural Economies. *Ethnos* 64:57–81.

Lockwood, C. A., C. G. Menter, J. Moggi-Cecchi, and A. W. Keyser. 2007. Extended Male Growth in a Fossil Hominin Species. *Science* 318:1443–1446.

Lombard, Denys, and Jean Aubin (editors). 2000. *Asian Merchants and Businessmen in the Indian Ocean and the China Sea*. Oxford University Press, Oxford.

Lombard, Maurice. 1975. *The Golden Age of Islam*. Translated by Joan Spencer. American Elsevier, New York.

Lomnitz, Larissa. 1988. Informal Exchange Networks in Formal Systems: A Theoretical Model. *American Anthropologist* 90:42–55.

———. 2002. Reciprocity, Redistribution and Market Exchange in the Informal Economy. In *Economy and Society: Money, Capitalism and Transition*, edited by Fikret Adaman and Pat Devine, pp. 172–191. Black Rose Books, Montreal.

Markovits, Claude. 2000. *The Global World of Indian Merchants, 1750–1947: Traders of Sind from Bukhara to Panama*. Cambridge University Press, Cambridge.

Meneses, E. H. H. 1987. Traders and Marginality in a Complex Social System. *Ethnology* 26:231–244.

Milne, Gustav, and Damian Goodburn. 1990. The Early Medieval Port of London, AD 700–1200. *Antiquity* 64:629–636.

Milisauskas, S. 2002. *European Prehistory: A Survey*. Academic Press, New York.

Moore, B., Jr. 2000. *Moral Purity and Persecution in History*. Princeton University Press, Princeton, New Jersey.

Moore, J. 2001. Evaluating Five Models of Human Colonization. *American Anthropologist* 103:395–408.

Morrison, Kathleen D. 1997. Commerce and Culture in South Asia: Perspectives from Archaeology and History. *Annual Review of Anthropology* 26:87–108.

Morrison, Kathleen D., and Laura L. Junker (editors) 2002. *Forager-Traders in South and Southeast Asia: Long Term Histories*. Cambridge University Press, Cambridge.

Nwabughuogu, Anthony I. 1981. From Wealthy Entrepreneurs to Petty Traders: The Decline of African Middlemen in Eastern Nigeria, 1900–1950. *Journal of African History* 23:365–379.

Odling-Smee, F. John, Kevin N. Laland, and Marcus W. Feldman. 2003. *Niche Construction: The Neglected Process in Evolution*. Princeton University Press, Princeton, New Jersey.

Ofek, Haim. 2001. *Second Nature: Economic Origins of Human Evolution*. Cambridge University Press, Cambridge.

Oka, Rahul C. 2006. Network or Bust: Network Stability through Co-operation for Trade Continuity among Merchant Communities of Afrasia. Paper presented at the Annual Conference of the American Anthropological Association, Washington, DC.

———. 2008. Resilience and Adaptation of Trade Networks in East African and South Asian Port Polities, 1500–1800 C.E. Unpublished PhD dissertation, Department of Anthropology, University of Illinois, Chicago.

Oka, Rahul C., and Chapurukha M. Kusimba. 2008. Archaeology of Trading Systems. Part 1: Towards a New Trade Synthesis. *Journal of Archaeological Research*. 16(4): 339–395.

Parkins, Helen, and Christopher Smith (editors). 1998. *Trade, Traders and the Ancient City*. Routledge, London.

Ray, Himanshu Praba. 2003. *The Archaeology of Seafaring in Ancient South Asia*. Cambridge World Archaeology. Cambridge University Press, Cambridge.

Redman, Charles, and Ann P. Kinzig. 2003. Resilience of Past Landscapes: Resilience Theory, Society, and the Longue Durée. *Conservation Ecology* 7(1):14. Electronic document, http://www.consecol.org/vol7/iss1/art14.

Richerson, P. J., and R. Boyd. 2005. *Not By Genes Alone: How Culture Transformed Human Evolution*. University of Chicago Press, Chicago.

———. 1998. The Evolution of Human Ultra-Sociality. In *Indoctrinability, Ideology, and Warfare: Evolutionary Perspectives*, edited by I. Eibl-Eibisfeldt and F. Salter, pp. 71–95. Berghahn Books, Oxford, UK.

Seidenberg, Dana April. 1996. *Mercantile Adventurers: The World of East African Asians, 1750–1985*. New Age International, New Delhi.

Smith, Adam. 2004 [1759]. *The Theory of Moral Sentiments. With an introduction by Pat Mulroney*. Barnes & Noble, New York.

Soffer, Olga. 1985. *The Upper Paleolithic of the Central Russian Plain*. Academic Press, Orlando.

Stein, Gil J. 1999. *Rethinking World-Systems, Diasporas, Colonies, and Interaction in Uruk Mesopotamia*. University of Arizona Press, Tucson.

Subramanian, Lakshmi. 1996. *Indigenous Capital and Imperial Expansion: Bombay, Surat and the West Coast*. Oxford University Press, New Delhi.

Terrell, John E., John P. Hart, Nico Cellinese, L. Antonio Curet, Timothy Denham, Chapurukha M. Kusimba, Sibel B. Kusimba, Kyle Latinis, Rahul Oka, Joel Palka, Mary Pohl, Kevin Pope, P. Ryan Williams, Helen Haines, and John Staller. 2003. Domesticated Landscapes: The Subsistence Ecology of Plant and Animal Domestication. *Journal of Archaeological Method and Theory* 10:323–368.

Webb, Malcolm C. 1975. The Flag Follows Trade: An Essay on the Necessary Interaction of Military and Commercial Factors in State Formation. In *Ancient Civi-*

lization and Trade, edited by Jeremy A. Sabloff and C. C. Lamberg-Karlovsky, pp. 155–210. University of New Mexico Press, Albuquerque.

Wilmsen, Edwin. 1989. *Land Filled with Flies: A Political Economy of the Kalahari.* University of Chicago Press, Chicago.

Wilson, David S., and Eliott Sober. 1994. Reintroducing Group Selection to the Human Behavioral Sciences. *Behavioral and Brain Sciences* 17(4):585–608.

Wood, B., and D. Strait. 2004. Patterns of Resource Use in Early Homo and Paranthropus. *Journal of Human Evolution* 46:119–162.

Yoffee, Norman, and Patricia McAnany. 2006. Exploring Scholarly and Best-Selling Accounts of Social Collapse and Colonial Encounters. Invited Panel at the 105th Annual Meeting of the American Anthropological Association, San Jose, November 2006.

2

Market Integration and Prosocial Behavior

Evidence from the Standard Cross-Cultural Sample

E. Anthon Eff, Middle Tennessee State University
Malcolm McLaren Dow, Northwestern University

Two actors participate in the ultimatum game. One (the *proposer*) is given a sum of money and told that she must divide it with another—anonymous—person (the *responder*). The proposer is given one chance to propose a division of the money. If the responder rejects her offer, then both get nothing; if the responder accepts her offer, then both receive their agreed-on share.

A narrow and somewhat naive definition of rationality as income maximization would suggest that the proposer offer a tiny fraction of the prize to the responder, who would accept that tiny fraction since something is always better than nothing. Experiments have shown, however, that subjects (mostly university students) do not behave as strict income maximizers (Henrich et al. 2004:8–9). Modal offers are typically around 50 percent, with a mean close to 45 percent of the prize, and if the proposer offers too little to the responder, the responder is likely to reject it (Henrich et al. 2004:19). Clearly, subjects behave in a much more prosocial way than a narrow definition of rationality would assume.

In 1996, experiments done among the Machiguenga in the Peruvian Amazon attracted a great deal of interest. The Machiguenga behaved much more like strict income maximizers, and much less prosocially, than did the subjects of experiments conducted in affluent industrialized countries (Henrich et al. 2004:11). Subsequently, ethnographers carried out work in a variety of cultures around the world (Efferson et al. 2007; Henrich et al. 2004; Lesorogol 2007). These results showed that players in different cultures behaved in strikingly different ways. While the modal offer in affluent industrialized cultures is consistently 50 percent, the modal offers across ethnographic samples range from 15 to 50 percent (Henrich et al. 2004:19).

Henrich et al. (2004:33–35) found that individual-level data such as age, sex, exposure to markets, and wealth do not explain individual-level variations in offers and rejections; the crucial determinants are group-level measures in market integration[1] and payoffs to cooperation. Lesorogol (2007:924) also found that individual-level characteristics failed to predict the results of dictator games[2] played among the Samburu, except in *contextualized* games where players were encouraged to apply prevalent social norms for meat division as the context for their offers. Efferson et al. (2007:917) conducted dictator games in two locations: altiplano Bolivia and a multiethnic village in Tanzania. They found that individual-level measures of market integration and participation in cooperative activities did, in fact, partially predict game results for Bolivia, while ethnic affiliation was overwhelmingly the most important determinant of game results in Tanzania. These results suggest that variations in game behavior are more likely to be determined by the culture in which the individual is embedded, rather than by the unique position or life history of the individual within the culture. And, taken together, these factors raise interesting questions regarding the cultural determinants of prosocial behavior.

In some ways these results are not particularly surprising. Years of experiments with college students in industrialized countries have also failed to explain offers or rejections with demographic data such as sex, age, or income (Henrich et al. 2005:798). Querying players on their ideological or social preferences typically yields variables that explain game results quite well (Henrich et al. 2005:799). What is new is the notion that results could vary so much across different societies, and that market integration of each society could explain a significant portion of that variation.

Market integration, as formulated by Henrich et al., reflects the frequency and importance of contact with strangers. Societies organized in semi-autarkic households, with scant need to interact with strangers, might therefore exhibit little prosocial behavior when interacting with the anonymous other of a game (Henrich et al. 2004:40). Likewise, cooperation with non-kin would be low in societies with semi-autarkic households, since the household can furnish most of its own needs. From this perspective, prosocial behavior would be emphasized in societies where persons come in frequent contact with others, requiring that contact in order to gain their livelihood. For example, the society with the most prosocial behavior in the Henrich et al. sample, the Lamalera, engages in whale hunting, which requires that men work together in boat crews, dividing the catch (Henrich et al. 2004:39).

Similar work has been done comparing game behavior across modern nation-states. While the results of "basic games" such as the ultimatum game show little variation across nations, variation is quite pronounced in games that allow "norm enforcement" (i.e., punishment) (Gächter et al. 2005). Herrmann et al. (2008) conducted games with university students in 16 cities across 15 countries. They used a *public goods game*, in which four participants are each given 20 tokens, redeemable for money. Each participant can put tokens in a common fund, which the experimenter increases by 1.6 and then redistributes equally among all participants. If each player puts in her entire endowment, she will receive 32 tokens at the end of the game. However, if she keeps her 20 tokens and the other players each put in 20 tokens, then she will do even better, receiving 24 tokens from the common fund, giving her a total of 44 tokens. If she is the only one to contribute, and she contributes her entire endowment, then she will lose heavily, ending the game with only eight tokens. From the narrow income-maximizing perspective of rationality, players should anticipate that other players will not contribute and therefore not contribute themselves.

Generally, public goods games are played for multiple rounds. Contrary to predictions assuming narrow rationality, the average contribution to the common fund will start out high; eventually, however, contributions fall to very low levels. But if players are allowed to "punish" one another, then typically those who fail to contribute are punished by high contributors and will subsequently also contribute, so that the game ends with all players contributing their full endowment. "Punishment," in the Herrmann et al. games, consists of a three-token fine, but the player who initiated the punishment must pay one token as a cost. The Herrmann et al. study examined the fact that punishment takes on not only prosocial forms (punishing those who failed to contribute) but also antisocial forms (usually revenge attacks on high contributors by those who had been punished). Nations with stronger traditions of rule of law had much less antisocial punishment (Herrmann et al. 2008:1366). Herbert Gintis (2008:1346) considers the most likely reason for this to be that societies with well-developed rule of law are those in which people often interact with strangers, and who therefore react with guilt to punishment by strangers and correct their own behavior. Those societies with weaker rule of law are those in which people primarily cooperate with family and friends, and are likely to respond with anger to punishment by strangers.

Using both ethnographic and international samples, empirical studies have attempted to uncover the determinants of prosocial behavior in economic games. In all cases, the most prosocial behavior is seen in players from societies in which people are accustomed to interacting with strangers. Since markets are the primary means through which strangers voluntarily interact, this suggests that market relationships encourage prosocial behavior.

In what follows we will examine the extent to which markets are associated with prosocial behavior, using the Standard Cross-Cultural Sample

(SCCS), a database containing variables for 186 well-documented societies. The advantage of the SCCS is that it contains well-studied societies from the entire range of human experience: from foragers to advanced civilizations, from the Arctic to the tropics, sampled from every major cultural region of the world. Only by testing against such a complete sample can one make generalizations claiming to encompass all humanity (Ember and Ember 2000).

This chapter is divided into five parts. First, we briefly review some of the literature on determinants of prosocial behavior. Next, we describe the variables selected from the SCCS. We then briefly discuss three major econometric issues encountered when estimating models with data from the SCCS. The fourth section describes the estimation and the results. We conclude with a discussion of our findings.

THE DETERMINANTS OF PROSOCIAL BEHAVIOR

Henrich et al. (2005:814) note that their experimental outcomes could be either the expression of behavioral rules cued by the context of the game or the expression of "generalized behavioral dispositions." For the former, the researchers offer a few examples: the Orma interpreted the public goods game as similar to a funding practice called *harambee* used to build schools or roads, and contributed generously; the Au interpreted the ultimatum game as similar to gift giving by powerful men, where recipients fall under an onerous obligation to repay, and therefore rejected generous offers (Henrich et al. 2005:811). These are instances of behavior explicitly cued by *specific* norms. Some societies may try harder to inculcate prosocial behavior, and the variation in game results could be due to these generalized dispositions.

Socialization research (Henrich et al. 2005:813; Ross 1992; Whiting 1965; Whiting and Whiting 1975; Broude 1990) has documented how different child-rearing practices can lead to different levels of prosocial behavior. Cross-cultural methods have established that different kinds of values are instilled in different kinds of subsistence economies (Barry et al. 1959; Barry et al. 1976). For example, obedience and responsibility are valuable in pastoral or agricultural societies, where children must learn to care for stocks of food; self-reliance is valuable in forager societies, where children must learn to roam about and gather food (Barry et al. 1959). Generalized prosocial behavior would tend to be established in a society where members would find it useful. As discussed below, agents in a market economy have an incentive to display generalized prosocial behavior.

Evolutionary theory suggests a partitioning of sociality into three forms: nepotism, reciprocity, and coercion (van den Berghe 1981). The first two represent the two theoretical perspectives that can explain the existence of cooperation: cooperation that benefits consanguineous kin (Hamilton 1964), and cooperation with non-kin that is paid back in future benefits (Trivers 1971). Coercion encompasses noncooperative behavior. These three forms are conceived as ideal types, since any specific social structure will embody all three forms, though one might predominate. For example, the nuclear family includes elements of coercion (parents coerce children) and reciprocity (the parents are not close consanguineous kin), though nepotism predominates.

A society in which reciprocity is particularly predominant, relative to nepotism and coercion, will be one in which prosocial behavior is particularly useful. Coercive relationships require only that subjects be obedient—not honest, trustworthy, or generous—so the need for prosocial behavior is low in a society characterized by hierarchy and force. Nepotistic relationships require that subjects discriminate in favor of close consanguineous kin, and do not require generalized prosocial behavior. Prosocial behavior is especially useful whenever non-kin freely enter into cooperative activities.

Reciprocity, as used here, embraces any exchange in which the partners are not consanguineous kin, and are not strictly bound by formal rules or authority to perform the exchange. Voluntary exchange in a market would meet these criteria, as would freely entered-into cooperative behavior.[3] Reciprocal relationships usually entail a prisoner's dilemma problem: the agents collectively benefit most from cooperation, but individually benefit most from cheating. Since the best strategy for an agent faced with a cheating partner is also to cheat, one would expect both agents to cheat in the absence of trust.

Explaining the existence of human reciprocal relationships has therefore become an interesting theoretical problem for biologists and social scientists. One of the first important theoretical advances came in 1981, when the political scientist Robert Axelrod and the evolutionary biologist William Hamilton showed that the optimal solution to a repeated, two-agent prisoner's dilemma game was tit for tat: start out cooperating, then on each subsequent move simply repeat what the other party did on the previous move (Axelrod and Hamilton 1981).

Tit for tat, however, is unable to explain cooperative behavior in cases where multiple agents interact, or where interactions with a particular agent are not repeated. Richard Alexander (1987:85) developed the concept of "indirect reciprocity" to explain situations where humans behave altruistically, even though there is a near-zero chance of further interactions (e.g., the tipping of a waiter at a restaurant that one will not visit again). Here, the altruistic act is for display, to inspire trust in potential partners. A large number of models subsequently emerged in which the agents cultivate "reputations" that determine the quality of their interactions with others (for example, Gintis et al. 2001; Panchanathan and Boyd 2003; Pacheco et al. 2006).

Over two centuries ago[4] Adam Smith (1978:538–539) made the argument that agents engage in prosocial behavior in order to build reputations that inspire trust, thus receiving benefits from that trust through improved access to reciprocal relationships. Specifically, he argues that *market relationships* promote honesty, because honesty builds trust, and trust brings customers:

> Whenever commerce is introduced into any country, probity and punctuality always accompany it. . . . Of all the nations in Europe, the Dutch, the most commercial, are the most faithfull to their word. The English are more so than the Scotch, but much inferiour to the Dutch, and in the remote parts of this country they are far less so than in the commercial parts of it. This is not at all to be imputed to national character. . . . It is far more reduceable to self interest. . . . A dealer is afraid of losing his character, and is scrupulous in observing every engagement. When a person makes perhaps 20 contracts in a day, he cannot gain so much by endeavouring to impose on his neighbours, as the very appearance of a cheat would make him lose. Where people seldom deal with one another, we find that they are somewhat disposed to cheat, because they can gain more by a smart trick than they can lose by the injury which it does their character. . . . When the greater part of people are merchants they always bring probity and punctuality into fashion, and these therefore are the principal virtues of a commercial nation.

Morton Deutsch (1962) maintains that the following four conditions are sufficient to create trust in experimental games: the participants can work out a system of procedures; the participants both have control over outcomes; the participants know each other; and there is the possibility of involving a third party to resolve disputes (Erasmus 1977:50). The first two of these conditions require that parties to an exchange can work out the rules themselves, and that they retain control of the exchange, so that exchange is both decentralized and voluntary. One can see that these conditions would be more pervasive in a society with a long-established tradition of liberty and egalitarianism, and that market transactions can meet these two conditions. The third condition—that the parties know each other—involves the cultivation of reputation, as in the models based on indirect reciprocity.

The final condition—that third parties can be involved as arbiters—is implicit in Adam Smith's recognition that a market economy needs an impartial court system to enforce contracts (e.g., Smith 1937:576 [1776]), and in Mancur Olson's (1965) idea that "selective incentives" can force free riders to contribute to public goods. Contemporary research (e.g., Boyd and Matthew 2007; Boyd and Richerson 1992; Gintis 2008) recognizes that punishment for uncooperative behavior maintains cooperation, as discussed above in the context of the public goods game. Even among nonhuman primates, such as chimpanzees and capuchin monkeys, experiments have shown that actors are willing to punish others when outcomes are unfair (Brosnan and de Waal 2005; Silk 2007). Thus successful reciprocity requires some coercion.

Coercion can therefore support reciprocity insofar as it punishes uncooperative behavior. Group selection models consider coercion aimed at outgroups, and conclude that *external* war should promote prosocial behavior (Choi and Bowles 2007). Thus coercion both in the form of sanctions against uncooperative behavior and in the form of external war should promote prosociality. Socialization studies find prosocial behavior to be incompatible with a male ideal of aggressive toughness (Ross 1992:278); warfare would be particularly likely to call forth this male ideal, so war could lower prosocial behavior.

DATA

The Standard Cross-Cultural Sample (SCCS) contains 186 cultures, each selected as a relatively well-documented representative of a local cultural region (Murdock and White 1969). Over time, scholars have combed the ethnographies for these 186 cultures, coding about 2,000 variables for a wide variety of cultural traits.[5] The descriptive statistics for the variables used in our models are presented in Table 2.1.

Three variables, coded by Barry et al. (1976), measure the degree to which a society, during the process of childhood socialization (ages 4 through 12), attempts to inculcate the prosocial traits of generosity, trust, and honesty. These prosocial traits will serve as dependent variables. Figure 2.1 shows the geographic distribution of values for the mean of these three variables.

Our hypothesis is that prosocial traits are most likely to be inculcated in societies where non-kin engage in voluntary exchanges, whether these are part of a web of ongoing cooperation, or sharply delimited onetime market exchanges. Three independent variables measure the intensity of market exchange. Two variables measure the extent of cooperation. Two other variables give some sense of the rules governing the inheritance of property.

Societies in which coercive relationships predominate will have less need for prosocial behavior, and we include one variable to measure the degree of coercion from political authorities within the society. We also include one variable for internal war, one for external war, and one to indicate the number of neighboring societies. Likewise, societies where nepotistic relationships predominate will have less need for general prosocial behavior, and we employ three variables to measure the degree of nepotism.

Table 2.1. Descriptive Statistics for Data from SCCS

Variables	*Description*	*Sign*	*SCCS*	*mean*	*max*	*min*	*sd*	*nobs*	*trust*	*gener*	*honest*
Markets											
markin	Internal markets	+	v1733	2.792	4	1	1.187	96	-0.226*	-0.070	-0.111
markout	External markets	+	v1734	3.333	4	1	0.969	99	-0.061	0.128	-0.053
money	True money	+	v155	2.511	5	1	1.479	186	-0.200**	0.027	-0.048
Cooperation											
commland	Communality of land	+	v1726	2.306	3	1	0.817	98	-0.056	-0.048	-0.047
sharefood	Shared food	+	v1718	4.461	7	1	1.895	89	0.136	0.390***	0.141
Property											
inhreal	Inherit land and structures	+	(v278 > 1)	0.619	1	0	0.487	155	-0.229**	-0.225**	-0.220**
inhmove	Inherit movables	+	(v279 > 1)	0.862	1	0	0.346	152	-0.167*	-0.160	-0.166
Religion											
moralgods	Gods support morality	+	v238	2.149	4	1	1.192	168	-0.068	-0.056	-0.052
Scarcity											
marrgood	Goods exchanged at marriage	-	(v208 < 4)	0.597	1	0	0.492	186	-0.101	0.037	-0.085
polygamy	Polygamy	-	v79	3.118	4	1	0.711	186	-0.114	0.115	-0.211**
foodscarc	Chronic hunger	-	v1685	2.139	5	1	1.277	144	0.014	-0.176	-0.067
ecorich	Rich environment	+	v857	3.554	6	1	1.265	186	-0.112	-0.214**	-0.071
Warfare											
warintern	Frequent internal warfare	-	v1649	7.250	17	1	6.483	152	-0.192**	0.012	-0.215**
warextern	Frequent external warfare	+	v1650	8.097	17	1	6.663	154	-0.136	-0.028	-0.110
nsoc150	Number of societies within 150 miles	+	(v1865 + v1875)/2	4.194	27	0	4.995	183	-0.225***	0.026	-0.105

Nepotism											
famsize	Size of family	-	v80	3.231	5	1	1.237	186	-0.091	0.016	-0.049
ncmallow	Restrictions on cousin marriage	+	v227	4.810	8	1	2.572	174	0.104	-0.124	0.124
exogamy	Exogamy	+	v72	3.195	5	1	1.200	185	0.031	0.085	0.042
Coercion											
sanctions	Coercion enforces authority	-?	v1743	1.776	3	0	1.145	98	-0.039	-0.259*	-0.102
Valuation of children valuechil	Degree children valued	+	(v473 + v474 + v475 + v476)/4	6.006	9	2	1.425	171	0.395***	0.378***	0.236**
Dependent variables											
trust	Trust inculcated		v335	5.152	10	0	2.234	138		0.447***	0.453***
gener	Generosity inculcated		v334	6.010	10	1	1.830	104	0.447***		0.399***
honest	Honesty inculcated		v336	4.418	10	0	2.034	110	0.453***	0.399***	

Notes: "Sign" is the expected sign of coefficients when regressed on the dependent variables. "SCCS" shows how the variable is constructed, using the variable numbers from the Standard Cross-Cultural Sample; variables are described fully in the codebook (http://eclectic.ss.uci.edu/~drwhite/courses/SCCCodes.htm). The final three columns report the Pearson correlation coefficients for the variables with the three dependent variables; significance levels are indicated with "***" (p-value < 0.01), "**" (p-value < 0.05), and "*" (p-value < 0.1).

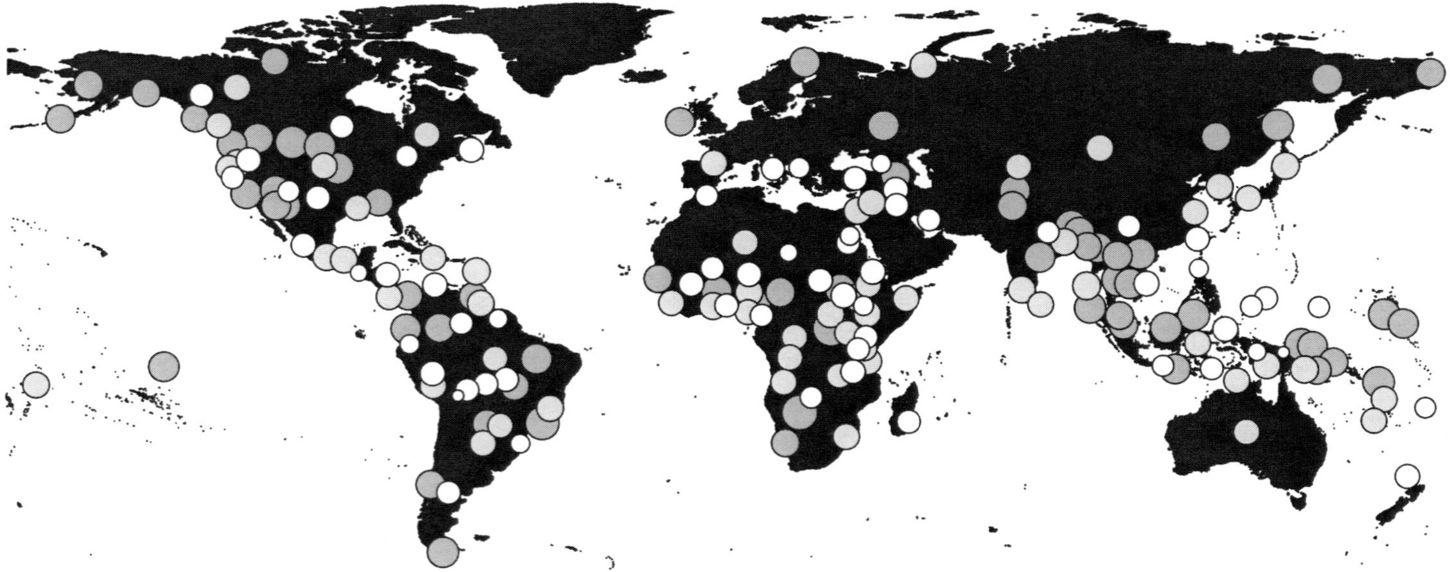

Figure 2.1. Mean prosocial behavior. Each circle is an SCCS society. The size and shade of each circle represents the average of the values for generosity, honesty, and trust, with larger sizes and darker shades representing higher levels of prosocial behavior.

To avoid omitted variable bias, one must control for other likely determinants of prosocial behavior. One consideration would be the costs of prosocial behavior: prosocial behavior would be more costly in a society experiencing scarcity and hence be less likely to be observed. Two variables reflect the scarcity of food, and two others reflect the difficulty of obtaining a spouse. Since religion plays a role in most moral systems, a variable is included indicating that gods actively support human morality.

Finally, since variation in the degree to which a society tries to instill prosocial behavior may simply be due to variation in the degree to which a society pays attention to children, we include a variable for the value a society places on children.

ESTIMATION ISSUES FOR SCCS DATA

Three issues are of particular importance when estimating regression models with the SCCS data. The first is the fact that the observations are not independent, since some societies are related through common descent or through cultural borrowing. This problem, usually called "Galton's problem," can be addressed by using spatial lag models (Dow 1984, 2007; Dow et al. 1984), an approach we follow here:

$$y = \mathbf{X}\beta + \lambda_L \mathbf{W_L} y + \lambda_D \mathbf{W_D} y + \varepsilon$$

where y is an *nx1* vector representing our dependent variable; $\mathbf{X}$ is an *nxk* matrix representing the independent variables; β is a *kx1* vector of coefficients; $\mathbf{W_L}$ and $\mathbf{W_D}$ are weight matrices for language (Eff 2008) and distance, respectively; λ_L and λ_D are scalar coefficients; and ε is a vector of errors. The scalars λ_L and λ_D are the spatial lag parameters, allowing an estimate of the effects of common descent or cultural borrowing on y. The model is estimated using two-stage least squares, as detailed in Dow (2007).

The second issue is the large number of missing values in the SCCS data (Dow and Eff 2009a, 2009b). The usual procedure for handling missing data is *listwise deletion*. In a regression model of the form $Y = \mathbf{X}\beta$, one drops any row where data are missing in Y or in one of the columns of $\mathbf{X}$. However, this method forgoes the information present in the dropped observations, and in turn has the potential to cause sample selection bias, so that the estimated coefficients are misleading.

An alternative is *multiple imputation*, which uses iterated estimation methods to estimate missing values based on all extant values. Gibbs sampling is used to take m random draws from the probability distribution for the missing values, conditional on the variables used to estimate them. One then has m (typically 5 to 10) duplicates of the original data set, each with different values imputed for the missing data. The equation $Y = \mathbf{X}\beta$ is estimated once for each of the m imputed data sets. This gives m estimates of the parameters β, their standard errors, and any model diagnostics. These estimates are then combined to give final estimates, as shown in Rubin (1987:76–81). In general, multiple imputation produces estimates that are more efficient and have less bias than estimates produced using listwise deletion (King et al. 2001:50–51).

The third issue is that of causation. Examining functional relationships in cross-cultural data raises two kinds of issues related to causation: endogeneity and the distinction between proximate and distal causes. Strictly speaking, functional relationships are teleological, and not relationships of efficient cause. Insofar as it is possible to speak of efficient cause in a functional relationship it is mutual causation that is implied. In the econometric setting, such mutual causation leads to the problem of endogeneity, which implies that the estimated regression coefficients will be biased. Nevertheless, there are theoretical reasons to think that some cultural features have a kind of causal primacy over other cultural features. Specifically, a *cultural materialist* perspective suggests that a society's environment and technology condition its social organization, which conditions its ideology. A materialist perspective gives a theoretical reason to think that the problem of endogeneity can be avoided: if the dependent variable is a feature of ideology, and the independent variables are features of the environment, technology, or social organization, then none of the independent variables should be endogenous.

The distinction between proximate and distal causes is seldom discussed in cross-cultural work, but it is potentially important. Socialization practices such as father absence have long been known to influence the inculcation of prosocial traits. These are proximate causes, directly responsible for the appearance of prosocial behavior. But behind these are more distal causes, such as the existence of chronic warfare, which provide the prosocial behavior with its functional rationale. The layers of causation are unlike those in a traditional econometric setting, where the layering is ordered temporally (more recent phenomena are caused by older phenomena), but are rather organized in terms of immediacy, such that efficient causes are proximate and final causes are distal, with gradations between.

The key issue for model specification is that variation in the dependent variable will be captured by both the proximate and distal causes, leading to a problem of multicollinearity. Since both proximate and distal causes are part of the same process, one should avoid including independent variables representing different layers of causation. In the present study, we are interested in the effects of markets on prosocial behavior, and we therefore avoid introducing independent variables for socialization practices (such as father absence) that are more proximate causes of the behavior.[6]

ESTIMATION AND RESULTS

Tables 2.2 through 2.5 present the estimation results for four different two-stage least squares models, where lag variables (for distance and language effects) are first estimated, and the fitted values from this first stage are used as "instruments" (i.e., replacements for endogenous independent variables) in the second stage. The first three models are for the dependent variables generosity, honesty, and trust. The fourth model has trust as the dependent variable, but includes instruments for generosity and honesty among the independent variables. All variables were first standardized, so that the coefficients can be interpreted as the number of standard deviations the dependent variable will change for a one-standard deviation increase in the independent variable. For all models an unrestricted model was estimated across 50 imputed data sets, and the *p*-values from the unrestricted model were used to rank the variables. Independent variables were then dropped, beginning with the variables with the highest *p*-values, until an *F*-test on the restrictions attained a *p*-value below 0.05. The last variable dropped was then reintroduced into the final model.

Listwise deletion would have left us with between 26 and 30 observations in our four unrestricted models; since these models estimated 20 parameters, the degrees of freedom would have been unacceptably low, and there would have almost certainly been a problem of sample selection bias in the particular societies deleted. Multiple imputation therefore offered the opportunity to estimate a model over the full range of societies, with a large number of independent variables.

A number of diagnostic tests are conducted for each of the restricted models. A RESET test (Ramsey 1969) has the null hypothesis that the model's functional form is adequate. A LaGrangian multiplier test for heteroskedasticity (Breusch and Pagan 1979) has the null hypothesis that the regression residuals are homoskedastic. The LaGrangian multiplier tests for spatial error and spatial lag effects, using the two weight matrices (language and distance), under the null hypothesis that there are no spatial effects (Anselin 1988). Finally, the Variance Inflation Factor (VIF) is calculated for each variable in each model to examine the extent to which multicollinearity is present (Greene 2003:57). The VIFs and the R^2 reported in the tables are the mean values from the 50 imputed data sets.

Table 2.2. Generosity: Unrestricted and Restricted Models

		Unrestricted Model		*Restricted Model*		
Variable	*Description*	*coef.*	*p-value*	*coef.*	*p-value*	*VIF*
Spatial lags						
gd	Spatial lag (Distance)	0.0905	0.3903	0.0968	0.3922	1.6539
gl	Spatial lag (Language)	0.0504	0.6185			
Markets						
markin	Internal markets	0.0662	0.6832			
markout	External markets	0.2613	0.0541	0.2308	0.0525	1.5910
money	True money	-0.0007	0.9955			
Cooperation						
commland	Communality of land	-0.1641	0.1874	-0.1683	0.1073	2.1242
sharefood	Shared food	0.2227	0.1143	0.2315	0.0326	1.7492
Property						
inhreal	Inherit land and structures	-0.2140	0.1030	-0.2117	0.0483	1.9581
inhmove	Inherit movables	-0.2200	0.0210	-0.1783	0.0314	1.3888
Religion						
moralgods	Gods support morality	0.0491	0.5809			
Scarcity						
marrgood	Goods exchanged at marriage	0.0810	0.4265			
polygamy	Polygamy	-0.1081	0.3498	-0.0672	0.5167	1.3428
foodscarc	Chronic hunger	-0.1585	0.0621	-0.1750	0.0343	1.6208
ecorich	Rich environment	0.0833	0.4040	0.0773	0.3936	1.4409
Warfare						
warintern	Frequent internal warfare	0.1056	0.4749			
warextern	Frequent external warfare	-0.0089	0.9566			
nsoc150	Number of societies within 150 miles	0.0606	0.5347			
Nepotism						
famsize	Size of family	-0.0757	0.3830	-0.0788	0.3595	1.3115
ncmallow	Restrictions on cousin marriage	-0.0299	0.7211			
exogamy	Exogamy	0.1368	0.0767	0.1487	0.0510	1.7822
Coercion						
sanctions	Coercion enforces authority	-0.0540	0.6924			
Valuation of children						
valuechil	Degree children valued	0.3441	0.0000	0.3305	0.0000	1.6216

Notes: All coefficients are standardized. *F-test on Restrictions*, p-value = 0.099. For the restricted model: $R^2 = 0.4305$. $m = 50$. *RESET test, p*-value = 1; *Heteroskedasticity, p*-value = 1; *LM test for spatial error* (Language), *p*-value = 0.3741; *LM test for spatial lag (Language), p*-value = 0.467; *LM test for spatial error (Distance), p*-value = 0.2827; *LM test for spatial lag (Distance), p*-value = 0.7226.

Table 2.2 reports the estimation results for a model with generosity as the dependent variable. Coefficients and *p*-values for both unrestricted and restricted models are given. All the cooperation and property variables enter the restricted model, as does one of the market variables.

The final restricted model diagnostics indicate no problems with heteroskedasticity, autocorrelation, or misspecification. Five of the independent variables are insignificant, even though an *F*-test rejects adding any of these insignificant variables to the list of variables already dropped. Usually such a situation indicates multicollinearity, but that is not the case here since all the VIFs are low. The variables are sorted by ascending size of coefficient (these are standardized so that they can be directly compared to one another). The surprise here is that the two property variables (*inhreal* and *inhmove*) are negative and significant, suggesting that rules of property inheritance discourage generosity. Norms of food sharing, however, promote the inculcation of generosity, as does the presence of external markets. Of the other variables entered into the model as controls, the positive coefficient for exogamy is the most interesting; this indicates that as nepotistic ties become less salient, generosity is more encouraged. As expected, scarcity (*foodscarc*) discourages generosity.

Table 2.3 contains the results for a model with *honest* as the dependent variable. The two property variables and one of the cooperation variables, but none of the market variables, enter the restricted model. Again, the final restricted model passes all the diagnostic tests, but many of the coefficients are insignificant despite the *F*-test's indicating that these variables should remain in the model. Only one property variable is significant (*inhreal*) in the restricted model, and this is negative, suggesting that rules of inheritance of real property discourage honesty. Of the control variables, exogamy is again positive and significant. And, similar to the case with generosity, scarcity (*polygamy*) discourages honesty.

A model with *trust* as the dependent variable is presented in Table 2.4. The diagnostic tests show no problem with heteroskedasticity, autocorrelation, or specification. Two of the market variables (*markin* and *money*), one of the property variables (*inhreal*) and one cooperation variable (*sharefood*) emerge from the unrestricted model, but only *inhreal* is significant in the final restricted model. Once again, the results suggest that prosocial behavior is less encouraged in societies with rules for the inheritance of real property. The most interesting of the control variables is *nsoc150*, which has a negative coefficient; this indicates that trust is less pronounced in societies that have a large number of neighboring societies. Unlike the previous models, the spatial lag (based on physical distance) is significant; this indicates that trust may diffuse among neighboring societies.

Table 2.3. Honesty: Unrestricted and Restricted Models

Variable	*Description*	*Unrestricted Model* *coef.*	*p-value*	*Restricted Model* *coef.*	*p-value*	*VIF*
Spatial lags						
hd	Spatial lag (Distance)	0.0758	0.4911			
hl	Spatial lag (Language)	0.0485	0.6344			
Markets						
markin	Internal markets	-0.0076	0.9557			
markout	External markets	-0.0741	0.5716			
money	True money	0.0603	0.5652			
Cooperation						
commland	Communality of land	-0.0515	0.7254			
sharefood	Shared food	0.2137	0.1086	0.1775	0.1569	1.7416
Property						
inhreal	Inherit land and structures	-0.2572	0.0606	-0.2607	0.0172	1.5647
inhmove	Inherit movables	0.1098	0.3726	-0.0644	0.5833	2.1221
Religion						
moralgods	Gods support morality	-0.0012	0.9907			
Scarcity						
marrgood	Goods exchanged at marriage	-0.0099	0.9261			
polygamy	Polygamy	-0.2068	0.0251	-0.2398	0.0053	1.4412
foodscarc	Chronic hunger	-0.0650	0.5388			
ecorich	Rich environment	0.1302	0.2250	0.1331	0.1612	1.6173
Warfare						
warintern	Frequent internal warfare	-0.0949	0.5241			
warextern	Frequent external warfare	-0.1187	0.4500	-0.1675	0.1268	1.9840
nsoc150	Number of societies within 150 miles	-0.0905	0.3471	-0.0477	0.5953	1.7649
Nepotism						
famsize	Size of family	-0.0076	0.9394			
ncmallow	Restrictions on cousin marriage	0.0552	0.5444			
exogamy	Exogamy	0.1477	0.1001	0.1520	0.0797	1.5825
Coercion						
sanctions	Coercion enforces authority	-0.0577	0.7010			
Valuation of children						
valuechil	Degree children valued	0.1961	0.0255	0.2191	0.0116	1.3871

Notes: All coefficients are standardized. *F-test on Restrictions*, p-value = 0.0587. For the restricted model: R^2 = 0.2418. *m* = 50. *RESET test*, *p*-value = 0.5737; *Heteroskedasticity*, *p*-value = 0.4494; *LM test for spatial error (Language)*, *p*-value = 1; *LM test for spatial lag (Language)*, *p*-value = 1; *LM test for spatial error (Distance)*, *p*-value = 0.4813; *LM test for spatial lag (Distance)*, *p*-value = 0.6341.

Table 2.4. Trust: Unrestricted and Restricted Models

		Unrestricted Model		*Restricted Model*		
Variable	*Description*	*coef.*	*p-value*	*coef.*	*p-value*	*VIF*
Spatial lags						
td	Spatial lag (Distance)	0.1667	0.1081	0.1888	0.0225	1.5790
tl	Spatial lag (Language)	0.0311	0.7563			
Markets						
markin	Internal markets	-0.1461	0.1894	-0.1286	0.1605	1.5533
markout	External markets	0.0379	0.7466			
money	True money	-0.1569	0.0982	-0.0878	0.2661	1.7568
Cooperation						
commland	Communality of land	-0.1375	0.2828			
sharefood	Shared food	0.1618	0.1618	0.1285	0.1852	1.7615
Property						
inhreal	Inherit land and structures	-0.2538	0.0323	-0.1784	0.0505	1.6195
inhmove	Inherit movables	-0.0080	0.9361			
Religion						
moralgods	Gods support morality	0.0253	0.7948			
Scarcity						
marrgood	Goods exchanged at marriage	0.0029	0.9722			
polygamy	Polygamy	-0.0398	0.6615			
foodscarc	Chronic hunger	0.1572	0.1116	0.1111	0.1772	1.9845
ecorich	Rich environment	0.0629	0.4915			
Warfare						
warintern	Frequent internal warfare	-0.0054	0.9660			
warextern	Frequent external warfare	-0.1083	0.4124			
nsoc150	Number of societies within 150 miles	-0.1834	0.0247	-0.2163	0.0028	1.7817
Nepotism						
famsize	Size of family	-0.0879	0.2741			
ncmallow	Restrictions on cousin marriage	0.1085	0.2150	0.1106	0.1832	2.0840
exogamy	Exogamy	0.0513	0.4910			
Coercion						
sanctions	Coercion enforces authority	0.1139	0.2900			
Valuation of children						
valuechil	Degree children valued	0.2925	0.0001	0.2949	0.0001	2.0000

Notes: All coefficients are standardized. *F-test on Restrictions,* p-value = 0.1027. For the restricted model: R^2 = 0.3148. *m* = 50. *RESET test, p*-value = 1; *Heteroskedasticity, p*-value = 1; *LM test for spatial error (Language), p*-value = 1; *LM test for spatial lag (Language), p*-value = 0.7152; *LM test for spatial error (Distance), p*-value = 0.5015; *LM test for spatial lag (Distance), p*-value = 0.5525.

Table 2.5. Trust (Generosity and Honesty as Independent Variables)

		Unrestricted Model		Restricted Model		
Variable	*Description*	*coef.*	*p-value*	*coef.*	*p-value*	*VIF*
Spatial lags						
td	Spatial lag (Distance)	0.1892	0.0568	0.2038	0.0096	1.8732
tl	Spatial lag (Language)	0.0256	0.7753			
Instruments for gener & honest						
geni	Instrument for Generosity	0.3136	0.0106	0.2844	0.0028	2.0342
honi	Instrument for Honesty	0.2498	0.0361	0.2551	0.0059	1.6720
Markets						
markin	Internal markets	-0.1634	0.1477	-0.1563	0.0788	1.8193
markout	External markets	-0.0209	0.8740			
money	True money	-0.1827	0.0488	-0.2004	0.0078	1.8098
Cooperation						
commland	Communality of land	-0.0612	0.6431			
sharefood	Shared food	0.0214	0.8727			
Property						
inhreal	Inherit land and structures	-0.0794	0.5326			
inhmove	Inherit movables	0.0279	0.7896			
Religion						
moralgods	Gods support morality	0.0153	0.8711			
Scarcity						
marrgood	Goods exchanged at marriage	-0.0230	0.7989			
polygamy	Polygamy	0.0697	0.4603			
foodscarc	Chronic hunger	0.2271	0.0151	0.2070	0.0130	2.5568
ecorich	Rich environment	-0.0009	0.9924			
Warfare						
warintern	Frequent internal warfare	-0.0007	0.9957			
warextern	Frequent external warfare	-0.0713	0.6075			
nsoc150	Number of societies within 150 miles	-0.1765	0.0393	-0.1589	0.0285	2.1968
Nepotism						
famsize	Size of family	-0.0648	0.4380			
ncmallow	Restrictions on cousin marriage	0.0968	0.2808			
exogamy	Exogamy	-0.0477	0.5403			
Coercion						
sanctions	Coercion enforces authority	0.1468	0.1901	0.1126	0.2148	2.1386
Valuation of children						
valuechil	Degree children valued	0.1132	0.1893	0.1317	0.0838	2.1589

Notes: All coefficients are standardized. *F-test on Restrictions,* p-value = 0.1322. For the restricted model: $R^2 = 0.3976$. $m = 50$. *RESET test, p*-value = 1; *Heteroskedasticity, p*-value = 1; *LM test for spatial error (Language), p*-value = 1; *LM test for spatial lag (Language), p*-value = 0.7234; *LM test for spatial error (Distance), p*-value = 0.4766; *LM test for spatial lag (Distance), p*-value = 0.4885.

The fourth model, presented in Table 2.5, again has trust as the dependent variable, but it includes instruments for generosity and honesty as independent variables. As one would expect, both of these are positive and highly significant, suggesting that trust is higher where honesty and generosity are higher. Two of the market variables (*money* and *markin*) pass to the restricted model. Contrary to our initial expectations, both of these are negative and significant. The control variable *nsoc150* again has a negative and significant coefficient, showing that the presence of strangers from *outside* one's own society diminishes trust. Again, the diagnostic tests show no problems with the restricted model.

Considering all four estimated models, our initial expectation that markets would tend to encourage prosocial behavior is not borne out by the results. The only exception appears to be for the trait of generosity, where the presence of external markets is associated with greater inculcation of generosity.

Our variables for cooperation return mixed results. Sharing of food is associated with greater inculcation of generosity, while communality of land is never significant and never takes on the expected positive sign even in the unrestricted model. The results for our property variables are unambiguously contrary to expectation: societies with clear rules of property inheritance are less likely to instill prosocial behavior in children.

DISCUSSION

The results failed to confirm our initial expectation that generalized prosocial behavior will be more pronounced in societies where reciprocity—especially reciprocity embodied in market relationships—is more important. There are several possible reasons for this negative result.

The first pertains to the nature of our dependent variables. Rather than measuring the extent to which prosocial behavior is observed among adults, the variables measure the extent to which adults attempt to inculcate the behavior in children. Since children learn by example and by explicit instruction, it could be that societies with plentiful good examples (i.e., adults tend to behave prosocially) would not need to make much effort to inculcate prosociality in children, and hence would rate low on the values of our dependent variables.

The second reason is that our prosocial behaviors, and especially generosity, do not always act so as to build reputations in support of reciprocity, and indeed cannot always be considered "prosocial." Among the Kwakiutl, generosity may serve to display leaders' status (Bliege Bird and Smith 2005:227); among the Au and Gnau of Papua New Guinea, ambitious men seek status by giving expensive gifts that create often-unwelcome obligations in the recipients (Henrich et al. 2004:39); among the Meriam of Queensland, generosity during funeral feasts signals "lineage strength" (Bliege Bird and Smith 2005:227). For Aristotle, who maintained that property should be privately held but used in common (Aristotle 1946:49), generosity was the enabling virtue, and in typical Aristotelian fashion it was defined as a middle-path behavior between miserliness and wastefulness (Aristotle 1985:88). Here generosity is part of the ethic of noblesse oblige, and elite expenditure becomes community consumption, as it does in the "corporate communities" described by Eric Wolf (1955:458). In all these cases, rather than signaling one's suitability as a partner in a reciprocal exchange relationship, generosity signals and builds status; in the language of Thorstein Veblen (1953 [1899]), it creates "invidious distinctions."

The third consideration is the possibility that general prosocial dispositions have little to do with the ethnographic experimental game outcomes discussed above, and that those outcomes are due entirely to the cuing of culturally specific norms. But this begs the question, how is it that specific norms were cued such that the size of offers in ultimatum games correlated with levels of market integration? There must be some way in which norms are systematically affected by markets. One possibility is that markets and capitalism lead to a weakening of shared norms.

One experiment by Carolyn Lesorogol explicitly looked at the effect of shared norms. In some of her experiments, proposers were encouraged to contextualize the dictator game by thinking of it as the sharing of goat meat. Framing the game in this way led proposers to make significantly *lower* offers than they did in a much more abstract game. Lesorogol (2007:921) points out that shared norms make the behavior of other agents predictable and, as Charles Erasmus (1977:49) notes, trust is based on predictability. A likely interpretation of Lesorogol's results is that the shared norms gave the proposer confidence that her offer would be acceptable to the responder, whereas in the abstract game, the proposer felt compelled to make higher offers in order to avoid offending the responder.[7] In other words, the absence of a shared norm gives rise to a kind of risk premium in the initial offer, so that initial offers become higher.

As Georg Simmel (1978 [1900]) has described, capitalism erodes traditions: pecuniary valuation displaces traditional ways of valuation; relationships among people become instrumental and restricted within the bounds of a contract, rather than becoming than ongoing whole-person relationships. Capitalism creates a world in which people and things are commodified, so that one person or thing is much like another, where all people are strangers and strangers really aren't that strange. Capitalism creates a much more *abstract* world, in which general notions of fairness in exchange (modeled on bargaining among equals in a market) replace specific cultural norms mediating exchanges among actors occupying specific roles. Friedrich Hayek (1976:109), in fact, argues that capitalism is simply an efficient means, allowing the coexistence of people with very different ends, so that in the resulting pluralistic society there are no norms shared by all people. Thus, players from capitalist societies may not only be primed to treat strangers with relative sympathy but also may have few shared norms available to guide offers and responses other than the norm of fair exchange in a market.

In this view, if specific shared norms are guiding offers and responses in experimental games, and those norms are different from one society to another (which is quite likely to be the case), then one would observe wide variation in offers and responses—which in fact *is* what one observes. Further, to the extent that a society has been affected by capitalism, shared norms will be weakened, leading to offers that are somewhat high since there is a greater probability of offending the responder without a shared norm. Viewed in this way, there is no reason to expect members of societies with economies integrated by markets to have any greater tendency toward generalized prosocial behavior than members of societies without markets.

CONCLUSION

A number of ethnographers have conducted experimental games among the people they study. The results have attracted a great deal of interest, for several reasons. First, they show a great deal more variation in game results than one sees in the large number of studies conducted among university students in industrialized nations. Second, ultimatum-game offers in many of the studied societies are more "rational" (i.e., less generous) than what one sees in industrialized societies. Third, variation in game results cannot be explained by individual-level demographic data, but much can be explained by society-level variables, with the striking discovery that more generous offers in ultimatum games are made in societies with higher levels of market integration.

There remains the question of whether the generous offers were made because of generalized prosocial dispositions, or because the offers were cued by specific shared norms. If the former, then it appears that societies with economies integrated by markets may socialize children to display high levels of generalized prosocial behavior. There are strong theoretical reasons to believe in such an association, beginning with ideas from Adam Smith and continuing through the work of contemporary game theory in evolutionary biology and social science. These perspectives argue that prosocial behavior helps to build an actor's reputation, with the goal of gaining the trust of other actors, so that the other actors are willing to engage in cooperative activities.

Using the Standard Cross-Cultural Sample of 186 societies representing the full spectrum of human diversity, this chapter attempted to test the association between generalized prosocial behavior and markets. Since many of the variables have missing values, we used multiple imputation in order to retain the full diversity of societies with the SCCS. Galton's problem is widely recognized as the single most critical problem of cross-cultural research; we employed the spatial econometric methods presented in Dow (2007) to correct for Galton's problem. The dependent variables in our models represent the degree to which a society attempts to inculcate the values of generosity, trust, and honesty during socialization. The independent variables include several variables pertaining to markets (the existence of internal markets; the existence of external markets; the existence of true money); two variables on the existence of assignable property rights; and 14 control variables.

The results of our models give no support to the notion that societies with markets are more likely to inculcate prosocial values in their children. We interpret this negative result as implying that societies with market-organized economies are no more likely to instill high levels of prosociality in their members than are any other kind of society, and that the results of the ethnographic experiments can most likely be interpreted as due to the cuing of shared norms. We explain the fact that ultimatum-game offers are higher in societies with higher levels of market integration by pointing to the writings of Georg Simmel and Friedrich Hayek, who show that capitalism leads to the erosion of shared norms. The relative lack of shared norms reduces the predictability of a responder's reaction in an ultimatum game, and therefore causes the proposer to make a higher offer in order to ensure against rejection.

NOTES

1. The term *market integration* as employed by Henrich et al. (2004:28–29) refers to a composite measure containing three variables: (1) frequency of market exchange (market integration), (2) amount of centralized decision making taking place above the household (sociopolitical complexity), and (3) size of local settlements (settlement size). Each of these variables is formulated as the rank of a particular society (among all of the Henrich et al. societies) for that dimension. The composite is simply the mean of the three ranks.
2. The dictator game is like the ultimatum game, except that the player who receives the offer cannot reject it.
3. This definition of reciprocity therefore potentially encompasses much of both *reciprocity* and *markets* in Karl Polanyi's influential schema (Polanyi 1957).
4. Smith's *Lectures on Jurisprudence* are based on notes by students attending his lectures at Glasgow University between 1752 and 1764 (Smith 1978:2).

5. The data and documentation are available at http://eclectic.ss.uci.edu/~drwhite/sccs/.

6. The working paper version of this chapter provides a much fuller discussion of Galton's Problem and missing data: http://econpapers.repec.org/paper/mtswpaper/200803.htm.

7. This was a dictator game, so the responder could not reject the proposer's offer. The responders and proposers were kept in separate areas, without contact, and were randomly called to participate in the anonymous game (Lesorogol 2007:923). Nevertheless, all players were from the same ethnicity and the same community, and proposers may have had the sense that they were playing with members of their in-group. Proposers may have also expected gossip to spread of their winnings. Unfortunately, the experimenters were unable to conduct postgame interviews for the abstract game, so we lack proposers' own testimony on why they made such high offers (Lesorogol 2007:924).

REFERENCES

Alexander, Richard D. 1987. *The Biology of Moral Systems*. New York: Aldine De Gruyter.

Anselin, Luc. 1988. *Spatial Econometrics: Methods and Models*. Dordrecht: Kluwer Academic Publishers.

Aristotle. 1946. *The Politics of Aristotle*. Translated by Ernest Barker. Oxford: Oxford University Press.

———. 1985. *Nicomachean Ethics*. Translated by Terence Irwin. Indianapolis: Hackett.

Axelrod, Robert, and William D. Hamilton. 1981. "The Evolution of Cooperation." *Science* 211:1390–1396.

Barry, Herbert, III, Irvin L. Child, and Margaret K. Bacon. 1959. "Relation of Child Training to Subsistence Economy." *American Anthropologist* 61 (1): 51–63.

Barry, Herbert, III, Lili Josephson, Edith Lauer, and Catherine Marshall. 1976. "Traits Inculcated in Childhood: Cross Cultural Codes 5." *Ethnology* 15:83–114.

Bliege Bird, Rebecca, and Eric Alden Smith. 2005. "Signaling Theory, Strategic Interaction, and Symbolic Capital." *Current Anthropology* 46 (2): 221–248.

Boyd, Robert, and Peter J. Richerson. 1992. "Punishment Allows the Evolution of Cooperation (or Anything Else) in Sizable Groups." *Ethology and Sociobiology* 13:171–195.

Boyd, Robert, and Sarah Matthew. 2007. "A Narrow Road to Cooperation." *Science* 316 (5833): 1858–1859.

Breusch, T. S., and Pagan, A. R. 1979. "A Simple Test for Heteroscedasticity and Random Coefficient Variation." *Econometrica* 47:1287–1294.

Brosnan, Sarah F., and Frans B. M. de Waal. 2005. "A Cross-Species Perspective on the Selfishness Axiom." *Behavioral and Brain Sciences* 28 (6): 818.

Broude, Gwen J. 1990. "Protest Masculinity: A Further Look at the Causes and the Concept." *Ethos* 18 (1): 103–122.

Choi, Jung-Kyoo, and Samuel Bowles. 2007. "The Coevolution of Parochial Altruism and War." *Science* 318 (5850): 636–640.

Deutsch, Morton. 1962. "Cooperation and Trust: Some Theoretical Notes." *Nebraska Symposium on Motivation* 10:275–319.

Dow, Malcolm M. 1984. "A Biparametric Approach to Network Autocorrelation: Galton's Problem." *Sociological Methods and Research* 13 (2): 201–217.

———. 2007. "Galton's Problem as Multiple Network Autocorrelation Effects." *Cross-Cultural Research* 41 (4): 336–363.

Dow, Malcolm, Michael Burton, Douglas R. White, and Karl Reitz. 1984. "Galton's Problem as Network Autocorrelation." *American Ethnologist* 11:754–770.

Dow, Malcolm M, and E. Anthon Eff. 2009a. "Cultural Trait Transmission and Missing Data as Sources of Bias in Cross-Cultural Survey Research: Explanations of Polygyny Re-examined." *Cross-Cultural Research* 43 (2): 134–151.

———. 2009b. "Multiple Imputation of Missing Data in Cross-Cultural Samples." *Cross-Cultural Research* 43 (3): 206–229.

Eff, E. Anthon. 2008. "Weight Matrices for Cultural Proximity: Deriving Weights from a Language Phylogeny." *Structure and Dynamics: eJournal of Anthropological and Related Sciences* 3 (2), art. 9.

Efferson, Charles, Masanori Takezawa, and Richard McElreath. 2007. "New Methods in Quantitative Ethnography: Economic Experiments and Variation in the Price of Equality." *Current Anthropology* 48 (6): 912–919.

Ember, Melvin, and Carol R. Ember. 2000. "Testing Theory and Why the 'Units of Analysis' Problem Is Not a Problem." *Ethnology* 39 (4): 349–363.

Erasmus, Charles. 1977. *In Search of the Common Good: Utopian Experiments Past and Future*. New York: Free Press.

Gächter, Simon, Benedikt Herrmann, and Christian Thöni. 2005. "Cross-Cultural Differences in Norm Enforcement." *Behavioral and Brain Sciences* 28 (6): 822–823.

Gintis, Herbert. 2008. "Punishment and Cooperation." *Science* 319 (5868): 1345–1346.

Gintis, Herbert, Eric Alden Smith, and Samuel Bowles. 2001. "Costly Signaling and Cooperation." *Journal of Theoretical Biology* 213:103–119.

Greene, William H. 2003. *Econometric Analysis*. Upper Saddle River, NJ: Prentice Hall.

Hamilton, W. D. 1964. "The Genetical Evolution of Social Behaviour I and II." *Journal of Theoretical Biology* 7:1–16 and 7:17–52.

Hayek, Friedrich. 1976. *Law, Legislation, and Liberty: The Mirage of Social Justice*. Chicago: University of Chicago Press.

Henrich, Joseph, Robert Boyd, Samuel Bowles, Colin Camerer, Ernst Fehr, and Herbert Gintis et al. 2004. *Foundations of Human Sociality: Economic Experiments and Ethnographic Evidence from Fifteen Small-Scale Societies*. Oxford: Oxford University Press.

———. 2005. "'Economic Man' in Cross-Cultural Perspective: Behavioral Experiments in 15 Small-Scale Societies." *Behavioral and Brain Sciences* 28 (6): 795–855

Herrmann, Benedikt, Christian Thöni, and Simon Gächter. 2008. "Antisocial Punishment across Societies." *Science* 319 (5868): 1362–1367.

King, Gary, James Honaker, Anne Joseph, and Kenneth Scheve. 2001. "Analyzing Incomplete Political Science Data: An Alternative Algorithm for Multiple Imputation." *American Political Science Review* 95 (1): 49–69.

Lesorogol, Carolyn K. 2007. "Bringing Norms In: The Role of Context in Experimental Dictator Games." *Current Anthropology* 48 (6): 920–926.

Murdock, George P., and Douglas R. White. 1969. "A Standard Cross-Cultural Sample." *Ethnology* 9:329–369.

Olson, Mancur. 1965. *The Logic of Collective Action: Public Goods and the Theory of Groups*. Cambridge, MA: Harvard University Press.

Pacheco, Jorge M., Francisco C. Santos, and Fabio A. C. C. Chalub. 2006. "Stern-Judging: A Simple, Successful Norm Which Promotes Cooperation under Indirect Reciprocity." *PLOS Computational Biology* 2 (12): 1634–1638.

Panchanathan, K., and Robert Boyd. 2003. "A Tale of Two Defectors: The Importance of Standing for Evolution of Indirect Reciprocity." *Journal of Theoretical Biology* 224:115–126.

Polanyi, Karl. 1957. "The Economy as Instituted Process." In *Trade and Markets in the Early Empires: Economies in History and Theory*, edited by Karl Polanyi, Conrad M. Arensberg, and Harry W. Pearson, 243–270. Glencoe, IL: Free Press & Falcon's Wing Press.

Ramsey, J. B. 1969. "Tests for Specification Errors in Classical Linear Least Squares Regression Analysis." *Journal of the Royal Statistical Society B* 31 (2): 350–371.

Ross, Marc Howard. 1992. "Social Structure, Psychocultural Dispositions, and Violent Conflict: Extensions from a Cross-Cultural Study." In *Aggression and Peacefulness in Humans and Other Primates*, edited by James Silverberg and J. Patrick Gray, 271–289. Oxford: Oxford University Press.

Rubin, Donald B. 1987. *Multiple Imputation for Nonresponse in Surveys*. New York: J. Wiley & Sons.

Silk, Joan B. 2007. "Chimps Don't Just Get Mad, They Get Even." *Proceedings of the National Academy of Sciences* 104 (34): 13537–13538.

Simmel, Georg. 1978 [1900]. *The Philosophy of Money*. London: Routledge & Kegan Paul.

Smith, Adam. 1937 [1776]. *An Inquiry into the Nature and Causes of the Wealth of Nations*. New York: Modern Library.

———. 1978. *Lectures on Jurisprudence*. Oxford University Press.

Trivers, Robert .L. 1971. "The Evolution of Reciprocal Altruism." *Quarterly Review of Biology* 46:35–57.

Van den Berghe, Pierre L. 1981. *The Ethnic Phenomenon*. New York: Elsevier.

Veblen, Thorstein. 1953 [1899]. *The Theory of the Leisure Class*. New York: Mentor Books.

Whiting, Beatrice B. 1965. "Sex Identity Conflict and Physical Violence: A Comparative Study." *American Anthropologist* 67, no. 6, pt. 2: *The Ethnography of Law* (December): 123–140.

Whiting, John W. M., and Beatrice B Whiting. 1975. "Aloofness and Intimacy of Husbands and Wives: A Cross-Cultural Study." *Ethos* 3, no. 2 (Summer): 183–207.

Wolf, Eric R. 1955. "Types of Latin American Peasantry: A Preliminary Discussion." *American Anthropologist* 57 (3): 452–471.

3

Critique of Reciprocity

Shifting Uses and Meanings of Ayni *among Andean Groups*

Matthew Bird,
University of Chicago and
Harvard Business School

Reciprocity has served as a basic analytical category for understanding nonmarket social exchange and as such has been contrasted with money-mediated market transactions (Malinowski 1962 [1922]; Mauss 1990 [1924]; Polanyi et al. 1957; Polanyi 2001 [1944]; Sahlins 1972). However, social scientists have also, somewhat paradoxically, used the concept to explain the formation and functioning of institutions needed to lower transaction costs and improve market performance (Axelrod 1984; North 1990; Ostrom 1990; Putnam 1992). Can the concept of reciprocity apply equally to both nonmarket and market economic contexts or does a qualitative difference exist between the two uses?

A historical and ethnographic analysis of the shifts in Andean reciprocity or *ayni* from one mediated by kinship and community mechanisms to one mediated more fully by market exchange indicates that there is a qualitative difference. Originally, *ayni* emerged in the pre-Colombian Andes to help organize agricultural production in the face of ecological demands. Money and markets did not exist until Spanish colonization, when *ayni* was used to access the labor needed for production in a new mercantile economy. The development of a liberal export economy in the 19th century accelerated the erosion of Andean communities, leading to rural–urban migration in the 20th century and the use of *ayni* upon arrival to Lima, where it served as a boon subordinate to contractual market exchange. These moorings were soon jettisoned as Andean groups entered more fully into urban markets. As seen in transactions in Lima's textile, food, and artisan marketplaces, the practice of market exchange taught migrants to privilege profit and specific notions of freedom, equality, property, and self-interest. Within such a context, reciprocal practices were relegated to microsociological niches in response to the lack of trust in third-party institutions. While the core act of *ayni* persisted, its uses and meanings changed with shifting economic contexts.

The transformation of *ayni* suggests that the reciprocity concept should be both delimited and affirmed as an analytical category for studying exchange. Caution must be taken in applying it, for if researchers overemphasize its narrow "contractual" aspect—that is, as the meeting of two people or groups who are obligated to give and receive—they risk importing an unduly utilitarian frame into the analysis, ignoring distinct mental conceptions associated with reciprocal practices in nonmarket contexts. Broadly, the uses and meanings of reciprocity should be distinguished from trust, and both should be understood within the context of the full economic system of production and exchange, however organized and motivated.

THE STRANGE CAREER OF RECIPROCITY

The paradoxical uses of the reciprocity concept stem from two distinct models: the gift and collective action. Reciprocity is assumed to mean the same in both models, but the assumptions and internal logics of the two frameworks are not easily reconcilable.

Reciprocity and the Gift

The first model seeks to explain social exchange in premodern, precapitalist "archaic," or primitive, societies. The reciprocity concept stems from the sociological desire to analyze relations between people as organized by mechanisms other than market exchange.

Although Bronislaw Malinowski (1962 [1922]) posited the concept of the pure gift—giving something freely and without interest or expectation of return—both Malinowski and Marcel Mauss (1990 [1924]) concluded that a premodern system of the gift and reciprocity rested on an agonistic give-and-take. Mauss pushed this model the furthest by making three claims: there is no such thing as a pure gift, reciprocal exchange is an essential component of all societies, and there is a historical descent from a system of total *prestations* to modern, contract-based market exchange.

Although Malinowski and Mauss sought to develop an anthropological critique of neoclassical economic principles, they went about this endeavor in different ways. Malinowski (1962 [1922]), for example, argued that the psychological wants of Trobriand chiefs differed from those of modern entrepreneurs. The chieftain's motivation in the famed Kula ring was the continuous engagement in the transfer of things, in giving and receiving as an end in itself, while the modern entrepreneur's objective was wealth accumulation. Mauss moved the critique in a sociological direction. He replaced market exchange with the gift system and substituted the invisible hand for the gift cycle. "Increasingly," Mary Douglas wrote, "we are finding that the gift economy comprises all the associations—symbolic, interpersonal, and economic—that we need for comparison with the market economy" (1990: xiv).

Karl Polanyi (1957, 2001 [1944]) and Marshall Sahlins (1972) later attempted to codify the distinctions between market and reciprocal exchange. Polanyi identified differences among reciprocity, redistribution, and the market. The first applied to noncentralized communities, the second to more centralized societies, and the third to modern economies. Sahlins organized reciprocity into three categories—generalized, balanced, and negative. The mode of reciprocal exchange shifts from generalized to balanced to negative the farther one moves outward from circles of group membership—from the house to kin to the village to the tribe and so on.

Despite critiques of the gift model—for example, against the proposed universality of reciprocal practices, the use of typologies, or inattention to the sociocultural embeddedness of exchange (Gudeman 2001; Hann 2006)—the framework remains a theoretical counterpoint to market exchange models and associated neoclassical principles of scarcity, utility maximization, and equilibrium on which the second model of reciprocity grew.

Reciprocity and Collective Action

The second framework stems from game theory and rational choice models of collective action and the free-rider problem, which make different assumptions about human behavior.

Mancur Olson framed the basic issue: "It is *not* in fact true that the idea that groups will act in their self-interest follows logically from the premise of rational and self-interested behavior," he wrote. "Indeed, unless the number of individuals in a group is quite small, or unless there is coercion or some other special device to make individuals act in their common interest, *rational, self-interested individuals will not act to achieve their common group interests*" (1965:1–2; emphasis in original). When groups provide public goods—a resource that does not disappear when used and from which people cannot be excluded from using—individuals are tempted to not contribute to the good's production or conservation since they can still benefit from it even if they shirk collective responsibility. Examples of these dilemmas abound, for all social groups encounter collective action problems of some kind, whether they fish in the same area, have animals that graze on the same land, or draw benefits from the same government good.

Game theory models the issue as a prisoner's dilemma (e.g., Axelrod 1984). Imagine that you and someone else are held by the police and can't communicate. If you give up the other person, you can leave. If you remain silent, and your partner implicates you, you'll face a more severe punishment. However, if you both remain silent, you'll both escape with a lighter punishment. What do you do? In game theory, the dominant strategy is to "defect," or squeal, because there is no guarantee that the other won't do the same. By blaming the other person, you avoid the worst punishment. However, this is only the third-best solution.

Real-world collective action problems possess a similar structure. Imagine herders sharing common grazing land or fishermen using the same section of the sea. Each person gains direct benefit from access to these resources. But since the costs of overgrazing and overfishing are delayed or indirectly felt, rational self-interested actors will continue to add more herds and increase their catch, leading to unintended resource depletion. Common pool resources, in whatever guise—be it international cooperation, global warming, or government spending—are all susceptible to these kinds of collective action failures (Ostrom 1990).

Yet we also know that in the real world, better solutions than the prisoner's dilemma's dominant strategy appear. How do they function and how did they come about? Thomas Hobbes (1994 [1651]) argued that a third-party enforcer in the form of the state—a Leviathan—was necessary for ensuring mutual benefit and social harmony. But who enforces the state? Some scholars returned to game theory in search of a solution. People do not cooperate in the prisoner's dilemma scenario because it is a one-shot game, they reasoned. Yet if the game were infinitely repeated, thus better approximating reality, players would respond "tit for tat," reciprocating each other's actions based on past experience, thus building mutual trust (Axelrod 1984). The strategy's success, however, depends on the amount of information flow about the actor's reputation and prior behavior. As social groups become larger and more complex, the tit-for-tat strategy is harder to maintain.

For this reason, others posited that social capital or norms of reciprocity and networks of trust were the key to solving collective action problems and explaining the rise of formal third-party institutions (Bates 1988; North 1990; Ostrom 1990). The full argument rests on three related assertions: individuals adopt norms of trust and reciprocity; this leads people to behave in certain ways; and these behaviors aggregate to create governance institutions that foster economic growth (Coleman 1990; Putnam 1992). The argument assumes shared ends for all actors and the desire to reach Pareto-optimal outcomes—a situation when welfare is maximized as best as possible for all members of a group. The means for realizing this objective depends on reciprocal norms and trust networks, which enable self-interested actors to overcome collective action and free-rider problems. Out of this research agenda, scholars began to search for the "essence" or sources of human sociality through cross-cultural economic experiments (Henrich et al. 2004) while others hypothesized universal biological and evolutionary psychological substrates explaining reciprocity and trust (Hoffman et al. 1998; Zak 2004).

But the two models lie in fundamental contradiction. The first construes reciprocity as a mode of exchange distinct from the market. The second conflates reciprocity with trust and sees it as essential for the formation and functioning of market institutions. Meanwhile, many seek to universalize reciprocity biologically, psychologically, or sociologically. An analysis of shifts in Andean *ayni* practices—based on ethnographic fieldwork in Lima, Peru, and triangulated with primary and secondary historical sources (Bird 2009)—reveals certain weaknesses in both approaches and points toward an alternative model that subsumes existing frameworks by explaining how the uses and meanings of reciprocity change with shifting economic contexts.

ANDEAN *AYNI*

Scholars have applied Polanyi's concepts of reciprocity and redistribution to archeological, archival, and ethnographic sources to decipher the logic of the pre-Columbian Andean economic system (Alberti and Mayer 1974; Mayer 2001; Murra 1980, 2002; Zuidema 1964, 1990).

Andean economic organization emerged to address ecological demands. Between its river valleys, mountain slopes, and highland plains, the region possessed a dizzying array of microclimates. Specific staples grew only in certain production zones. Maize was found in the river valleys; tubers flourished above designated altitudes; and on the high plains, or *punas*, at a height too inhospitable for agriculture, four varieties of camelids grazed in their natural habitat. To meet subsistence needs, communities settled between the major maize and tuber growing areas to gain better "vertical control" of the surrounding ecological zones (Murra 1972).

Kinship and community relations mediated access to land and labor. Villages were organized according to concentric kinship relations—from the household, to a web of households extending to third cousins descended from a great-great-grandfather, to a web of household networks, or an *ayllu*, which was endogamous and claimed a common ancestor, to an *ayllu* of *ayllus*, and so forth, until an ethnic group formed. Households were apportioned land for each ecological floor, while worker settlements, or *mitmaqs*, colonized distant zones to provide one's ethnic group with salt, coca leaf, or other goods.

Labor demands required for harvesting or tilling one's fields were met by calling on *ayni*, or reciprocal help. One day someone from your household helps our household and later someone from my household helps your household. The exchange did not take place between two people, but between two groups of people that lived under separate roofs. Labor exchange was understood as the equal and horizontal sharing of labor time. However, households were also required to contribute to the building of roads, terraces, or irrigation canals. The *mit'a*, as it was called, was organized by the village leader, or *kuraka*, and often included labor for the chieftain. In return, the *kuraka* provided gifts in kind, but not labor, since the reciprocal exchange was vertical. The entire system operated without the use of money-mediated exchange and barter was an ancillary activity (Murra 2002). Variations of this model existed throughout the Andes.

The Incan empire grew by extending reciprocal practices to the state level. The Cuzco-centered Incans made *mit'a* labor demands on conquered ethnic groups and forcibly resettled rebellious populations. Households were required to send labor to work on Incan lands, and permanent retainers were kept to serve the nobility. Regardless, a community's social viability was still conceived according to its degree of self-sufficiency. The Quechuan word for "poor" referred less to material goods and more to one's lack of social networks, which mediated access to resources.

Mentally, the *ayllu* member construed him- or herself through the commune and not as a "dot-like" individual who, when aggregated, constituted a group. This does not imply that the psychological concept of the person or self was absent. Rather, land did not belong to the individual but to the commune first; the commune then allotted it to households following distribution rules. *Ayni* was conceptualized as an exchange of household labor for working on apportioned lands redistributed periodically among a small, circumscribed clan. Since Andean subsistence did not rely primarily on specialized trade or barter, pre-Columbian Andean organization could be considered as noncapitalist.

INTRODUCING MARKETS

The Spanish Conquest in the Andes introduced a new mercantile economic organization, which used reciprocal practices as a means for accessing the labor needed for commodity production.

The raison d'être of the colonial economy was the extraction of silver and gold for export to Spain. To fulfill this objective, a complex of intra- and interregional trade networks linking peasant villages, haciendas, mines, and urban administrative centers emerged and coalesced, with cyclical rises and falls, from the mid-16th to the 19th century (Assadourian 1982; Larson and Harris 1995). The Andes possessed the land for agriculture and mining and the Spaniards provided the capital and technology, but the system lacked a major factor of production—labor. Large amounts of it were needed for the mines and for producing secondary inputs (such as mercury to amalgamate the silver ore), and domestic goods (such as tools, clothing, and foodstuffs for the non-self-subsistent population). But who would work the mines, extract the mercury, till the hacienda lands, and labor in the *obrajes* or textile and manufacturing workshops? No labor market existed. Potential workers remained "locked" in subsistence agriculture organized by practices of reciprocity and redistribution.

After conquest in 1532, the Crown initially addressed this issue by instituting an *economienda* system, which in feudal-like manner "entrusted" groups of natives to a lord, who held labor and tribute rights over his subjects as well as the responsibility for evangelizing and civilizing them. But the system soon reached a crisis point (Stern 1982). The *encomendero* relied on the *kuraka* for providing labor, which was supplied by calling on *mit'a* obligations. But this required the *kuraka* to reciprocate in kind with his population. As the labor demand increased with mining expansion and commercial growth, indigenous subjects threatened rebellion. Why, they asked, should they contribute if they received nothing in return? The colonial government responded in the 1570s with a series of reforms that tapped into and exploited Andean *ayni* and *mit'a* logics.

To gain tighter control over a dispersed, rebellious, and dwindling native population, the Crown ordered *reducciones*, or forced resettlement to new village centers. Once people had relocated, the Crown placed labor and tribute obligations on the population. It created a forced labor draft, or *mita*,[1] which required each household to send workers for periods of time to the mines and haciendas. The natives also had to pay a tax in money or goods and were forced to purchase manufactured commodities produced within the empire (Spalding 1974). These demands put the indigenous population in a difficult economic position: they had to contribute *mita* labor, pay tributes, and buy goods while eking out a subsistence living within the context of massive demographic collapse and geographic relocation. A subsistence system was forced to produce a surplus, whether in labor, goods, or money, to meet state obligations.

Although the reforms disrupted subsistence practices, they did not eliminate them. The *reducciones* cut off many *mitmaqs* in distant ecological zones from their *ayllus*, but much of the indigenous population reorganized in new settlements using principles of reciprocity and redistribution. Since access to communal lands was protected by colonial law, the native population maintained, albeit in modified form, a subsistent agricultural lifestyle

(Wightman 1990).[2] When a household needed to turn over its fields, harvest crops, or build a roof, it called on kin and community members for *ayni* help. The household was then beholden to the others for when they needed assistance. Village leaders also continued to call on either the *mit'a* or communal labor for projects.

This does not imply that wage labor was absent during the colonial era. It existed—in the mines, on the haciendas, and within urban centers. Rather, alternative labor regimes operated side by side: forced labor, whether in *mita* or slavery form; debt-peonage; and *yanaconaje* (serflike retainers). Free wage labor was in scarce supply because of demographic collapse and because Andean communities remained relatively self-subsistent. This lack of pressure on land made it even more difficult to entice (as opposed to force) natives from their government-recognized communal lands and subsistence lifestyles.[3] Andean migrants didn't arrive en masse to urban and coastal areas until Peru inserted itself into global markets following independence in 1821 (Gootenberg 1989).

By the turn of the 20th century, the country began to diversify exports—sugar, cotton, minerals, wool, oil, and rubber (Thorp and Bertram 1978). New labor and resource demands affected the subsistence communities in different ways given distinct organizations needed for production. In general, however, economic linkage effects accelerated the long-term erosion of Peru's Andean communities. Hacienda encroachment and demographic growth placed pressures on land and water resources, forcing community members to abandon semisubsistent lifestyles and migrate permanently. Despite variations, the result was the same: the near final and systematic divorcing of communities from subsistent ways of life—from access to kinship- and community-mediated land, water, and labor resources (Deere 1990; Jacobsen 1993; Klarén 1973).

It took several centuries for Peru to develop a free labor market, to create individuals who began to perceive themselves in dot-like isolation. This is why the *mita* draft was created, slaves were brought from Africa, and debt-peonage systems were used. Despite coercive methods and the gradual rise of wage labor, the indigenous masses were not yet divorced from subsistence lifestyles. They didn't depend on the sale of their labor and the use of earnings to live. Different mental conceptions and economic relationships existed. Andean access to land and labor resources remained mediated more through kinship- and community-mediated reciprocal practices, a system whose deterioration took generations to erode. But when it did, a new kind of economic necessity appeared, based not on ecological demands but on the need for monetary income.

AYNI AS URBAN BOON

It is a common, Dickensian story. Migrants arrived to Lima through a multistep process buoyed by kinship and community networks, which mediated information and opportunities. They left because a parent or family member sent them to the local capital to work, or perhaps even to escape abuse. Upon arrival, they sought out relatives or community members. Some stayed, satisfied with their new situation, while others left. The economic reality often failed to meet their expectations, so they continued their journey, sometimes alone and other times with family or friends, going to places where they heard of opportunities. Most migratory streams ended in Lima. Once a critical mass formed in the capital, migrants arrived there directly. Between 1920 and 2007, the number of migrants living in Lima grew from 84,000 to 2.8 million, with nearly three-quarters of the city's eight million people coming from provincial, mostly Andean, descent (INEI 2009).

But in Lima, the streets were not lined with gold. The initial challenges were to find housing and secure income. Migrants used reciprocal practices as an economic boon to solve these problems and access resources. In the process, market exchange further mediated reciprocal practices.

Migrant social organization emerged on the back of neighborhood associations, which in most cases formed with the founding of squatter settlements (Collier 1976; de Soto 1986). Given housing scarcity, Lima's *criollo* and Andean poor began to invade private and public lands surrounding the city. The San Cosme settlement in 1945 initiated this process and continued, in various forms, over the following decades (Degregori et al. 1986; Matos Mar 1977). San Cosme arose organically when Andean workers began to build makeshift homes on land near Lima's new central market, La Parada, where they worked. But they were evicted from the private land, and later they tried to negotiate a price. When the owners rejected the offer, the migrants organized a land invasion timed to coincide with other political events. The government eventually intervened in support of the new settlement, initiating four decades of informal but contested state sponsorship of squatter communities.

The organization of San Cosme and other settlements relied on a modified model of Andean reciprocal practices. Residents were expected to contribute to a common resource pool. The obligation was financial, but also included work. The neighborhood organization called on communal labor to complete public projects such as the building of a road or the digging of a drainage ditch. Residents followed similar principles to build homes, ritualizing the workday, as in the Andes, except the labor pool was not as tightly organized around a relatively closed kin and community group. While the circle remained concentric, it loosened. Existing kin were called on, then friends and migrants from the community of origin, and then members of the squatter settlement (Lobo 1982). Those who called the workday were obligated to provide food, alcohol, and perhaps coca leaf, though the last practice began to disappear. Once someone donated work to the other family, that family was indebted to him. In the traditional Andean setting, labor obligations were calculated and reconciled according to the household. Anyone living under the same roof could repay the labor debt to the other. But with transient kin or community members moving in and out of the home, the household was defined by who ate out of the same *olla*, or pot, making it more difficult to rationalize reciprocity corporatively. As such, *ayni* labor obligations became more individualized. It soon became not so much the household that was in debt, but the person.

While the use of networks made the clustering of kin and community members inevitable, not all members lived in the same neighborhoods. Regional associations also formed, linking migrants from the same area of origin and providing them with social support and resource access (Golte and Adams 1987). Take the case of those from the town of Unicachi, located on the shores of Lake Titicaca in Peru's Puno region. The first migrants arrived in the late 1940s and worked in La Parada as salted meat merchants, a specialization stemming from their contacts with Puno's cattle-raising region. Mass migration from the area began in the 1960s. Most migrants came to work either in La Parada or in the fishmeal industry in Lima's port city, Callao, and over time they managed to accumulate capital. This growth occurred through reliance on close kinship and community ties. As in many towns and provinces, Unicachi members used a *mit'a* logic to organize a regional club, which collected monthly quotas and sponsored public works projects (e.g., construction of schools and plazas) not only in Lima but also in Unicachi.

In the field of commerce and production, the *ayni* logic also persisted, albeit in modified form, as the firm came to replace the land as the site of reciprocal practices. Since Lima's formal economy could not absorb the mass of rural–urban migrants, newcomers created their own employment opportunities and sources of income by becoming merchants and small-scale producers. The firm, like the land, became a family's source of livelihood. Instead of calling on *ayni* for tilling fields or harvesting the crops, they used social networks and reciprocal practices to support entrepreneurial activities.

The objective of a migrant entrepreneur, repeated ad infinitum, was to *independizarse* (to become independent) by starting a business as soon as he or she saved enough capital and the opportunity presented itself. The goal mirrored that of creating an independent household in the Andes. In a village, one was not a full-fledged member of the community until he set up an independent home, from which *ayni* obligations could be drawn. After all, the Quechuan word for "poor" does not mean rich in material goods but in an abundance of relations through which someone accesses resources. While the drive to become independent continued in Lima, a new concept of wealth as material property evolved as market exchange mediated reciprocal practices.

Informal marketplaces appeared throughout the city. As in the squatter settlements, group members agreed to organize to share the financial and labor costs for public goods. They paid for security and they self-policed, staying on the lookout for thieves because they knew that the reputation of an unsafe environment would hurt all the group members. They set up communal dining, in which they ate from the same *olla*. They also extended credit to one another and traded small favors such as looking after another's stall or helping to fulfill an order. While the stringent reciprocal rules found in villages did not map perfectly onto these practices, a general "spirit" of reciprocity—of understanding that if I help you today, you will help me tomorrow—remained. Networks were tight enough in small marketplaces that shirking would damage a person's reputation and shut him or her off from future resources. But these sociological conditions would soon change.

ENTERING THE EDEN OF RIGHTS

Voluntary market exchange—the act of two free agents seeking to increase personal gain by setting a price for the contractual trade of goods and associated rights—is a cultural practice distinct from instances when production and exchange are organized through kinship, community, or network mechanisms (Marx 1993 [1858]). The market's increasing mediation of economic life infused migrants with the drive to maximize wealth, understood more as money and material goods rather than the density of social relations. In the process, the uses and meanings of *ayni* fundamentally changed.

Take the example of merchants and small producers, the source of economic livelihood for most migrants. The original heart of migrant activity in Lima centered on La Parada, the site of the city's bus terminal and its major market. It was there that San Cosme formed and it was there that Gamarra, Latin America's largest textile cluster consisting of over 15,000 firms and nearly $1 billion in annual sales, took shape (Bird 2007).

The majority of Gamarra's entrepreneurs began as poor Andean migrants or as their sons and daughters. Most started as street vendors, with nothing more than the small amount of capital they scraped together and a ferocious drive to improve their situation. The cluster's founders benefited from first-mover advantage in the 1960s and 1970s. "Anything you made was sold," one pioneer said. "You couldn't manufacture fast enough." Although firms confronted both *ex ante* property rights and *ex post* contract enforcement problems, they initially addressed these obstacles through reciprocal practices.

Gamarra's entrepreneurs came to adhere to the holy trinity of the logic of capital—work, save, reinvest. They labored on average 60–70 hours per week. Unlike many of Peru's status-conscious white-collar employees, they were frugal and they privileged business expenses over the home. Many avoided investing in additional goods or home improvement, such as a roof, because, as one daughter of a Gamarra businessman who owned her own firm said, "To invest in the home is dead capital." Such investment did not offer any return. This woman, like many in Gamarra, possessed an insightful understanding of what capital is—an asset that must be thrown back into circulation as quickly and efficiently as possible in order to self-valorize. When entrepreneurs spoke about their businesses they admitted to becoming consumed by it. María, one of 11 children from San Martín, a transitional area between the Andes and the Amazon, explained her transformation: "When I came [to Lima], I never imagined having my own business. But now, it's like a drug or an addiction. I can't stop, I'm always thinking about the business."

This mental shift was also present in worker reasoning. Entrepreneurs were split on whether they preferred to pay workers based on a salary or piece-rate. They admitted that the quality of salaried employees was higher, but with time constraints they often had to hire piece-rate workers. However, the more experienced, skilled, and efficient sewing machine operators learned to accept only piece-rate pay because they calculated it as the best way to maximize their earnings; many workers eventually used this income to start their own businesses.

The experience of migration infused actors with the logic of capital. A capitalist mentality, according to Weber, is "the idea of the duty of the individual to work toward the increase of his wealth, which is assumed to be an end in itself" (2002:11 [1905]). By contrast, a noncapitalist mentality is that which "does not 'by nature' want to make more and more money, but simply to live . . . in the manner in which he is accustomed . . . and to earn as much as is necessary for this" (2002:16 [1905]). Andean peasant mentalities, once concerned with maintaining subsistence and later supplementing incomes, had morphed into fuller, wealth-maximizing actors.

Market practices generated different mentalities, forms of labor, and ways of relating objectively and subjectively to property. In this context, the uses and meanings of reciprocity fundamentally shifted. Take as examples two entrepreneurial strategies—splintering and agglutinating—that developed in response to two leading barriers to firm growth: the lack of formal property rights (i.e., legal recognition of the right to use, derive income from, or alter an asset) and poor contract enforcement (i.e., the inability to complete an agreed exchange due to information and measurement costs).

By the 1980s, the high cost of formalization—of obtaining the proper licenses and registrations—was the leading limiter of firm size (de Soto 1986). Although staying informal was a rational economic decision, extralegality exacted a greater long-term price. When you are not legal, the costs of avoiding detection lead you to disperse activities, shun publicity, and spend on sanction-dodging bribes. You are forced to deal exclusively in cash within an inflationary environment and save in tangible goods rather than in cash. You may benefit from avoiding taxes and labor laws, but this compels you to hire less-qualified workers and become more labor intensive than capital intensive. You have no guarantee over your ability to use an asset, appropriate returns from it, or change its form or substance. You thus lack the incentive to invest in your own property and cannot use it as collateral for credit. You have trouble enforcing contracts and since many exchanges rest on oral agreements, you cannot easily resolve a dispute through a judicial court mechanism.

Ayni-supported market exchange could operate under conditions of thin markets and dense networks because it helped foster information flow about buyer and seller reputations. But with the growing anonymity—the transition from personal to impersonal exchange—more robust third-party institutions were needed to enforce contracts. In this context, *ayni* practices were reduced to smaller social circles and were superseded by a concern with *confianza*, or trust, a concept distinct from reciprocity. Reciprocity applied to exchange within a system of personal interaction, in which actors had information on one another, made judgments based on cultural frames of what is good or bad, and were obligated in some way to return favors. Trust took precedence within a system of impersonal market exchange, when anonymous actors, who had limited information about people or organizations, had to take a leap of faith that the other would honor a contractual commitment. The "new Limeños" made a strategic decision based on this distinction; the decision prompted them to use reciprocal practices in two distinct ways to address contract enforcement problems: "splintering" as demonstrated in Gamarra and "agglutinating" as seen with Unicachi urban investment groups.

Gamarra: A Splintering Model

The solutions Andean migrants and their children and grandchildren developed to adapt to the market-mediated business environment reached scalable limits by the 1980s. In the late 1980s and early 1990s, the Peruvian state addressed this through business legalization reform. The results were astonishing (Jaramillo 2004). In the early 1980s, it took 289 days and $1,231 paid in either fees or bribes to formalize a business. After reform in the 1990s, it took 100 days and $510 to complete the process. By 2003, Gamarra's formalization costs had fallen to 61 days and $163. Meanwhile, access to microcredit expanded significantly. With formalization, microfinance, and the willingness of banks to extend loans, a plethora of credit options became available.

But these reforms had unintended consequences. They fostered a pernicious firm multiplier effect that weakened the already-limited informal enforcement mechanisms, thus preventing firms from specializing in order to capture gains from trade. The new industry environment created greater *ex post* enforcement problems both between and within firms; these problems squeezed businesses and forced them to "rationally" stay small.

One of the most striking characteristics of Gamarra's entrepreneurs was neither their work ethic nor the capacity to save and reinvest, but their drive for independence.[4] More than a motif, this theme appears as a low and consistent bass line in nearly every conversation. The goal of hired workers, street vendors, and the sons and daughters of entrepreneurs was to "be independent"—to establish their own income stream by starting a business. Becoming a self-sufficient business owner offered many people pride and self-respect, consummating them as full-fledged members of society. But low entry barriers and meager worker salaries, which made ownership an attractive option, also incentivized this step. The drive for independence initiated a firm multiplier effect that led to fierce rivalry and greater anonymity.

Both created problems. Low entry barriers and setup costs, resulting from improved formalization procedures and the labor-intensive nature of the industry, crowded the marketplace and eroded profit margins. Competitor rivalry turned Gamarra into a buyers' market. Lower purchasing and production costs could offset this, but economies of scale weren't achievable. Smaller firms didn't have bargaining leverage with suppliers, and they had low levels of technology and limited market reach. Greater anonymity increased opportunistic or shirking behavior. These obstacles could not be checked by *ayni*-based enforcement mechanisms.

Experience taught Gamarra's entrepreneurs that each transaction presented a risk of loss. A couple approaches your stand and orders 500 T-shirts. They leave a down payment, but upon return they renege and refuse to pay. Since the agreement was oral you couldn't demand payment, and given Peru's high court-enforcement costs you never bothered to sign a contract. Owners combated these problems with the same informal solutions identified in the 1980s—reputation, investment in information, social networks, collective organizations, and even violence. But they had limited efficiency due to

Gamarra's growth and anonymity. As a result of this and an increasingly competitive market, owners jealously guarded their goods and services. They extended less credit, depended more on formal financing, and demanded more up-front cash payments. Most owners could tell cautionary tales of how prosperous businesses went under because of one bad deal. So high were these risks that entrepreneurs opted to reduce them by eliminating market activities and integrating them into their firm.

Failed attempts at joint production accentuated these between-firm obstacles. In general, when firms ally to fill large orders, they must set the conditions of association by specifying liability, property rights, and quality-control procedures. The challenge was twofold: to specify rights and operational protocol *ex ante* and to enforce the agreement *ex post* should a firm not fulfill its obligation. But again, anonymity and the absence of effective enforcement (because either courts are inefficient or informal strategies are limited) created problems. Since businesses used joint production to fill short-term orders, the risk of partners' "stealing" designs and taking advantage of supplier contacts afterward impeded the development of trust. In light of such costs, owners again rationally chose to integrate activities into their firm.

Given this, one would think Gamarra's firms had extra incentive to expand. But they were squeezed. The push to integrate ran up against internal agency costs. Owners had difficulty enforcing worker contracts. How could a firm incentivize employees to work in the owner's best interest when many workers also sought to start businesses once the opportunity arose? Gamarra's owners resorted to four strategies: rely heavily on piece-rate labor, since workers responded to production incentives; hire only those recommended by friends or family; delegate major firm responsibilities only to "trustworthy people" such as family members or friends who constituted the owner's inner circle, thus approximating a reciprocal model since exit from the group was less of an option; or subcontract activities, an option that had grown given the excess capacity of some businesses. But piece-rate and service contracting just brings us back full circle to between-firm enforcement issues.

After the reforms, the leading cause of firm size shifted from *ex ante* property rights to *ex post* contract enforcement. Gamarra's firms stayed small because they were squeezed. On the one hand, they were pushed to integrate activities. On the other, they avoided internal agency costs by returning to the market. In the end, they opted to do the work themselves—sewing, accounting, purchasing, and marketing. Productivity suffered because they couldn't achieve gains from the division of labor. Capital must be defined and protected, but it also must be allowed to circulate and self-valorize through specialization.

In sum, increasing market reliance, aided by property-rights reforms and increased credit, eroded reciprocal practices, spurring a shift from a "traditional" mentality to a more opportunistic mind-set that progressively resembled the *Homo economicus* model, but without the third-party institutions needed to solve the new collective action problems accompanying the shift from personal to impersonal exchange. Contrary to the argument of adherents to the social capital model of reciprocity, Gamarra's problems did not result from "deficient" preexisting cultural practices. Andean migrant groups brought strong and elaborate reciprocal practices with them to Lima. Rather, the transition from agricultural subsistence to market relations created a new type of collective action dilemma.

Unicachi: An Agglutinating Model

Unlike many in Gamarra, the Unicachinos combated collective action problems by releveraging reciprocal practices.

In the mid-1980s, several of Lima's district mayors initiated discussions about relocating the city's wholesale market from La Parada due to urban congestion. This sparked a speculative spiral in other marketplaces, hurting Unicachi merchants in La Parada. For this reason, the merchants proposed the construction of their own retail and wholesale market. However, due to the political and economic crisis in the late 1980s and early 1990s, neither the municipality nor the Unicachinos made headway in this plan. During that time, Peru suffered from a double-helix spiral of hyperinflation and political violence, the latter spurred by the emergence of the Shining Path guerrilla group.

In 1996, once stability returned and growth ensued, 29 Unicachinos pooled $720,000, bought a lot in Caquetá, and built Plaza Unicachi. On the heels of this success, 280 Unicachinos formed a commercial association, raised $2.4 million between them, outbid 13 other interested firms, and bought 7.5 hectares of prime real estate next to the city's major north–south highway, where they constructed Megamercado Unicachi. Afterward, six other multimillion-dollar projects appeared, bringing total investment to over $50 million (Niezen 2005). While these eight projects were distinct, consisting of different Unicachi shareholder groups, they were closely linked through the same kinship and community reciprocal ties used upon arrival to Lima. Only after the success of their first investment projects did other Unicachi groups gain formal access to bank financing, an avenue closed to them for initial investments.

What explains Unicachi's ability to create strategic alliances, especially if they relied on the same practices used by Peru's other Andean migrants? Why did the alliances agglutinate and not splinter? A local explanation may exist in the unique communal tightness seen in the Puno region, but this answer does not suffice. The Puno region has a reputation for possessing particularly tight kin and community relationships. But why Unicachi and not others from Puno?

The answer may lie in three additional factors. First, the success achieved by the Unicachinos' regional club projects, which fostered decades of repeated exchange and reinforced and extended the reciprocal relationships and strategies brought to Lima. Their foray into real-estate projects was modeled after earlier public works projects in both Unicachi and Lima, but on a greater scale. In comparison, many other regional clubs dissolved after a couple of decades once community members integrated more fully into Lima society. Second, the nature of real-estate investment shielded the group from the type of intense contract enforcement difficulties confronted daily in commercial clusters like Gamarra. The investment group sizes were relatively small, ranging from 29 to 280 people, compared to Gamarra's 15,000 firms. Given previous group success, little gain from shirking existed, since that would ostracize individuals from a relatively small investment community. These costs were not only financial but also cultural and psychological, a sanction arguably more powerful than monetary loss. And third, success created both a network of support and a precedent for other Unicachinos to model.

Unicachi was not the only example of agglutinating success; it was simply the most prominent and impressive, for other groups even in Gamarra managed to create successful alliances. Moises arrived to Lima from Cuzco in 1999. He came for *necesidad*, or necessity, because, as he said, the land he worked was getting smaller and didn't provide a living. He came alone—"I didn't know anybody"—with a small amount of savings and rented a small room. After arriving, he saw a newscast about Gamarra and decided to go there. He bought some T-shirts and sold them on the street. With these earnings, he extended his hotel stay, ate, and reinvested in more T-shirts. At one point, he almost went bankrupt when his inventory was stolen, but he recovered to the point that he rented a workshop in one of Gamarra's scores of galleries. On the same floor, he befriended three or four other men with whom he organized an *ayni* trading community. They assisted one another when needed and eventually applied for funding from Prompyme, a government arm dedicated to the promotion of small businesses.

Although the anonymity created in Lima pushed the limits of extralegal solutions, creating greater tendencies to shirk, there existed microsociologies, or "gobs," within which reciprocal practices were built daily; opportunism even in Lima could be foreclosed with ever more complex network- and information-sharing relationships, which took advantage of sociological niches in the marketplace to re-create *ayni* conditions. But these reciprocal practices fundamentally changed as they became more fully subordinate to market-mediated exchange, for they were grounded in different objective relations (kinship- and community-mediated exchange versus the market) and subjective conceptions (conceiving one's relationship to property through communal and household ownership *first* versus one modeled on a market-mediated understanding of the individual rights to use, change the form of, and derive income from one's private property).

CRITIQUE OF RECIPROCITY

In the spirit of critique, the reciprocity concept should be both delimited and affirmed. This requires the crafting of a framework that reconciles real contradictions, valid insights, and legitimate critiques.

Real contradictions. The reciprocity concept rests on two distinct frameworks that make fundamentally different assumptions about human behavior. The gift model does not assume that people maximize individual utility. Although the collective action model loosens expected utility axioms, it adheres to a basic *Homo economicus* framework.

Valid insights. The gift model focuses on the agonistic, psychological nature of give-and-take within kinship- and community-mediated groups. The collective action model provides crucial sociological insights about the importance of group size, information flow, network density, and reputation effects.

Legitimate critiques. The assertion of the universal and essential nature of reciprocal behavior, whether grounded in sociological, psychological, or biological origins, can be questioned. Attempts to typologize reciprocity can be critiqued. Greater attention should be given to the sociocultural embeddedness of exchange.

These contradictions, insights, and critiques can be reconciled if we (1) focus on the fundamental difference between nonmarket and market organization as lying not in exchange alone, but in the mode of exchange made possible by changes in economic production; and (2) recognize that this shift, while initially brought about by a transformation in social relations, prompted cultural changes emergent from the normative logic of market exchange.

The act of market exchange gives birth to specific notions of freedom, equality, property, and self-interest. However, these notions do not appear in identical form wherever market transactions have become the fundamental mode of exchange and production. Markets come to mediate differing existing practices to forge new varieties of economic mentalities. These interactions are akin to a dye, which when poured into different-colored paints produces ever more similar but multifarious hues. A historical analysis subsumes insights about reciprocity by offering a new framework for understanding its changing uses and meanings in different economic contexts.

Accounting for the Gift Model

The gift model of exchange construes the reciprocity concept as an agonistic give-and-take. It identifies a fundamental difference between "archaic" and modern market economies according to the mode of exchange. The movement of goods was not mediated by money nor motivated by the insatiable thirst to increase one's wealth. Other principles applied, such as the concern for status and honor. Mauss pushed the rationale the furthest, replacing the logic of the market with the logic of the gift. He did so with the goal of identifying the historical genesis of the modern form of the contract.

But the narrow focus on reciprocity as the meeting between two people or entities that obligate each other to give and receive does not capture the fundamental shift in social relations from which modern market exchange emerges. The underlying mode of production matters. In the Andes, for example, different mental notions about one's relationship to property existed. Prior to the arrival of markets, access to property was mediated through kinship and community mechanisms, and village members construed themselves through this framework. *Ayni*, and its associated rules and customs, stemmed from this context. Forced migration and entrepreneurial activities in Lima made Andeans "free to choose." They gradually ceased to view resource access through kinship and community as *ayni* practices became subordinate to market exchange to the point that resource access became more fully mediated by market exchange. Only then did reciprocity become something narrower—as a contractual and enforceable give-and-take. The sociology of trust, characterized by anonymity, the lack of information, and the need for third-party enforceability, took precedence in a system where production was organized by market exchange.

Accounting for the Collective Action Model

The collective action model conflates reciprocity and trust. And in cases that concern a form of reciprocity, such as among delimited social groups where gossip acts as a social enforcement, the reciprocal practice is distinct from that used, for example, in the North American Indian potlatch or the Melanesian *kula*. Sociological insights of network density, reputation, and information flow may apply. However, the economic organization of a 15th-century Andean village and the social networks in 21st-century business clusters in Gamarra differ greatly. Specifically, the subjective conceptualization of the relationship between the person and the group and property are not the same. In Andean *ayni*, resources were mediated by kinship and community—not contributing labor was akin to social suicide. In Gamarra, property was understood in its market-mediated form—as individually owned and fungible.

Cultural expectations held the system in place in the Andes and, to an extent, in Lima, where practices became more fully mediated by market exchange. Thus, the game theory argument that reputation, information flow, and repeated plays determine cooperation or defection is only partially correct. Social networks and collective organizations that give rise to organic private-order mechanisms may serve the same bare ends, but the *means*—the cultural practices—used for realizing these ends may vary. In the field, the creation of reputations and the flow of information can take several forms and be enabled by different belief systems. Regardless, the argument that extralegal solutions in places like Gamarra fail to achieve economies of scale holds because game theory's assumptions asymptotically come to match the sociological conditions and psychological attitudes created by market contexts.

Accounting for Culturalist Critiques

Finally, culturalist critiques have been directed at both reciprocity models. First, Malinowski and Mauss claim that the essence of human sociality was found in reciprocity, but critics cite the importance of sociocultural embeddedness. Second, Polanyi admits that economic principles apply to modern market societies, but some refuse to cede disciplinary ground, asserting that all economies are socially and culturally embedded. Third, the collective action argument rests on a claim about the superiority of cultural norms and values, but critics consider this a fallacious resurrection of white man's burden arguments.

However, the three culturalist critiques do not fully construe market exchange as a mode of social relations that generates its own cultural forms, thus making the critiques or dichotomies appear both valid and false. By focusing on exchange alone, Malinowski and Mauss inadvertently risk, at times, a utilitarian conception of reciprocity that they never quite work through, thus providing the appearance of continuity from the potlatch and *kula* to the modern contract. Polanyi identifies legitimate sociological differences between economic modes, causing him to "cede" modern economic principles to the modern market economy. His critics seize on the cultural nature of market economies, consequently questioning the universal validity of economic principles even in the midst of modern capitalist societies. And finally, the "culture matters" school recognizes the importance of certain cultural values for making market economies work more efficiently, while critics correctly highlight the perils of making such generalized claims (Harrison and Huntington 2000).

But the dichotomies are false when viewed according to a mediation model. Differences between "archaic" and capitalist economies are grounded in more than exchange alone. Kinship- and community-mediated production gives rise to reciprocal practices distinct from the market-mediated issues of general trust and niche reciprocity. The question is not whether reciprocity has always existed, but what forms it takes in distinct contexts and to what uses. Andean *ayni* was different from give-and-take in Gamarra. Distinct economic modes do exist, but the fact that principles of supply, demand, utility maximization, scarcity, and equilibrium take precedence does not eliminate the fact that market relations can mediate existing practices in different ways to generate ever more multifarious or kaleidoscopic "modern" cultural forms.

In this sense, the "culture matters" school is not wrong; they just aren't right. New concepts of freedom, equality, property, and self-interest emerge. Among Gamarra's entrepreneurs especially, the birth of unfettered profit maximization redefines their concept of self-interest. The unceasing search for wealth creation takes precedence, gives rise to impersonal exchange, and creates new collective action dilemmas. Within such a framework, reciprocity is far removed from what it once was. But to understand how, we must understand the concept by interpreting it within the context of how societies organize to produce wealth and sustenance, however conceived.

***

Research for and preparation of this chapter was supported by grants from the National Institute of Mental Health, Fulbright-Hays, and the National Science Foundation.

NOTES

1. The term is written without an apostrophe to distinguish it from the pre-Columbian *mit'a*.
2. The exceptions were the few who left and engaged in entrepreneurial activities—in the mines or as traders.
3. In fact, much of the colonial era was characterized by a ruralization of the population (Morse et al. 1971).
4. These conditions for entrepreneurship may not be limited to Gamarra. In fact, an international study of entrepreneurship ranked Peru as the most entrepreneurial country in the world. (Minniti et al. 2005).

REFERENCES

Alberti, Giorgio, and Enrique Mayer, eds.
1974. *Reciprocidad e intercambio en los Andes Peruanos*. Lima: Instituto de Estudios Peruanos.

Assadourian, Carlos Sempat.
1982 *El sistema de la economía colonial: Mercado interno, regiones, y espacio económico*. Lima: Instituto de Estudios Peruanos.
Axelrod, Robert.
1984 *The Evolution of Cooperation*. New York: Basic Books.
Bates, Robert.
1988 Contra Contractarianism: Some Reflections on the New Institutionalism. *Politics and Society* 16:387–401.
Bird, Matthew.
2007 Traveling Down the Other Path: Learning to See Extra-legality as an Investment Opportunity. In *Business and Development: The Private Path to Prosperity*, ed. Michael Klein. Washington DC: IFC/Financial Times. Available at http://www.ifc.org/competition.
2009 Practice Makes Perfect: Comparative Economic Performance, the Cultural Psychology of Decision Making, and Middle-Class Transformation in Lima, Peru. PhD diss., University of Chicago.
Coleman, James
1990 *Foundations of Social Theory*. Cambridge: Harvard-Belknap Press.
Collier, David.
1976 *Squatters and Oligarchs: Authoritarian Rule and Policy Change in Peru*. Baltimore: Johns Hopkins University Press.
Deere, Carmen Diana
1990 *Household and Class Relations: Peasants and Landlords in Northern Peru*. Berkeley: University of California Press.
Degregori, Carlos Iván, Cecilia Blondet, and Nicolás Lynch.
1986 *Conquistadores de un nuevo mundo: De invasores a ciudadanos en San Martín de Porres*. Lima: Instituto de Estudios Peruanos.
de Soto, Hernando, with Enrique Ghersi and Mario Ghibellini
1986 *El otro sendero*. Lima: Instuto de Libertad y Democracia.
Douglas, Mary
1990 Foreword: No Free Gifts. In *The Gift*, by Marcel Mauss, vii–xviii. New York: W. W. Norton.
Golte, Jurgen, and Norma Adams
1987 *Los caballos de troya de los invasores: Estrategias campesinas en la conquista de la Gran Lima*. Lima: Instituto de Estudios Peruanos.
Gootenberg, Paul
1989 *Between Silver and Guano: Commercial Policy and the State in Post-Independence Peru*. Princeton, NJ: Princeton University Press.
Gudeman, Stephen
2001 *Anthropology of Economy*. Oxford: Blackwell.
Hann, Chris
2006 *The Gift and Reciprocity: Perspectives from Economic Anthropology*. In *Handbook of the Economics of Giving, Altruism, and Reciprocity*, vol. 1, ed. Serge-Christophe Kolm and Jean Mercier Ythier, 207–223. Amsterdam: North-Holland.

Harrison, Lawrence, and Samuel Huntington
2000 *Culture Matters: How Values Shape Human Progress*. New York: Basic Books.
Henrich, Joseph, Robert Boyd, Samuel Bowles, Colin Camerer, Ernst Fehr, and Herbert Gintis, eds.
2004 *Foundations of Human Sociality: Economic Experiments and Ethnographic Evidence in Fifteen Small-Scale Societies*. Oxford: Oxford University Press.
Hobbes, Thomas
1994 [1651] *Leviathan*. Indianapolis: Hackett.
Hoffman, Elizabeth, Kevin McCabe, and Vernon Smith
1998 Behavioral Foundations of Reciprocity: Experimental Economics and Evolutionary Psychology. *Economic Inquiry* 36 (3): 335–252.
INEI (Instituto Nacional de Estadística e Informática), Dirección Técnica de Demografía e Indicadores Sociales
2009 "Perú: Migraciones Internas 1993–2007." Lima: Talleres de la Oficina Técnica de Administración del INEI.
Jacobsen, Nils
1993 *Mirages of Transition: The Peruvian Altiplano, 1780–1930*. Berkeley: University of California Press.
Jaramillo, Miguel
2004 *Starting a Garment Manufacturing Firm in Peru: Background and Case Study*. Ronald Coase Institute Research Report Series, Research Report No. 1.
Klarén, Peter
1973 *Modernization, Dislocation, and Aprismo: Origins of the Peruvian Aprista Party, 1870–1932* Austin: University of Texas Press.
Larson, Brooke, and Olivia Harris, with Enrique Tandeter.
1995 *Ethnicity, Markets, and Migration in the Andes: At the Crossroads of History and Anthropology*. Durham: Duke University Press.
Lobo, Susan
1982 *A House of My Own: Social Organization in the Squatter Settlements of Peru*. Tucson: University of Arizona Press.
Malinowski, Bronislaw.
1962 [1922] *Argonauts of the Western Pacific: An Account of Native Enterprise and Adventure in the Archipelagoes of Melanesian New Guinea*. New York: E. P. Dutton.
1921 "The Primitive Economics of the Trobriand Islanders." *Economic Journal* 31 (121): 1–16.
Marx, Karl
1993 [1858] *Grundrisse: Foundations of the Critique of Political Economy*. New York: Penguin.
Matos Mar, José
1977 *Las barriadas de Lima, 1957*. Lima: Instituto de Estudios Peruanos.
Mauss, Marcel
1990 [1924] *The Gift: The Form and Reason for Exchange in Archaic Societies*. New York: W.W. Norton.

Mayer, Enrique
2001 *The Articulated Peasant: Household Economies in the Andes*. Boulder, CO: Westview Press.
Minniti, Maria, with William Bygrave and Erkko Autio
2005 *Global Entrepreneurship Monitor, 2005 Executive Report*. Wellesley, MA, & London: Babson College and London School of Business.
Morse, Richard, with Michael Conniff and John Wibel
1971 *The Urban Development of Latin America, 1750–1920*. Palo Alto, CA: Stanford University, Center for Latin American Studies.
Murra, John
1972 El "control vertical" de un máximo de pisos ecológicos en la economía de las sociedades andinas. In *Visita de la provincial de León de Huánuco en 1562*, vol. 2., ed. John Murra, 427–476. Huánuco, Peru: Universidad Nacional Hermilio Valdizán.
1980 *Social and Economic Organization of the Inka State*. Greenwich, CT: JAI Press.
2002 *El mundo andino: Población, medio ambiente, y economía*. Lima: Instituto de Estudios Peruanos.
Niezen, Cecilia
2005 *Puno en alto*. *El Comercio*, Suplmento Día Uno, January 10.
North, Douglass
1990 *Institutions, Institutional Change, and Economic Performance*. Cambridge: Cambridge University Press.
Olson, Mancur
1971 [1965] *The Logic of Collective Action: Public Goods and the Theory of Groups*. Cambridge: Harvard University Press.
Ostrom, Elinor
1990 *Governing the Commons: The Evolution of Institutions for Collective Action*. Cambridge: Cambridge University Press.
Polanyi, Karl
2001 [1944] *The Great Transformation*. Boston: Beacon Press.
Polanyi, Karl, Conrad Arensberg, and Harry Pearson, eds.
1957 *Trade and Market in the Early Empires: Economics in History and Theory*. New York: Free Press.
Putnam, Robert, with Robert Leonardi and Raffaella Nanetti
1992 *Making Democracy Work: Civic Traditions in Modern Italy*. Princeton, NJ: Princeton University Press
Sahlins, Marshall
1972 *Stone Age Economics*. Chicago: Aldine-Atherton.
Spalding, Karen
1974 *De indio a campesino: Cambios en la estructura social del Perú colonial*. Lima: Instituto de Estudios Peruanos.
Stein, Steve
1980 *Populism in Peru: The Emergence of the Masses and the Politics of Social Control*. Madison: University of Wisconsin Press.

Stern, Steve
1982 *Peru's Indian Peoples and the Challenge of Spanish Conquest: Huamanga to 1640*. Madison: University of Wisconsin Press.
Thorp, Rosemary, and Geoffrey Bertram
1978 *Peru 1890–1977: Growth and Policy in an Open Economy*. London: Macmillan.
Weber, Max
2002 [1905] *Protestant Ethic and the Spirit of Capitalism and Other Writings*. New York: Penguin.
Wightman, Ann
1990 *Indigenous Migration and Social Change: The Forasteros of Cuzco, 1570–1720*. Durham: Duke University Press.
Zak, Paul
2004 Neuroeconomics. *Philosophical Transactions of the Royal Society* 359:1737–1748.
Zuidema, R. Tom
1964 *The Ceque System of Cuzco: The Social Organization of the Capital of the Inca*. Leiden: E. J. Brill.
1990 *Inca Civilization in Cuzco*. Austin: University of Texas Press.

4

Commerce and Cooperation among the Classic Maya

The Chunchucmil Case

Scott R. Hutson, University of Kentucky
Bruce H. Dahlin, Shepherd University
Daniel Mazeau, University at Buffalo, State University of New York

In 1971, William Rathje provided one of the first systematic models of long-distance exchange for the lowland Maya. Beginning from a then prominent cultural ecology paradigm that held that complex societies emerged only in areas with environmental heterogeneity, Rathje attempted to explain how the ancient Maya produced an illustrious civilization in an apparently homogeneous and resource-poor environment. Rathje argued that because scarce resources such as salt, obsidian blades, and basalt for grinding stones were located far away, individual households could not acquire them on their own. Instead, households cooperated. They banded together to organize production of surpluses for exchange and to outfit long-distance trade expeditions. Such cooperation provided the necessary and sufficient conditions for the emergence not only of social and political complexity but also of Maya religion. Though Rathje's model has been superseded, it generated a legacy of research on trade and political economy that runs strong today (see chapters in Masson and Freidel 2002).

If there is a place in the Maya lowlands where fragments of Rathje's model may still work, it is the northwest tip of the Yucatán Peninsula. Here, the ancient Maya faced thin soils and scarce rainfall (Leyden et al. 1996), but populated several massive sites, such as Chunchucmil, the largest Early Classic period city in this corner of the peninsula (figure 1). The Pakbeh Regional Economy Program has sought to understand how Chunchucmil thrived at the end of the Early Classic period (A.D. 400–600; Dahlin 2003). This research has led to the proposal that survival depended on long-distance exchange. In this chapter, we focus on the durable evidence for long-distance trade and how trade goods were distributed at Chunchucmil. Though other nearby centers such as Komchen and Dzibilchaltún are also understood to have depended on

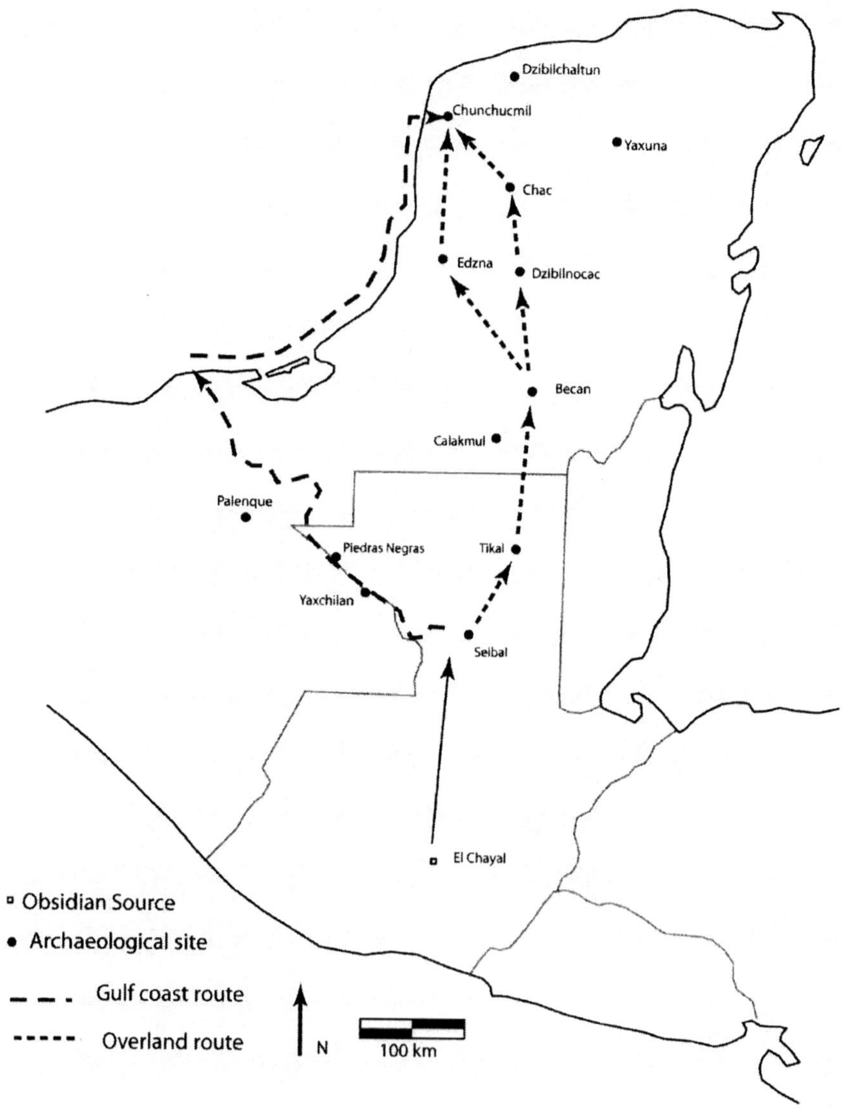

Figure 4.1. Map of the Maya area showing possible Classic period overland and Gulf Coast trade routes for El Chayal obsidian

trade, Chunchucmil's economy stands out in two ways. First, it has abundant imported obsidian in comparison to other sites in the northern Maya lowlands. This suggests that Chunchucmil served as a gateway community and that many of its residents worked to support long-distance trade. Second, Chunchucmil's obsidian is evenly distributed across the site at a time—the Early Classic—when it is concentrated in the hands of elites at many other sites.

This suggests the presence of a marketplace. These two conclusions imply two forms of cooperation. First, fulfilling the role of a trade center required cooperation across the social spectrum to ensure a supply of long-distance goods. Second, the creation of a marketplace required cooperation among the multiple governing factions at the site and integration among producers, consumers and merchants. The core of this chapter presents the data to substantiate these points. Neither point squares cleanly with orthodox views of ancient Maya economies. Nevertheless, our results join a tide of recent studies that are transforming what we know about trade and exchange in the lowlands. We therefore begin by contextualizing our research within broader understandings of ancient Maya economies.

CHANGING VIEWS ON MAYA ECONOMIES

Since Rathje proposed his model, research has shown that the Maya lowlands were neither environmentally homogeneous nor resource deficient (McAnany 1989). Most households could meet their basic needs without the aid of long-distance exchange. Long-distance trade did flourish during the Classic period, but most trade goods served to create and reinforce status distinctions. In several places, elites controlled long-distance trade and limited the distribution of its spoils (Aoyama 2001; Rice 1987). Studies of chert tool production at the Belizean site of Colha (Potter and King 1995:28) and ceramic production on the periphery of Tikal (Fry 1979) suggest that elites took little part in the organization of local production. The producers of pottery and stone tools distributed their goods not through centralized markets, but through balanced reciprocal exchanges (Rice 1987:77; cf. Sahlins 1965). Thus there came into focus a two-tiered model of Maya economies in which elites procured and redistributed prestigious long-distance goods and commoners produced utilitarian goods for reciprocal exchange. The model minimizes cooperation between elites and commoners and reifies two social classes (cf. Chase and Chase 1992). Researchers believe that Maya economies underwent major transformations from the Classic to the Postclassic period, ushering in market centers and much broader participation in long-distance exchange (Sabloff and Rathje 1980).

By presenting evidence for markets and evidence for broader involvement across the social spectrum in the production of finished goods, recent studies justify revisions to the two-tier model. Though the two-tier model allowed for elite sponsorship of attached specialists producing painted vases, codices, and other arts in palace workshops (Inomata and Stiver 1998; Reents-Budet 1994), evidence from Aguateca suggests an even broader range of goods produced in elite contexts (Emery and Aoyama 2007). Data from excavations in elite contexts at Calakmul (Dominguez Carrasco et al. 1996) and Copan (Hendon 1997) document the production of textiles and mundane stone tools, likely by actors of varied social status (Robin 2003). Furthermore, evidence from Cancuen (Kovacevich et al. 2003), Tikal (Moholy-Nagy 1997) and elsewhere (Guderjan 2007) suggests that nonelites played a role in the production of high-status goods such as jade ornaments and obsidian eccentrics. At Cancuen, specialists living in very modest houses located well beyond the site center appear to have been contracted to perform the first stages of jade ornament manufacture.

Evidence for ancient marketplaces is notoriously difficult to recover because the actual residues of market transactions are extremely ephemeral. However, as Hirth (1998) has emphasized, market exchange entails a series of conditions that manifest themselves in the archaeological record. Such data have been reported for an increasing number of sites, such as Tikal (Jones 1996), Caracol (Chase and Chase 2004), Sayil (Wurtzburg 1991), Ceren (Sheets 2000), and Trinidad de Nosotros (Moriarty 2004). In this chapter we strengthen earlier evidence for a market at Chunchucmil (Dahlin and Ardren 2002; Dahlin et al. 2007) by adding distributional data (Hirth 1998). We will also show that powerful social groups worked to ensure access to long-distance goods for nearly all residents. Finally, we will comment on what we infer as an unusual degree of cooperation between competing factions at the top of a segmentary political system.

COOPERATION IN OBSIDIAN PROCUREMENT

To understand potential cooperation involved in getting obsidian to Chunchucmil we must first establish the sources of Chunchucmil's obsidian, the specific forms of obsidian that came to the site, and the scale on which Chunchucmil imported obsidian. This information enables a tentative reconstruction of the regional exchange system as well as an assessment of Chunchucmil's role in this system. We also assess the degree to which fulfilling this role required cooperation between different social groups within the city.

Prismatic blade fragments account for 95 percent of the 2,746 obsidian artifacts at Chunchucmil that have received preliminary analysis. Research and experimentation on prismatic blade production reveals a patterned series of steps in blade manufacturing, only the later stages of which occurred at Chunchucmil. The process begins by obtaining raw obsidian from the source. At Chunchucmil, 96 percent of the blades in a sample of 120 analyzed by X-ray fluorescence were made from material originating at the El Chayal source, located 670 km away in highland Guatemala. This complements data from visual sourcing of 2,230 artifacts performed by Daniel Mazeau (trained by Geoffrey Braswell; cf. Moholy-Nagy 2003).

At Chunchucmil, we have evidence—in the forms of exhausted cores, core rejuvenation flakes, and blades with hinge fractures—only for the final stage of prismatic blade production (i.e., removing blades from polyhedral cores by applying pressure flaking techniques). Such production debris suggests an exchange model in which polyhedral cores were traded long distances. Several authors (but cf. Rovner 1976) have noted that in long-distance exchange systems it is more efficient to transport obsidian in the form of cores as opposed to finished blades (Clark 1987; Rice 1984, 1987:80; Rovner and Lewenstein 1997:45). The ratio of cores to blades at Chunchucmil indicates that blades were produced on-site from cores rather than being imported.

Two general trade routes—overland and Gulf coast—can account for the passage of obsidian from El Chayal to Chunchucmil (figure 1). Both begin with overland portage from El Chayal to the navigable rivers of the western Petén, such as the Chixoy and Pasión. In the overland route, obsidian moving along the Pasión River stops at Seibal, where porters would have taken it overland to Tikal and eventually all the way north to northern Yucatán. In the Gulf coast route, obsidian moves down the Pasión River to the Usumacinta River, which drains to the Gulf of Mexico. Having reached the Gulf, the obsidian would have been taken northeast along the coast of the Yucatán Peninsula until it reached the mouth of the Celestún estuary, from which it is 27 km overland to Chunchucmil. Disagreement exists with regard to whether the Gulf route was popular only in the Postclassic period (Nelson 1989; Sabloff and Rathje 1980) or earlier (Hammond 1972; Rovner 1976).

Quantities of obsidian at Chunchucmil and inland sites do not follow expectations for overland trade. Once obsidian left the western Petén rivers and began its overland route north to Chunchucmil, it would pass through a series of central places, beginning with Tikal, as suggested by directional models (Renfrew 1977). In the directional model each central place represents a peak in the multimodal fall-off curve for obsidian (Renfrew 1977:86, figure 5). In other words, the next center after Tikal will have more obsidian than secondary sites between it and Tikal. Nevertheless, this center will have slightly less obsidian than Tikal: each peak in the directional fall-off curve is lower than the previous peak. Thus, if we look at central places alone and disregard secondary sites, the "law of monotonic decrement" (Renfrew 1977) should prevail: from Tikal to Chunchucmil, each central place should have less obsidian because only a portion of the obsidian entering these sites from the south would get passed on to the north.

One way to test the expectation is to gauge the degree to which consumers economize on obsidian. For example, sites with less access to obsidian—for instance, those sites on the overland route that are farther from the source—should make thinner blades, therefore getting more cutting edge out of the same amount of material (Rovner 1976; Rovner and Lewenstein 1997:45). However, blade widths among Early Classic lowland sites using El Chayal obsidian are similar regardless of distance from the source. Mean blade width at Chunchucmil, 670 km from El Chayal, is 1.004 cm. Mean blade width from a sample of 130 Early Classic blades from Becán, located 440 km from El Chayal, is 0.93 cm (Stoltman 1978). A separate sample of 64 Early Classic blades from Becán and Chicanná has a mean width of 0.99 cm (Rovner and Lewenstein 1997:51). Mean width of a sample of 306 third-series Early Classic blades from Ojo de Agua, Chiapas, located 280 km from El Chayal, is 0.94 cm (Clark 1997:115). The average width of Early Classic El Chayal blades from Edzna is 0.93 cm (Matheny et al. 1983:166–167). Thus, in the Early Classic lowlands, there is little difference in blade width regardless of distance from the source, El Chayal being the predominant source in all these samples.

A different, more direct way of measuring access to obsidian at a particular site examines ratios of obsidian to some other entity. Sidrys (1977) measured obsidian as a ratio with volume of excavation, and then multiplied the result by distance from the source. Chunchucmil would rank highly in Sidrys's "trade index," but this index does not account for differences in the length of occupation (the ratio of artifact to matrix at Chunchucmil increases the longer the site is occupied due to the relative lack of sources of sedimentation), nor for differences in depositional contexts (Rovner 1989b). Expressing obsidian as a ratio to utilitarian artifacts such as pottery avoids this problem. Unfortunately, few sites have quantified obsidian data appropriate for intersite comparison.

As predicted by the overland trade route in the directional model, Tikal appears to have more obsidian than Calakmul. Though obsidian from the University of Pennsylvania project at Tikal was not collected systematically, a recent estimate of well over 300,000 artifacts seems highly plausible (Moholy-Nagy 1997). Unlike the sample at Chunchucmil, most of the obsidian recovered at Tikal is debitage. At Calakmul, extensive excavations at four major structures recovered only 107 obsidian artifacts (Dominguez Carrasco et al. 1996). This lesser amount of obsidian at Calakmul might also be explained by the notoriously hostile relation between the two sites during the Classic period.

North of Calakmul, Nelson's proposed overland route stipulates that Becán is the next central place (figure 1). Like Calakmul, Becán has far less obsidian than Tikal: 235 artifacts from the 1969–1971 Tulane excavations (some of these artifacts are from neighboring sites; Rovner and Lewenstein 1997:119) and 147 artifacts from excavations in 1973 (Stoltman 1978). Without precise information on the volume of excavation or ratios with ceramics, Becán cannot be compared with Calakmul. Furthermore, most deposits at Becán were not screened.

North of Becán, Nelson's model stipulates Dzibilnocac as the next central place, but excavations at Dzibilnocac revealed almost no Early Classic occupation (Nelson 1973:136). This reflects the fact that for portions of the proposed overland route between Tikal to Chunchucmil, we do not know exactly which sites the route passed through. Nearer to Chunchucmil, however, quantitative data are available from Early Classic components at two sites that would be good candidates as central places on the purported overland obsidian chain: Chac and Edzna.

At Chac, Michael Smyth's excavations in Early and Middle Classic contexts yielded 110.4 g of obsidian (79 artifacts, 81 percent of which come from El Chayal) and 377.51 kg of pottery (Michael Smyth, personal communication, 2008). The ratio of grams of obsidian to kilograms of ceramics is therefore 0.29. At Chunchucmil a sample of excavations from the Early Classic yielded 597.4 g of obsidian (858 artifacts) and 603.38 kg of ceramics, yielding a ratio of 0.99. At Edzna, 96 obsidian artifacts have been reported (Nelson et al. 1977, 1983), though only nine of these come from Early Classic contexts. Excavations of approximately 133 m^3 in residential contexts in the northwest portion of the site yielded six obsidian blades from contexts where Early Classic ceramics dominated or made up a large portion of the ceramic debris (Matheny et al. 1983). Quantification of obsidian as a ratio with ceramics is difficult for Edzna because ceramic weights are not given. Furthermore, not all excavations were screened. However, assuming a modest average of 10 g per sherd, the ratio of grams of obsidian per kilogram of sherds at Edzna is 0.15 versus 0.99 at Chunchucmil. The ratio of obsidian to volume of excavation at Edzna was approximately 0.14 g of obsidian per cubic meter, as opposed to 2.20 g of obsidian per cubic meter at Chunchucmil.

Thus, both Edzna and Chac received much less obsidian than Chunchucmil. This does not fit the model of directional trade overland, in which Chunchucmil, located farthest from the source, should have the smallest amount of obsidian. We therefore conclude that the main obsidian trade route for Chunchucmil was not overland. The comparison with Edzna and Chac suggests that Chunchucmil was a gateway community (Hirth 1978) for obsidian that would eventually be distributed across the western side of northern Yucatán (Dahlin and Ardren 2002). In other words, obsidian went to Chunchucmil first via the Gulf route and then to sites farther inland such as Chac,

Dzibilchaltún, and Yaxuna. Excavations at Dzibilchaltún from 1957 to 1965 were of greater or comparable scale to those at Chunchucmil, but recovered only 444 obsidian artifacts compared to the nearly 3,000 obsidian artifacts at Chunchucmil. However, dirt from the excavations at Dzibilchaltún was not screened, and most lithics date to the Late Classic. Researchers screened excavations of comparable scale at Yaxuna, which had a substantial Early Classic occupation, but they recovered a total of only 199 obsidian artifacts (Dave Johnstone, personal communication 2006).

We argued that the high volume of obsidian at Chunchucmil compared to other sites in northern Yucatán, such as Yaxuna and Chac, suggests that Chunchucmil was the gateway for obsidian that would eventually be distributed across the western side of northern Yucatan. Alternatively, it may be possible to argue that Chunchucmil had more obsidian than other sites because chert was scarce. Our excavations recovered nearly four times as many obsidian artifacts as chert artifacts. At Rio Bec, there are nearly 25 times as many chert artifacts as obsidian artifacts (Rovner 1989b). However, good chert sources in the Puuc hills were not far away from Chunchucmil (30–60 km to the west), and Chunchcumil certainly had the demographic strength in the Early Classic period to brush aside any Puuc hills site whose inhabitants may have attempted to deny access to chert. Thus, we conclude that the relative abundance of obsidian at Chunchucmil has little to do with access to chert. Finally, it may be possible to argue that Chunchucmil had more obsidian than other sites because Chunchucmil was involved in craft activities not performed at other sites. We discuss craft production in more detail later, but note for now that systematic testing for craft workshops revealed very little nonperishable evidence for specialized production at Chunchucmil (Hutson and Dahlin 2008).

The fact that Chunchucmil has substantially more obsidian than other sites in northern Yucatán makes sense only if the obsidian that arrived to northern Yucatán entered the peninsula by sea near Chunchucmil, which acted as a gateway for distribution to sites farther inland. The evidence from obsidian quantities in northern Yucatan sites thus fits well with Dahlin's earlier comments on Chunchucmil's favorable position as a point of entry. Chunchucmil's port site, Punta Canbalam, has one of the few sheltered harbors on Yucatán's Gulf coast (Dahlin et al. 1998). The evidence for Chunchucmil's role as a gateway in the redistribution of obsidian also fits well with subsistence and demographic data reported earlier for Chunchucmil (Dahlin et al. 2005; Hutson et al. 2008). These data show that Chunchucmil's population was too large to be supported by local agriculture and therefore must have relied on additional sources of income, such as long-distance trade.

In sum, many lines of evidence suggest that Chunchucmil received an abundance of obsidian, mostly in the form of polyhedral cores, from a Gulf coast trade route and served as a redistribution center for obsidian to other inland sites. The possibility of cooperation enters the picture when we consider precisely who managed the long-distance exchange of obsidian. This question is, admittedly, difficult to answer (Rice 1987:77). Earlier studies proposed that an enclave of Teotihuacán merchants at Kaminaljuyú, located close to the El Chayal source, oversaw the exchange of El Chayal obsidian. Teotihuacán was the dominant central Mexican site in the Early Classic period. Santley (1983) proposed that Teotihuacanos managed El Chayal obsidian to ensure that obsidian from El Chayal would not compete with obsidian from central Mexican sources directly controlled by Teotihuacán. However, revisions of our understanding of the extent of Teotihuacán's obsidian business (Clark 1986) and reconsiderations of the evidence of Teotihuacán influence at Kaminaljuyú (Braswell 2003) make it difficult to claim that Teotihuacán merchants had control of the El Chayal source.

Perhaps trade collectives from Chunchucmil managed long-distance commerce. The logistics and other considerations for acquiring obsidian imply the coordination and cooperation of many actors (Clark 1987:273; Rathje 1971; Rice 1987:80). These logistics include stimulating the production of surplus goods (probably salt from the Celestún salt flats, approximately 35 km to the northwest of Chunchucmil, but also other perishable materials from the estuaries and forests to the west) to exchange for obsidian; outfitting trading expeditions with canoes and other equipment to make the journey to the source area; gaining knowledge and access to provisioning stations and freshwater sources along the route; negotiating safe passage through multiple feuding Early Classic polities (e.g., Piedras Negras and Yaxchilan; Houston et al. 2003) along the Gulf coast route; maintaining trade relationships with producers of polyhedral cores near the source; and conducting the exchange itself, possibly in different languages.

The scale of the obsidian trade puts the notion of powerful trade groups in perspective. Presuming a conservative estimate of 10 obsidian blades per year per family of five (Clark 1986), and that each polyhedral core was good for 200 blades, Chunchucmil's estimated 8,000 to 8,500 families would need a total of at least 400 polyhedral cores per year. Given the data presented above in support of Chunchucmil as a gateway, we estimate that Chunchucmil's merchants were serving perhaps five times as many consumers living throughout the northwestern corner of the peninsula during the Early Classic. Thus, Chunchucmil merchants may have acquired and transported an additional 2,000 polyhedral cores for exchange with people living farther inland.

Presuming that polyhedral cores weigh at least 700 g and that a small quantity of additional obsidian was transported for bifaces and other obsidian tools, a minimum estimate for the total annual burden of transport would be in the range of 2,000 to 2,500 kg of obsidian.

Such a scale is not large enough to require management by centralized institutions. Yet this scale and complexity of the undertaking are too much for individual households. We propose that trade was managed by collectives. We should also note that obsidian might have been the nonperishable tip of a vast commercial iceberg composed largely of perishable goods. If this were the case, polyhedral cores would be one of many commodities in the canoes, and the volume of trade may have required the guidance of the large, resourceful corporate groups that we suspect were headquartered at compounds called *quadrangles*.

Quadrangles are the largest architectural compounds at Chunchucmil. They consist of a large temple on one side of a quadrangular patio with range structures on the other three sides and a performance platform in the middle. At Chunchucmil, 15 quadrangles are connected to one another by raised stone causeways. Though one particular quadrangle stands above the rest insofar as it has the largest pyramid, the most voluminous and complex auxiliary architecture, the site's only ball court, and a central position, this quadrangle does not dominate Chunchucmil's cityscape (Dahlin forthcoming; Dahlin and Ardren 2002:267). Unlike many other Maya cities, Chunchucmil does not appear to be centralized around a paramount, divine king. People had options as to which quadrangle to support (see Lucero 2007:423); this implies that elite factions needed to maintain harmonious ties with supporters in order to retain such mutually beneficial relations (see also Sheets 2000).

The quantities of labor required to construct the pyramids within the quadrangles suggest that authority was concentrated within the quadrangles. Since coordinating trade also required authority, the quadrangles are likely to have been trade headquarters. In fact, Dahlin (forthcoming; Dahlin and Ardren 2002:269) argues elsewhere that quadrangles existed to receive merchants, negotiate deals, store trade surpluses, and so forth. Exploring this further will require broadscale horizontal excavations in more quadrangles. Thus far, most horizontal excavations have targeted other architectural contexts. These excavations indicate that involvement in trade was probably not limited to the quadrangles. For example, Traci Ardren's (2003) excavations in the Lool houselot revealed that this group's shrine had a talud tablero facade. Such facades are widely common at Teotihuacán. Though talud tablero facades can no longer be considered unambiguous signatures of Teotihuacán influence (García Cook 1984), they nonetheless manifest participation in a pan-Mesoamerican sphere of interaction. Horizontal excavations in the 'Aak houselot uncovered 670 obsidian artifacts, 58 jade ornaments, and fragments of a Teotihuacán-style cylinder tripod vessel. In their familiarity with cosmopolitan styles and easy access to exotic foreign goods, the rather modest Lool and 'Aak houselots (and probably others not yet explored intensively) appear to have been well integrated in Chunchucmil's long-distance commerce. This differs from patterns observed at most other sites where elites monopolized long-distance trade in the Classic period (McAnany 1993). At Chunchucmil, it appears that elites (presumed to reside in the quadrangles) cooperated with lower-status households at the site.

COOPERATION IN OBSIDIAN DISTRIBUTION

The distribution of obsidian within Chunchucmil can also gauge the degree of cooperation at the site. The distribution of obsidian at other sites during the Early Classic suggests that it was a wealth good controlled by elites and not readily accessible to commoners (Aoyama 2001; Stoltman 1978; Rice 1984). Rice (1987:80) concludes that "as wealth, obsidian procurement and distribution may have been a narrowly guarded perquisite of high status, the stone being obtained for purposes of making offerings on ceremonial occasions." If obsidian were a ceremonially restricted wealth good at Early Classic Chunchucmil, we would expect to find very little of it beyond Chunchucmil's quadrangles and elite residences. Alternatively, if obsidian were a mundane household tool, we would expect equal frequencies of obsidian in high- and low-status households.

To evaluate these models, we provide data from test pitting (841 units measuring 1 × 1 m) in 162 architectural contexts at the site (seven of these contexts were also excavated horizontally). Of these contexts, 141 received excavations substantial enough to be included in the analysis. This comprises an 11.3 percent sample of the approximately 1,250 architectural groups mapped at the site. Eleven of the 141 contexts were not dominated by Early Classic ceramics and were therefore dropped from the current study to ensure contemporaneity of the contexts. We divided the remaining 130 contexts into four categories that we thought would best represent different social statuses. The highest status category included architectural groups with massive pyramids. Twelve of the 15 groups in this category are quadrangles. Though the large temples in these groups suggest ritual activities serving larger sections of the population, excavations indicate that these groups were also residences. The next three categories of architectural contexts consist of residential groups with one or more houses often facing onto one or more patios. These groups are not purely residential because they tend to contain gardens, work areas, and small shrines for the veneration of ancestors. The three categories include large groups with 11 or more stone platforms ($n = 13$), medium-sized groups with 6 to 10 stone platforms ($n = 38$), and small groups with 5 or fewer stone platforms ($n = 64$). All but 11 of the groups in these three categories are encircled by low stone walls. We refer to such encircled groups as *houselots*. We initially thought that the division of patio groups into large, medium, and small would correspond roughly to social status because patio groups with more buildings tend to have more residents, implying greater wealth, and larger buildings, implying greater control of labor and resources (Netting 1982). However, larger groups and smaller groups have nearly equal access to potential status indicators, such as fancy pottery (see table 4.1; differences are not statistically significant). On average, 1 percent of the ceramics in each of the four categories are fine wares (polychromes—Timucuy, Aguila—or thin service vessels—Chencoh, Acu, and Kochol; Varela Torrecilla 1998). Thus we cannot be certain that we have captured status differences with these four categories of architectural context.

The groups excavated at Chunchucmil were selected in such a way as to produce a representative sample. In addition to stratifying the site's 1,250 architectural contexts by category, we stratified them by area so that at least some examples of all four categories in each km^2 block of the site were excavated. Within each category and km^2 block, we used random numbers to select the contexts to be excavated.

Table 4.1 shows the average quantities of obsidian for each of the four group types. When quantified as a ratio to ceramics, the data in table 1 show that the smaller the houselot, the more access to obsidian. The only statistically significant difference is the one between small residential groups and groups with large pyramids ($t = -2.77$, $p = 0.002$, $df = 77$). When obsidian is quantified as a ratio to volume of excavation, the three categories of houselot have nearly identical quantities, though the quantities in pyramid groups are low. Insofar as our four categories mark status distinctions, this finding challenges the notion of obsidian as a wealth good.

Table 4.1. Quantities of Fine Pottery and Obsidian Recovered from Excavations in Four Common Architectural Groups at Chunchucmil

	Pyramid Groups	*Large Houselots*	*Medium Houselots*	*Small Houselots*
n	15	13	38	65
% fine pottery	1.14	0.71	0.89	1.16
Grams Obsidian to kg pottery	0.67	0.95	1.27	1.70
Standard Dev.	0.57	0.72	1.61	2.72
Grams Obsidian to m^3 excavation	1.50	2.58	2.15	2.34

These data on access to obsidian across the site also allow us to explore whether obsidian was distributed by redistribution, balanced reciprocity, or market exchange. As discussed above, obsidian entered the site in the form of slightly reduced polyhedral cores. Since blade production debris was found in a small number of household contexts, some mechanism must have functioned to move blades from the few producers to the multiple consumers. If these producers sold blades at what Dahlin et al. (2007) have identified as Chunchucmil's central market, blades would be spread relatively evenly across the site (Hirth 1998). However, even though obsidian does not appear to be a wealth good, its superior sharpness does make it desirable, so we might expect access to obsidian to vary with purchasing power. Thus, even with market distribution, obsidian could be distributed unevenly (again in proportion to purchasing power), especially if there were disruptions in supply. The fact that obsidian at Chunchucmil came from foreign lands not controlled by Chunchucmil meant not just that acquiring it was a complex logistical undertaking but that steady access to it in times of distant political upheaval could not be guaranteed. It may in fact be the case that Chunchucmil's seventh-century collapse was tied to the intensified warfare and rivalry between southern lowland polities at this time.

As alternatives to market exchange, reciprocity or redistribution may have moved blades from producers to consumers. Both these systems have spheres of distribution smaller than that of the market because they are not as efficient in moving large volumes of goods (Hirth 1998:454). In particular, redistribution may reproduce status hierarchies. If blades were redistributed at Chunchucmil, this most likely occurred at quadrangles since quadrangles most likely played a major role in organizing the expeditions that procured the polyhedral cores from which blades were produced. As to quadrangles' motivations for redistribution, John Clark (1987) has argued that political factions within a site could gain larger followings if they organized trade expeditions for acquiring obsidian and then distributed obsidian blades to households in exchange for loyalty and service. In this model, it was in the interests of political factions to supply their supporters with obsidian. Though obsidian could therefore be broadly available in this model, Clark and Hirth both argue that the distribution of obsidian would replicate status hierarchies to some degree.

Side by side, the marketing and redistribution models introduce a problem of equifinality. When households of different purchasing power participate in the same market, households of higher status will end up with more obsidian. This dovetails with the expectation of a redistributive system: redistribution replicates status hierarchies. Fortunately, the data from Chunchucmil help mitigate this problem.

The data presented in table 4.1 suggest that obsidian at Chunchucmil was distributed by a market as opposed to reciprocity or redistribution. In the redistribution model, we would expect more obsidian in the quadrangles/groups with large pyramids. Pyramid groups have less obsidian than patio groups. The ratio of obsidian to ceramics in pyramid groups was significantly smaller than that for the other three categories ($t = 2.93$, $p = 0.002$, $df = 127$). This may be the result of different discard practices in the two different kinds of groups, but we are unable to test this possibility at present. The lower quantities of obsidian in pyramid groups may be the product of a sampling error since we did not excavate special deposits in the largest groups. At Tikal and Quirigua, special deposits contain the lion's share of obsidian (Moholy-Nagy 1989; Sheets 1979). However, Moholy-Nagy (1997) argues that obsidian in special deposits at Tikal is not necessarily an indicator of elite access to obsidian. Finally, quadrangles may have had less need for obsidian. In other words, the suite of domestic and workshop activities involving obsidian that took place in other architectural contexts, such as food preparation, leather-working, processing of maguey fiber, and so forth, may not have occurred at the quadrangles.

Insofar as the four group size categories express status distinctions, obsidian is spread too evenly to suggest the status hierarchies predicted by redistribution. Figure 4.2 shows that the groups pertaining to the quartile with the most obsidian and the quartile with the least obsidian are spread evenly across the site. This is not in keeping with reciprocity, whose inefficiencies predict a limited spatial distribution of obsidian across a site (Hirth 1998).

Thus, our data appear to support the presence of a market. Nevertheless, there is substantial variation in access to obsidian within the four categories of houselots. We see this variation in the large standard deviations seen in table 4.1 and in the fact that in six of the 64 small houselots we recovered no obsidian, whereas one had over 10 times the mean. Thus, the relative equality between categories of houselots of different size masks inequality among houselots of the same size. This inequality of access might be reconciled with market distribution if we could show that the groups with more obsidian required it for specialized productive activities. Our excavation data reveal that, unlike other urban sites such as Caracol (Chase and Chase 2004:141) and Tikal (Moholy-Nagy 1997), very few of Chunchucmil's households specialized in productive activities that left durable remains (Hutson and Dahlin 2008). Systematic research on refuse patterning at Chunchucmil shows that the absence of debris from craft production is not a function of site formation processes (Hutson et al. 2007). Chunchucmil therefore presents a paradox insofar as markets in urban centers of Chunchucmil's magnitude are expected to stimulate craft production.

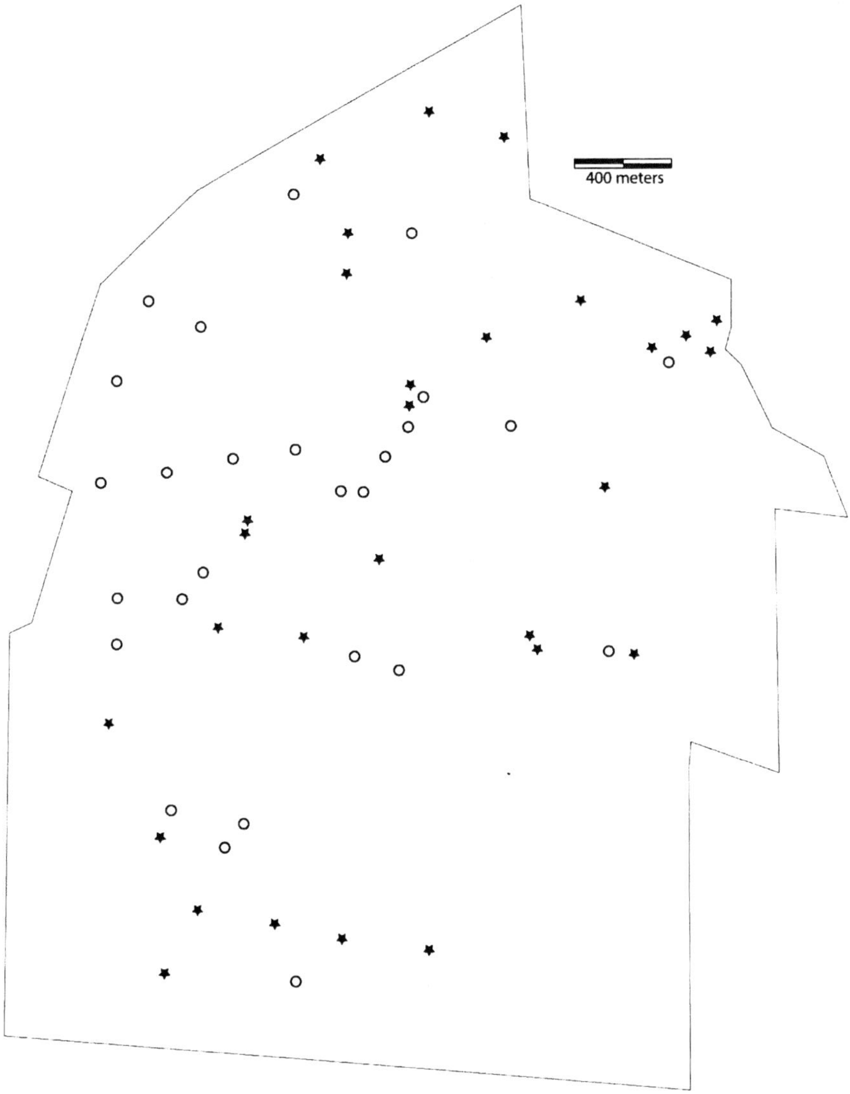

Figure 4.2. Map of Chunchucmil showing the distribution of excavated architectural contexts with high quantities of obsidian (the top quartile, marked with stars) and low quantities of obsidian (the bottom quartile, marked with circles)

We complete the discussion of obsidian distribution by examining access to obsidian in Chunchucmil's hinterland. Though our data do not support Rice's conclusion that obsidian was a status-reinforcing good in the Early Classic, Rice's conclusion was in fact built on a distinction between urban and rural access to obsidian. Despite even distribution of obsidian within

Chunchucmil, the frequency of obsidian drops in its hinterland. Households at a distance of 2.5 to 5 km from the site center had a third of the obsidian of those within 2.5 km. Households beyond 5 km from the site center had one-twentieth of the obsidian of those within 2.5 km of the site center. The decrease in access to blades in the hinterland matches Rice's (1987) data from the Yaxha region, Aoyama's data at Copan (2001), and Moholy-Nagy's data (1989; personal communication, March 2008) from Tikal.

In closing, is there a connection between market exchange and cooperation? Chunchucmil's site structure strongly suggests the kind of segmentary political organization that lies at the core of models of factional competition (Brumfiel 1994; Clark 1987). As mentioned above, one quadrangle is larger than all the others, but it does not tower over the others. Furthermore, the site's layout—15 nearly identical quadrangles connected to one another by causeways—provides an excellent case for an oligarchic political organization. Using the notion of co-opetition (Brandenburger and Nalebuff 1996), Dahlin has argued that each of these quadrangles are headquarters of trade organizations that competed with one another but cooperated, in the absence of a strong central government, to protect common interests. In this case, it was in their interest to cooperate in maintaining markets. Such a system was the keystone to Chunchucmil's stability. Not only did it integrate the society, polity, and economy (see Freidel 1981), it also made possible Chunchcumil's role as a gateway for the entrance of highland goods into the northern lowlands, allowing the massive site to survive in one of the most agriculturally marginal regions.

CONCLUSION

The data presented in this chapter support the following conclusions. First, Chunchucmil received polyhedral cores from the Gulf coast trade route in the Early Classic. Second, the high quantities of obsidian at Chunchucmil indicate that it was an economic central place in its region and a gateway community for much of the northern lowlands. We cannot know precisely who managed this trade, but the scale and logistics suggest that suprahousehold collectives based at Chunchucmil's quadrangles were heavily involved. Competition among quadrangles engendered cooperation between quadrangles and households: the success of quadrangles would have depended on recruiting households by sharing prosperity. Indeed, excavations in domestic contexts show that multifamily households located beyond the quadrangles, such as the Lool and 'Aak houselots, played important roles in these collectives. Third, once obsidian arrived at Chunchucmil, it was distributed at a market, though households in the hinterland were not well serviced by this market. The distributional evidence for a market presented in this chapter complements contextual and configurational lines of evidence. The existence of market distribution at Chunchucmil would have required a second form of cooperation, this time between the competing quadrangles that shared a joint interest in providing venues to stimulate trade and commerce. A market system implies an even broader form of cooperation: the site's authorities helped producers, merchants, and consumers by providing a central venue for efficient exchange. This cooperation likely served the important function of integrating economic networks that extended beyond the site but were crucial in securing subsistence goods that do not grow well locally. Households in Chunchucmil's hinterland may have participated in this economic system, but their participation did not give them access to obsidian.

As discussed in the introduction, our proposal of cooperative entanglements that cross status hierarchies does not follow the two-tiered model of Maya economies that has prevailed for the last few decades. Though trade was peculiarly important in the northern lowlands, our study joins recent research from the southern lowlands that is beginning to highlight cooperative ties across the two tiers in other realms of the economy, such as production.

Our argument for cooperation may be seen as a throwback with regard to broader trends in the study of ancient economies. By the late 1970s, managerial models were beginning to be replaced by political economy models in which elite participation in the economy was understood to serve not the good of society as a whole but rather the elites' own strategic interest in reproducing or increasing inequality (Brumfiel and Earle 1987). However, we do not see our view of northwest Yucatán, with its suprahousehold collectives that help fulfill basic subsistence needs while also achieving equitable distributions of long-distance goods, as being at odds with political economic perspectives. Rather, we believe our conclusions are attuned to recent discussions in social archaeology that recognize the mutual engagement of all sectors in the production and reproduction of ancient economies.

Acknowledgments: We thank Chris Pool, Payson Sheets, and Hattula Moholy-Nagy for comments on this chapter. We also thank the National Science Foundation for funding and INAH for permission to conduct archaeological fieldwork at Chunchucmil.

REFERENCES

Aoyama, Kazuo

2001 Classic Maya State, Urbanism, and Exchange: Chipped Stone Evidence from the Copan Valley and Its Hinterland. *American Anthropologist* 103:346–360.

Ardren, Traci

2003 Excavations in the Lool Group. In *Pakbeh Regional Economy Program: Report on the 2002 Field Season*, edited by B. Dahlin and Daniel Mazeau. Sociology and Anthropology Department, Howard University, Washington, DC.

Brandenburger, A., and B. Nalebuff

1996 *Co-opetition*. Currency/Doubleday, New York.

Braswell, Geoffrey E.

2003 Understanding Early Classic Interaction between Kaminaljuyu and Central Mexico. In *The Maya and Teotihuacan: Reinterpreting Early Classic Interaction*, edited by G. E. Braswell, pp. 105–137. University of Texas Press, Austin.

Brumfiel, Elizabeth M.

1994 Factional Development and Political Competition in the New World: An Introduction. In *Factional Competition and Political Development in the New World*, edited by E. M. Brumfiel and J. W. Fox, pp. 3–13. Cambridge University Press, New York.

Brumfiel, Elizabeth M., and Timothy Earle

1987 Specialization, Exchange, and Complex Societies: An Introduction. In *Specialization, Exchange, and Complex Societies*, edited by E. Brumfiel and Timothy Earle, pp. 1–9. Cambridge University Press, Cambridge.

Chase, Diane Z., and Arlen F. Chase

2004 Archaeological Perspectives on Classic Maya Social Organization from Caracol, Belize. *Ancient Mesoamerica* 15:139–147.

Chase, Diane Z., and Arlen F. Chase, eds.

1992 *Mesoamerican Elites*. Norman: University of Oklahoma Press.

Clark, John E.

1986 From Mountains to Molehills: A Critical Review of Teotihuacan's Obsidian Industry. In *Economic Aspects of Prehispanic Highland Mexico*, edited by B. Isaac, pp. 23–74. Economic Anthropology, Supplement 2. JAI Press, Greenwich, CT.

1987 Politics, Prismatic Blades, and Mesoamerican Civilization. In *The Organization of Core Technology*, edited by J. K. Johnson and C. A. Morrow, pp. 259–284. Economic Anthropology, Supplement 2. Westview Press, Boulder, CO.

1997 Prismatic Blademaking, Craftsmanship, and Production: An Analysis of Obsidian Refuse from Ojo de Agua, Chiapas, Mexico. *Ancient Mesoamerica* 8:137–160.

Dahlin, Bruce H.

2003 Chunchucmil: A Complex Economy in Northwest Yucatan. *Mexicon* 25:129–138.

Forthcoming The Dimensions of Power: Interpreting the Built Environment at Chunchucmil, Yucatan, Mexico. In *Urbanismo en Mesoamerica*, edited by R. Cobean and W. T. Sanders. Penn State University Press, State College.

Dahlin, Bruce H., Anthony Andrews, Tim Beach, Clara Bezanilla, Patrice Farrell, Sheryl Luzzader-Beach, and Valerie McCormick

1998 Punta Canbalam in Context: A Peripatetic Coastal Site in Northwest Campeche, Mexico. *Ancient Mesoamerica* 9:1–15.

Dahlin, Bruce H., and Traci Ardren
2002 Modes of Exchange and Regional Patterns: Chunchucmil, Yucatan, Mexico. In *Ancient Maya Political Economies*, edited by M. Masson and David Freidel, pp. 249–284. AltaMira, Walnut Creek, CA.

Dahlin, Bruce H., Tim Beach, Sheryl Luzzader-Beach, David Hixson, Scott R. Hutson, Aline Magnoni, Eugenia B. Mansell, and Daniel Mazeau
2005 Reconstructing Agricultural Self-Sufficiency at Chunchucmil, Yucatan, Mexico. *Ancient Mesoamerica* 16(2):229–247.

Dahlin, Bruce H., Chris T. Jensen, Richard E. Terry, David R. Wright, and Tim Beach
2007 In Search of an Ancient Maya Market. *Latin American Antiquity* 18(4):363–384.

Dominguez Carrasco, M., William J. Folan, and Joel D. Gunn
1996 Calakmul, Campeche: Sus áreas de actividades ceremoniales, cívicas y domésticas, derivadas de sus materiales líticos y cerámicos. *Investigadores de la Cultura Maya* 4:80–106.

Earle, Timothy K.
1977 A Reappraisal of Redistribution: Complex Hawaiian Chiefdoms. In *Exchange Systems in Prehistory*, edited by T. K. Earle and J. E. Ericson, pp. 213–229. Academic Press, New York.

Emery, Kitty, and Kazuo Aoyama
2007 Bone, Shell, and Lithic Evidence for Crafting in Elite Maya Households at Aguateca, Guatemala. *Ancient Mesoamerica* 18:69–89.

Freidel, David A.
1981 The Political Economies of Residential Dispersion among the Lowland Maya. In *Lowland Maya Settlement Patterns*, edited by W. Ashmore, pp. 371–382. University of New Mexico Press, Albuquerque.

Fry, Robert
1979 The Economics of Pottery at Tikal, Guatemala: Models of Exchange for Serving Vessels. *American Antiquity* 44(3):494–512.

García Cook, Ángel
1984 Dos elementos arquitectónicos tempranos en Tlalancaleca, Puebla. *Cuadernos de Arquitectura Mesoamericana* 2:29–32.

Guderjan, Thomas H.
2007 *The Nature of an Ancient Maya City: Resources, Interaction and Power at Blue Creek, Belize*. University of Alabama Press, Tuscaloosa.

Hammond, Norman
1972 Obsidian Trade Routes in the Mayan Area. *Science* 178:1092–1093.

Hendon, Julia A.
1997 Women's Work, Women's Space, and Women's Status among the Classic Period Maya Elite of the Copan Valley, Honduras. In *Women in Prehistory: North America and Mesoamerica*, edited by C. Claassen, and Rosemary Joyce, pp. 33–46. University of Pennsylvania Press, Philadelphia.

Hirth, Kenneth G.
1978 Interregional Trade and the Formation of Gateway Cities. *American Antiquity* 43:35–45.

1998 The Distributional Approach: A New Way to Identify Marketplace Exchange in the Archaeological Record. *Current Anthropology* 39(4):451–476.

Houston, Stephen D., Hector L. Escobedo, Mark Child, Charles Golden, and Rene Munoz

2003 Moral Community and Settlement Transformation among the Classic Maya: Evidence from Piedras Negras, Guatemala. In *Social Construction of Ancient Cities*, edited by M. L. Smith. Smithsonian, Washington, DC.

Hutson, Scott R., and Bruce H. Dahlin

2008. Desenredando una paradoja: Asentamiento y economía en Chunchucmil, Yucatán. *Los Investigadores de la Cultura Maya* 16.

Hutson, Scott R., David Hixson, Aline Magnoni, Daniel E. Mazeau, and Bruce H. Dahlin

2008 Site and Community at Chunchucmil and Ancient Maya Urban Centers. *Journal of Field Archaeology* 33(1):19–40.

Hutson, Scott R., Travis W. Stanton, Aline Magnoni, Richard E. Terry, and Jason Craner

2007 Beyond the Buildings: Formation Processes of Ancient Maya Houselots and Methods for the Study of Non-architectural Space *Journal of Anthropological Archaeology* 26:442–473.

Inomata, Takeshi, and Laura Stiver

1998 Floor Assemblages from Burned Structures at Aguateca, Guatemala: A Study of Classic Maya Households. *Journal of Field Archaeology* 25:431–452.

Jones, Christopher

1996 *Excavations in the East Plaza of Tikal*. Tikal Report Number 16. University Museum, University of Pennsylvania, Philadelphia.

Kovacevich, Bridget, Ronald Bishop, Hector Neff, and Karen Pereira

2003 Sistemas económicas y de producción maya: Nuevos datos y retos en Cancuen. In *XVI Simposio de Investigaciones arqueológicas en Guatemala*, edited by J. P. Laporte, B. Arroyo, H. Escobedo, and H. Mejia, pp. 143–158. Museo Nacional de Arqueología y Etnología, Guatemala City.

Leyden, Barbara, Mark Brenner, Jason H. Curtis, Dolores Piperno, Tom Whitmore, and Bruce Dahlin

1996 A Record of Long- and Short-Term Paleoclimatic Variation from Northwest Yucatan: Cenote San José Chulchaca. In *The Managed Mosaic: Ancient Maya Agriculture and Resource Use*, edited by S. L. Fedick, pp. 30–52. University of Utah Press, Salt Lake City.

Lucero, Lisa J.

2007 Classic Maya Temples, Politics, and the Voice of the People. *Latin American Antiquity* 18(4):407–428.

Masson, Marilyn A., and David A. Freidel (editors)

2002 *Ancient Maya Political Economies*. AltaMira, Walnut Creek, CA.

Matheny, Ray T., Deanne Gurr, Don W. Forsyth, and Forest R. Hauck

1983 *Investigations at Edzna, Campeche, Mexico, Vol. 1, Part 1: The Hydraulic System*. Papers of the New World Archaeological Foundation, No. 46. Brigham Young University, Provo, UT.

McAnany, Patricia

1989 Economic Foundations of Prehistoric Maya Society. *Research in Economic Anthropology* Suppl. 4:347–372.

1993 Resources, Specialization and Exchange in the Maya Lowlands. In *The American Southwest and Mesoamerica*, edited by J. Ericson and T. J. Baugh, pp. 213–245. Plenum, New York.

Moholy-Nagy, Hattula

1989 Who Used Obsidian at Tikal? In *La obsidiana en Mesoamerica*, edited by M. Gaxiola and J. E. Clark, pp. 379–390. INAH, Mexico City.

1997 Middens, Construction Fill, and Offerings: Evidence for the Organization of Classic Period Craft Production at Tikal, Guatemala. *Journal of Field Archaeology* 24(3):293–313.

2003 Source Attribution and the Utilization of Obsidian in the Maya Area. *Latin American Antiquity* 14(3):301–310.

Moriarty, Matthew D.

2004 Investigating an Inland Maya Port: The 2003 Field Season at Trinidad de Nosotros, Peten, Guatemala. Report submitted to the Foundation for the Advancement of Mesoamerican Studies, Inc.

Nelson, Fred W.

1973 *Archaeological Investigations at Dzibilnocac. Campeche, Mexico*. Papers of the New World Archaeological Foundation, no. 33. New World Archaeological Foundation, Brigham Young University, Provo, UT.

1989 Rutas de intercambio de obsidiana en el norte de la península de Yucatán. In *La obsidiana en Mesoamerica*, edited by M. Gaxiola and J. E. Clark, pp. 363–368. INAH, Mexico City.

Nelson, F. W., Kirk K. Nielsen, Nolan F. Mangelson, Max W. Hill, and Ray T. Matheny

1977 Preliminary Studies of the Trace Element Composition of Obsidian Artifacts from Northern Campeche Mexico. *American Antiquity* 42(2):209–225.

Nelson, F. W., D. A. Phillips, and Alfredo Barrera Rubio

1983 Trace Element Analysis of Obsidian Artifacts from the Northern Maya Lowlands. In *Investigation at Edzna, Campeche, Mexico*, Appendix A. R. Matheny, ed. Provo: New World Archaeological Foundation.

Netting, Robert M.

1982 Some Home Truths on Household Size and Wealth. *American Behavioral Scientist* 25(6):641–661.

Potter, Daniel R., and Eleanor M. King

1995 A Heterarchical Approach to Lowland Maya Socioeconomies. In *Heterarchy and the Analysis of Complex Societies*, edited by R. M. Ehrenreich, C. L. Crumley, and J. E. Levy, pp. 17–32. American Anthropological Association, Arlington, VA.

Rathje, William L.

1971 The Origin and Development of Lowland Classic Maya Civilization. *American Antiquity* 36:275–285.

Reents-Budet, Dorie
1994 *Painting the Maya Universe: Royal Ceramics of the Classic Period*. Duke University Press, Durham, NC.
Renfrew, Colin
1977 Alternative Models for Exchange and Spatial Distribution. In *Exchange Systems in Prehistory*, edited by T. K. Earle and J. E. Ericson. Academic Press, New York.
Rice, Prudence M.
1984 Obsidian Procurement in the Central Peten Lakes Region, Guatemala. *Journal of Field Archaeology* 11:181–194.
1987 Economic Change in the Lowland Maya Late Classic Period. In *Specialization, Exchange and Complex Societies*, edited by E. M. Brumfiel and T. K. Earle, pp. 76–85. Cambridge University Press, Cambridge.
Robin, Cynthia
2003 New Directions in Classic Maya Household Archaeology. *Journal of Archaeological Research* 11(4):307–356.
Rovner, Irwin
1976 A Method for Determining Obsidian Trade Patterns in the Maya Lowlands. *Katunob* 9(1):43–51.
1989a Patrones anómalos en la importación de obsidiana en el centro de las tierras bajas Mayas. In *La obsidiana en Mesoamerica*, edited by M. Gaxiola and J. E. Clark, pp. 369–373. INAH, Mexico City.
1989b Theories and Methods in Obsidian Analysis: Methodological Problems at Trade Recipient Sites. In *La obsidiana en Mesoamerica*, edited by M. Gaxiola and J. E. Clark, pp. 427–431. INAH, Mexico City.
Rovner, Irwin, and Suzanne M. Lewenstein
1997 *Maya Stone Tools of Dzibilchaltún, Yucatán, and Becán and Chicanná, Campeche*. Middle American Research Institute Pub. No. 65. Tulane University, New Orleans.
Sabloff, Jeremy A., and William Rathje
1980 The Rise of a Maya Merchant Class. In *Pre-Columbian Archaeology: Readings from Scientific American*, pp. 139–149. W. H. Freeman, San Francisco.
Sahlins, Marshal
1965 On the Sociology of Primitive Exchange. In *The Relevance of Models for Social Anthropology*, edited by M. Banton, pp. 139–236. Tavistick, London.
Santley, Robert S.
1983 Obsidian Trade and Teotihuacán Influence in Mesoamerica. In *Highland-Lowland Interaction in Mesoamerica: Interdisciplinary Approaches*. Dumbarton Oaks, Washington, DC.
Sheets, Payson
1975 A Reassessment of the Precolombian Obsidian Industry at El Chayal, Guatemala. *American Antiquity* 40(1):98–103.
1979 Lithic Artifacts. In *Quirigua Report*, edited by Robert Sharer. University Museum, University of Pennsylvania, Philadelphia.
2000 Provisioning the Ceren Household. *Ancient Mesoamerica* 11:217–230.

Sidrys, Raymond V.
1977 Mass-Distance Measures for the Maya Obsidian Trade. In *Exchange Systems in Prehistory*, edited by T. K. Earle and J. E. Ericson, pp. 91–107. Academic Press, New York.
Stoltman, James B.
1978 *Lithic Artifacts from a Complex Society: The Chipped Stone Tools from Becán, Campeche, Mexico*. Middle American Research Institute, Occasional Paper No. 2. Middle American Research Institute, New Orleans.
Varela Torrecilla, Carmen
1998. *El Clásico Medio en el noroccidente de Yucatán*. Paris Monographs in American Archaeology 2 (BAR International Series 739).
Wurtzburg, Susan
1991 Sayil: Investigations of Urbanism and Economic Organization at an Ancient Maya City. PhD dissertation, Department of Anthropology, State University of New York, Albany.

II

COOPERATION AND HIERARCHY

5

Cooperation in Conflict

Negotiating Inequality in Midwestern U.S. Hog Contracting

Ronald Rich, Eastern Michigan University

Rob Simpson[1] runs a 2,000-acre grain farm in east-central Illinois that has been in his family since the 1950s, and on which they have raised hogs for as long as Rob can remember. When I interviewed Rob, he owned about 1,400 sows and a swine herd numbering perhaps 12,000 animals. Rob practices multiple-site hog production, meaning he breaks his herd into age- and function-based groups/stages housed on separate sites. Sows are on his home gestation site, where he also farrows, and he has animals in his own nursery and finishing buildings at different places around his farm.[2] But most of his pigs are housed on sites owned by other farmers/hog producers. Rob organizes the stages through contracts to create a "contract operation," a single production unit through which animals move in a coordinated flow. Contract operations like Rob's intersect yet are organizationally distinct from the simple commodity production farms of which they are a part. "Contractors" like Rob own the hogs and hire "contractees," or growers, to raise the animals on their own farms/sites, paying them a predetermined fee. Rob's growers maintain the fixed resources on their property and provide labor to raise his animals, and he is able to increase scale and better position his marketing.

Since the end of World War II, hog production in the Midwest has gone from a widespread, small-scale, low-capital, market-based form of simple commodity production involving many small hog producers selling on spot commodity markets to a highly specialized process conducted by a small number of producers often organized administratively through production and marketing contracts. Nowhere is this better illustrated than in Illinois, where the number of hog farms has plummeted over the past 50 years. As late as 1965, about 62,000 farms had hogs; this figure represented over 40 percent of all Illinois farms. By 1990 that number was 15,300, by 2000 it was only 5,100, and by December 2007 there were only 2,900 hog farms in Illinois. Contract production began in earnest in Illinois in the early 1990s, intensifying concentration. In 1990, hog farms having less than 500 animals made up 80 percent of the hog farms in Illinois and held 32 percent of the Illinois hog inventory. By 2000, those same farms still constituted 63 percent of Illinois hog farms, but held only 8 percent of the state's inventory; in 2007 the percentages were 52 and 3.9 respectively. In Illinois in 2007, fewer than 1,000 extremely large producers (those having over 1,000 animals on-site) held over 90 percent of the state's hog inventory (National Agricultural Statistics Service 2008).

Contracting fundamentally changes the way hog production is organized. Production and market contracts replace input/output markets in pork commodity chains, including live hog spot markets (Rich 2006), and create new ones in labor and barn space. Contracts enable primary producers to access capital and erect the large automated confinement buildings that are the hallmark of contemporary industrial hog production. The internal organization of contract operations like Rob Simpson's centralizes production and marketing authority in the hands of hog owners, creating hierarchical and unequal relations of production between contractors and contractees. In neoliberal analyses, centralized authority in contract operations is necessary to meet the retail consumers' changing demands, which include prepared foods and foods with characteristics like leanness and enhanced nutritional qualities (Martinez 1999:21; Barkema 1993; Frank and Henderson 1992). In the presence of highly competitive retail markets, upstream market-based exchanges through which simple commodity producers acquire inputs and sell their animals, and on which pork commodity chains have long been based, are understood to be inefficient and are theorized as forms of risk and cost. Contracts iron out market "imperfections" and "irregularities," minimize risk (McBride and Key 2003), and contribute to greater control (by contracting entities) of markets by rendering exchanges more dependable and regular (Acheson 2002; Schrader 1998). Contracting is often depicted as the best of U.S. agriculture in this regard: a rational and progressive form of development using cutting-edge production methods and technology, and employing advanced marketing relationships that make pork products, and thereby all pork producers, more competitive for consumers' meat dollars (see Boehlje 1995).

Neo-Marxist political economy analyses read centralized authority somewhat differently. Contractees do not sell the commodities produced in their barns, but rather sell their labor to the owner of the hogs they raise. Contract fees often involve incentives and so in practice are a form of risk and cost allocation instituted through a piece-rate wage (Davis 1980; Mooney 1983; Wilson 1986). Such "disguised" proletarianization (Clapp 1994; Durrenberger 1996:47–48) creates structural relations of dependency and authority that echo those in industrial wage labor. Centralized decision making means that contractors rather than contractees control inputs and production (Heffernan 1984; Rhodes 1993; Watts 1994:27–28). Contractees raise animals but lack the authority to control the kinds of animals they raise, how they raise them, and how and to whom they market them. Ownership, management, and labor become separated, and contractees are "de-skilled" (Welsh 1997:494, 495). Excluded from much decision making and mental labor, contractees perform only manual labor, functioning as a kind of "hog janitor" (Thu and Durrenberger 1994).

Neoliberal and neo-Marxist analyses emphasize contract production as a hierarchical centralization of production and marketing authority that involves relations of inequality and conflict. From an ethnographic perspective that accounts for the experience of animal producers, centralized authority and the conflict and inequality it generates capture only part of contract organization. Hog contracting involves a contradiction between centralized authority and decentralized production that creates substantial "moral hazard" (Wolf et al. 2001) for both contractors and contractees. In industrial hog production, multiple site organization is a biosecurity measure necessary for scale-based production of biologically fragile animals. Authority for production rests in the hands of contractors, while production itself is spread over multiple growers. As a result, direct labor oversight is impractical for contractors, who are dependent on the husbandry of their contractees. Since many production decisions are removed from hog raisers, contractees are dependent on contractors to not manipulate production in ways that take undue advantage of them. Contract operations involve an underlying cooperation between contractor and contractees that mitigates the moral hazard generated by centralized authority and decentralized production. Contractors and contractees both recognize the inequality and conflict generated by contract organization, but they rarely characterize their relations as antagonistic. They use the terms "trust and honesty" to frame contract relations and they situate these characteristics in the personal integrity of those involved. Of the 27 contract operations I studied,[3] 20 are farm based like Rob Simpson's; that is, contract relations often follow existing lines of friendship, neighborhood, work, and kin. In these farm-based contract operations, cooperation becomes much more than a function of production. It is a way in which midwestern family farmers (contractors and contractees alike) manage their participation in exploitive agricultural development more generally.

MORAL HAZARD AND RAISING INDUSTRIAL HOGS

The biological characteristics of agricultural commodities always condition the ways that those commodities can be raised, even in highly industrialized contexts (Goodman and Watts 1994). In contracting, the primary characteristic conditioning production is the biological "fragility" of hogs that are bred genetically to be very lean. Leanness functions as a form of input standardization, and lean animals are preferred by large packers because they are more amenable to mechanized production lines (Whittemore 1998:5, 32). These lean animals, referred to as "indoor pigs" by growers I worked with, require controlled environments to be raised efficiently, and are fragile because they are susceptible to multiple forms of stress (Rich 2008). Susceptibility to stress is in part a genetic characteristic, unwittingly selected for by breeders as they selected for leanness (Schook and Clamp 1993). Indoor pigs also need constant access to feed and water, and their lack of fat reserves makes them less resilient than their outdoor counterparts. Animal fragility is linked also to the way that animal health is construed as efficiency, and efficiency is then measured by rate of growth in relation to feed inputs. Pathogens are addressed physically in animals by metabolizable energy provided by feed, and so fighting stressors requires energy that prevents maximization of feed efficiency (Curtis 1993:94). Production of protein molecules that enhance the body's immunological response to a pathogen also entails reduced secretion of growth hormones and chemical and neural processes that reduce an animal's feed intake and slow growth (Harris 2000:84–85; Kelley et al. 1993). Placing many animals in the enclosed spaces of confinement barns further increases the potential for pathogen transmission to other animals and threatens production efficiency (Pond et al. 1991:52).

The goal of production is to limit stressors that interfere with efficient growth. To this end, in the late 1980s and into the 1990s emergent-area firms[4] pioneered new capital-intensive methods and organizations of production that combined multiple-site methods, full confinement technologies, and contracting in order to raise large numbers of animals in a single production flow (Harris 2000). Multiple-site methods are based on the isowean principle in which piglets are weaned early from their mothers and then isolated or removed from the sow herd and raised on other sites. Animals raised on different sites prevent pathogens that may infect one site from infecting animals on other sites. Confinement technologies have been around for decades in Midwestern hog production, and emergent-area firms took confinement production to new levels in the form of buildings that maintain ideal growing environments by automatically controlling temperature, humidity, and feed and water access, and mechanizing manure removal. Firms offered contracts to potential growers, who used the guaranteed income assured by a contract to secure financing for capital-intensive facilities. Breaking a swine herd into age- and function-based groups housed on different sites and coordinated into a single production flow enabled integrating firms to build monumental swine herds by mitigating the effects of disease and illness and leaving to contractees the investment in fixed resources necessary to raise the animals.

Emergent-area firms were among the largest hog producers in the United States by the early 1990s (Rhodes and Grimes 1992:26), when they entered the Midwest and began competing directly with farm-based hog producers on live hog spot markets. They were more efficient than traditional midwestern farrow-to-finish producers,[5] and were preferred by packing plants because of the lean animals they produced and their regularized production schedules. As a result, midwestern hog producers experienced tremendous pressure to (re)capitalize, and over the 1990s two-thirds of Illinois hog producers left the industry. Many of those who survived accessed the new technologies through networking relationships, including contracting (Ziegenhorn 1998). Contemporary Illinois contracting is rooted in a highly developed infrastructure that included significant capitalization among many hog producers of various sizes. As a result, industrialization there spread through not only integrating firms but also farm-based producers like Rob Simpson who were once independent and who continue to raise hogs in conjunction with grain farming. The vast majority of contractees I interviewed were also independent hog producers at one time and continue grain farming on substantial land bases. Most also have some form of off-farm job, and are thus "part-time" farmers, combining simple commodity grain production, contract hog production, and wage labor in diversified subsistence strategies. Industrialization of hog production has thus proceeded in Illinois, to a good extent, through relationships between otherwise independent simple commodity producers.

MORAL HAZARD AND "CRISIS POINTS" IN LABOR DISCIPLINE

Raising fragile commodities on multiple sites and the structural dependency of contractees on contractors create moral hazard in contract operations. According to Wolf et al. (2001), moral hazard develops in production situations characterized by asymmetric information, and in contracting refers to contractees' "perfect" knowledge of their actions, and contractors' "imperfect" knowledge of contractees' actions. Contracts function as "policing mechanisms" through which contractors discipline labor by "exercising control over growers' practices" and mitigating the ever-present potential for contractees to shirk responsibility (Wolf et al. 2001:366). But moral hazard is more than just production risk for contractors. It involves the way risks and responsibilities give contractors and contractees different and sometimes competing interests. Contractees face considerable moral hazard because they assume production risk through incentives in their fees, and are responsible for production costs associated with operating, maintaining, and financing the buildings in which animals are raised. Their contractors' actions impact the costs and risk they absorb. Just as contractors do not have perfect knowledge of their contractees' actions, so do contractees not have perfect knowledge of (or control over) how contractors make decisions that affect them. What Wolf et al. describe as policing mechanisms are more appropriately discerned in hog contracting as what Wells (1996) calls "crisis points." In hog contracting, crisis points occur in every production cycle requiring contractors to sensitively make production decisions that affect the costs and risks borne by their contractees. These decisions fall into three different categories: input provisioning, residual claimancy, and labor versus capital expenses.

Input Provisioning

Input provisioning refers to production factors that contractors provide and/or pay for to ensure that their hogs receive necessary materials and services. They include hog genetics; providing animals; providing feed, medication and related equipment; and veterinary services. When, how, the quality of, and under what conditions inputs are provided are repeated areas of negotiation in contract operations. To illustrate, I describe three problems associated with contractors provisioning animals to contractees: understocking, overstocking, and animal health and quality. Since pigs are farrowed year-round in industrial hog farming, there are always pigs awaiting space in a barn, and contractors must coordinate the movement of groups of animals from building to building. Managing such a flow can be costly if not coordinated well, and it can cause conflict if contractors repeatedly make decisions that take undue advantage of contractees.

Filling a barn incompletely, or leaving it empty for a time, can increase contractee operating cost. When temperatures are cool, the bulk of warming in confinement barns is provided by the bodies of the animals. If a barn is only partially filled, heaters will be used more, resulting in increased fuel costs for contractees. When contractee pay hinges on the number of animals that move through their buildings (which is often the case), underfilling a barn also reduces the absolute income of the contractee. Nursery growers for a large vertically integrated agricultural firm that I call International Pork Finishing (IPF) are paid eight cents per day per pig for every day that pigs are on feed in their barns. IPF moves their pigs in "routes," each route stocked by a series of sow centers. As a biosecurity measure, animals are moved from these sow centers to the same nurseries, and from the nurseries to the same finishing barns. Animals from multiple routes are not mixed even if there is room in grower buildings, so understocking is common. IPF contracts guarantee that nursery contractees will always receive payment as though their buildings are at least half-full. However, that leaves considerable room for them to manipulate pig flows and contractee pay.

Overstocking also affects contractee income. Sometimes contractors pay for less pig space than a barn can hold; this allows them to fill the barns to capacity and pay for less pig space than they are actually using. When contractors are paying on the basis of pig space,[6] it is somewhat common for them to overstock their contractee barns by bringing in more pigs than the standard pig-space allowance recommends for healthy confinement animals. Smaller pigs require less space per animal, and overstocking does not become inefficient until pigs are older. Since some death loss is expected, mild overstocking of young pigs is remedied through the death of some animals over the cycle, allowing contractors to anticipate death loss and more efficiently manage their pig flows. Overstocking can also occur when a contractor has not acquired sufficient space to hold all the animals in the flow. Ralph Thomas, a farm-based contractor who underwent dramatic expansion in the 1990s, was forced to overstock his growers' barns because his sow herd growth far outpaced his contracted space. The overstocking led to health problems in the barns, and pigs moved through nursery sites more quickly than normal. Contractee labor increased as buildings required more frequent cleaning and because increased health problems meant more injections and removal of dead pigs.

One of the advantages of contracting that contractees enjoy is a regular and single source of high-quality healthy animals. Repeatedly getting animals that are underweight, in poor health, or mixed from several sow centers or nurseries increases labor costs for contractees. Underweight animals lengthen the turnaround time of a barn, thus leading to reduced long-term income. Since the health of pigs a grower receives is affected by conditions and management practices at previous sites, if pigs have health trouble in a nursery, and/or if a nursery grower lacks management skills, then the animals may not be up to weight and may not perform as well in finishing barns; this impacts labor and income for the finisher. Brian and Wendy Short, who finish for Rob Simpson, had this problem. Pigs frequently arrived from the nursery with respiratory problems related to improper ventilation. Ammonia from the manure pits beneath the building acted as a stressor and exacerbated some endemic health problems Rob had at the farrowing center. Animals leaving the farrowing center were not in great shape, and by the time the Shorts got the animals, stress was quite evident and the Shorts' job more difficult.

"Residual claimancy" refers to sharing revenue between contractors and contractees through incentives in contractee wages. Contract fees often consist of two parts. One is a predetermined and guaranteed base fee that takes into account the age, size, structure, quality, and location of the buildings in which the hogs are raised. The second part consists of incentives that involve performance standards and structure total pay received in part on the basis of the quantity and quality of the commodity raised. Of the 37 contractees I interviewed, 21 (57 percent) have a fee that includes incentives. Incentives transfer some production and marketing risk to contractees and function as labor discipline by vesting contractees in the performance of the animals they raise. Contractors use incentives to mitigate their own moral hazard, typically paying a smaller base fee so that contractees are motivated to capture the "full" fee by meeting production standards. Incentives in hog contracting include mortality, sort loss, and feed conversion. Mortality incentives involve hogs that die while on a grower's site. Sort loss incentives refer to the number of culls that should not move on to the next phase of production but leave a grower's site anyway. And feed conversion incentives are based on the amount of feed it takes to bring a hog to market weight, figured on a per pig or per pound basis.[7]

Contractors can use incentives to unfairly shift production cost to contractees. I was told of one contractor who manipulated his pig flow so as to not have to pay feed conversion incentives he had with his nursery and finishing growers. Pigs put on weight in different proportions to feed intake in different stages of growth (Ensminger and Parker 1997:134). The younger a pig is, the less amount of feed is required to produce growth. This contractor sabotaged both his nursery and finishing growers by extending the time the animals were in the nursery; this raised the feed conversion at the nursery stage while at the same time denying the finisher full access to the "easy pounds" that come in the first weeks that animals are in the finisher. Frank Keys faced a situation like this. He was never able to achieve the feed conversion bonus in his contract because he raises two kinds of pigs for his farm-based contractor: maternal line replacement gilts and terminal line market hogs.[8] The replacement gilts are slower growers than terminal line hogs because the maternal line genetics that this contractor uses are selected not for rate of gain, but for durability and lactation. Since Frank's fee was somewhat less than he would get if no incentives were in place, his contractor was unfairly sharing production cost under conditions that made it virtually impossible for Frank to achieve a bonus.

IPF grower John Walker is another example. Walker at first had a typical finishing arrangement with IPF, raising feeder pigs to market weight. After some time he was made part of its gilt multiplication program, raising gilt replacements and receiving a lucrative $1.50 bonus for every animal that left his site. He was forced by the way IPF brought him gilts to run more of a continuous flow operation rather than follow all-in/all-out procedures,[9] and he was never able to completely empty and clean his site. This led to endemic disease in his barns that he could never get rid of. IPF stopped sending him gilts, and wanted him to again finish commercial hogs. At the same time, IPF was beginning to sell more of its feeder pigs instead of finishing them on contract. But it still contracted with a few growers to finish the small, damaged, and/or sick animals that they could not sell but that still had market value. John raised these hogs, often called "off pigs," or "junk pigs." The animals were mixed from numerous nurseries and their health problems were exacerbated by the endemic disease in his barns. In addition, he thinks that IPF provided him with lower-grade feed that it could not sell to its regular feed customers. John's death loss and labor costs were astronomical. Even though he was raising off pigs, he did so under the terms of the original finishing contract that had incentives linked to quotas for weight and quality. It was virtually impossible for him to meet the quotas, and he lost money on every group of pigs that went through his barns.

Capital versus Labor Interests

Incentives and risk allocation are supposed to keep contractor and contractee "on the same page," one contractor expressed to me, by making their interests the same: producing the best quality product at the lowest cost. However, responsibility for costs associated with their buildings and performing labor on hogs that are not theirs gives contractees interests that differ from contractors. For instance, contractees pay for utilities, but utilities cost bears no direct correlation to the fee they receive and cannot be coordinated with that fee in a cost-benefit analysis. Propane, which fuels the heaters in hog buildings, is an excellent example. Contractees' interest is to conserve propane and reduce their utility cost while contractors' interest is to use heaters to ensure that as much feed energy as possible goes to weight gain. Contractees lack the proper incentive to assure that buildings are kept as warm as contractors might want.

Norman Salt raises hogs for a farm-based contractor named John Braun. A small independent producer for decades, Norman has buildings that are in good shape but not equipped with the most recent technology. John wants the buildings heated so as to maximize feed efficiency, keeping temperatures higher in order to direct more feed energy to growth and less to maintaining body temperature during colder seasons. But Norman's contract does not have a feed efficiency bonus, and so he has no incentive to heat the building as John would. Instead, Norman heats the buildings to maintain what he refers to as "adequate health." For him, the issue is who pays for animal growth: does he pay for it by heating the building, or does Braun pay for it through more feed usage? "I'm somewhat of the opinion that you can buy feed cheaper than you can buy heat, especially now, lately. . . . Why should I spend money that I'm not getting back to do something that I'm not sure [about]?" Propane prices at the time of our interviews were high, and the previous winter had been a cold one. Corn prices had been dropping for several years and feed costs were low. To Norman, when all things were considered it made more sense to pay for animal growth through a little more feed rather than a little more propane.

Labor versus capital expenditures is another area where contractor and contractee interests conflict. Contractees want to limit their labor costs while contractors try to utilize contractee labor to limit their capital costs. Medicating animals is a good example. Hogs are medicated in confinement barns through feed or water distribution, and by injection. Water and feed medicating are capital intensive and can treat an entire barn of animals at once with a minimum of labor, while injections are labor intensive and treat individual animals. Contractees frequently want to water or feed medicate, for it limits their labor. But it is much more costly to medicate an entire herd than it is to inject several hogs that might be sick, and so contractors often prefer to inject individual animals to see if the medication prevents an outbreak before it becomes necessary to medicate an entire barn. What form of medication to administer (shots or feed/water), or when to administer feed/water medication, are constantly negotiated. Most contractees do not have free rein to administer water or feed medication as they see fit, but vials of antibiotics are almost always present on contractee sites for injections. If a contractee thinks that water or feed medication is required, the contractor must provide it.

Implications

Contractors and contractees face different risks, costs, and responsibilities. Contractors must delicately manage crisis points and mitigate moral hazard for their contractees. Contractees are tolerant of some manipulation, seeing it as part of doing business. But excessive or repeated violations undermine the willingness of contractees to cooperate. If contractees think that contractors are using their labor to deal with health issues that would be more appropriately addressed through more capital-intensive measures, then they feel taken advantage of. When this occurs, contractee motivation is diminished, and they can engage in actions that increase contractor moral hazard. In my experience, contractee "shirking" of responsibility, one of the worst things a contractee can do in a production system that is devoted to raising biologically fragile animals and that dramatically heightens contractor moral hazard, tends to be a contractee response to contractors who take undue advantage of their position rather than contractees simply exploiting conditions of asymmetrical knowledge. In order to prevent shirking, contractors maintain a personalistic relationship by consistently providing single-sourced healthy pigs, applying incentives in a fair manner, and not taking undue advantage of risk and cost allocation to serve their own narrow interests.

MORAL HAZARD AND PERSONALISM

Wells (1996) describes the informal relationships between strawberry field laborers and the field bosses who oversee them as a form of personalism. Strawberry production involves considerable moral hazard situated around raising a fragile commodity in which sharecroppers rely on skilled pickers for some production decisions, labor recruitment, and labor discipline. Contract hog operations in Illinois involve a similar personalist ethic linked to multiple-site production and contractor reliance on the skill of their contractees. Contractors and contractees alike characterize this personalism by the terms "trust" and "honesty," and use it to frame the way contractors (ought to) manage crisis points in ways that mitigate contractee moral hazard and make the contract experience more egalitarian. "A contract is no better than the person who signs it" is something I commonly heard in the field. In interviews, contractors often expressed the need to have faith in the character of the people raising their animals, and many placed characteristics of honesty, trustworthiness, and self-motivation above experience and skill when describing the qualities of a good contractee. I asked one contractee what prevents him from not adequately caring for the hogs he is in charge of. He answered "honesty," while his wife put in "values." Then he said, "Yeah, that's the only thing there is there, 'cause . . . if I wanted to steal from them I could steal them blind and all they could do is just say, 'Hey, enough's enough,' and they come and get their hogs, you know. Because it's your honesty and integrity that they rely on."

In exchange for performing their responsibilities honestly, contractees expect contractors to negotiate crisis points in a personalistic manner that takes contractees' interests into account. For example, Frank Keys, who could never make the feed conversion bonus in his contract because he raised both replacement gilts and terminal market hogs, brought up the issue when he renewed his contract. Because his buildings are good and he does an excellent job with the animals, his contractor, Brandon Trotter, agreed to eliminate the incentive and pay him a larger base fee. Ralph Thomas cultivates personalistic relationships with his contractees even though it costs him.

> There's times when we've done what I'd call cosmetic medication. . . . It may be a situation where I'm pretty sure that I don't have any magic in a bottle that's gonna cure the pig. But if it makes him feel good to go out and give a few shots, or if it makes him feel good that we put something in the water, sometimes it's worth a little bit of cost to show him that you care, show him that you're trying, and that you're trying to support him.

Contractees often say the good contractor is one "who does what he says he is going to do," which means abiding by the terms of the contract and enforcing those terms without taking undue advantage. Ralph resolved the conflict generated when he was forced to overstock his nursery barns by not changing the terms of his contracts. Thomas growers were upset at the overstocking and clumsiness with which the pig flow was managed. Ralph recognized the problem and was sensitive to the increased labor demands that resulted. Most of Ralph's growers at the time were paid by the head, so with all the pigs moving through their barns, they were making a great deal more money than they would otherwise have made because more animals were moving through the barns. In a show of trust and honesty, Ralph "did what he said he would do" and stuck to the terms of the contracts instead of changing the terms to minimize his losses. Carl Anderson, one of Ralph's nursery growers, told me that he was able to make over 20 percent of his entire building loan repayment in the few turns that Ralph overstocked.

Another sign of a trustworthy contractor is his allowing a contractee to contribute to the mental and manual labor involved in the contract operation so that the work relationship is characterized by negotiation and cooperation rather than hierarchical mandate. Contracting separates mental from manual labor as it shifts production authority from hog raisers toward hog owners. However, it also involves a distribution of labor and responsibilities that is not fully captured by a simple distinction between mental and manual labor. Kohls (1958) observes that there are two categories of labor in contract operations: routinized repetitive "production-specific" mental and manual labor associated with contractees, and nonrepetitive strategic "structural-specific" mental and manual labor associated with contractors. The vast majority of contractees in Illinois are highly experienced husbandmen, and the personalist ethic creates a context in which they can utilize their husbandry skills and assume responsibility for production-specific decisions and labor.

Many contractees make production-related decisions in their barns and manipulate barn conditions, timing of feed budgets, feeder adjustments, and sorting, so long as production numbers are satisfactory. John Braun takes this approach with Norman Salt and propane usage. While he wants Norman to increase the heat in order to maximize feed efficiency, his oversight is irregular, and Norman is able to manipulate the heat as he sees fit. So long as his decisions do not cost John too much (which is almost always the case), there is no problem. To take another example, Mike Pence, a contract finisher for a family-firm contracting entity named Pork Gard, has had several "battles" with owner Walt Gard over sorting pigs in his barns. Walt wants him to sort into three size-based groups (big, medium, and small) in order to maximize feed efficiency. But this causes Mike problems when moving the animals to market, for when the first cut of pigs is taken at the end of a cycle he ends up with most pigs being pulled out of the "big" pens, half being pulled out of the "medium" pens, and only a few out of the "small" pens. This makes it harder for him to get those "small" pigs to weight because as they approach market weight they grow more slowly. He also ends up with uneven pen placement, some pens having a few hogs and others being full, and this extends the time needed to get the remaining animals to weight. Mike prefers to sort into two size groups: large/medium and medium/small. By mixing some medium-sized pigs with the bigs, and some with the smalls, at the first market cut he can pull some pigs out of each pen. He does not have to re-sort as much, his labor is reduced, and animal growth is more even. Mike says that his production numbers are good, so Walt lets him go his own way.

Contractors manage crisis points by recognizing what Brandon Trotter told me: "You want to protect your interests, but yet you need these guys, these buildings, to make money. . . . You walk a tightrope." Brandon needs the buildings that his growers own. He needs their conscientious labor. The way he deals with grower concerns impacts how his growers tend to his hogs, which could cost him a great deal of money in the long run rather than a little in the short term. Mitigating contractee moral hazard means sometimes assuming responsibility for unexpected and excessive costs, applying incentives fairly, and encouraging contractees to follow their own experience in their barns. Contractors do not want "hog janitors" raising their animals. They want concerned husbandmen who have opportunities to exercise their substantial skill and experience. Contractees reciprocate this trust by treating pigs as if they themselves owned the animals.

Personalism in Illinois hog contracting creates a context in which the hierarchical contract relation is refigured into a cooperative relationship between independent farmers/producers. Nevertheless, the personal bonds between contractors and contractees are, like the animals they raise, fragile. Personalism is not equipped to challenge the basic inequality of the contract relation. Once the personalist ethic is violated it is difficult to restore the trust on which it rested. Communication becomes haphazard and unreliable, and negotiating crisis points is contentious. Contracts are rarely enforced (or challenged) legally. I have data on many contract relationships that were "broken," but not one of them involved dispute resolution in the courts. When personalism falters, contractors and contractees prefer to just go their own ways. John Walker's situation with IPF is a good illustration. The way that IPF continued to enforce his original contract terms despite sending him inferior animals grossly violated the personal ethic. Once John discovered that he was losing money raising the off pigs, he didn't want legal dispute resolution or even compensation. He wanted out of his contract. IPF agreed so long as the new contractor agreed to use IPF feed products in its barns. John went with Pork Gard, which had taken over the contracts of other IPF finishers under similar terms, and was able to continue production under much more satisfying circumstances.

DISCUSSION: CONTRACTING, REPRODUCTION, AND DEMOCRATIZATION?

Neoclassical and neo-Marxist analyses of contracting are conflict-based approaches, capturing the shift of authority from primary producers to off-farm actors that generates dependency of contractees on contractors. From the perspective of neoliberal theory, centralizing authority empowers producers by making their production more competitive on retail markets. In political economy analyses, centralizing authority disempowers primary producers by restructuring hog production through wage relations and rendering spot hog markets incapable of accommodating the many smaller producers who once participated in midwestern hog production. A more ethnographic approach that places contracting in the context of the farms on which it is practiced suggests also that cooperation is vital to relations of conflict and hierarchy in contract hog operations. Cooperation is a function of production, linked to the multiple-site organization necessary to raise fragile commodities. Contractors mitigate their own moral hazard by not taking undue advantage of contractees. Personalism circumscribes legitimate contractor actions and thereby creates a moral basis on which contractees can evaluate the behavior of their partners as they negotiate crisis points. Cooperation is not in practice distinct from conflict, for personalism is a context through which inequality and dependency are negotiated.

Much hog contracting in Illinois remains tied to family-based farms, and so the reproduction of contract production units and their relations of inequality are now entailed in reproducing Midwestern family farms. The eminent sociologist of agriculture Frederick Buttel (1983:88), writing at the beginning of the 1980s Midwestern farm crisis, argues that the beauty of "family farming" has always been that it stands as "a democratic alternative to the frequently grossly unequal landholding systems of Western Europe" and to slavery in the U.S. South. Midwestern family farming has been not an end unto itself, but a means to a greater end of "democratization," in Buttel's terms. Perhaps "a system of atomistic, independent family farms in a context of contemporary market institutions is not a viable means to sustain the position of household ownership and labor in farming," he says, and perhaps we should be looking "beyond the family farm" for other means of making agriculture a more democratizing enterprise (Buttel 1983:99). Buttel's observations, made more than a quarter century ago, describe contract hog production today: the highly integrated nature of commodity/supply chains in which spot hog markets are dominated (and circumvented) by corporate entities makes control over the means of hog production by atomized family labor-based simple commodity production units no longer tenable. The vast majority of those hog producers no longer exist, and the reproduction of those who remain is secured no longer through production of self-owned market animals, but through wage-based contract relations of conflict and inequality.

It is difficult to argue that contracting is a means to democratization in the way Buttel meant it. However, in a context of rapid industrialization, Illinois hog producers take advantage of the structural cooperation required to produce fragile commodities to fashion contracting in a manner through which the democratizing element of family-labor farming still has meaning and relevance to the structure of Midwestern agriculture. Consider Dick Simon, a contract grower whose farm has been part of his family since his great-grandfather founded it in 1882. Dick has raised hogs his whole life. He laments the loss of family-based independent hog producers and recognizes the role of contracting in this process. However, he still makes contracting an extension of relations he has with other farmers. One of these is a partnership he has had for years with a longtime friend and neighbor in which they farm their land separately, but share machinery and labor. Contracting as he practices it is similar to this kind of partnership, a cooperative enterprise based in shared cost between partners who also share a history. His contractors are a nearby team of brothers who also farm family land. They went to the same high school as he did, graduating a year or two after him. The two families have known each other for years, and their father hauled hogs for Dick's father years ago. "Maybe its because I'm friends with the people I'm working with, but I look at it as a shared risk working together, a way of surviving. These are people with the same framework of farming, family farm, trying to survive, raise a family, and by working together maybe we can all make it." Dick fits contracting into patterns and sets of existing relationships, and so contracting is made familiar and personal even while it institutes new inequalities between him and people he has known all his life and through which he must now reproduce his farm.

I found similar patterns through many of the farm-based contract operations I studied in Illinois. Unlike firm-based contractors, farm-based contractors and their contractees are much more likely to have ties of neighborhood, friendship, employment, and kin. Eric Leaf, one of Rob Simpson's contractees, has worked on Rob's farm since high school, and he and Rob have been best friends for over 30 years. Rob helped Eric purchase a farm several years ago and puts hogs in the barns on Eric's farm. Frank Keys, one of Brandon Trotter's growers, worked on Brandon's hog farm before contracting with him. Three of Ralph Thomas's growers are also former (and current) employees, and one of his nursery growers is a neighbor. John Braun has known Norman Salt since they served on a county committee together years before they contracted. John also contracts with three of his cousins who live nearby and farm some 1,500 acres together, and his nursery grower is a friend he went to high school with.

Larry Stanson finishes hogs for a neighbor with whom he went to school and has known pretty much all his life. He knows his farm, his family, and especially his hogs, and when he made the decision to contract after years of being independent he deliberately turned to local people rather than the big corporations that were active in his area. In our interview, Larry described his contract as consisting of only one page, in contrast to the sometimes excessive and elaborate contracts offered by firm-based contractors, and he wanted to show it to me. As we talked, he rummaged through his cluttered office, checking drawers in his desk and looking through his file cabinet. He failed to find it, and I never did see it. The piece of paper itself is not important enough for Larry to keep track of. For him, contracting is but one facet of a long-term relationship between his own and his contractor's families that extends beyond contracting and that is now reproduced in part through contracting. Through cooperation in farm-based contract operations, contracting farmers like Larry and Dick exert a "democratizing" influence on industrialized hog production in a manner that echoes Buttel.

In the final analysis, though, cooperation has ambivalent results. It does help reproduce (some) midwestern family-type farming and some semblance of the relationships to which producers are accustomed, and it does mitigate relations of inequality and conflict in contract production. But it cannot challenge those relations of inequality, nor can it challenge the long-term concentration of power and authority in U.S. agriculture. Cooperation mitigates structural inequalities, but to mitigate them is to reproduce them, and thereby to perpetuate the industrialized commodity chains in which family-labor hog producers as a group are captured, controlled, and exploited. Perhaps the most important conclusion to draw in an ethnographic approach to contracting that explores the role of cooperation is that reproducing family-labor farming through cooperation reproduces the very relationships that threaten the ongoing viability of simple-commodity producing farms more generally.

NOTES

1. All names used are pseudonyms.

2. *Gestation* is a phase of production consisting of sows in various stages of pregnancy. *Farrowing* refers to birthing new pigs. The nursery stage is where weaned pigs are raised from about three to twelve weeks of age. When leaving the nursery the animals are known as *feeder pigs*, and they are raised to market weight in the finishing stage. New methods are also employed in some operations that divide the process into only two stages. Weaned pigs are moved from farrowing directly to a finishing site equipped for newly weaned animals. I did much of my participant observation work in these new "wean-to-finish" buildings.

3. Fieldwork was conducted between 1998 and 2002. I performed participant observation labor in industrial contract hog barns in northwestern Illinois, mostly cleaning buildings and doing other related work between groups of pigs. I also traveled with contract field supervisors for several different contract operations. Finally, I conducted taped interviews with 64 contracting hog producers from all over the state (37 contractees and 27 contractors), representing 27 different contract operations.

4. A massive geographical shift in hog production from the Midwestern United States to the South and West occurred in the 1980s and 1990s. McBride (1995:21) labels these areas of new hog growth as "emergent," and refers to Midwestern areas of hog production as "traditional." Corporate firms, rather than farm-based producers, initiated these production and organizational changes in emergent areas, hence the label "emergent-area firms."

5. A "farrow-to-finish" hog producer conducts all three (or two) stages of production (see note 2) on a single site, or if the producer employs multiple-site methods, the stages may be on different sites yet still on the producer's own land. The assertion that contract production is more efficient than farrow-to-finish production is based on data from 1992 Farm Costs and Return Surveys (summarized in McBride 1995:25), which show that emergent area producers using contracts (and by implication confinement technologies) and specializing in finishing hogs had better feed efficiency, better labor efficiency, and lower total feed costs than did Midwestern farrow-to-finish producers.

6. The term "pig space" refers to the number of animals that can be raised in a particular confinement building. All confinement buildings are divided into pens that can hold a certain number of animals based on the size of the pen and age of the animals in the barns. When contractors pay a contractee on the basis of pig space they pay a predetermined amount for each space in the barn.

7. Mortality incentives are the most common in hog contracts. Of the 21 contractees I interviewed who have incentive-based contracts, every one has a death loss incentive. Sort loss and feed conversion incentives are each present in 14 percent of

incentive-based contracts on which I have data (3/21). The feed conversion incentive is a bit more common than reflected here. I spoke with several contractors who reported using such an incentive with their contractees, but because I never spoke with the contractees themselves, they are not reflected here.

8. Gilts are female hogs yet to be inseminated and give birth. Maternal line replacement gilts are animals raised specifically to repopulate the sow portion of a swine herd. Terminal line market hogs are raised specifically for commercial meat production; that is, they are destined for slaughter.

9. "All-in/all-out" procedures are important biosecurity measures and refer to pigs flowing in discrete groups through the phases of industrial animal production, entering and leaving buildings/sites together. The advantage is that the entire facility can be cleaned and disinfected so that any pathogens left by the exiting group are removed before the next group arrives. "Continuous flow" methods pre-date industrial hog production and refer to production in which animals are not moved in distinct groups, but rather a few at a time so that there are always at least some animals on-site. Continuous flow methods make it difficult to thoroughly clean a building/site.

REFERENCES

Acheson, James

2002 Transaction Cost Economics: Accomplishments, Problems, and Possibilities. In *Theory in Economic Anthropology. Society for Economic Anthropology Monographs*, No. 18, ed. Jean Ensminger, 27–58. Walnut Creek, CA: AltaMira.

Barkema, Alan

1993 Reaching Consumers in the Twenty-First Century: The Short Way Around the Barn. *American Journal of Agricultural Economics* 75:1126–1131.

Boehlje, Michael

1995 Vertical Coordination and Structural Change in the Pork Industry: Discussion. *American Journal of Agricultural Economics* 77:1225–1228.

Buttel, Frederick

1983 Beyond the Family Farm. In *Technology and Social Change in Rural Areas*, ed. Gene Summers, 87–107. Boulder, CO: Westview Press.

Clapp, Roger

1994 The Moral Economy of the Contract. In *Living under Contract: Contract Farming and Agrarian Transformation in Sub-Saharan Africa*, ed. Peter Little and Michael Watts, 78–94. Madison: University of Wisconsin Press.

Curtis, S. E.

1993 The Physical Environment and Swine Growth. In *Growth of the Pig*, ed. Gilbert Hollis, 93–105. Wallingford: CAP International.

Davis, John

1980 Capitalist Agricultural Development and the Exploitation of the Propertied Laborer. In *The Rural Sociology of the Advanced Societies*, ed. Frederick H. Buttel and Howard Newby, 133–154. Montclair, NJ: Allanheld, Osmun.

Durrenberger, E. Paul
1996 *Gulf Coast Soundings: People and Policy in the Mississippi Shrimp Industry*. Lawrence: University Press of Kansas.
Ensminger, Marion, and Richard Parker
1997 *Swine Science*. 6th ed. Danville, IL: Interstate Publishers.
Frank, Stuart, and Dennis Henderson
1992 Transaction Costs as Determinants of Vertical Coordination in the U.S. Food Industries. *American Journal of Agricultural Economics* 74:941–950.
Goodman, David, and Michael Watts
1994 Reconfiguring the Rural or Fording the Divide?: Capitalist Restructuring and the Global Agro-Food system. *Journal of Peasant Studies* 22:1–49.
Harris, D. L.
2000 *Multiple-Site Pig Production*. Ames: Iowa State University Press.
Heffernan, William
1984 Constraints in the U.S. Poultry Industry. In *Research in Rural Sociology and Development*. Vol. 1, *A Focus on Agriculture*, ed. Harry Schwarzweller, 237–260. Greenwich, CT: JAI Press.
Kelley, K., S. Kent, and R. Dantzer
1993 Why Sick Animals Don't Grow: An Immunological Explanation. In *Growth of the Pig*, ed. Gilbert Hollis, 119–132. Wallingford: CAP International.
Kohls, R. L.
1958 Decision-Making in Integrated Production and Marketing Systems. *Journal of Farm Economics* 40:1801–1811.
McBride, William
1995 *U.S. Hog Production Costs and Returns, 1992: An Economic Basebook*. Agricultural Economic Report No. 724. Washington, DC: Economic Research Service, USDA.
McBride, William, and Nigel Key
2003 *Economic and Structural Relationships in U.S. Hog Production*. Agricultural Economic Report No. 818. Washington, DC: Economic Research Service, USDA.
Martinez, Steve
1999 *Vertical Coordination in the Pork and Broiler Industries: Implications for Pork and Chicken Products*. Agricultural Economic Report No. 777. Washington, DC: Economic Research Service, USDA.
Mooney, Patrick
1983 Toward a Class Analysis of Midwestern Agriculture. *Rural Sociology* 48:563–584.
National Agricultural Statistics Service.
2008 Illinois Data, Hogs & Pigs—Operations: Number by Size Group, 1965–2007. Electronic document, http://www.nass.usda.gov/QuickStats/PullData_US.jsp, accessed August 12, 2009; Illinois Data, Hogs & Pigs–Operations: Percent of Inventory by Size Group, 1983—2007. Electronic document, http://www.nass.usda.gov/QuickStats/PullData_US.jsp, accessed August 12, 2009; *Hogs and Pigs, Quarterly Report*. December. Washington, DC: USDA.

Pond, Wilson, Jerome Maner, and Dewey Harris
1991 *Pork Production Systems: Efficient Use of Swine and Feed Resources*. New York: AVI.
Rhodes, V. James
1993 Industrialization of Agriculture: Discussion. *American Journal of Agricultural Economics* 75:1137–1139.
Rhodes, V. James, and Glenn Grimes
1992. *U.S. Contract Production of Hogs: A 1992 Survey*. University of Missouri Agricultural Economics Report 1992–2. Department of Agricultural Economics. Columbia: University of Missouri.
Rich, Ronald
2006 "This Little Piggy Went to Market; This Little Piggy Stayed Home": Contracts and Live Hog Markets in Illinois, 1993–2000. *Culture and Agriculture* 28 (1): 45–63.
2008 Fecal Free: Biology and Authority in Industrial U.S. Contract Hog Production. *Agriculture and Human Values* 25 (1): 79–93.
Schook, L. B., and P. A. Clamp
1993 Mapping Genes for Growth and Development. In *Growth of the Pig*, ed. Gilbert Hollis, 75–91. Wallingford: CAP International.
Schrader, Lee
1998 *Coordination in the United States Hog/Pork Industry*. Staff Paper No. 98–19. Department of Agricultural Economics. West Lafayette, IN: Purdue University.
Thu, Kendall, and E. Paul Durrenberger
1994 North Carolina's Hog Industry: The Rest of the Story. *Culture and Agriculture* 49:20–23.
1998 Introduction. In *Pigs, Profits, and Rural Communities*, ed. K. M. Thu and E. P. Durrenberger, 1–20. Albany: State University of New York Press.
Watts, Michael
1994 Life under Contract: Contract Farming, Agrarian Restructuring, and Flexible Accumulation. In *Living under Contract: Contract Farming and Agrarian Transformation in Sub-Saharan Africa*, ed. Peter Little and Michael Watts, 21–77. Madison: University of Wisconsin Press.
Wells, Miriam
1996 *Strawberry Fields: Politics, Class, and Work in California Agriculture*. Ithaca, NY: Cornell University Press.
Welsh, Rick
1997 Vertical Coordination, Producer Response, and the Locus of Control over Agricultural Production Decisions. *Rural Sociology* 62 (4): 491–507.
Whittemore, Colin
1998 *The Science and Practice of Pig Production*. 2nd ed. Oxford: Blackwell.
Wilson, John
1986 The Political Economy of Contract Farming. *Review of Radical Political Economics* 18:47–70.

Wolf, Steven, Brent Hueth, and Ethan Ligon
2001 Policing Mechanisms in Agricultural Contracts. *Rural Sociology* 66 (3): 359–381.
Ziegenhorn, Randy
1998 An Alternative Model: Swine Producer Networks in Iowa. In *Pigs, Profits, and Rural Communities*, ed. Kendall Thu and E. Paul Durrenberger, 170–182. Albany: State University of New York Press.

6

Cooperation, Equality, and Difference

Loyalty and Accountability in Ghana's Marketplace Commodity Groups

Gracia Clark, Indiana University

The organizational structure of traders in Ghanaian marketplaces features paradoxes that contradict many commonsense assumptions of contemporary social science. The stereotype of communalist African villagers emerging from primordial isolation to face the rude shock of individualism brought by colonial commerce melts away especially quickly under the light of West African historical experience. Market traders in present-day Ghana can trace their linkages with global trade networks back centuries, directly through the Portuguese before Columbus and indirectly to ancient Rome and Carthage. Fierce loyalty to Asante traditional values and institutions, such as land management by chiefs and lineage heads, is compatible with market relations because the precolonial culture was already built around trade.

Analyzing cultures like Asante requires expanding the model central to Bird's chapter in this volume. He proposes that cooperation and reciprocity characterize a preexchange economy that persists in opposition to the dominant commercial system. In Asante, cooperation and reciprocity provide the backbone of competition in the marketplace, and kinship and chiefship relations incorporate individual self-interest. Since Asante nonmarket relations grew up in an already commercialized context, in general they support trading relationships rather than discourage commitment to trading. For example, a husband reciprocates his wife's domestic services with cash—a regular food allowance called "chop money" in Ghanaian English. This individual income frees the wife to devote her own expected income to personal advancement or lineage responsibilities, including raising her children. Both family heads and chiefs keep custodial authority over inherited property, but use some of its income to give capital loans that further the trading careers of their followers.

Asante practices confound another opposition, that between reciprocity and trust. Bird and Rich (also in this volume) both place reciprocity in nonmarket societies, without explicit rules of payment or calculations of the amount paid. Rich further contrasts the personalized character of reciprocity, grounded in relationships with specific people, with the anonymous system of enforced rules that generate trust. Reciprocity is associated with the remnants of the preexchange economy and trust with the profit motive. But Asante funeral donations and other lineage assessments at the heart of family obligations are assessed in cash, carefully recorded and calculated rather than freely pooled. Marketplace commodity groups facilitate credit and other forms of measured trust alongside unmeasured reciprocity in respecting market norms and institutions. Members use personalized reputations to enforce these rules, and more diffuse group membership to protect shared assets that may be material (control of market space) or nonmaterial (a shared pool of credit knowledge).

Like so many proudly maintained Ghanaian traditions, market women's groups emerged in response to historically specific needs and continue to respond sensitively to shifting economic and political conditions (Berry 2001). Local markets still maintain their predominance in the distribution of foodstuffs and consumer goods, despite Ghana's extensive experience with the formal sector, both public and private, and its now exemplary but long-standing openness to multinational firms. Fluid membership and leadership patterns give groups their strength under conditions of recurrent crisis that place a premium on both flexibility and persistence.

Paradoxically, the strength and continuity of the central core of leadership in market traders' groups turns out to be exactly what sustains the notable flexibility and resilience of Ghanaian marketplace institutions (Clark 1991a). Market trading repeatedly revived with dramatic speed after episodes of government repression and other economic shocks (Robertson 1983; Clark 1988). Fluctuations in the form and function of market organizations signal their continuing vitality and centrality in contemporary urban life.

METHODOLOGY

Studying the organizations of Ghanaian market traders forms part of a larger inquiry into economic aspects of market life that began with dissertation research in 1978 and continues to the present. Details of leadership practices such as dispute settlement were documented most fully from 1978 to 1980, during that period of full-time participant observation and interviewing in Kumasi Central Market. I spent most days with traders in the market or accompanying them on buying trips to other rural supply areas or other regional markets. Three regime changes in rapid succession enabled close observation of interactions between market leaders and both military and civilian officials. Three heads of state followed one another: General Akuffo in 1978; the first brief term in office of Flight Lt. Jerry Rawlings from June to December 1979; and elected president Hillal Limann in office in 1980. The effect of price controls and other commercial policy changes on ordinary traders was also evident in the traders' personal accounts and a sample survey of the central portion of the market, conducted in 1979.[1]

Assessment of historical trends comes from combining ethnographic and archival sources. Dramatic enforcement strategies such as beatings, market demolitions, and confiscation of traders' goods stimulated much discussion of current and past market conditions. Older, more experienced traders commented on how these episodes intensified police practices seen intermittently over the past several decades, since they had started trading. Likewise, further fieldwork with Kumasi traders on other subjects since 1980 indicates that the general outlines of group activity remain recognizable, albeit adapting to the changing political and economic environment. Searching archival collections at the Asantehene's Record Office in Kumasi and the National Archives branches in Accra and Kumasi turned up petitions from traders to colonial officers and the Asantehene over Kumasi market disputes, wartime price controls, and market construction and taxation policies during the colonial period.[2]

Additional periods of fieldwork in Ghana enabled me to monitor changing economic and political conditions and their effects on market trade. Subsequent projects related to rural crop processing and women traders brought me back to Kumasi during 1982–1984, 1990–1991, 1994–1995, 1999, and 2006. An International Labour Organization (ILO) consultancy kept me in Ghana during 1983, when the second government of Flight Lt. Jerry Rawlings brought the most intense attacks on traders and their national marketplace system. Life histories of older Asante women traders, recorded in 1994–1995, gave especially rich information from market leaders and on the first half of the 20th century. Reorganization made national archival collections more accessible and brought to light additional documents related to trade. These opportunities for long-term research and the relatively deep historical record allow the identification of trends in market organization and leadership throughout the long 20th century.

GROUP STRUCTURE

The current system of commodity-based organizations took shape during the early years of the 20th century, when the need for negotiations with colonial authorities seems to have provided the major impetus for group formation.

Immediately upon British conquest of the Asante Confederacy, British authorities dismantled the hierarchy of chiefly officials and border controls that had regulated trade. They demolished the royal palace of the Asantehene, abolished his office, and exiled him to the Seychelles. Rebuilding the city of Kumasi, they relocated the main market from in front of the old palace to a space left behind the main street lined with British firms. This downtown site, ringed with Lebanese shops, soon became overcrowded, and the market moved again, to an open area recently drained to construct the railway line. Market traders needed to negotiate the moves, settle internal disputes, and develop commercial procedures to cope with increased volume as the city grew. They met these new political and economic needs by choosing leaders in each major commodity for Kumasi Central Market, and eventually for neighborhood markets as these expanded.

Group members say "we know ourselves," whether or not they have any formal group structure with officially recognized leaders. Traders who habitually do the same type of buying or selling in the same location soon become known to one another. Their usual opposite numbers in those transactions constitute another group or subgroup (of traders) or a distinct group (of non-traders such as farmers.) In Kumasi Central Market, each locally important agricultural commodity has a named group that integrates the wholesalers, retailers, and traveling buyers who trade in that commodity. The larger Kumasi commodity groups run wholesale yards—open areas at the edges of the market—where trucks unload and purchases must be made in large units, by the sack or the hundred. Their market queen, called *ɔhemma*, spends the peak trading hours there, in a small kiosk, or "office." Commodity group leaders have the tightest control within their wholesale yards, where the high daily volume puts the highest premium on fast dispute settlement and other commercial services they manage.

The wholesale yard acts as a spatial focus because all three categories of traders come there regularly, making them accessible for meetings and dispute hearings. The wholesalers spend their working hours there, waiting for goods to arrive and selling them off when they get some. Many do not have a personal stall but can be found in the group area, which may have facilities such as a covered rest area, office, or meeting rooms. The commodity queens, or *ahemma* (pl.), must spend most of their working hours in the wholesale yard, available for consultation, and they are usually wholesalers themselves. They also use the group spaces for settling disputes between traders and negotiating with outside groups.

Other categories of members need to appear periodically in the wholesale yards. Retailers have their own stalls, either within the Central Market or in nearby neighborhood or small town markets, but they must visit the wholesale yard regularly to renew their supplies. Travelers shuttle back and forth constantly to specialized producing districts, where they buy at village markets or at the farmgate. They link Kumasi Central Market to other regional markets and to scattered small farms, sometimes counting as members in several urban markets they frequent. Traders in the same commodity from different towns also meet or join in negotiations occasionally.

Within Kumasi Central Market, the queen of the yam traders, the *bayerehemma*, has seniority over the others. The high capital required to trade in yams, the prominent role of the *bayerehemma* in major Asante rituals, and the preeminence of Kumasi in the national yam distribution network combine to give this seniority to the yam queen here. In other Ghanaian markets, the cloth queen has this senior rank. On ceremonial occasions or in negotiations with high officials, she leads the delegation of *ahemma* and speaks for them. They do not acknowledge her authority to advise or manage them in their internal group operations or routine duties, but they follow her lead in joint actions.

The other market *ahemma* act like her council of elders in some respects. In 1979, the *ahemma* of yams, cassava, tomatoes, cocoyam, cocoyam leaves, oranges, and snails constituted a respected set that remained in informal contact about market affairs. The *bayerehemma* could not make a major decision without consulting them. They must be summoned and they have a duty to appear for formal meetings of the *ahemma*. Because of this unified front, the yam queen could represent Kumasi Central Market traders as a whole in negotiations with the market manager and other nontraders, and not only during periods of crisis such as the price control raids of 1979.

Leaders of male or non-Asante market groups had their own external linkages to coethnic or male hierarchies, but spoke there only for their own members. Two associated peer groups of men are the truck drivers and pushcart carriers who specialize in transporting that commodity. Their male leadership may support or confront women traders on specific issues, such as gasoline prices or freight rates. On marketwide issues they all follow the lead of the *ahemma*.

STRONG AND WEAK LOYALTIES

The commercial relations specific to traders in agricultural commodities foster relatively strong groups among them. Traders in farm produce had more autonomy in relating to farmers than those buying imports or manufactures had from the large import firms or factories. Both leaders and followers have more scope for developing loyalty through effective negotiations and dispute settlement. As one provisions seller put it, "If we had a chief, it would be someone in a store." In the specialized retail sections of the market, where long lines of stalls each display the same items, traders also show firm allegiance to their commodity groups. This retail area offers enough advantages in information access and foot traffic that both stallholders and their buyers take care to keep in good standing there; this motivates them to work for consensus and abide by dispute settlements. Outside buyers do not actually join the group, but do take any disputes with group members to its *ɔhemma*.

When there is no wholesale yard for their commodity, traders select a leader from among the stallholders. These leaders have a less authoritative style and actions, which are often hard to distinguish from those of independent elders recognized only by their immediate neighbors. Stall-based retail traders have tighter neighborly relations. In a specialized location, these will reinforce commodity group ties, but in a mixed location they will weaken them. In locations that mix traders selling many different commodities, ties of neighborhood alone support basic leadership functions. Disputes between neighbors there cross commodity lines, so localized elders rather than commodity group leaders are the appropriate senior mediators.

Group negotiations do not always have a presiding figure whom both sides recognize as senior and impartial, although sometimes such a figure was sought out. In intractable cases, or when traders were the weaker part, the yam queen (*bayerehemma*) can invoke a standard dispute settlement option by appealing to a mutual superior. In such circumstances the *bayerehemma* becomes one of the disputants and the superior takes the presiding role. This senior figure should have ties to both parties to ensure that both sides abide by the agreed-on settlement out of respect for him. Market leaders had been known to take disputes before the market manager, the regional commissioner, and the *Asantehemma*, depending on the kind of settlement they sought. In disputes involving farmers or markets outside Kumasi, they could also approach chiefs with local jurisdiction. The government also went though the *Asantehene*, *Asantehemma*, and local chiefs to mediate with traders in Kumasi and elsewhere.

LEADERSHIP MODELS

Kumasi Market traders have drawn on aspects of culturally legitimized patterns of leadership from both contemporary and historical Ghana, reassembling and modifying them to meet their changing commercial and political needs. From Akan culture, Kumasi traders have incorporated the office of *ɔhemma* (female chief), *ɔhene* (male chief), and *ɔpanyin* (elder). Male traders from northern Ghana draw on the Hausa *sarkin* model of chiefship. Western models, featuring officers, committees, and secretaries, supplement but do not supplant those of chiefship.

Locally grown vegetable foodstuffs are sold overwhelmingly by Asante women traders in Kumasi, so the groups organized for those commodities find a powerful precedent in the *ɔhemma* title, a political office Asante culture reserves for women. Market *ahemma* follow the chiefly pattern in some respects, but deviate significantly in others. Like community-based male and female chiefs, the market *ahemma* and *ahene* are elected for life by their elders, must consult them on important decisions, and can be destooled by them in case of bad conduct. Each *ɔhemma* has complete authority within her own commodity group, shared with its elders. Most distinctively, market *ahemma* define their followers by occupation rather than residence or citizenship, as in community leadership, or by kinship, as in lineage leadership. Her constituency consists of women, rather than a community of men and women. She also rules alone, rather than in tandem with a male chief or lineage head. When an *ɔhemma* dies or is destooled, her successor is elected from among the council of group elders, rather than from a royal lineage.

Unlike town and village chiefs, market *ahemma* have no place in the official chiefly hierarchy and cannot directly invoke its political or ritual authority. In attending funerals and settling disputes, market *ahemma* follow general Asante procedural models rather than the specific chiefly ones. When they are newly elected or when they go to the royal palace to greet the *Asantehemma* or the *Asantehene* on public holidays or ritual occasions, they do so as private citizens, albeit important ones. In 1979, the *Asantehemma* cooperated with government attempts to delegitimize market leaders by announcing that market leaders had no right to use the title of *ɔhemma*, which was bestowed only by the *ɔhemma*'s predecessors on town and village leaders. News reports said they should henceforth be called headmen; this led market leaders to joke aboout their sex-change operations.

Traders show considerable creativity in incorporating Western terms and institutions into indigenous patterns of chiefship and elderhood without disrupting them substantially. Frequently, an existing hierarchy simply layers on extra titles. For example, when yam traders registered their commodity group as a cooperative in 1974, their *ɔhemma* became the president, leading elders became vice president and treasurer, and the council of elders became the executive committee. Several groups employ secretaries to keep minutes and financial accounts. Market women also become familiar with committee ritual through church women's groups. They continue to welcome new titles that give access to new forms of legitimacy, for example, when the yam *ɔhemma* became a member of the Kumasi District Assembly and enjoyed her air-conditioned office.

Superficial addition of Western models had little effect on the day-to-day activities of the commodity groups because these Westernized elements were adopted instrumentally, not as the major purpose of group formation. As in the "reinvention" of tradition that took place during the codification of customary law (Hay and Wright 1982), Africans represented market institutions that were sometimes highly innovative as long-standing traditions and inserted them into respectable European classifications. These added prestige and stood ready for self-defense when operating within the Eurocentric framework of the colonial and national political arenas.

Like public office, official cooperative status was worth seeking because it improved relations with the government. Yam traders expressed the hope that such public endorsement of their group would deflect government hostility; it did not. They also hoped that it would improve their chances, admittedly slim, of receiving a cheap loan for a truck or other major improvement, since these seemed to be extended to cooperatives only. Cooperative status had brought tangible benefits to others in the past. For example, a defunct tobacco traders' cooperative formerly received a regular bulk allocation of government-supplied tobacco and a share of the scarce consumer goods distributed to cooperatives.

BENEFITS OF GROUP MEMBERSHIP

Being known as a group member carries definite commercial advantages. The smooth conduct of transactions in retail and wholesale areas alike depends on mutual respect for a complex network of trading etiquette and conventional procedures. Colleagues can trust one another to conform to bargaining etiquette, thus streamlining transactions. Market retailers, wholesalers, and travelers take messages and placate customers for one another, and watch over one anothers' goods. They know the others will reciprocate favors and pass on helpful information, consequently reducing risk for all. During serious public challenges, such as the 1979 currency exchange, these groups met frequently to exchange information and to discuss and coordinate ways of dealing with problems.

Market *ahemma* have no enforceable legal jurisdiction, and many commercial conventions have no legal standing. Traders abide voluntarily, if not cheerfully, by the *ɔhemma*'s decisions because they need a speedy decision by a panel familiar with market conditions, both in their present dispute and for the future. The ability to take disputes immediately to a nearby elder, or to the *ɔhemma* if necessary for final settlement, reduces the uncertainty over general compliance with trading conventions. Those services were strategically located within Kumasi Central Market, improving long-term survival and capital accumulation even for the majority of traders who did not participate actively in a commodity group.

A comparison of strongly and weakly organized commodities and locations confirms the primacy of internal dispute settlement in group dynamics. Where a recognized leader settles disputes over credit and other issues, traders not "known" to her find it difficult to do business. They cannot easily bring cases or defend themselves against accusations, since she cannot easily judge their actions accurately or bring pressure on them to comply with her decisions. Other traders are reluctant to deal with them without this protection in case of problems.

The paramount aim of dispute settlement is to preserve the smooth flow of business for the disputants and other traders. The loss of time and income involved discourages traders from appealing too often to the *ôhemma*, for fear others will avoid dealing with them. Even traders in the middle of a dispute exclaim at frequent intervals their great reluctance to press the issue with the refrain "I don't like to argue."

Creditors could take their debtors to court, but the expense and time of a lawsuit would cost more and disrupt more social relations than would losing the case in the market. Rapid internal settlement avoids the loss of time involved in a protracted quarrel and the high cost and risk of complaints to police or courts unfamiliar with trading procedures. Traders distrust the impartiality of the courts and suspect someone bringing a court case of wanting to ruin her opponent at any cost. One would not want to do business with such a person, who becomes in a sense an outlaw for resorting to the law.

Representing traders in negotiations with outside institutions or groups is another primary function of the market *ahemma*. Market leaders spent considerable time in negotiations with government officials, military representatives, chiefs, farmers, drivers, porters, and other nontraders during all the fieldwork periods. Traders also mentioned external negotiations as one of the major services provided by leaders, since as individuals they could not afford to leave the market for these frequent summonses. Almost all such negotiations observed could be considered an extension of dispute settlement. They took place in response to a dispute or problem, which they aimed to resolve, between traders and outside groups or institutions. The *ahemma* tried to implement the norms and procedures of dispute settlement between individuals in these intergroup negotiations, but could do so only to the extent that nontraders respected them.

Commercial regulation by leaders as individuals was minimal. Leaders exercise their authority mainly through settling disputes over the interpretation of commonly acknowledged rules, and rarely take positive legislative action. They clarify or emphasize these established norms by proclamation, after consulting their elders, when repeated disputes show confusion on a particular subject, perhaps under changing conditions. The potential for selective or distorted enforcement of rules by the *ôhemma* is sharply restrained by the constant consultation with elders required over disputes and policy decisions. Ordinary members can also passively refuse to comply or to enforce unpopular decisions. For example, when one *ôhemma* wanted to monetize her customary dues, she had to negotiate the rate with her elders and put up with delays in collection when traders pleaded slow sales. The more modest routine functions of the *ahemma* nonetheless positioned them well to rapidly expand their regulatory role temporarily in times of crisis. They still innovated from within the framework of negotiation, rather than authority, by coordinating negotiations between different categories of members and nonmembers on new rules and procedures to handle the new conditions.

Other aspects of market leadership, though valued by traders, are less central than negotiating skill, which they listed as a primary criterion for selecting new leaders. A candidate's personal wealth, for example, which promotes group ceremonial display, takes second place to personality characteristics of patience and unselfishness, which are needed for effective dispute settlement but which inhibit accumulation. Group members did strongly value leaders' ceremonial functions, however, in attending funerals and community celebrations. This public visibility cements group loyalty and maintains the leaders' prestige and connections, which can then be drawn on during negotiations.

Group affiliation also gives traders access to some significant economies of scale in transport. For example, traveling traders operating out of the same wholesale yard often get together in the village to fill a whole truck and head straight back to Kumasi, rather than wait for mixed passenger transport. Yam traders run a truck parking lot in Kumasi, where travelers can leave their full trucks with a watchman until it is their turn to unload. The yam group also supports the services of full-time market porters, who provide expert counting, handling, and delivery services. Orange wholesalers hire full-time checkers, literate young men who record individual buyers' names with the price and quantity they have purchased and collect payment later in the day.

During the 1970s and 1980s, the challenge of scarce, unreliable transport motivated a complex division of labor between intermediaries. Specialized travelers were constantly "on the road," maintaining the knowledge and contacts to arrange for transport from the farm gate or village market to an urban center. Goods had to be constantly accompanied by their owner, who had the authority in case of vehicle breakdown to arrange for a new carrier or rapid disposal. Buyers from other cities bought at the Kumasi wholesale yards partly because they might hire a truck for onward shipment from among those unloading. Traveling traders cultivated special relationships with truck drivers as well as farmers, earning preferential access that made it difficult to bypass the traders' mediating services.

INFORMATION AS COMMON PROPERTY

Credit, dispute settlement, and bargaining procedures in Kumasi Central Market all stem from the high level of mutual information among these sets of colleagues. Buyers and sellers prefer to patronize their wholesale yards and concentrated retail areas to dealing directly with one another because the supply-and-demand information available there reduces their risk of accepting a bad bargain. Wholesale yards in large urban marketplaces like Kumasi Central Market offer sellers immediate access to local retailers and cooked-food vendors, and they offer wholesale buyers from schools and prisons reliable bulk supplies. During periods of shortage, the wholesale yard will bring together available supplies for easier access by the public.

The need for information to bargain effectively and extend credit when necessary explains both the boundaries and the functions of commodity-based collegial sets in Kumasi Central Market. Physical presence functions as an effective boundary marker between collegial groups and informal sets, laying a foundation for the basic division of labor between retailers, travelers, and wholesalers. A resident wholesaler must be physically present in the wholesale yard during all normal business hours to offer information and other services that attract and keep her customers. Although a traveler bringing supplies could collect fairly accurate supply-and-demand information within a few hours of her arrival, her goods would deteriorate and her fatigue after a night on the road would impair her bargaining ability. Selling through a wholesaler puts her back on the road more quickly and in better health. She can check her wholesaler's performance at her leisure by comparing with her own colleagues the prices they received from their own wholesalers. She concentrates her main information-gathering activities in her preferred supply areas. Customers buying food in bulk for institutions or for cooked-food preparation likewise save time for their main work and reduce the risk of acting on incomplete information.

Given the open layout of Ghanaian markets, the major limit to mutual information is physical presence. Visual inspection readily reveals the amount of goods and the numbers of buyers and sellers then present, even to casual passersby. It would be impossible to maintain the level of secrecy Geertz reports for Moroccan bazaars (Geertz et al. 1979). In many market locations, those transacting business can easily see adjacent traders and overhear the prices they are bargaining. High levels of price information result in high levels of price uniformity within a given location. Hoarding and concealment of goods or transaction takes place outside the market, in homes and office buildings.

High levels of information within the collegial set govern credit with considerable efficiency. A wholesaler can with confidence extend credit to one of the known retailers in her commodity. She hears about her buying habits, credit history, and outstanding debts from other members of her own set. In case of default, she can intercept the debtor on her return to renew supplies from another wholesaler, or visit her local stall to harass her. Fellow retailers will encourage repayment of credit in order to protect their general reputation as a set, and other wholesalers will cooperate in penalizing a persistent defaulter.

The most common types of credit extended did not establish long-term dependency between debtor and creditor. Retailers often collected goods for payment later the same day. In several commodities this arrangement was not considered credit, but a procedural convenience to avoid counting and handling large sums of cash during the morning rush. Nonetheless it enabled very capital-short traders to buy in larger quantities, since they could sell at least part of the goods before payment. Peer pressure also inhibited exploitative credit terms, since the unreasonable creditor might suffer later when asking for goods on credit or other favors from the debtor's colleagues.

Credit is needed to move goods at certain times of year, so transactors without the information needed to identify creditworthy people could not survive those periods. Credit is extended when conditions warrant along the chain of collegially linked sets to any member of the appropriate set who is in good standing. For very perishable foodstuffs such as tomatoes, for example, rapid clearance of incoming goods from the wholesale yards during the peak morning hours demanded nearly universal short-term credit. Wholesalers collected their money later the same day. Horizontal collegial ties provide essential support to credit through information and dispute settlement services, but they do not themselves transmit capital. All capital transfers observed in the Ghanaian marketplace system were vertical, between buyer and seller.

The direction of longer-term credit reversed seasonally for most foodstuffs. Traders experienced the need to give credit as a sign of the weakness of their commercial position, rather than as a way to establish domination over the borrower. Farmers and wholesalers advanced goods on credit during the glut season, collecting payment after resale. During the dry season, Kumasi traders sent money back out with travelers in search of scarce goods. Travelers in turn advanced their money to farmers for harvest expenses and sometimes the final weeding. Those who demanded excessive price concessions in return for such credit faced ostracism from the same group of farmers they would later the same year ask to give them goods on credit or in times of scarcity.

FLEXIBILITY AND SURVIVAL

The leaders of organized commodity groups in Kumasi Central Market had a critical role to play in facilitating the swift recovery of the market from the wide range of political and economic crises it faced during the 1970s and 1980s. Their negotiating skills had been honed on a daily basis through providing the valued internal service of dispute settlement to group members. These skills were then taxed to the full by external negotiations with government and military officials and with other economic actors such as drivers and porters.

The Ghana currency exchange in March 1979 clearly demonstrated the importance and limits of this adaptive ability in Kumasi Central Market. After closing all the borders, the Ghana government announced on Friday, March 9, that all existing banknotes would have to be exchanged through the banks, at a rate of ten old to seven new cedis, before they became valueless on March 26. Commodity group leaders spread information, coordinated discussions within each group of traders, and briefly closed some wholesale yards to minimize losses and chaos. During this crisis, the ordinary mediation duties of the *ahemma* between debtors and creditors were still as much in demand as these extraordinary functions. Likewise, during extreme price control enforcement episodes, elders met to exchange information on new regulations or initiatives and on conditions in different towns and villages.

These information and service considerations define boundaries for sets of colleagues that are resistant but permeable to individual movement. The sets constantly admit new members, but these only gradually filter through to the dense network of relations at the center, although sponsorship by an established trader helps a new entrant to penetrate more rapidly. Newcomers and less-successful traders remain marginal, along with those who deliberately maintain membership in more than one local group. The lack of rigid boundaries allows individuals to enter or exit on their own initiative and at reduced transaction cost. Those who leave retain the skills and the knowledge of people needed to collect from the remaining core members up-to-date information on supply and demand when they decide to return. This allows the set to contract and expand rapidly as conditions permit; this is a flexibility that paradoxically gives the group increased stability in the long run.

The relations between core and marginal members in these collegial groups legitimize and preserve the members' unequal positions but carry some benefits for both. The marginal members clearly absorb more than their share of economic fluctuations, as the collegial group sheds or attracts them. The core group of long-established members can remain unchanged for many years. These core members reap the benefits of longer experience and longer mutual observation of successful transactions and disputes, but also preserve this knowledge base for the use of the trading system as a whole. Their continuous presence enables marginal members to reenter market positions very rapidly when conditions improve, when these core members welcome back former participants they remember well.

The combination of the two status groups thus maintains more elasticity than either could provide alone. This elasticity was an important factor in Ghana's rapid supply response during and after disastrous droughts and political crises during the 1970s and 1980s. The traders' ability to efficiently switch between varied and innovative geographic and commodity specializations and financial arrangements greatly helped restabilize food supply levels (Clark 1991b). Close comparative analysis of other urban food supply systems in Africa shows that flexibility and access to alternative marketing channels make critical contributions to efficiency and equity in distribution for many of them (Guyer 1987).

CONCLUSION

The configuration of tradition and innovation with respect to hierarchies and commonalities within these marketplace trading networks raises interesting questions about the conceptual relationships between cooperation and competition and between trust and personalism. The intersection of tradition and 20th-century innovation is just as salient for Asante as for the Andean migrants analyzed by Bird in another chapter here. Andeans on the coast invoke the cherished precedent of the *ayllu* as an organizing tool for both entrepreneurial and communal initiatives. In an analogous way, Asante traders invoke the legitimacy and continuing significance of Asante chiefship and kinship by appropriating terminology and structural or procedural features selectively for new purposes in their marketplace groups. In the Asante empire, chiefship and kinship are not antithetical to the market, as Bird suggests for the Inca empire. Asante expect both kin and chief to foster market participation and to benefit from it through contributions that are assessed in cash.

The long historical continuity of marketplace systems in towns like Kumasi makes the systems credible examples of indigenous institutions adapting successfully to contemporary economic conditions; at the same time, they are examples, unfortunately, of backward traditions impeding national development. The more dynamic concept of tradition held by most Asante comes closer to that held by contemporary ethnographers. This enables market groups, like chiefships, to appropriate features from a range of Western organizational models as well, without loosening their indigenous roots.

Close attention to the importance of dispute settlement further challenges the conventional opposition between cooperation and competition. Cooperation appears not to eliminate competition but to facilitate fierce competition for customers and profits. Traders cooperate in enforcing procedural conventions and credit agreements to keep a high volume of goods flowing smoothly. The commodity group system preserves market access as a shared asset that increases in value with wider access and higher attendance to the specific marketplace. Considering the social process of the marketplace as a common property asset helps explain how strong loyalties coexist with strong inequalities within commodity groups. Keeping the market highly attractive benefits all the diverse categories of traders. Commodity groups maintain a social arena with a pool of information about supply, demand, and reputation that reduces costs for retailers, wholesalers, and their customers. Procedural conventions streamline bargaining and reduce information demands, while dispute settlement services reduce the costs of credit default. Even though the institutions that preserve this arena clearly advantage an elite core group of relatively prosperous wholesalers, the services provided by this core group both require and reward the participation of all categories of buyers and sellers. By facilitating strategies such as moving into different trading roles or different commodities, group ties reduce overall risk for even the poorest members, rather than simply shifting it onto them.

In Kumasi Central Market, risks and losses arise with harrowing frequency from climate, politics, and global economic conditions. Under high-risk conditions in Asia and Latin America, socially or economically vulnerable individuals often attach themselves to a powerful patron who reduces their risk by making transactions more predictable and controllable, if not always more profitable (Buechler 1973; Szanton 1972). Many similar benefits and protections were secured in Kumasi through commodity groups. The contrast drawn by Rich between the personalism governing clientship and the more impersonal, rule-governed foundation of trust dissolves in this case. Kumasi traders trust in their commercial self-regulation because intensely personal reputations operate within the group. They trust that most of their buyers and sellers will follow the rules due to fear of a bad reputation. Reputation equally informs them whom not to trust and reassures them that even defaulters will abide by a market queen's ruling.

Dyadic clientship is quite familiar to, but relatively rare among, traders in Kumasi Central Market. Committed dyadic relations with steady customers were more brittle and more vulnerable during periods of intense upheaval in 1979 and 1983. Collegial relations were more flexible, more useful, and easier for traders with relatively modest means to sustain over the long term. Credit and other services exchanged within the group structure enable smaller enterprises to survive economic shocks at the personal or societal levels that might easily topple them into bankruptcy. Recognized commodity groups or less-formal sets of colleagues provided efficient, centralized access to scarce information and transport. Their flexibility proved more effective than more rigid legal contracts in maintaining a flow of goods during acute crisis periods.

Traders' strength and resilience under fierce economic pressures drew some admiration as role models of ethnic and gender solidarity or popular resistance to elite accumulation. At the same time, public deprivation and government frustration frequently fed suspicion of their power. Urban markets carry a symbolic charge as the most visible face of the wild and unruly informal sector. The pressure to demonstrate their civilization pushes some market groups to appropriate modernist values of liberty, equality, and transparency. Market traders are conversely said to cling from ignorance or personal ambition to a backward way of life that cannot contribute to national stabilization and growth. Ironically, markets meanwhile provide very significant financial support to the same authorities that regard them with suspicion. Precolonial and colonial rulers had also found it much easier to collect market tolls than head tax or other levies. In Kumasi, revenues collected from both legal and supposedly illegal market locations fund almost half the total city budget, equal to the national government subvention (King 1999).

Leaders and their groups show considerable creativity in combining and transforming varied cultural models of leadership to suit their changing economic and political environment, but they still face very real external constraints. Factors affecting the character and potency of external negotiations have been especially influential on the emergence and strength of the current market group framework. During the turbulent period just before independence, market *ahemma* were allowed or even compelled to join in competition between political parties for traders' votes. In tense contestations over the role to be allowed Europeans, Lebanese, and Africans from other countries in the new national regulatory structure, local market women briefly represented local interests as "our mothers."

Ideological boundaries shifted as political parties were repressed in the 1960s through the 1980s, and government hostility intensified against women traders and their leaders in particular. They seemed the chosen symbol for frustratingly incomplete government control of the national economy during a painfully long period of economic decline. The most hostile portrayals condemn group solidarity as a conspiracy to monopolize supplies, raise prices and profits, and sabotage legitimate planning efforts. These incidents and campaigns reduced not only leaders' prestige but also their ability to function effectively as market leaders. Their negotiating role as traders' representatives presumed tacit recognition of their standing by other social groups, such as the military. Internal dispute settlement required traders to assemble openly and conduct their business within calling distance of others; this was impossible under constant threats of confiscations, beatings, and arrests. The Kumasi *ahemmafo* never ceased to function entirely during price controls, but the offices became much less attractive to potential candidates. Leadership lapsed completely in groups selling the imported and manufactured commodities subject to extended attacks, such as cloth.

The neoliberal SAP reforms implemented after 1985 did include dismantling price controls and significantly reducing physical and ideological attacks on market traders and their leaders. Austerity budgets created economic stresses that undermined the autonomy and prosperity of traders in other ways, but market leaders were able to resume a more open role in community affairs. In Kumasi, the *bayerehemma* was appointed to serve on the city council. The Kumasi cloth sellers accepted a new, young queen in the 1990s, and a newly elected *bayerehemma* led delegations of *ahemmafo* to meet with the market manager and the regional commissioner, as well as to congratulate the newly elected *Asantehene*. The election of a new plantain queen was hotly contested, and the successful candidate was affiliated with the ruling party. Electoral democratization enabled many traders to participate openly in various political parties and run for local office as individual citizens. In Accra, the capital, traders were occasionally consulted by national or city policy commissions.

Still, the second-class status of market trading compared to other occupations continues to bring serious political and economic disadvantages that undermine the market leaders' effectiveness. Market leaders are still not regularly consulted on policy decisions that affect their constituents; they are simply informed. The city market committee included none of them, although it sets tax rates and oversees maintenance of buildings and enforcement of regulations. City officials attending gender sensitization workshops organized by a local nongovernmental organization (NGO) in 1999 openly referred to traders as "a nuisance." Traders were not involved in planning for an ambitious rebuilding of roads and pedestrian access in and around the Central Market that is still in progress. Several years of the resulting traffic congestion seriously hampered trade. Some wholesale functions have physically dispersed to more accessible suburban crossroads, weakening the commercial position of the group leaders based in Kumasi Central Market wholesale yards.

The relationship between the market leadership and local or national government institutions may be more distant than that enjoyed by formal-sector institutions such as import firms, but it is still important to both sides. Market queens expect and usually enjoy a considerable degree of autonomy in their normal operations. Government leaders implicitly tolerate this autonomy because they implicitly rely on the marketplace system to keep supplying food, jobs, tax revenues, and other necessities during difficult times. Conversely, market leaders need to maintain sufficient authority to negotiate the changes continually needed to keep providing those social necessities under shifting economic and political conditions. They depend on the continuous recognition of underlying norms of representation and negotiated settlement in Ghanaian society on the whole, including among government officials, in order to fulfill both their internal and external responsibilities. This broader social recognition, even without explicit legal standing, enables leaders to maintain loyalty and discipline among group members and to keep markets running smoothly enough to perform their key economic and political functions.

NOTES

1. More details on these research methods are included in my thesis and a subsequent book (Clark 1984; Clark 1994.). I would like to thank the Economic and Social Research Council (UK), the International Labour Organization (ILO), the Social Science Research Council (SSRC), the Fulbright Commission, and the United States Department of Education for funding various of these fieldwork opportunities.
2. I am especially grateful to historians Gareth Austin, Larry Yarak, and Thomas McCaskie for directing my attention to valuable files.

REFERENCES

Berry, Sara
2001 *Chiefs Know Their Boundaries: Essays on Property, Power and the Past in Asante, 1966–1996*. Portsmouth, NH: Heinemann.
Buechler, Judith-Maria
1973 Peasant Marketing and Social Revolution in the State of La Paz. PhD diss., McGill University.
Clark, Gracia
1988 Traders versus the State (ed., with chapter and introduction). Boulder, CO: Westview Press.
1990 Class Alliances and Class Fractions in Ghanaian Trading and State Formation. *Review of African Political Economy*, December 1990, 73–82.

1991a Colleagues and Customers in Unstable Market Conditions in Kumasi, Ghana. *Ethnology* 1991 (1): 31–48.

1991b Food Traders and Food Security in Ghana. In *The Political Economy of African Famine: The Class and Gender Basis of Hunger*, ed. R. E. Downs, D. O. Kerner, and S. P. Reyna. London: Gordon and Breach.

1994 *Onions Are My Husband: Survival and Accumulation by West African Market Women*. Chicago: University of Chicago Press.

Geertz, Clifford, Hildred Geertz, and Lawrence Rosen

1979 *Meaning and Order in Moroccan Society: Three Essays in Cultural Analysis*. Cambridge: Cambridge University Press.

Guyer, Jane

1987 *Feeding African Cities: Studies in Regional Social History*. Bloomington: Indiana University Press with the International African Institute, London.

Hay, Margaret Jean, and Marcia Wright, eds.

1982 *African Women & the Law: Historical Perspectives*. [Boston]: Boston University, African Studies Center.

King, Rudith

1999 The Role of Urban Market Women in Local Development Processes and Its Implication for Policy: A Case Study of Kumasi Central Market. PhD diss., University of Sussex, Brighton, UK.

Robertson, Claire

1983 The Death of Makola and Other Tragedies: Male Strategies against a Female-Dominated System. *Canadian Journal of African Studies* 17 (3): 469–95.

Szanton, Maria Cristina

1972 *A Right to Survive; Subsistence Marketing in a Lowland Philippine Town*. University Park: Pennsylvania State University Press.

Yankah, Kwesi

1995 *Speaking for the Chief: Okyeame and the Politics of Akan Royal Oratory*. Bloomington: Indiana University Press.

7

Testing the Limits of Nonzero

Cooperation, Conflict, and Hierarchy in Ancient Near Eastern Marginal Environments

Benjamin W. Porter, University of California, Berkeley

Over the last decade, public intellectuals have taken the issue of economic anthropology into their own hands, producing narratives that discuss social evolution in terms of cooperation and competition that have become enormously popular with readers beyond the academy. Leading the conversation are Jared Diamond's two works *Guns, Germs, and Steel: The Fates of Human Societies* (1997) and *Collapse: How Societies Choose to Fail or Succeed* (2005). Both books narrate the rise and fall of civilizations in terms of conflict and competition, pitting societies that manage their environments and structure their societies according to complex, apparently "rational" means, against societies that abuse natural resources and make unwise decisions about subsistence and social organization. The rate of public consumption of Diamond's books suggests that the public continues to desire grand narratives that reduce human history to simple explanations of conflict and conquest. So one might think that reading *Nonzero: The Logic of Human History*, Robert Wright's tracing of human social evolution through the lens of cooperation (2000), might counter Diamond's themes of violence, competition, and conquest. For Wright, human societies advance in the most productive ways when individuals and groups cooperate. Whether or not this cooperation consists of intentional face-to-face interactions, or self-interested, yet symbiotic global economic transactions is irrelevant. For Wright, stone tools, farming, commerce, and the Internet are all born of humans' abilities to cooperate.

While it may be pleasing to see so many public readers thinking critically about human history in scientific and anthropological terms, Diamond's and Wright's narratives ultimately produce prescriptive cookbooks for cultural success that gloss over, and at times, disregard the details that social scientists have amassed over the past few centuries regarding the human condition.

Upon finishing these two books, readers are left to decide between either competition or cooperation as the modus operandi of human social evolution. This choice that readers are required to make, I argue, ultimately matters. For whichever prescription readers choose, whether they are Washington policymakers or Baltimore homemakers, will likely inform their interpretation of current events and guide their future actions. And nowhere do the effects of these interpretations play out more than in the modern Middle East. The region is featured early in Diamond's and Wright's narratives as the stage on which the generative moments of agriculture, bureaucracy, technologies, and religious organization occur (e.g., Diamond 1997:134–142; Wright 2000:109–111). Once these contributions have been made to human society—usually passed on to early European societies—the ancient Near East and the modern Middle East make only cameo appearances, usually as unfortunate foils for more successful actors and events occurring elsewhere in the world. Such characterizations betray the knowledge that scholars have accumulated over the past two centuries of investigation that details the diversity of social life in the region (Meyers 1997; Sasson 1995). There is not only an abundance of archaeological data spanning more than eight millennia of human history, but also a vast, albeit uneven, historical record documenting the last five millennia of political and economic transactions. The region additionally boasts a diversity of microclimates and an uneven distribution of natural resources that make it impossible to generalize about the region's environment. Given their concerns with the ways that societies manage unfavorable environmental conditions, Wright and Diamond seem to have missed an interesting opportunity to examine configurations of ancient Near East social life under various environmental regimes.

In light of this brief critique, this chapter presents a case study from the ancient Near East where communities combined modes of cooperation and competition in unexpected ways. In west-central Jordan, a collection of agricultural villages were founded and abandoned during the early Iron Age between approximately 1250 BCE and 1000 BCE. What makes west-central Jordan an interesting context is that many of the settlements subsisted in a marginal semi-arid setting. Archaeological evidence and historical sources indicate that households organized subsistence in a flexible manner that permitted them to shift between corporate and competitive modes depending on political, economic, and environmental contingencies. This reconstruction leads me to argue that we should think about cooperation and competition in antiquity as more than simply discrete behaviors, but also as flexible strategies that help communities adjust their organizational relationships to the whims of shifting circumstances. Such a conclusion acknowledges the nuances of social life in ancient societies in ways that Wright's and Diamond's discourses on competition and cooperation did not grasp.

COOPERATION, COMMUNITY, AND HIERARCHY IN ANCIENT NEAR EASTERN MARGINAL ENVIRONMENTS

Despite the problems with Wright's insistence that human social evolution be viewed strictly through the lens of cooperation, he does depend on a productive framework, the Prisoner's Dilemma. When applied appropriately, this model can be used to draw out the ways individuals and groups decide to cooperate and compete in social life. A cornerstone of game theory, the prisoner's dilemma is a non-zero-sum game championed by cooperation theorist Robert Axelrod in *The Evolution of Cooperation* (1984). In the most basic version of this hypothetical arrangement, two prisoners can cooperate with or betray each other when deciding to plea bargain. If neither gives the other one up (i.e., they cooperate with each other), they both are punished but with lighter sentences than if one (or both) were to inform on the other. A non-zero-sum interaction, then, is one in which all participants benefit in some way when they choose to cooperate rather than compete. Wright extends this basic model to behavior in past societies to argue that when human societies chose cooperation over competition, social evolution saw its most notable advancements. Wright's argument is as prescriptive as it is descriptive, suggesting that humanity acknowledge and learn from these cooperative successes. Yet with the prisoner's dilemma, Wright seems to have taken a right step in the wrong direction, ignoring how competitive and cooperative behavior productively alternate to motivate changes in social life. Alternatively, if one recognizes non-zero-sum interactions as sets of strategic alternatives that help humans negotiate social life under collective circumstances, rather than as a formula that determines the outcome of "positive" human behaviors, the lessons of prisoner's dilemma are enormously insightful. Time, for example, is an important element in fostering non-zero-sum interactions: in any given transaction, if participants are aware they will encounter each other in future events, they are more likely to choose reciprocity over defection. As reciprocal acts occur over several events between the same individuals or groups, participants become intertwined in a web of social relations and dependencies. Yet at the moment when reciprocity—cooperative action—ceases or becomes less frequent, these entanglements loosen, raising the possibilities of defection and even conflict.

The sensitivity to strategy and choice that non-zero-sum interactions brings to the analysis of social life speaks to the recent turn that archaeologists have made toward agent-based frameworks to explain human behavior in past societies (e.g., Dobres and Robb 2000). Within non-zero-sum interactions, the course that human interactions will take is highly unpredictable and contingent on the conscious and unconscious decisions of participants as well as the structural conditions that mediate human actions. This is especially true when human behavior is observed within preindustrial agricultural communities. Compared to archaic cities and states, the microstrategies of cooperation, competition, and defection are potentially more visible in communities, where social life consists of collections of dependent, often face-to-face relationships that include, but often extend beyond, the immediate kin group (Canuto and Yaeger 2000; Porter 2007). Preindustrial communities are often mediated by unspoken and potentially coercive social contracts based on mutual prosperity, defense, and subsistence. As members acquire, share, and exchange capital—wealth, resources, labor, or knowledge—it becomes differentially distributed across space, forging symmetrical and asymmetrical social relationships. This framework helps to identify how members amass capital and assume decision-making positions in communities. It also recognizes that members can concurrently defy this concentration by amassing their own wealth, resisting exchange, or abandoning the community altogether.

Non-zero-sum interactions grow even more complex in communities persisting under marginal political, economic, and environmental conditions. The unstable and unanticipated configuration of marginal settings places the constellations of power and wealth under frequent reorganization as resource availability, trade networks, and political polities shift or decline. Although different aspects of a community's social life can be examined, a regime that strikes at the core of a community's persistence is production, a practice that creates the substance—the capital—over which people negotiate social hierarchies. How such production takes place—by individuals, households, or the entire population—is central to the number and types of relationships between members. Production's role is even more critical in communities that subsist in marginal environments with limited precipitation, poor soil quality, and frequent droughts and famines. Communities often implement strategies that maximize production and distribute risk to reduce uncertainties like storing a food surplus, managing herd structure, and building infrastructure such as cisterns that capture precipitation, and terraces that preserve soil beds. Organizing production routines at different levels of specialization also helps to distribute risk.

Production in marginal environments can also potentially yield unequal amounts of capital. To reduce competition over resources, communities may manage production and wealth collectively. However, even when household and communal production co-occur, individual households might still accrue more wealth than their neighbors. During droughts or famine, households that accumulate surplus wealth increase their chances for survival. This wealth may also be shared with other households, such that relationships of dependency are formed. Yet such emergent asymmetrical relationships do not necessarily bring an end to cooperative conditions. Rather, debts and dependencies can be temporary, since the arrangements of power have been carefully set for the whims of marginal environments. Moreover, shifting between cooperative and competitive conditions might ultimately be viewed as a strategy for the group's long-term survival.

An analysis of non-zero-sum interactions in ancient Near Eastern communities placed in marginal settings brings a fresh perspective to economic practices in that region. Current scholarly consensus about economic practices has been constructed using economic records—contracts, laws, and receipts, for example—from contexts where they have been most abundant, usually in the personal and administrative archives of urban centers. When we view this evidence collectively, however, it is clear that economic practices varied tremendously over time and space. Furthermore, attempts by local authorities to impose regulations on exchange rarely succeeded in actual practice. Given the variance and fragility of economic practices even in the core urban centers of the ancient Near East, it is not surprising to discover that such practices in marginal settings would yield unpredictable results given the instability of production and social life. Indeed, economic practices in marginal settings like those examined in this chapter depended on relatively informal modes of exchange that structured the basis of cooperation such as gifting or reciprocity. Such modes of exchange would include feasts, cooperation in household and community-building projects, mutual defense, and agricultural production. Because reciprocity and cooperation are embedded in larger networks of events and agents, social life in marginal settings depends on such reciprocal acts to maintain collective social cohesion. But the rate at which such acts occur and the effects that they have on communities are unpredictable and demand close investigation, especially in marginal settings where scarcity and political instability influence exchange.

COOPERATION AND COMPETITION IN EARLY IRON AGE WEST-CENTRAL JORDAN

Such shifts between cooperative and competitive strategies in ancient Near Eastern social life took place during the early Iron Age (1250–1000 BCE) in west-central Jordan. During this period, ancient Egyptian sources as well as the Hebrew Bible indicate that this region was home to several different groups including the Ammonites, Moabites, and Israelites (Boling 1988). Discerning these groups in the archaeological record is frustrated by the homogeneity in physical evidence, however. Archaeological surveys over the past several decades have identified small and midsize agricultural settlements sparsely distributed throughout the region (e.g., Glueck 1940; Ibach 1987; Ji and Lee 2000; Miller 1991) (Figure 7.1). Several settlements have been excavated including Balu'a (Worschech 1989; Worschech and Ninow 1994, 1999; Worschech et al. 1986), Lahun (Homes-Fredericq 1992), Khirbat al-Mu'ammariyya (Ninow 2004), Khirbat al-Mudayna al-'Aliya (KMA hereafter) (Routledge 2000; Routledge and Porter 2007), Khirbat al-Mudayna al-Mu'arradja (Olavarri 1977–1978, Olavarri 1983), and 'Umayri (Herr 2000).[1]

Those settlements whose remains are exposed at or near the surface (e.g., Lahun, Khirbat al-Mu'ammariyya, Khirbat al-Mudayna al-'Aliya, and Khirbat al-Mudayna al-Mu'arradja) share several characteristics (Figure 7.2). Oval fortifications with defensive towers bound each settlement, their total area ranging between one and two hectares. Inside these fortifications are open plazas surrounded by buildings, many of which are still visible today on the sites' surfaces. This repeated pattern across settlements suggests that intersite settlement communication was common. But even more intriguing is that despite the settlements' close proximity to one another, no single one stands out as a dominant administrative center. That is to say, west-central Jordan's early Iron Age settlement patterns do not reflect the ranked settlement hierarchy typical of ancient Near Eastern polities where one large settlement dominates smaller satellite towns. To make matters even more complex, these settlements were occupied for brief periods of time despite the relatively large human investment it took to construct buildings and fortifications. Current knowledge of the region's ceramic vessel sequence suggests that occupation lasted for no more than a century. Furthermore, settlements' chronologies suggest that occupational episodes did not always overlap in time. Rather, as Routledge has observed (Routledge 2004:111–112), settlement growth moved from north to south over a 250-year period before disappearing altogether by the mid-10th century BCE.

Recognizing that these communities were situated in politically and environmentally marginal locations partly explains this brief and staggered settlement pattern. Just prior to the early Iron Age, the New Kingdom Egyptian Empire controlled much of the southern Levant, although the extent to which west-central Jordan was managed by the empire is unknown. Egyptian historical sources only suggest that Pharaoh Ramses II campaigned through the region at least twice (Kitchen 1992). It is likely that at least the southern half of west-central Jordan—the area today known as the Karak Plateau—

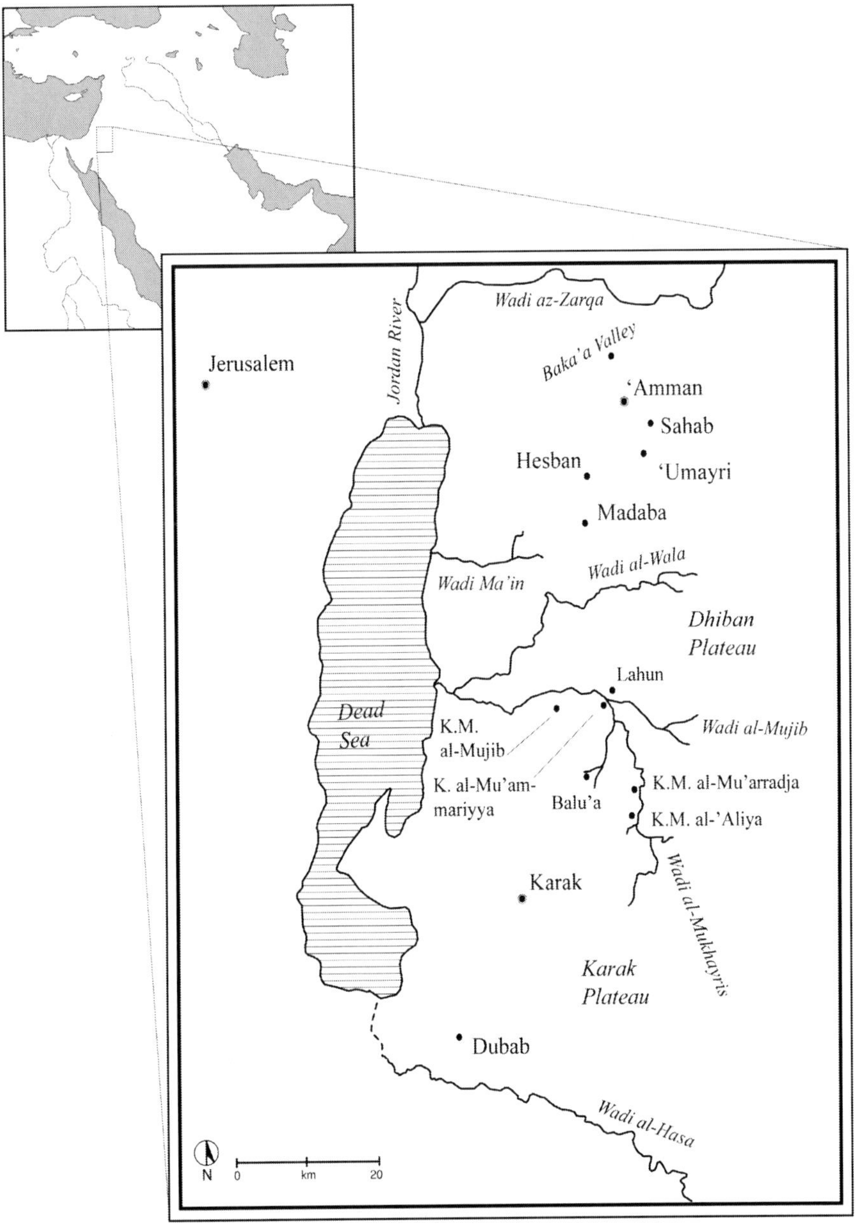

Figure 7.1. Map of west-central Jordan detailing early Iron Age settlements, modern settlements, and natural features

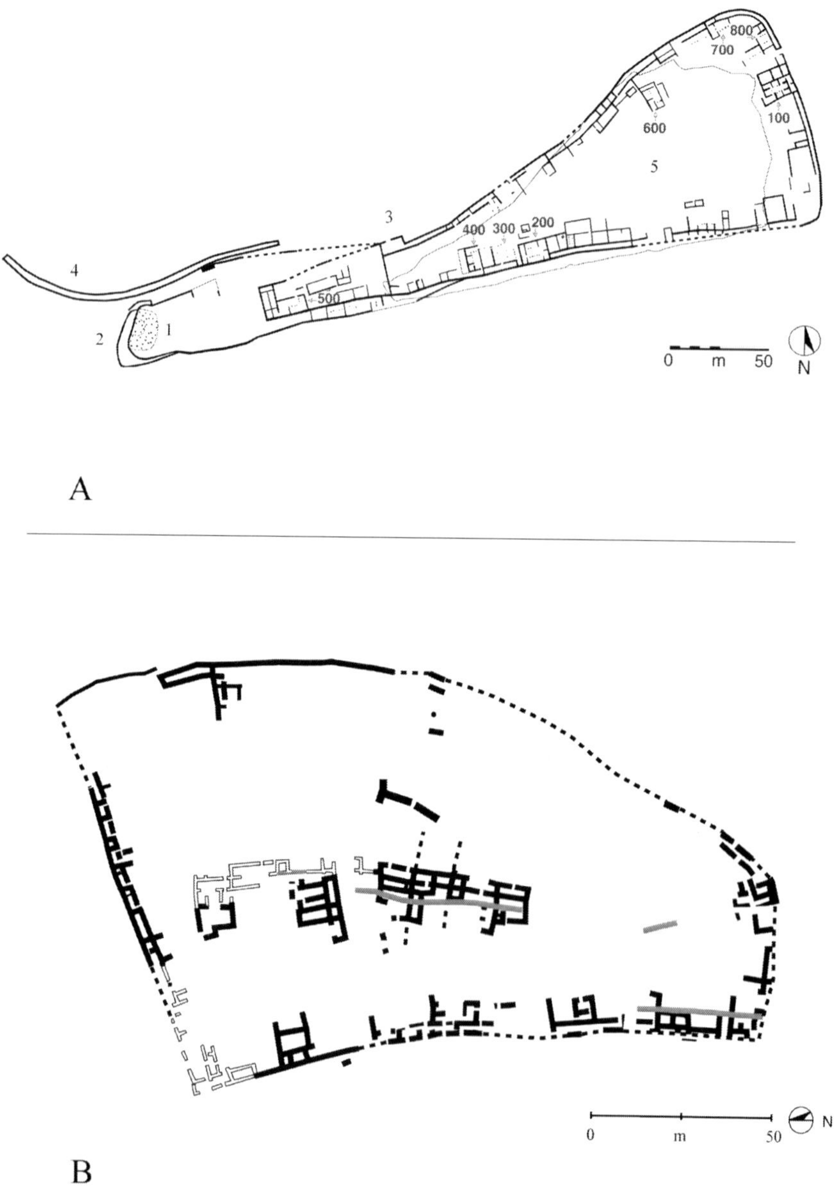

Figure 7.2. Settlement plans of Khirbat al-Mudayna al-'Aliya (A) and Lahun (B). The KMA plan shows Buildings 100 through 800, a tower (1), moat (2), a possible gated entrance (3), a paved pathway (4), and courtyard (5). (KMA plan courtesy of B. Routledge; Lahun plan after Homes-Fredericq 1997: Fig. 41.)

saw limited Egyptian activity compared to areas west of the Jordan River.[2] During the transition from the Levantine Bronze Age to the Iron Age—the late 13th and early 12th centuries BCE—much of the eastern Mediterranean experienced a dramatic upheaval that instigated, among other things, Egypt's gradual withdrawal from the Levant, the collapse of local economies, and the migration of groups away from urban centers and toward rural settings (Gitin et al. 1998; Ward and Joukowsky 1992). It is in this milieu that the communities under investigation begin to generate in the northern half of west-central Jordan, gradually fissioning southward.

West-central Jordan's uneven and, in places, marginal environment also helps to explain this staggered settlement pattern. Oddly, the best-known early Iron Age settlements are those that were founded in the region's most environmentally challenging contexts. These settlements were perched on the cliffs of the Wadi Mujib canyon and its tributaries. Because the region lacks a major water source like Egypt's Nile River or Iraq's Tigris and Euphrates, ancient societies depended on limited winter precipitation—between 200 and 250 millimeters—for year-round subsistence. These amounts were barely adequate to sustain rain-fed agricultural production. Luckily, aquifer-fed springs in the bottom of the canyon created a narrow riparian zone where limited agriculture was possible. Soil quality is also uneven across the region, and the topsoil necessary for Iron Age agricultural production had already begun to erode during earlier settlement episodes (Cordova 2000). Droughts and famines also made agricultural production in this region uncertain.

PRODUCTION STRATEGIES IN EARLY IRON AGE WEST-CENTRAL JORDAN

Just how these early Iron Age settlements organized production in this marginal context is clear when five routines are examined: house building, agriculture, animal husbandry, food production, and fortification construction.[3] House building, the first production routine, was a cooperative endeavor that often required participation beyond the household. Each settlement's residences exhibit similar blueprints and they line the interiors of each settlement. Excavated artifacts associated with food and textile production suggest these buildings were houses for families ranging in size from four to six people. House building was no casual affair in the early Iron Age and required a substantial amount of resources and labor. The construction of the floor, both exterior and interior walls, ceilings, and the second story using a combination of mudbrick, stone, wood, reeds, and lime was a labor-intensive activity. Clark has determined from his reconstruction of one house at 'Umayri that a minimum of 2,000 calories per day was required to sustain house-building projects (Clark 2003). These extreme labor demands meant families were required to depend on their neighbors to help them build and repair buildings. Cooperating in such projects meant that when assistance was needed, neighbors could be persuaded to return the favor.

Agricultural production was also a corporate endeavor. Flora (Simmons 2000) and fauna (Lev-Tov, Porter, and Routledge in press) evidence from excavated settlements shows that grains, vegetables, olive oil, and meat made up a typical Mediterranean diet. Some of this food, such as the freshwater crabs and wild fowl that live in the canyon's riparian zones, was available naturally in the community's vicinity. But food also had to be grown, and production could be difficult in a marginal environment where soils were poor and precipitation limited. In order to manage this challenge, communities planted crops on sloping hills, where they could capture runoff precipitation, or next to canyon streams. In many areas, soils were not rich; this required communities to maintain the landscape's productivity by constructing infrastructure such as terraces that slowed soil erosion and dams that directed runoff. Nutrient depletion was bulwarked with manuring and fallowing, a common strategy in rain-fed agricultural production in the Middle East (Palmer 1998). Like house building, these projects were labor-intensive activities that required cooperation and organization between households.

Communal animal husbandry also appears to have been common in early Iron Age west-central Jordan. Excavated faunal evidence shows that communities maintained mixed sheep and goat herds for wool, meat, and dairy products (Lev-Tov, Porter, and Routledge in press). In the Middle East, herd size is a common marker of wealth, especially because herds are "storage on the hoof" (Palmer 1998). Yet despite this perception, communities would often cooperate in herding practices. During droughts and famine, communities could cull their herds when additional meat was needed to supplement grain shortages. A large granary at KMA, Building 100 (Figure 7.3), and possibly a second at Mu'ammariya (Ninow 2004:Figure 4), serves as evidence for communal animal husbandry practices. Both buildings exhibit unique designs different from the surrounding residences. A bent-axis entrance gives way to a central room (Room 105) lined with storage installations (Rooms 101–102, 104, and 106–110). Two installations (Rooms 102 and 106) that have been excavated reveal that the floors were paved with flagstones, a feature that raised produce off the ground, protecting it from moisture and rodents. In Room 106, carbonized barley mixed with an unusual amount of weeds and stems was recovered (Simmons 2000), suggesting this building stored animal fodder to supplement grazing. Herds could enter the community through a small gate near the building to be stabled when they were not pastured at

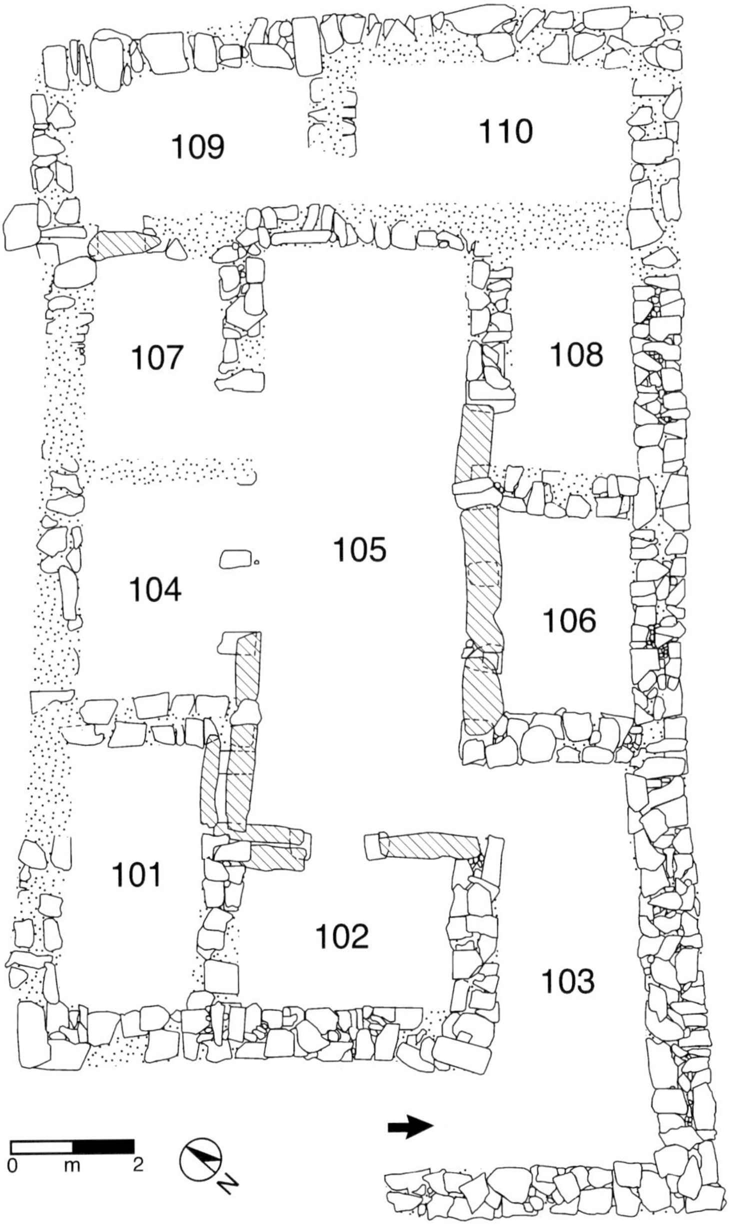

Figure 7.3. Plan of KMA's Building 100. A bent-axis entrance (Room 103) gives way to a central room (Room 105) lined with storage installations (Rooms 101 –102, 104, and 106–110). (Courtesy of B. Routledge.)

the spring beneath the settlement. This evidence for communal animal husbandry demonstrates that communities were willing to manage certain types of wealth—herds and fodder, in this case—in common.

While house building, agricultural production, and animal husbandry had their communal elements, grain storage and food production took place at the household level. In a resource-scarce, marginal environment like west-central Jordan, successfully keeping food surplus guaranteed families a buffer against famine and drought. Most houses had well-protected granaries positioned in the backs of buildings, farthest from the entrance. The best-preserved examples are found in 'Umayri's Buildings A and B (Herr et al. 1997:63–64, 2002:97–99). These rooms were approximately ten meters square, and their floors were covered with protective flagstones. These storage rooms contained large ceramic jars that protected dry goods from moisture and rodents and prevented evaporation of water, wine, and olive oil. Like the rooms themselves, these vessels were essential for effective storage. Small kitchens and cooking pots found inside each house indicate that most food was produced by and for the household. The repetition of these facilities in individual houses across the early Iron Age settlements indicates that foodstuffs were considered household property reserved for families' consumption.

Evidence for organized labor projects is also visible in the communities' fortified walls, gates, and towers. These fortifications protected the community's herds and agricultural surplus from neighboring settlements that would have sought to steal this wealth during droughts and famine. One tower excavated at KMA is over 10 meters tall and 32 meters wide, and is among the largest early Iron Age structures excavated in the southern Levant. Such large fortifications indicate that intensive projects demanded the entire community's labor. Yet how these labor projects were organized is difficult to determine. There is the possibility that fortifications were communally planned, since it is reasonable to consider the mutual benefits fortifications offered all community members. But supposing that wealthier households had the most to protect, they may have needed to persuade their neighbors to undertake these ambitious labor projects.

GOVERNING COOPERATION

The entanglement of corporate and household production routines raises the question of leadership and governance in the early Iron Age communities of west-central Jordan. How did these communities manage to cooperate in the scheduling of labor projects and the redistribution of surplus? Under what conditions did communities reach the limit of these iterated non-zero-sum interactions? Historical sources provide a window into the organization of collective governance in the sedentary and nomadic communities across the Bronze and Iron Age ancient Near East (Fleming 2004; Seri 2005). These sources describe how assemblies and councils consisting of the eldest male drawn from each household adjudicated conflicts between households and made decisions about subsistence, defense, and external affairs. What is clear from these sources is that it is impossible to generalize about the role, size, and composition of these corporate decision-making bodies across the ancient Near East. Closer to early Iron Age west-central Jordan, the Hebrew Bible's books of Judges and Samuel describe such governing bodies (Hebrew: *zakhain*) in early Iron Age agricultural settlements associated with ancient Israel (McKenzie 1959; Reviv 1989).[4] Although located in the Central Highlands of Palestine, these settlements are comparable in size and similar in date to those in west-central Jordan (Finkelstein 1988).

Evidence for these assemblies and councils is suggested in the mortuary remains of early Iron Age west-central Jordan. Mortuary remains implicitly or explicitly express social hierarchies that function in living communities, making west-central Jordan's early Iron Age tombs an appropriate context for examining authority in social life. There are several tombs available (Albright 1932; Dajani 1965; Harding 1953; Saller 1965–1966; Thompson 1986; Worschech 2003), although the quality of preservation and publication limits the extent to which their internal arrangements can be discerned. Baq'ah Valley Cave A4, however, stands as a notable exception (McGovern 1986:53–61). Nearly five meters wide by five meters long, the tomb consists of two parts: a forecourt and a burial cave. Commingled individuals (n = 233), varying in age and sex, were excavated from the back of the tomb. The large number of individuals indicates that communities, rather than individual households, buried their deceased members in the tomb. Once bodies had decomposed, skeletal remains were integrated with the rest of the community's deceased. Social rank in the mortuary evidence would be almost impossible to discern if it were not for two subtle lines of evidence. First, prestige objects including copper and iron jewelry, a pendant, seals, a scarab, and a sickle blade were found scattered around the tomb (McGovern 1986:Figure 21). The dramatically unequal ratio of prestige objects to individuals suggests that only some individuals received elaborate burials. A second indication of rank is found in the twelve human crania arranged on a shelf in the tomb's northwest corner. The display of these crania suggests that the community sought to commemorate individuals of social import, possibly members of the elder councils described in ancient Near Eastern sources.

This mortuary evidence, as well as available historical sources, suggests that assemblies were a common form of governance in early Iron Age agricultural communities. Yet the Hebrew Bible also conveys an anxiety about authority in early ancient Israel, characterizing this time as politically chaotic despite the presence of patrimonial councils. Judges 18:1 and 21:25, for example, report: "In those days, there was no king in Israel; all the people did what was right in their own eyes." The Hebrew Bible explains that to manage these uncertainties, judges emerged in periods of crisis or need, claiming an irregular charismatic authority from the Israelite deity, Yahweh (Malamat 1976; Weisman 1977). Acting almost as proto-kings, judges served several functions in early Israelite society. Deborah, Ehud, and Gideon exercised authority in military matters, while Samuel and Deborah did so in legal and theological affairs. As leaders, judges could accumulate wealth and be male or female, young or old. In the Judges narratives, the charismatic authority of judges operated in tandem with the patrimonial authority of elder assemblies, the latter often seeking the former's help in emergencies (e.g., 1 Samuel 8:4).

Symptoms of an emergent hierarchy are visible in the early Iron Age settlements when one examines the differences between residences. At KMA, seven buildings range in area from 71 to 238 square meters (Routledge 2000:Table 3). One building, Building 500 (Figure 7.4), greatly surpasses its neighbors in size and wealth. Although a typical pillared building is recognizable in the complex (Rooms 501–503), there are several additional rooms surrounding it, only some of which have been documented (e.g., Rooms 504–509). Three features indicate the occupants' wealth, the first being the large granary attached to the back of the pillared building (Rooms 504–509). Storage bins (508b and 509) are accessible only after one passes through a narrow corridor (Rooms 504b, 505–507). Here, carbonized barley and storage jars were excavated in two large bins (508b and 509). A second indication of wealth is the large kitchen adjacent to the storage area (Room 503). Complete with ovens, grinders, and stone bowls, this kitchen could produce enough food to feed multiple families. This evidence for large-scale food production suggests that the residence's occupants could muster the efforts and resources to hold feasts to reward those who cooperated in large labor projects.[5] Likewise, during famine and drought, Building 500's owners could distribute surplus wealth through gifts that created dependent relationships. But the most obvious sign of Building 500's wealth is its size. Although its full extent is not yet known, this building is at least 238 square meters. The large walls and second story required the building's owners to solicit and organize their neighbors' labor for its construction. One might take these differences in house size for granted if it were not for the textual sources ranging from economic documents to epic poetry that convey the practical and metaphorical importance of the house in ancient Near Eastern society (Schloen 2001). A house's size was a visual indication of its owner's wealth and status, indicating how much surplus could be stored within the house's walls. Near

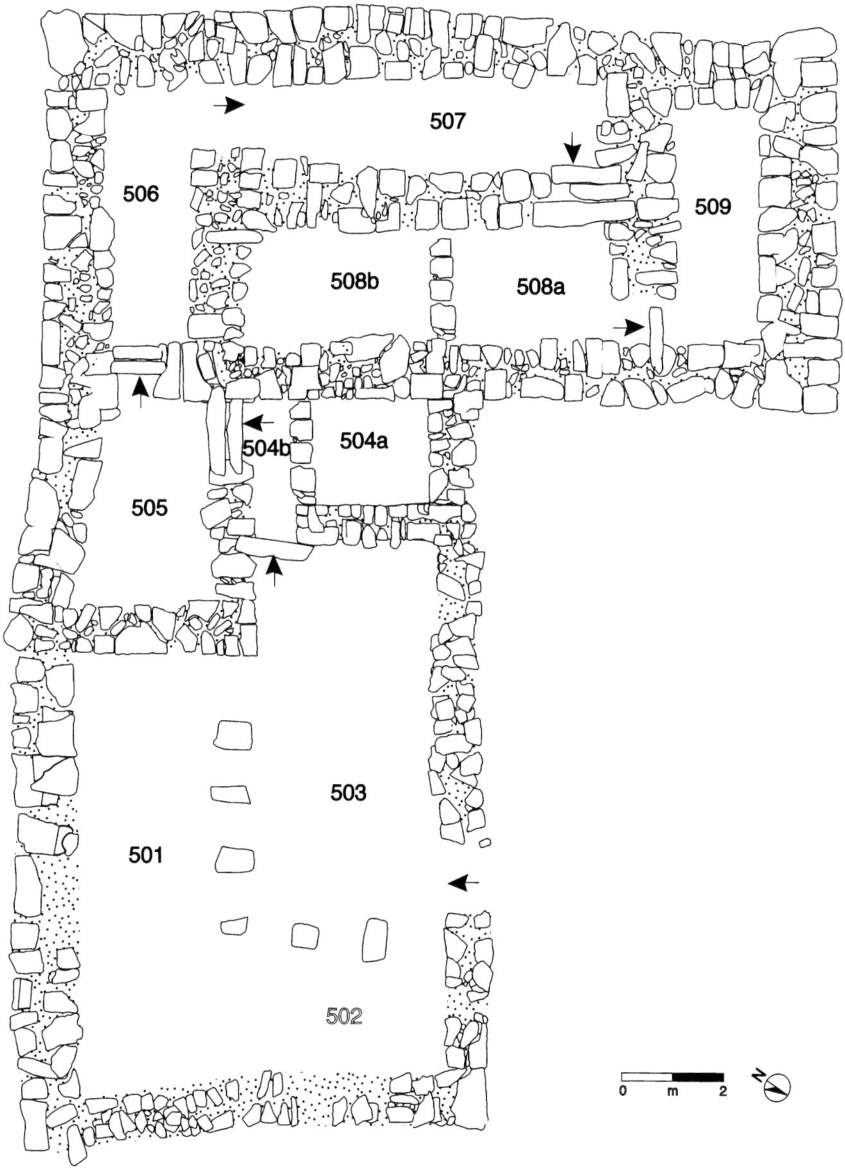

Figure 7.4. Plan of KMA's Building 500. (Courtesy of B. Routledge)

Eastern texts commonly applied the term for house (*bait*) regardless of scale, referring even to palaces as "houses" of the king.

When comparing textual representations of assemblies and judges in the Hebrew Bible, we see that patrimonial and charismatic genres of authority appear to coexist in the same communities. Although the books of Judges and Samuel often characterize the relationship between elders and judges as compatible, we might imagine moments when conflict could erupt, since the two genres would have disagreed over decisions concerning law, subsistence, and surplus management. These charismatic and patrimonial genres, in part, explain the contrasting strategies of cooperation and competition discussed earlier in connection with the archaeological evidence. Elder assemblies employed corporate production strategies like land allocation, animal husbandry, vessel production, and possibly fortification construction. But if one elder grew wealthy through his own successful household production, the community's commitment to communal production and ownership of wealth was challenged. Inequalities must have been greater in periods of environmental stress, when wealthy households could gain dependents through gifts and feasts. Less-fortunate households would have been obligated to return these debts with labor, from which only the wealthy household benefited. If this pattern repeated over several agricultural cycles, then a wealthy household could consolidate authority over the entire community.

REFLECTIONS ON COOPERATION: RECIPROCITY, DEFECTION, AND SHADOWY COLLABORATORS

This reconstruction presents opportunities to reflect on the themes that Axelrod discusses in his *Evolution of Cooperation*, particularly the important role that reciprocity, defection, and time play in structuring cooperative practices. It also presents an opportunity to extend this theory to understand the role that nonhuman agents play in the iterated non-zero-sum interactions that structured social life in the early Iron Age.

The co-occurrence of patrimonial and charismatic modes of governance in west-central Jordan's early Iron Age is in some ways not surprising in light of archaeological investigations that have appreciated the variety of leadership strategies in ancient societies (e.g., Haas 2000). But in this particular case, this co-occurrence held implications for the durability of social life. As political and environmental contingencies shifted, communities made organizational adjustments that attempted to maintain cohesion between households, even if this meant that a hierarchy emerged. Yet, the power to reorganize and lead the community appears to have had its limits. Once environmental conditions improved and the community no longer depended on wealthy households for sustenance, new leaders lost their ability to justify their authority in terms of their wealth. Instead, leaders attempted to naturalize their authority through charisma and ideology. Households could escape these new regimes of governance by leaving the community—maybe to found their own. Indeed, excavations at KMA suggest these defections were common (Routledge 2004:106–108). Buildings 200 and 700 contained a large number of artifacts in the fills above the surface, suggesting that the rest of the community used this house as a midden following its abandonment. Construction materials from the building were also missing; they were probably reused for new houses in the community. Building 700's state contrasts with other buildings at KMA like Building 500, whose preservation, especially the kitchen, was excellent. This pattern of gradual abandonment explains the unusual fissioning process of early Iron Age settlement patterns. Households like Building 700 that defected from the communities likely founded new settlements in the region, likely recruiting other households to join them. The current understanding of settlements' occupation and abandonment sequence suggests that this process moved from north to south and occurred gradually over two and a half centuries.

In the iterated non-zero-sum interactions that structured cooperative strategies, then, leaders who had amassed too much wealth faced the problem of household defections. These defections are symptomatic of the importance as well as the challenges of maintaining reciprocal relationships in the early Iron Age communities. So long as households engaged in material (e.g., grain surplus) and immaterial (e.g., labor) acts of reciprocity, the community's ethos of cooperation was sustained. Yet such reciprocal acts were difficult to maintain in a resource-scarce environment. Wealthy households were forced to choose between two inconvenient choices. On one hand, they could redistribute their wealth as gifts to less-fortunate households. In doing so, social cohesion was maintained and the community could endure short-term hardships. Yet at the same time, wealthy households risked losing the wealth on which their authority was based. The other choice was to hoard surplus wealth and abstain from reciprocal relationships, acts that would result in extreme asymmetries, mass defections, or worse, insurrections. Wealthy households likely practiced a combination of these strategies that they adjusted as environmental and political contingencies arose and subsided.

In this scenario, time plays a challenging role in managing reciprocity and preventing defection. Recall that Axelrod suggests that cooperation is more likely when participants perceive that they will encounter each other again in the future (Axelrod 1984:126–132). If a household develops a reputation for not "playing nice," as Axelrod might describe it, its neighbors will anticipate that future interactions will be similar. Hence, this emphasis on the future not only encouraged cooperation, but also urged households to avoid conflicts that would leave them isolated from the rest of the community. But the uncertainty of the future, a hallmark of subsistence in a marginal environment, makes such projections very difficult. As defected or alienated households came together to form new communities, they promoted this sense of future obligation by establishing alliances through covenant ceremonies and marriage alliances that formed the basis of new iterated interactions.

Uninvestigated until now is the implicit hierarchy between humans and nonhumans in reconstructing these networks of cooperation and competition. In the above scenario, animals—domesticated and nondomesticated alike—and objects such as building materials, ceramic vessels, and grain surplus, played a passive role in human decision making. The environment, too, was misconstrued; although it played an important role in structuring early Iron Age social life, the agentive role it was prescribed was overdetermined. Such hierarchies between human and nonhuman spheres denies the complexity of the cooperative games that took place in early Iron Age west-central Jordan, leading one to ask the nuanced question, who *or what* is cooperating? Recent critical calls in the social sciences suggest that the roles that nonhuman agents play as participants in social life be recognized (Latour 1993, 2005).

This position also requires a rethinking of the role that production plays in cooperative relationships. Once nonhuman agents are created, they are endowed with specific use or exchange values. They take on their own social life, participating in the network of exchanges that were documented earlier in the human world. What they reciprocate is their willingness to cooperate or betray their human counterparts in the difficult marginal environment. The scarcity of nonorganic portable objects excavated in the early Iron Age communities suggests that ceramic and metal objects possessed a high cultural value. For a household to be successful in agricultural production and storage surplus, it needed to create and maintain relationships with these objects. An analysis of the ceramic vessel evidence from these communities suggests that vessel production was organized at the communal level and then the vessels were distributed to households for their individual storage and cooking needs (Porter 2007:216–278).

Recognizing the potentially cooperative role that nonhuman agents play in social life contrasts with the ways Diamond and Wright consider humans as the main protagonists of their grand narratives of human history. In marginal environments, humans could collaborate all they wanted on animal husbandry, agriculture, and house and fortification building. But if there is no precipitation, soil nutrients are gone, insects have infested the grain surplus, and all the ceramic vessels are broken, then humans are required to rethink their strategies of cooperation, especially the roles that nonhuman agents play in subsistence.

CONCLUSION

When presented alongside Diamond's and Wright's books, west-central Jordan's early Iron Age communities suggest that narratives of conflict and cooperation are successful only when observed at the broadest resolutions. These early Iron Age marginal communities tested the limits of iterated non-zero-sum interactions in the ancient Near East. Did it simulate social complexity as Wright might have predicted? Not exactly—although households could defect from the community, they still held the abilities to reconstitute themselves in new, semi-sustainable configurations. What this suggests is that social life in marginal environments can be durable so long as actors are flexible in the ways they organize their production routines and modes of authority. Axelrod's lessons from the prisoner's dilemma resonate here: reciprocity, defection, and time were all mediating concerns for households. In contemporary times, with growing concerns about global warming, human migration, food shortage, and regional genocides, stories of ancient societies that mitigated adverse conditions are potentially more productive than grand narratives of conflict and collapse. Herein lies perhaps the greatest contribution by the relatively small and historically remote agricultural villages of early Iron Age west-central Jordan as we consider the future of cooperation in an increasingly competitive world.

ACKNOWLEDGMENTS

Thanks to Jordan's Department of Antiquities and my colleagues Bruce Routledge, Denyse Homes-Fredericq, Larry Herr, Doug Clark, Udo Worschech, Friedbert Ninow, and Tim Harrison for sharing their thoughts, evidence, and conclusions with me. The argument presented here remains my own.

NOTES

1. Only settlements where early Iron Age artifacts were associated with architectural features are discussed in this chapter. For a list of published early Iron Age settlements in west-central Jordan, see Porter 2007:132, no. 18.
2. See Worschech (1990:94–102, 131) and Timm (1989:14–33) for a counter-argument that the Egyptian empire did manage south-central Jordan during the Late Bronze and early Iron ages.
3. See Porter 2007 for complete descriptions of supporting data for the following conclusions.
4. Caution must be exercised when using the Hebrew Bible as a historical source for the early Iron Age southern Levant. These narratives of the early Israelite settlement were likely preserved through oral transmission but not written down until several centuries later, when Israelite scribal practices were at their peak. See Boling (1975) and Soggin (1981) for commentaries discussing Judges and Samuel.

5. The organization of ceramic vessel production was also examined to determine if individual households or the entire community carried out this labor-intensive task. See Porter 2007 for results and a detailed discussion.

REFERENCES

Albright, William F.
1932 An anthropoid clay coffin from Sahab in Transjordan. *American Journal of Archaeology* 36:295–306.
Axelrod, Robert M.
1984 *The evolution of cooperation*. New York: Basic Books.
Boling, Robert G.
1975 *Judges*. Garden City, NY: Doubleday.
1988 *The early biblical community in Transjordan*. Sheffield: Almond.
Canuto, Marcello, and Jason Yaeger
2000 *Archaeology of communities: A new world perspective*. London: Routledge.
Clark, Douglas
2003 Bricks, sweat, and tears: The human investment in constructing a "four-room" house. *Near Eastern Archaeology* 66 (1–2): 34–43.
Cordova, Carlos E.
2000 Geomorphological evidence of intense prehistoric soil erosion in the highlands of central Jordan. *Physical Geography* 21 (6): 538–567.
Dajani, Rafik
1965 Jabal Nuzha tomb at Amman. *Annual of the Department of Antiquities of Jordan* 10:48–52.
Diamond, Jared
1997 *Guns, germs, and steel: The fates of human societies*. New York: W. W. Norton.
2005 *Collapse: How societies choose to fail or succeed*. New York: Viking.
Dobres, Marcia-Anne, and John E. Robb, eds.
2000 *Agency in archaeology*. London: Routledge.
Finkelstein, Israel
1988 *The archaeology of the Israelite settlement*. Jerusalem: Israel Exploration Society.
Fleming, Daniel E.
2004 *Democracy's ancient ancestors: Mari and early collective governance*. Cambridge: Cambridge University Press.
Gitin, Seymour, Amihai Mazar, and Ephraim Stern
1998 *Mediterranean peoples in transition: Thirteenth to early tenth centuries BCE*. Jerusalem: Israel Exploration Society.
Glueck, Nelson
1940 *The other side of the Jordan*. New Haven, CT: American Schools of Oriental Research.
Haas, Jonathan, ed.
2000 *From leaders to rulers*. New York: Kluwer Academic Press.

Harding, G. Lankester
1953 *Four tomb groups from Jordan*. London: Palestine Exploration Fund.
Herr, Larry G.
2000 The settlement and fortification of Tell al-'Umayri in Jordan during the LB/ Iron I transition. In *The archaeology of Jordan and beyond: Essays in honor of James B. Sauer*, ed. L. Stager, J. Greene, and M. Coogan, 167–179. Winona Lake: Eisenbrauns.
Herr, Larry G., et al., eds.
1997 *Madaba Plains Project 3: The 1989 season at Tell el-'Umeiri and vicinity and subsequent studies*. Berrien Springs: Andrews University Press.
2002 *Madaba Plains Project 5: The 1994 season at Tell al-'Umayri and subsequent studies*. Berrien Springs: Andrews University Press.
Homes-Fredericq, Denyse
1992 Late Bronze and Iron Age evidence from Lehun in Moab. In *Early Edom and Moab: The beginning of the Iron Age in southern Jordan*, ed. P. Bienkowski, 187–202. Sheffield: J. R. Collis.
Ibach, Robert D.
1987 *Archaeological survey of the Hesban region*. Berrien Springs: Andrews University Press.
Ji, Chang-Ho, and Jong Keun Lee
2000 A preliminary report on the Dhiban Plateau Survey Project, 1999: The Versacare Expedition. *Annual of the Department of Antiquities of Jordan* 44:493–506.
Kitchen, Kenneth A.
1992 The Egyptian evidence on ancient Jordan. In *Early Edom and Moab: The beginning of the Iron Age in southern Jordan*, ed. P. Bienkowski. Sheffield: J. R. Collis.
Latour, Bruno
1993 *We have never been modern*. Cambridge: Harvard University Press.
2005 *Reassembling the social: An introduction to actor-network-theory*. Oxford: Oxford University Press.
Lev-Tov, Justin, Benjamin Porter, and Bruce Routledge
In press "Measusring local diversity in early Iron Age animal economies: A view from Khirbat al-Mudayna al-'Aliya (Jordan)," *Bulletin of the American Schools of Oriental Research*.
Malamat, Abraham
1976 Charismatic leadership in the book of Judges. In *Magnalia Dei: The mighty acts of God: Essays on the Bible and archaeology in memory of G. Ernest Wright*, ed. W. E. L. Frank Moore Cross and Patrick D. Miller, Jr., 152–168. Garden City, NY: Doubleday.
McGovern, Patrick E.
1986 *The Late Bronze and Early Iron ages of central Transjordan: The Baq'ah Valley Project, 1977–1981*. Philadelphia: University Museum.
McKenzie, J. L.
1959 The elders in the Old Testament. *Biblica* 40:522–540.
Meyers, Eric M., ed.
1997 *The Oxford encyclopedia of archaeology in the Near East*. Oxford: Oxford University Press.

Miller, J. Maxwell, ed.
1991 *Archaeological survey of the Kerak Plateau*. Atlanta: Scholars Press.
Ninow, Friedbert
2004 First soundings at Kirbat al-Mu'ammariya in the greater Wadi al-Mujib area. *Annual of the Department of Antiquities of Jordan* 48:257–266.
Olavarri, Emilio
1977–1978 Sondeo arqueológico en Khirbet Medeineh junto a Smakieh (Jordania). *Annual of the Department of Antiquities of Jordan* 22:136–149.
1983 La campagne de fouilles 1982 à Khirbet Medeinet al-Mu'arradjeh près de Smakieh (Kerak). *Annual of the Department of Antiquities of Jordan* 27:165–178.
Palmer, Carol
1998 "Following the plough": The agricultural environment of northern Jordan. *Levant* 30:129–165.
Porter, Benjamin
2007 The archaeology of community in Iron I central Jordan. PhD diss., University of Pennsylvania.
Reviv, Hanoch
1989 *The elders in ancient Israel: A study of a biblical institution*. Jerusalem: Magnes.
Routledge, Bruce
2000 Seeing through walls: Interpreting Iron Age I architecture at Khirbat al-Mudayna al-'Aliya. *Bulletin of the American Schools of Oriental Research* 319:37–70.
2004 *Moab in the Iron Age: Hegemony, polity, archaeology*. Philadelphia: University of Pennsylvania Press.
Routledge, Bruce, and Benjamin Porter
2007 A place in-between: Khirbat al-Mudayna al-'Aliya in the early Iron Age. In *Crossing Jordan—North American contributions to the archaeology of Jordan*, ed. T. Levy, P. M. Daviau, R. Younker, and M. Shaer, 323–329. London: Equinox.
Saller, Sylvester J.
1965–1966 Iron Age tombs at Nebo, Jordan. *Liber Annuus* 16:165–298.
Sasson, Jack M., ed.
1995 *Civilizations of the ancient Near East*. New York: Scribner.
Schloen, J. David
2001 *The house of the father as fact and symbol: Patrimonialism in Ugarit and the ancient Near East*. Winona Lake, IN: Eisenbrauns.
Seri, Andrea
2005 *Local power in Old Babylonian Mesopotamia*. London: Equinox.
Simmons, Ellen
2000 Subsistence in transition: Analysis of an archaeobotanical assemblage from Khirbet al-Mudayna al-'Aliya. MS thesis, University of Sheffield.

Soggin, J. Alberto
1981 *Judges: A commentary*. Philadelphia: Westminster Press.
Thompson, Henry O.
1986 An Iron Age tomb at Madaba. In *The archaeology of Jordan and other studies*, ed. L. Geraty and L. Herr, 331–363. Berrien Springs: Andrews University Press.
Timm, Stefan
1989 Moab zwischen den Mächten: Studien zu historischen Denkmälern und Texten. Wiesbaden: O. Harrassowitz.
Ward, William A., and Martha Joukowsky
1992 *The crisis years: The 12th century B.C. from beyond the Danube to the Tigris*. Dubuque: Kendall/Hunt.
Weisman, Ze'ev
1977 Charismatic leaders in the era of the Judges. *Zeitschrift für die alttestamentliche wissenschaft* 89.
Worschech, Udo
1989 Preliminary report on the second campaign at the ancient site of el-Balu' in 1987. *Annual of the Department of Antiquities of Jordan* 33:111–112.
1990 *Die Beziehungen Moabs zu Israel und Agypten in der Eisenzeit*. Wiesbaden: Otto Harrassowitz.
2003 *A burial cave at Umm Dimis north of el-Balu'*. Frankfurt: Peter Lang.
Worschech, Udo, and Friedbert Ninow.
1994 Preliminary report on the third campaign at the ancient site of el-Balu' in 1991. *Annual of the Department of Antiquities of Jordan* 38:195–203.
1999 Preliminary report on the excavation at al-Balu' and a first sounding at al-Misna in 1997 *Annual of the Department of Antiquities of Jordan* 43:169–173.
Worschech, Udo, Uwe Rosenthal, and Fawzi Zayadine.
1986 The fourth season in the north-westward el-Kerak, and soundings at Balu' in 1986. *Annual of the Department of Antiquities of Jordan* 30:285–310.
Wright, Robert
2000 *Nonzero: The logic of human destiny*. New York: Pantheon Books.

III

COOPERATION AND COOPERATIVES

8

Cooperation in the Informal Economy

The Case of Recyclers at a Brazilian Garbage Dump

Kathleen Millar, Brown University

DEBATING DUALISMS

In recent years, the implementation of neoliberal economic policies, shifts in the international division of labor, processes of deindustrialization, and rising rates of unemployment in many parts of the world have raised new questions for anthropological studies of labor and of social class (see, for example, Carbonella and Kasmir 2006; Collins 2002; Comaroff and Comaroff 2001). Many of these questions have centered on the issue of how to conceptualize work, labor organization, and social class in a global context in which two-fifths of the economically active population of the developing world does not participate in formal wage labor but rather earns a livelihood through a range of activities in what Keith Hart (1973) first termed the *informal economy* (Davis 2004:24). Studies of informal economic activities have thus gained increasing significance for an understanding of the nature and meaning of work in the current configuration of global capitalism.

This attention to urban informal economies in both anthropology and other social science disciplines has generated a plethora of debates, many of which relate directly to the unifying theme of this volume: cooperation in economic life. Many scholars have argued that the rise in informal labor has weakened trade unions and labor organizing; such scholars observe that many unions have been slow to include informal workers into their ranks (Ford 2004; Portes 1994). Others have pointed to the emergence of new forms of trade unionism and of class politics, maintaining that labor organizing has not declined in certain parts of the world but rather has been transformed into new kinds of social movements (Datta 2003; Gallin 2001). Some have seen the informal economy as increasingly a site of individualism, entrepreneurialism, and competition, often incited by neoliberal programs of self-help for the urban poor (Itzigsohn 2006). In contrast, studies focusing on the role of kinship ties and neighborhood networks in the informal economy have noted practices of reciprocity, collaboration, and exchange (Pahl 1984; Seligmann 1989; Weismantel 2001). Finally, many of those who have examined illicit practices in unregulated economies have argued that social trust both sustains and results from transactions that occur outside formal contracts and institutions (Hart 1988; Nordstrom 2007).

While these debates and studies have provided valuable perspectives on a diversity of informal economies, they have tended to portray these forms of employment as either individualistic or collective, competitive or cooperative. In what follows, I seek to complicate this dualism by scrutinizing the conditions in which cooperative practices are found in informal employment settings. In short, I argue that an account of the particular conditions and organization of labor in informal employment is central to understanding how and why cooperative practices at times emerge in informal economies and at times do not. My research findings ultimately suggest that conditions leading to cooperation in informal employment include workers' autonomy (that is, their ability to work independently of a higher authority); the integration of work-related activities with activities related to social and recreational life; and the presence of social networks that merge work, familial, and neighborly relationships. In addition, my research demonstrates that while these conditions *enable* cooperation, collective action on the part of informal laborers tends to occur specifically in response to a threat to their livelihood.

I base my analysis in this chapter on ethnographic research that I conducted from June through August 2005 among informal workers who collect, sort, and sell recyclable materials at the largest garbage dump in the metropolitan area of Rio de Janeiro, Brazil. This garbage dump receives an average of 8,000 tons of waste each day and has been in operation since 1976. Many of those who collect recyclables at this site live in the neighborhood that I call Jardim das Flores,[1] which is located outside of but adjacent to the dump. While the collection of recyclables might seem a marginal activity, this work has become increasingly common worldwide, accompanying the general expansion of informal employment. It is estimated that informal recyclers currently comprise 1 percent of the population in the urban developing world (Medina 2007:vii).

Throughout this chapter, I refer to those who collect recyclable material in Jardim das Flores as *catadores*. This word means "collectors" and is a shortened form of the term *catadores de materiais recicláveis* (collectors of recyclable material). Many of my research participants requested that I use "catadores" to refer to them rather than the more common terms, "garbage picker," "trash picker," or "scavenger." These other terms are not only derogatory, they also imply that catadores collect garbage. As many catadores frequently reminded me, "Garbage is that which is not worth anything" ("o lixo é o que não presta"). By this statement, they asserted that the material that they collect still has value and therefore cannot be considered waste.

In what follows, I provide a comparative analysis of cooperative practices among three distinct groups of catadores in Jardim das Flores. I begin with a description of the differences in the work environment and labor process of these three categories of catadores. I then examine how particular labor conditions shape the social relations and political practices that emerge in each work setting. Finally, I argue that the flexibility and autonomy characteristic of some work situations outside formal wage labor *enable* cooperative practices, while threats to the livelihood of informal laborers ultimately *motivate* collective organizing and political action.

LABOR CONDITIONS IN THREE WORK SETTINGS: DUMP, DEPOSITORIES, AND COOPERATIVE

Catadores in Jardim das Flores can be divided into three separate categories, each of which performs different activities in distinct labor conditions. The largest category consists of over one thousand catadores who work on the dump, retrieving recyclable materials from the waste of unloading garbage trucks. These catadores must work quickly to collect recyclables before a compactor, which follows the path of the garbage trucks, arrives to distribute, flatten, and effectively bury the freshly deposited waste. Catadores on the dump must also negotiate the constant movement of trucks so as not to be injured by a vehicle. The activity of catadores collecting on the dump appears hectic and aggressive though the frenzied nature of their work is less the result of interpersonal competition for material than the consequence of the race to reach material ahead of the compactor and to keep up with the constant traffic of garbage trucks.

The dump operates all twenty-four hours every day of the week, thus enabling these catadores to work during the day or at night and to choose their own flexible work schedules. Furthermore, catadores on the dump work for themselves without a boss or supervisor. At the end of the day, or in the morning for those who work at night, catadores bring their material down from the dump to one of the numerous depositories in the neighborhood where they sell their material by weight. In 1996, the company that operates the dump instituted policies that sought to regulate the number of catadores as part of a larger effort to improve the management of the dump. One of these policies requires that catadores wear vests to enter the dump; they must obtain the vests from the depositories to which they sell. If followed, this policy would control the number of catadores on the dump (since the company provided the depositories with a limited number of vests) and would also effectively tie a catador to a particular depository for all sales. However, catadores work to circumvent this policy by sharing and duplicating vests. In this way, they maintain independence from any one particular depository and continue to work autonomously on the dump, determining their own speed, frequency, and schedule of work.

Those who work in the depositories constitute a second category of catadores. Owners of depositories who buy material from the catadores on the dump hire workers to sort and bundle the various types of recyclable material. Though most of the depositories are unregistered and unregulated enterprises that pay weekly bribes to the police to overlook their operations and that therefore fall into the hazy category of the informal or illicit economy, the labor conditions in the depositories resemble aspects of formal waged employment. The catadores in the depositories work certain days of the week, usually Monday through Friday, and have a fixed work schedule with two set coffee breaks and a lunch hour. At the end of the week they receive cash payment that is similar to a wage; they must abide by the production-level demands of the manager of the depository; and they have the potential to be fired. In effect, catadores in the depositories are wage laborers who work without a *carteira assinada*[2] and therefore without employee rights or protections.

The third category of catadores consists of the 150 people who work at a recycling cooperative located at the base of the dump. This cooperative began in 1996 as part of the same effort by the company that operates the dump to manage the situation of catadores. The company intended that the cooperative replace the work of the catadores on top of the dump, but many catadores refused to leave their work situation on the dump for that of the cooperative. Furthermore, the cooperative could not accommodate the number of catadores in Jardim das Flores, which has continuously risen over the past ten years. The cooperative thus comprises a small fraction of the total catadores who work in Jardim das Flores.

At the cooperative, catadores retrieve recyclables from waste that moves down a production line on a conveyor belt. A few of the garbage trucks entering Jardim das Flores deposit their waste at the cooperative rather than at the top of the dump. The nonrecyclable material that remains after the waste passes along the conveyor belt is loaded onto trucks and then carried to the dump for final disposal. All catadores at the cooperative wear uniforms and gloves and have access to bathrooms in a building at the site, which houses an office as well as a space used for meetings and lunch breaks. The officers in the administration of the cooperative are elected and must be members of the cooperative. Despite this apparent democratic structure of the cooperative, however, clear divisions exist between the office and the production line. Officers do not work on the conveyor belt and they rarely identify as catadores. Workers on the production line frequently complain that the officers treat them poorly and profit from their work. The president of the cooperative at the time of research had served several terms and owned and operated several clandestine depositories. Many of those who have served as officers and subsequently lost an election have chosen not to return to the production line of the cooperative but rather to return to working on top of the dump.

In order to understand the failure of the cooperative to develop into a vibrant community organization, it is necessary to emphasize that the cooperative was created and continues to be maintained by the companies that have operated the dump and not by a grassroots initiative on the part of the catadores themselves. The buildings, machinery, and infrastructure of the cooperative were provided by the company managing the dump in 1996. The elected officials of the cooperative have the responsibility of overseeing the finances and daily administration of the cooperative, but the company hires and pays the salaries of the cooperative's manager and of a social worker who assists the cooperative's members. In 2002 a new company took charge of the dump and has continued to maintain the cooperative, including paying the manager and social worker. The company's involvement has contributed to unequal power relations in the cooperative; furthermore, few catadores expressed a sense of having any real ownership of the cooperative. Given that the capital needed to construct the cooperative came from the company operating the dump and that the companies in charge of the dump have continued to oversee and pay for the management of the cooperative, in actuality the cooperative is not owned by the member catadores but by the companies operating the dump.

It is important to note here that while all catadores have the option to work on top of the dump, those who work in the depositories or cooperative choose to do so primarily out of fear of injury on the dump or out of a concern about the physical conditions of their work site. All catadores interviewed in the depositories and cooperative stated that they had at least some experience working on the dump, ranging from a week to several years. When questioned in regard to their preference to work in the cooperative or in the depositories, where their work situation is less flexible and where they earn roughly 200 reals ($100)[3] less than catadores on the dump, they consistently replied that deadly accidents occur more frequently with machinery on the dump than in the cooperative and in the depositories, and that they found it unbearable to work under the harsh sun or winter rain on the dump. Those in the cooperative work under a tin roof; those in the depositories generally work under precariously hung tarps that provide minimal protection. It is certainly the case that more women than men opt to work in the cooperative or depositories. Roughly 60 percent of those who work in the cooperative and 70 percent of those in the depositories are women. However, nearly 50 percent of catadores who work on the dump are women and range in age from 18 to 72. Therefore, it is possible for women to work under the physical conditions of the dump, and many indeed choose to do so. The choice to work on or off the dump, then, often related to a lack of adaptation to the physical conditions of the dump (for those who worked on the dump for a brief stint) or to a close experience of danger on the dump. As the cooperative (usually preferred over depositories) is limited to 150 members, catadores who did not enter the cooperative in its early years and who do not wish to collect on the dump must work in depositories.

The three categories of catadores described above differ most significantly in relation to the degree of autonomy that they have in their work situation. Those who work on the dump are the most independent in that they determine their own schedules, their pace of work, the type of material they collect, the day that they sell, and the buyer to whom they sell. They also have virtually no work requirements, possess free access to their production, and own their products. In contrast, the catadores of the depositories must be "hired" (and can be sent away at any time), they have a boss who determines their work schedule and payment, and they sell their labor power rather than their products. Finally, the catadores of the cooperative demonstrate a mix of autonomy and dependence. Those who work in the office certainly control the production of the cooperative, and many who work on the line feel that they are in a boss-employee relationship, often stating, "We work so that they [the officers] earn." However, the catadores of the cooperative are more autonomous than those in the depositories in that they cannot be fired and can work as many days as they like. They also can work at the pace they choose and therefore are able to spend time collecting side items from the waste for their personal enterprises. Generally, this takes the form of collecting food for their families or for pigs that they raise on the side, though some also collect broken electronics and other objects to repair and resell.

The Production of Social Relations

The three work settings in Jardim das Flores—the first a situation of autonomous self-employment, the second a case of informal wage labor, and the third an example of an organized cooperative—enable a comparative investigation into the relation between the organization of work and the emergence of cooperative practices. Cooperative practices among catadores include the sharing of vests, communal meals, apprenticeship for novice catadores, the joint refusal to sell material when prices decline too sharply, and the recent creation of a work association. I begin this discussion by first exploring the social relations that are found in each of the three work settings and by drawing connections between the labor conditions and forms of sociality on the dump, in the depositories, and at the cooperative. I have chosen practices related to food and meals as one avenue through which to concretely examine questions of sociality. Anthropology has a long tradition of employing food as a lens through which to view larger issues such as social organization (Codere 1957), symbolic systems (Douglas 1996 [1966]), historical processes (Mintz 1985), and cultural values (Munn 1986). Furthermore, both anthropologists and sociologists of food have pointed to the sharing of meals as an act of sociality indicative of group inclusion, togetherness, intimacy, and fellowship.

A second reason for the use of food practices as an analytic window onto social relations among the catadores derives from their own comments, stories, and jokes regarding food. Food dominates discussion in Jardim das Flores in part because food, and more importantly its scarcity, constantly creates concern. For most of the catadores, who have built their makeshift homes in the informal settlement at the base of the dump and have minimal need for transportation, food expenditures often exceed any other cost of living. Furthermore, it is possible for catadores to delay the purchase of clothing and other household items until the necessary money can be saved, but catadores must face food expense daily. One woman, Ana, who injured her hand at a depository and could not work for over a week, spent an entire Saturday attempting to find the depository owner in order to plead with him to give her some money for food. The owner's wife repeatedly told Ana to return at a later time. When evening approached and Ana had still not found the owner, I naively suggested that she rest and try again on Monday. She replied, with a look of desperation, "What? How can I go back home and tell my mother that I was not able to get the money? There is nothing to eat in the house. No meat, no vegetables, no beans, no bread."

The scarcity of food has led many catadores to collect expired goods from supermarkets at the same time that they collect recyclables. Their work is therefore interwoven with their meals. In attempts to counteract stigmatized images of the catador as someone who eats garbage, many catadores express pride in the quality of their found food, which they jokingly call *podrão* (from the root word "rotten"). One woman inverted common assumptions about "safe" purchased food compared to "dangerous" scavenged food by asserting, "I've only been sick from food that I bought; I've never been sick from something that I found here [in the garbage]." Some catadores joke about their abilities to trick others into eating and liking food from the garbage. Two catadores laughed boisterously at another's story of having served her son-in-law some chicken that she had found. The son-in-law often asked the storyteller if the food that she cooked came from her work. This time she told him "no," and he ate it and then asked for seconds. Stories such as this one arise frequently among catadores, expressing both scorn at found-food stigmas and their close attention to who willingly does or does not eat podrão.

The significance of food to the work and words of catadores provides a focused lens through which to analyze their unity and division, cohesion and segregation, solidarity and discord. With this in mind, I comparatively consider the following questions for the catadores at the dump, depositories, and cooperative: During work, what do they eat? With whom do they eat? Where do they eat and in what surrounding context? I base responses to these questions on observations that I made while working in each of the three work environments and on unprompted comments made by catadores during interviews and informal conversations. I consider meal sharing both as a cooperative practice in and of itself—one that involves the distribution of found-food items and the joint use of containers and utensils—and as a situation that strengthens social relations necessary for further collective action.

Though work on the dump has no schedule and therefore no set lunch hour, most catadores working during the day pause around noon in order to eat and rest. The traffic of trucks on the dump tends to slow at midday and therefore provides good reason for catadores to stop for lunch. Though many catadores bring pastries, coffee, and juice as snacks for themselves or to sell to other catadores for extra income, a couple of older women provide the lunch for the majority of catadores. Irmã, a woman in her seventies who has worked on the dump since its beginning, cooks for the catadores. The meals that she serves, often large pots of stew or fried meat with cassava flour, are made from expired supermarket goods. Catadores contribute one real ($0.50) from time to time in order to compensate Irmã for the oil and seasoning that she usually has to buy for the meals and for her time, as she now works primarily as a cook on the dump. Catadores receive a share of Irmã's meal in found plastic containers and eat with old utensils brought from home. In the case of a shortage, the catadores share the containers and utensils. Half-filled burlap sacks and large overturned cans serve as seats for catadores eating and resting. Though a cluster generally gathers near Irmã, other small groups form throughout the area where catadores leave their sacks of material. Anyone who wishes can eat Irmã's meal, and only once in my presence did she run out of food toward the end of the informal lunch break.

In addition to food sharing, lunchtime on the dump often involves a variety of social activities. Soccer games on the dump, for example, are common sights in the afternoon. Many catadores also relax after eating and spend time chatting (*batendo papo*) with others. Such conversations frequently occur not only following lunch but at other times throughout the day. Thus the work of collecting recyclables on the dump is not kept separate from other dimensions of social life but rather is interspersed with moments devoted to leisure and social interaction.

In contrast to the catadores on the dump, those at the depositories cannot rely on found food for their lunches. Though a few food items might accidentally make it into the sacks sold to the depositories, nearly all the material sorted at the depositories consists of recyclables. Catadores who work at the depositories must therefore bring their lunches from home. During the morning, they leave their lunches with one of the few scattered street vendors in Jardim das Flores, who heat up their food for them in exchange for the catadores' exclusively purchasing their drinks. These catadores eat out of the containers that they bring from home and rarely share them with one another. The catadores who work in the same depository do tend to sit together when they eat, but they usually cannot lunch with those from other depositories due to the wide dispersal of the depositories throughout the neighborhood. Thus, unlike the situation on the dump, the catadores at the depositories do not share a central location for meals, relaxation, and social activities; as a consequence, their social network remains limited. Furthermore, the depositories do not provide adequate space for the catadores to sit together and eat, so most catadores choose to sit on the edge of the street outside the depository where they work. The din, dust, and discomfort on the street altogether discourage conversation and recreation during lunch. Finally, the work schedule at the depositories limits the catadores' lunchtime to a specified hour. The catadores at depositories do not have the liberty to decide at what time or for how long they will eat. This makes the meal part of the daily work routine rather than an activity set apart as a moment of diversion.

Like the catadores in the depositories, those who work in the cooperative have a set hour for lunch, during which all production ceases. Though the building at the cooperative includes a room with tables that can be used for meetings or for meals, few catadores choose to eat their lunches in this space, preferring instead to sit in the work site around the conveyor belt. When questioned about this choice, catadores explained that they did not like to lounge near the office or simply wished to keep to themselves. The majority of those who eat lunch at the cooperative eat either alone or with a couple of companions. Given the proximity of the cooperative to the informal settlement where many catadores live, many return home during the lunch hour. Such dispersal of the catadores during the only significant work break of the day inhibits group socializing and exchange.

Though catadores from the cooperative collect food from the garbage during their work, they do not eat this food for lunch as they have no way to prepare it. At times they will eat found fruit, a package of crackers, or other such items for a snack. Many eat nothing at all during lunch. I conducted most interviews during lunch when people could talk more easily. I always suggested that they eat first before we began the interview, but interviewees frequently responded that they did not intend to eat because they were observing a diet. One day, when I replied in a joking spirit that one woman could not possibly believe herself to be overweight, she and her friends laughed, "Oh, daughter, a compulsory diet!" (*uma dieta obrigada*). They did not eat lunch, because they had nothing to bring from home. This contrasts sharply with the practices of the catadores who work in the office of the cooperative. They always have a thermos of coffee on hand and frequently the president buys pastries to share with others in the office. Other catadores who enter the office for whatever reasons never receive an offering of coffee or bread. Those who work in the office also differ from the other catadores in that they eat an hour later. This enables them to keep the office open during the lunch hour at the cooperative in case catadores have questions or need an issue resolved. However, this means that the catadores in the office never eat with the catadores on the production line.

Food practices in Jardim das Flores both reflect and create social bonds or divisions within the three categories of catadores described above. First, whether or not catadores at a work site share food together depends at least in part on the presence or absence of relations in production conducive to commensality. This, in turn, depends on the particular labor conditions of the site. For example, catadores at the cooperative do not eat together partly as a result of the divisions and power inequalities between the catadores in the office and the catadores on the production line. The system of production further disconnects the catadores on the line, as it requires that each catador remain in a fixed place at the conveyor belt, thus prohibiting much joking, banter, gossiping, or other forms of interaction beyond two or three catadores working in close proximity. The tendency of catadores at the cooperative to split up during the lunch hour, returning to their respective homes or scattering to different spots around the conveyor belts (rather than congregating in the kitchen), indicates a generalized lack of social cohesion at the site. Their lunchtime practices manifest and re-create the social relations produced by the conditions and structure of the cooperative.

The opportunity to prepare food together and to engage in communal recreational activities during flexible lunch breaks, enabled by the particular work conditions on the dump, strengthens existing social bonds and group identity. Through the practices of eating meals intimately tied to their common work, passing around found plastic containers filled with soup, and chatting and joking during mealtimes, catadores on the dump come to know one another well. In particular, they come to know one another as fellow catadores. Likewise, the lack of such practices among catadores at the cooperative or at the depositories contributes to a continuation of the social fragmentation found in these two kinds of work sites. Little space exists within the structural constraints of their work sites for these catadores to engage in social activities that might facilitate group solidarity.

COOPERATIVE PRACTICES

The distinct work situations of catadores in Jardim das Flores and the varied types of social relations created in each context provide excellent cases for a comparative analysis of the emergence of cooperative practices in the informal economy. Catadores who work on the dump have long engaged in periodic collective actions. Their history of collective struggle began with the very first catadores who came to Jardim das Flores. Many of those who initiated work in Jardim das Flores came from other dumps in Rio de Janeiro that had closed. When they arrived in Jardim das Flores, "following the garbage," the company that owned and operated the dump prohibited them from entering. Each time that a catador entered, a guard evicted the person, sometimes beating the catador in the process. Eventually, the catadores formed a group to "invade" the dump together. Dona Marciana, who participated in this struggle and continues to work on the dump today, recounted this history:

> How was it in the past? Well, how to tell it? There was unity. You had to struggle for every *xepeiro* [scavenger]. We would say, "Let's go have a meeting. Let's go fight (*lutar*)." Everyone used to have to go through the swamp and we'd say, "Let's all go up [to the dump] together. Many people went together as a group. United. There were many women, many men, many older women. Many older women like my mother, like Dona Maria, like others. Really many people. We fought. It was not easy, it wasn't. . . . It was rough.

Catadores in Jardim das Flores thus gained the right to work on the dump through united struggle. In recent years, catadores have begun to organize again in order to defend their ability to work as informal recyclers. In 2004, catadores in Jardim das Flores formed an association in response to news that the dump would close in 2005[4] and be replaced by a planned sanitary landfill where it would be impossible to access deposited waste materials for collection. For the catadores, this news signified the imminent end to their work. They created the association with the aim of applying political pressure on the city governments of Rio de Janeiro and Duque de Caxias to help develop alternative means by which catadores could continue their work under the same conditions: as self-employed, autonomous workers. One alternative, for example, consisted of the implementation of a program of *coleta seletiva* in which the local government would establish recycling centers to be organized and operated independently by catadores. Since its initiation, the association has also taken up wider concerns, including the recognition of the work of catadores as a dignified profession and the betterment of infrastructure in the growing informal settlement of Jardim das Flores where most catadores live.

All three categories of catadores face similar problems related to their work and daily life in Jardim das Flores. They all will lose their source of income upon closure of the dump; they all endure the informal settlement's lack of infrastructure and poor living conditions; and they all suffer the stigmatization of their work. These three issues have comprised the majority of the association's battles, yet the catadores who work on the dump remain the only ones who have initiated or joined the association. In contrast, over one thousand catadores from the dump have signed on as members of the association.

I note three major factors that have influenced the capacity of each category of catadores to organize collectively: (1) the structural conditions of the work situation; (2) the scope of social activities at the work site; and (3) social solidarity and group formation. Based on previous descriptions of the structural and social characteristics of each category of catadores, I compare views and practices in each that are relevant to cooperation and ultimately suggest ways in which certain types of economic activity may lead to forms of collective action.

The flexibility in the work schedule of catadores on the dump enables them to participate in assemblies, attend meetings with politicians or nongovernmental organizations (NGOs), and assist with the daily work of organizing, whether that be distributing leaflets, visiting sick catadores in the hospital, or tracking down necessary documents or funds. Not only are catadores on the dump able to take a day off without fear of losing their employment as a result, they are also able to mitigate the consequences of losing a day of work (and therefore a day of pay) by working more hours the day before or the day after. This is not the case for catadores who work in a situation of semiemployment in the depositories. Cesar, who has worked in a depository for three years, explained that he knows about the association but has not found the opportunity to participate in its activities:

> I did not end up participating in anything, no. Because you have to work the whole week and during the week we can't miss work because they [the depository owners] discount our pay. Understand? I think, I think that there are more catadores from the dump, because they determine their own hours, understand? Up there [on the dump] they can say, "I'll go." They decide to go, understand? The movement belongs more to them than it does to the people in the depositories.

Those who work in the cooperative face similar difficulties. They are free to take any day off that they wish, but they are not compensated for the lost hours of work. Since the cooperative operates only mornings and afternoons Monday through Friday, and Saturday mornings, workers in the cooperative lack the possibility of working longer hours or extra days. Any loss of time, no matter how limited, becomes a sacrifice for those in the cooperative. The autonomy of the catadores on the dump makes it possible for them to extend their labor to include the work of political organizing in ways that are not available to the catadores who work in the depositories or at the cooperative.

The social activities that take place on the dump further facilitate efforts on the part of catadores to mobilize. Meetings and discussions concerning the association often occur during mealtimes or during moments of relaxation in the midst of work on the dump. Furthermore, many catadores have joined the association through social networks created through work on the dump. One catador, Marcos, thus described the process through which he became a member of the association:

> I entered in this struggle through Zezinho. Zezinho kept calling me all the time to participate, to go to meetings. I said no, that I didn't want to. But there on the dump in Jardim das Flores we would stop [work], we would converse, talk. He wanted to take me to meet other catadores in other states, to see how the organization is there, how other catadores were organized. I started listening and then I understood that we too have to organize in Jardim das Flores.

After joining the association, Marcos became active in mobilizing other catadores and began to help write the association's newsletter, *O Mensajeiro da Verdade*, which is both produced and distributed on the dump. Early one morning, I noticed one of the writers dictating his article to another catador who was not involved in this project but nonetheless helped him write the Portuguese. Because the dump becomes not only a space of work but also a space of organizing, the association is able to include a wide participation of catadores in the movement's activities as well as to integrate political actions into the everyday practices on the dump.

In contrast, the catadores in the depositories and at the cooperative do not share such a common space for political organizing. Social interaction among the catadores in depositories usually occurs only within a single depository. With the exception of the lunch hour, they do not have the opportunity to leave the depository and intermingle with other catadores. The scattered locations of over fifty depositories throughout the neighborhood impede spontaneous conversations and exchanges that have become fundamental to the formation of the association on the dump. Likewise, though the catadores at the cooperative share a common space for work, they do not share this same space for social life. During lunch they segregate into small groups or even eat alone. No other social activities bring them together or facilitate open and widespread interaction. Few catadores in the depositories and the cooperative know much about the ideas, objectives, and actions of the association despite the association's attempt to leaflet and announce meetings at the depositories and the cooperative. When interviewed about their familiarity with the Association or Movement of Catadores, these catadores all eventually responded that they had heard about it, often mentioning the names of the leaders or an invitation that they had received to attend a meeting. Beyond admitting that they knew about the association, none spoke about the specific efforts of the association or their opinions concerning them. In contrast to catadores on the dump, who often raised the subject of the association in interviews before I even broached the topic, offering their own opinions about its efforts, those in the depositories and cooperative hardly ventured a word. The following is an example of such an interview with Roberto, who works in the cooperative:

> *Author: Are you familiar with the association?*
> Roberto: No.
> *A: The Association of Catadores?*
> R. No, I don't know.
> *A: The Movement of Catadores?*
> R: Eh?
> *A: The movement that Zezinho leads?*
> R: Ah, the movement, this business of all those meetings?
> *A: Yes, that. Have you ever participated?*
> R: No, never. I have never participated. One time they called me to go to a meeting in the city, downtown, but I didn't go.

The lack of social interaction in the depositories and at the cooperative prevents the necessary process of *concientização* (consciousness-raising) from developing. These catadores may have heard of the association but know little about it and, as we will see, certainly do not feel a part of its larger group effort.

Finally, and perhaps most importantly, social relations on the dump helped create a group identity well before the association ever came into existence. Catadores on the dump share a common history; even those who are new to the dump (*novatos*) quickly became familiar with the older leaders and their stories. Experienced catadores also commonly train *novatos* to distinguish types of recyclable materials, to negotiate the seemingly chaotic system of collection, and to avoid common dangers. Through this experience, the *novatos* learn the histories, relationships, and personalities on the dump. They also learn slang that has developed on the dump and that sets catadores apart from others. In addition to the term *podrão* to refer to found food, catadores have created other words and phrases such as *Mãe Rampa* ("Mother Slope," referring to the dump), *mulher-homem*, which signifies a woman on the dump who can lift as much material as a man, and *ataque rápido*, the name given to young catadores who lounge for most of the day on the dump and then in the late afternoon collect quickly to make up for lost time. Because of a sense of community created through such shared practices and discourse, the association did not have to work to form a group identity in order to mobilize the catadores on the dump. The leaders of the association had only to appropriate this group identity for the purposes of organized action.

Neither the catadores in the depositories nor those in the cooperative associate themselves with the group of catadores on the dump. Due to the dispersal of depository catadores throughout the neighborhood and due to the internal divisions present in the cooperative, they also have not developed their own sense of community apart from that of the catadores on the dump. When questioned, the depository and cooperative catadores explicitly dissociated themselves from the catadores on the dump or even from an identity as catadores. Joseli, who worked in a depository, responded to the question, "Do you see yourself as a catadora?" with the following: "Well, we are all catadores, but we who work in the depositories call ourselves *deposistas*. If someone asks, 'Do you work on the dump?' I say, 'No, I work in the depository.'"

Catadores in the cooperative express stronger sentiments concerning the identity of the catador and group unity. Many of them believe that catadores who work in the office are corrupt and steal money from the cooperative. They speak frequently about their disillusionment with their earnings (which have dropped by 50 percent since the beginning of the cooperative in 1996) and with the treatment toward them by those who run the production line, designate tasks, or administrate. This sentiment had led to general distrust of other catadores, especially those attempting to organize, which they see as similar to the organizing of the cooperative. When I asked Franciele, who works in the cooperative, if she thought that the work of the association could better the situation of the catadores, she replied with a bitter tone in her voice: "It never gets better. No. It continues the same. It never gets better. Look at the cooperative. It did not amount to anything." Because the advocacy of catadores as a *categoria* (a class of work) has played a central role in the political organizing of the association, group segregation and discord in the depositories and cooperative have prevented the growth and dissemination of a sense of group solidarity in the struggle for a common cause.

CONCLUSION

The casualization of employment and the rise in urban informal labor in recent decades have generated concerns over the potential of workers in the informal economy to organize collectively for social and political gains. The experiences of the various catadores in Jardim das Flores offer possible insights into this issue. First, the significant differences among catadores on the dump, at the cooperative, and in the depositories point to the need to better understand the diversity of workers and work conditions that fall under the broad category of informal employment. All the catadores in Jardim das Flores engaged in similar activities and worked outside formal waged employment, yet the conditions in which they performed their work shaped the social relations at their work sites and in turn, influenced their ability to organize collectively.

Though drawing on a very different context—that of the historical transformations in the configuration of *ayni* in Andean communities—Matthew Bird similarly argues in this volume that practices of reciprocity are shaped by a community's organization of production. This insight not only enables us to distinguish different qualities and meanings of what may at first seem to be the same practice of reciprocity, as Bird demonstrates in his analysis of changes in the practice of *ayni* that accompanied the shift from community subsistence production to commodity production in the markets of Lima. It also allows us to consider why and how cooperative practices emerge at all. This certainly has implications for class politics today. The characteristics of the work conditions of the catadores on the dump that facilitated their ability to organize—their autonomy, lack of a boss, and ability to determine their own work schedules and pace—set them apart from those who work in formal wage labor. It is thus possible that certain conditions in the way production can be organized in the informal economy may at times lead to more, rather than less, political potential in comparison to that of the formal working class.

Furthermore, the case of the catadores in Jardim das Flores illustrates that cooperation can coexist with individualism, competition, and hierarchy. The catadores on the dump, who have participated the most in collective action, continue to collect their own materials individually. They never expressed a desire to develop work groups or begin a cooperative or similar organization in which their income would be administered and distributed collectively—whether equitably among members or, more commonly, according to each member's contribution to production. Yet at certain moments of their workday, such as mealtimes, and at certain historic moments, such as the recent news of the closure of the dump, they have worked together for a common cause. The absence of cooperative practices in a group thus does not signify the lack of a potential for cooperation. The possible periodicity of collective action suggests the need for not only ethnographic but also historical perspectives on this issue.

Finally, the catadores on the dump organized the association with the primary aim of defending their work. The defense of their work, as demonstrated by their proposed alternatives to working on the dump (which maintain their situation of self-employment), includes the defense of their control over their own work. Catadores in Brazil are not the only informal recyclers to value their autonomy and struggle for it. As I discovered during exploratory research in South Africa, a group of informal recyclers, called "reclaimers," fought for their continued access to the dump following a change in ownership of the dump that led to an agreement with a recycling company that the company would have total control over the collection of recyclables. This company offered the reclaimers formal employment, but the reclaimers rejected this offer, protested each day outside the dump, and eventually won a legal case that permitted them to return to the dump and collect independently. As many reclaimers explained in recounting this history, they did not want to work for anyone but themselves.

Asef Bayat has similarly noted that the goal of self-employed workers who mobilize is that of "attaining autonomy, both cultural and political, from the regulations, institutions, and discipline imposed by the state and by modern institutions" (2004:93). This anti-institutionalization on the part of many who work in the informal economy may appear at times like anticooperation. A recent study of informal recyclers (*cartoneros*) in Buenos Aires (Escliar et al. 2007), for example, describes how few cartoneros join cooperatives despite efforts on the part of members of existing cooperatives as well as NGOs to explain the benefits of collecting recyclables in association rather than individually. However, the authors argues that this desire to work independently rather than in a cooperative stems not so much from a spirit of individualism as it does from a spirit of resistance to institutional responsibilities, obligations, discipline, and regular schedules (46–47).

The actions of the Association of Catadores in Jardim das Flores have certainly demonstrated the potential for cooperation and collective action among workers in situations of informal employment. Their history and their experience of attempting to organize other catadores, however, draw attention to the need for greater inquiry into the work conditions, social relations, and broader political contexts that make cooperative practices possible.

NOTES

1. I also use pseudonyms for names of catadores.
2. A *carteira assinada* is a legal document in Brazil that an employer signs when hiring a worker, giving the worker the right to a salary of at least minimum wage, paid vacation days, an extra monthly salary per year, a pension, and maternity leave.
3. At the time of research, one U.S. dollar equaled roughly two Brazilian reals.
4. Since 2005, the closure of the dump has been continuously postponed.

REFERENCES

Bayat, Asef

2004 Globalization and the Politics of the Informals in the Global South. In *Urban Informality: Transnational Perspectives from the Middle East, Latin America, and South Asia*, ed. Ananya Roy and Nezar AlSayyad, 79–104. Lanham, MD: Lexington Books.

Carbonella, August, and Sharryn Kasmir

2006 Rethinking the Anthropology of Social Class. *Anthropology News* 47 (8):8–9.

Codere, Helen

1957 Kwakiutl Society: Rank without Class. *American Anthropologist* 59 (3): 473–486.

Collins, Jane

2002 Deterritorialization and Workplace Culture. *American Ethnologist* 29 (1): 151–171.

Comaroff, Jean, and John L. Comaroff

2001 Millennial Capitalism: First Thoughts on a Second Coming. In *Millennial Capitalism and the Culture of Neoliberalism*, ed. Jean Comaroff and John L. Comaroff, 1–56. Durham, NC: Duke University Press.

Datta, Rekha

2003. From Development to Empowerment: The Self-Employed Women's Association in India. *International Journal of Politics, Culture and Society* 16 (3): 351–368.

Davis, Mike
2004 Planet of Slums: Urban Involution and the Informal Proletariat. *New Left Review* 26:5–34.

Douglas, Mary
1996 [1966] *Purity and Danger: An Analysis of the Concepts of Pollution and Taboo*. London: Routledge.

Escliar, Valeria, with Valeria Matuberría Lazarini, Maria Florencia Rodríguez, and Paula Rodríguez
2007 *Cartoneros: Una práctica individual o asociativa?: Ciudad de Buenos Aires, año 2004–2005*. Buenos Aires: Centro Cultural de la Cooperación Floreal Gorini.

Ford, Michele
2004 Organizing the Unorganizable: Unions, NGOs, and Indonesian Migrant Labour. *International Migration* 42 (5): 99–119.

Gallin, Dan
2001 Propositions on Trade Unions and Informal Employment in Times of Globalisation. *Antipode* 33 (3): 531–549.

Hart, Keith
1988 Kinship, Contract and Trust: The Economic Organization of Migrants in an African City Slum. In *Trust: Making and Breaking Cooperative Arrangements*, ed. Diego Gambetta, 176–193. Oxford: Basil Blackwell.
1973 Informal Income Opportunities and Urban Employment in Ghana. *Journal of Modern African Studies* 11 (1): 61–89.

Itzigsohn, José
2006 Neoliberalism, Markets, and Informal Grassroots Economics. In *Out of the Shadows: Political Action and the Informal Economy in Latin America*, ed. Patricia Fernández-Kelly and Jon Schefner, 81–96. University Park: Pennsylvania State University Press.

Medina, Martin
2007 *The World's Scavengers: Salvaging for Sustainable Consumption and Production*. Lanham, MD: AltaMira.

Mintz, Sidney
1985 *Sweetness and Power: The Place of Sugar in Modern History*. New York: Penguin.

Munn, Nancy D.
1986 *The Fame of Gawa: A Symbolic System of Value Transformation in a Massim (Papua New Guinea) Society*. Cambridge: Cambridge University Press.

Nordstrom, Carolyn
2007 *Global Outlaws: Crime, Money and Power in the Contemporary World*. Berkeley: University of California Press.

Pahl, R. E.
1984 *Divisions of Labour*. Oxford: Basil Blackwell.

Portes, Alejandro
1994 When More Can Be Less: Labor Standards, Development, and the Informal Economy. In *Contrapunto: The Informal Sector Debate in Latin America*, ed. Cathy A. Rakowski, 113–129. Albany: State University of New York Press.

Seligmann, Linda J.
1989 To Be in Between: The *Cholas* as Market Women. *Comparative Studies in Society and History* 31 (4): 694–721.

Weismantel, Mary
2001 *Cholas and Pishtacos: Stories of Race and Sex in the Andes*. Chicago: University of Chicago Press.

9

Is It Possible to Overcome the "Tragedy of *Ubuntu*"?

The Journey of a Black Women's Economic Empowerment Group in South Africa

Katrina T. Greene, Biola University

This chapter examines how members of a Black[1] Women's Economic Empowerment (BWEE) group in Cape Town, South Africa, are attempting to negotiate and overcome the tensions that often arise from their participation in such groups in a post-apartheid and neoliberal-oriented South Africa. These groups seek to achieve financial enrichment in an economic climate that often requires depersonalized operation and management practices that focus on profit making. Such practices, while common in the context of business settings, often conflict with a long-ingrained cultural and social framework held by group members that mandates expressions of charitableness, sensitivity, and consideration among group members. These characteristics are a part of the cultural logic of *Ubuntu*, an ethos that is often translated as humanity in South Africa. It is one of the overarching logical frameworks for a belief and value system that governs the way that individuals live in relation to one another and ascribe behavior to various beliefs within the social system. The cultural logic of *Ubuntu* (humanness) defines what it means for a person or group of people to express their humanity to others.

Robert Thornton (2005), in his discussion of South African political culture and structures, argues that the exploitation of *Ubuntu* may lead to the "escape" of members of a social group from such a social context. He compares the "tragedy of *Ubuntu*" with the "tragedy of the commons" that is discussed in the seminal work of Garrett Hardin (1968). Hardin (1968) describes how unrestrained users of a common-pool resource eventually overexhaust that resource due to their desire to increase their individual short-term benefit or gain although it would be in the long-term interest of all users to exercise restraint.[2] However, Thornton (2005:29) suggests that unlike the commons, with *Ubuntu* there is an "escape," as people may choose to exit the group or social context that is putting pressure on their resources or hampering their individual enrichment or goals. The costs of that freedom or autonomy from a social group and the social controls that such groups maintain may include the loss of community security and identity (Thornton 2005:29). Some members of BWEE groups are seeking to overcome the "tragedy of *Ubuntu*" within the context of their commitment to advancing economically as a group. These individuals are attempting to maintain the solidarity group model for their investment endeavors instead of "escaping" to engage in individual investment opportunities for their individual economic advancement. They have sought to create ways to meet the challenges of *Ubuntu*.

In this chapter, I first focus on the goals and status of Black Economic Empowerment (BEE) as an objective of the South African government along with the government's promotion of neoliberal economic policies. Then, I discuss the cultural logic of *Ubuntu* and its continued meaning and use in the social context of South Africa. Next, I briefly examine my history with members of BWEE groups in South Africa before providing two case studies of BWEE groups. One BWEE group collapsed under the strain of *Ubuntu* and other management concerns. The second BWEE group formed out of the ashes of the first group. In conclusion, I will seek to understand the tensions experienced within some BWEE groups in relationship to the larger socioeconomic and political economic tensions generated by the neoliberal economic policies and philosophy promoted by the South African government.

SOUTH AFRICA AND BLACK ECONOMIC EMPOWERMENT

BWEE groups were created by their members in response to opportunities to participate in BEE opportunities in the post-apartheid period. These opportunities were encouraged by the South African government, which adopted the Reconstruction and Development Program after the first racially democratic elections of 1994. One of the objectives of the program was to employ black economic empowerment to deracialize business ownership and control—businesses were disproportionately owned and controlled by white South Africans at the end of apartheid (Department of Trade and Industry 2004:10). The goal of BEE was to redress the "existence of two nations within South Africa, one white and the other black, one prosperous and the other poor" (Williams 2005:478). In 1996, the Reconstruction and Development Program was replaced by the Growth, Employment and Redistribution Program, which signified the South African government's commitment to neoliberal economic policies. Such policies promoted liberal trade, less-regulated exchange, and other free-market initiatives (Williams 2005:478). They also focused on attacking poverty and bolstering the South African economy through market-led growth, privatization, and tax cuts (Cheru 2001:516).

The South African government encouraged BEE through its offer of government procurement contracts to enterprises that demonstrated that they were contributing to redressing the issues of inequality and disempowerment in South Africa by making efforts to diversify their ownership. Some businesses decided to offer stocks to disadvantaged groups as a way to begin healing the wounds left by apartheid. Investment opportunities were made available in multiple ways to most black investors, especially those who could not afford to invest in various South African companies. Special-purpose vehicles, for example, were created to provide blacks with financing to invest in companies through a process of banking institutions loaning money to blacks to purchase corporate stock at a discounted rate. In turn, investors would forfeit their dividends over a period of years in order to repay the loan with the hope that the stock price would increase. If the stock price did not increase, the stocks would revert to the financiers.

Other BEE initiatives by companies provided discounted public shares to historically disadvantaged citizens with the option that such investors could pay for their shares over a multiyear period through trust arrangements by investing an initial small down payment of about 10 percent of the stock price and then making subscription payments on the remaining balance at agreed-on intervals (see Greene 2002:159–160). In 1998, the Johannesburg Stock Exchange crashed, and many stocks lost their value; this hurt BEE investments. Many of these BEE "investments" often created much debt for investors and resulted in an increase of shareholders on company rolls, but not in changes in management (Harris 1999:1–2; Turner 1999:2).

Critics of BEE, as it was practiced in the mid-1990s and early 2000s, have called it "narrow-based empowerment" due to the fact that it did not lead to a transformation of ownership or management patterns that had excluded and disadvantaged the majority of South Africans during the apartheid period. Instead, they argue that "narrow-based empowerment" had resulted in the economic aggrandizement of a small black elite and was not transformative (Sutcliffe 2006). In 2004, in light of such a reality, the South African government passed Broad-based Black Economic Empowerment legislation. Such legislation recognized the fact that there continued to exist in the South African economy inequalities that were not being addressed by BEE practices. The legislation also recognized that more clarity and structure with regard to BEE practices were needed to promote poverty eradication. It was a government intervention to "address the systematic exclusion of the majority of South Africans from full participation in the economy." (Department of Trade and Industry 2004:6).

Broad-based Black Economic Empowerment not only seeks to redress past economic inequalities, it also is seen by the South African government as "a tool to broaden the country's economic base and accelerate growth, job creation, and poverty eradication" (Department of Trade and Industry 2004:11). The government expanded BEE to focus on encouraging management and skills training opportunities that would enable blacks to access control and decision-making structures within enterprises in addition to ownership equity. Codes of Good Practice were also established to evaluate South African firms on a scorecard to examine their qualifications for preferential government procurement opportunities based on their efforts to implement Broad-based Black Economic Empowerment (South African Government 2004). Among the objectives of this new structure for BEE were to increase black ownership and control of existing and new enterprises and to increase the number of new black enterprises, black-empowered enterprises, and black-engendered enterprises. It also sought to increase the representation of blacks in executive and senior management enterprises and to increase the levels of income of black people (Department Trade and Industry 2004:13). Various BWEE groups were seeking to carve out places for themselves in the new South Africa that had opened up opportunities for their investment in large-scale corporations as well as in various entrepreneurial projects.

UBUNTU

Ubuntu is an indigenous African term used to express an understanding that individuals exist in a social context of interdependence with other individuals in the group or community. It mandates that individuals within a community or group demonstrate such characteristics as charitableness, compassion, cooperation, solidarity, sharing, and trust toward one another (Marks 2000:182; Le Roux 2000:43; Barben 2006:6). Desmond Tutu described *Ubuntu* by stating:

> It [*Ubuntu*] has to do with what it means to be truly human. It refers to gentleness, to compassion, to hospitality, to openness to others, to vulnerability, to be available for others and to know that you are bound with them in the bundle of life, for a person is only a person through other persons. (Tutu 1994:121–122)

As this quotation implies, people must demonstrate mutual expressions of *Ubuntu* to acknowledge their humanness. During the apartheid period and post-apartheid period in South Africa, *Ubuntu* became a reference for many to explain a vision of a South Africa that was different from the apartheid

South Africa. The new South Africa would provide equitably for all of its people, especially those individuals who were systematically disadvantaged by apartheid (Greene 2002:30).

The concept of *Ubuntu* originally referred to an understanding of social action within feudal socioeconomic systems in which tribal chiefs, the clan, and extended family provided for the prosperity of and transmitted values to the larger social group (Venter 2004:150). Several informants during my research in some of the black townships of Cape Town informed me that the idea of *Ubuntu* had its roots in *ilima*, a communal rural farming activity in which neighbors in groups assist one another to till the soil and plant crops. Members assist in the success of everyone by working together toward a common cause in this communal activity (see Greene 2002:32). In these communities, mutual gain, cooperation, and interdependency are privileged while self-aggrandizement or gain and individual accomplishment and independence often become problematic. Individual rights and privileges are subsumed under one's duty to the social group, which make self-centeredness and individual greed forms of antisocial behavior and unacceptable acts (Venter 2004:151).

However, such a discussion is not to suggest that individuals do not engage in individual action in these contexts, but rather that such action may evoke various tensions within the social group and for the individual(s) seeking independence. These tensions may require nuanced explanations or responses by the offender, such as the public repudiation or denial of these actions if he or she wishes to remain within the group. Yet, "escape" may be the choice for those who achieve or acquire resources or status or who desire to do so in a less constricting context. Thornton (2005:30) argues that those who transgress the social rules by being uncharitable or uncaring to the needs of others often must "escape." In doing so, these "escapees" take with them the skills, distinction, resources, and other qualities that forced them to leave; consequently, the community assets are diminished "just as much as the exhaustion of grass in the commonage rangeland" (Thornton 2005:30). In the economic context of South Africa and among BWEE groups, tensions exist between a cultural logic that promotes modes of social action based on community well-being (*Ubuntu*) and a neoliberal economic logic that promotes Western economic practices. Such economic practices often are not community based, but rather focused on individual action and decision making. However, some of the members of a BWEE group that I examined during my research did not see "escape" from the group dynamic as their only solution to the tensions that they experienced. They were seeking ways to negotiate the cultural logic of *Ubuntu* and their desire to be successful as a group in their investment activities.

BLACK WOMEN'S ECONOMIC EMPOWERMENT GROUPS

As mentioned above, many BWEE groups formed in the early post-apartheid period to take advantage of the investment opportunities that resulted from the policies promoted by the post-apartheid government to deracialize South African business ownership. I conducted research in 1997, 1999–2000, and 2005 with multiple members of BWEE groups, including a group called *Siyalinga*,[3] which means "we are trying." After interviewing a member of *Siyalinga* in 1997, I continued and expanded my interaction with the group by including it as one of seven BWEE groups from which I interviewed members during my year of research in 1999–2000. That research focused on the cultural form of saving as a group among black South Africans and the flexible savings and credit strategies of what I called black women's long-term investment groups and small housing and savings and finance groups. Such strategies have their basis in the experience of groups along a continuum of savings and credit associations in South Africa, including more common rotating savings and credit associations and accumulating savings and credit associations in the black townships (see Greene 2002).

I returned to Cape Town in 2005 to conduct follow-up research with the same members of *Siyalinga*, as well as members of some of the other BWEE economic groups that I had previously researched, in order to examine and assess their status or progress after five years. My earlier research in 1999 and 2000 among BWEE groups had found that *Ubuntu* was a part of the flexible tendencies that positioned BWEE groups on a continuum of other cooperative economic financial groups. The groups were thriving and excited about their ability to participate in black economic initiatives. *Ubuntu* was being demonstrated in multiple ways, such as financial assistance to bereaved members within the BWEE groups. *Ubuntu* seemed to act as a bonding force among members of the group (see Greene 2002). However, my follow-up research in 2005 revealed a different reality. Many BWEE members were frustrated with the inability of BEE initiatives to redress inequality in South Africa. They also were frustrated with the role of *Ubuntu* in their groups, which had often become problematic over time. One group that was severely strained and had even collapsed was the group *Siyalinga*. The group had disbanded in 2003.

In 2005, I reinterviewed three members of *Siyalinga* whom I had interviewed in 1999 and 2000 during my earlier research. They included Ketiwe, Zanele, and Lindiwe. Ketiwe was 53 and a single mother of four children who ranged in age from 17 to 25 years of age. She worked at a small nongovernmental organization (NGO) in one of the black townships. Another interviewee, Zanele, who had been the unofficial director of *Siyalinga*, was also unmarried and the mother of a 23-year-old son. She was the director of a women's empowerment training NGO that reached out to women in the townships. The final interviewee, Lindiwe, was 54, divorced, and the mother of three children aged 18 to 25. Lindiwe was a lawyer by training but worked as an independent consultant to NGOs and other organizations on empowerment and skills-development initiatives for women. In fact, none of the members of *Siyalinga* were married, and this fact may have made it less difficult for the women to participate in the investment groups, as they each had power over their own money and did not need to consult with a husband about the use of their funds. The members of most BWEE groups, including *Siyalinga*, were middle-class professional black women who could afford to contribute to long-term investments. All the members of *Siyalinga* came from a social justice or community development professional work background and had met one another through various development networks.

SIYALINGA: A CASE STUDY

Siyalinga was formed in 1996 by a group of fourteen women who were interested in participating in BEE activities. All the members lived in Guguletu and Langa, which are two black townships outside Cape Town, or in the Southern Suburbs, which were all-white residential areas during apartheid. Each member knew the other members through personal friendship or through a tie to one or more members who would vouch for her trustworthiness to other members who may not have known her as well. Each member was also required to be gainfully employed and to contribute a R5,000[4] joining fee to create capital for the group to invest. Members of the group were seeking not to become rich, but to have a better life for themselves and their families through their participation in BEE activities. Ketiwe, for example, stated that she had joined *Siyalinga* because she desired to have money and a more comfortable life, which included being able to pay her children's school fees without difficulty, making home improvements, and enjoying life (Greene 2002:200–201).

Each month, the members of *Siyalinga* saved similarly to many rotating savings and credit associations and accumulating savings and credit associations, but unlike these groups, they did not redistribute the funds to themselves in turn or at the end of the year. Instead, they paid on their subscriptions to various companies from which the group had purchased stock or saved their joint funds for future investment opportunities that might arise (Greene 2002:191). Over time, the group invested with several BEE holding corporations that offered stocks to such groups at a discounted rate; among these corporations were the Women's Investment Portfolio Holdings Limited (Wiphold), Phuthuma Futhi, and Johnnic.

Upon my return to Cape Town in the summer of 2005, I hoped to discover if any of the BWEE groups had received any profits as well as how they had used them. However, I uncovered some puzzling information. In an interview at this time, Ketiwe stated:

> *Siyalinga* died. We tried to be investment businesswomen, and we were friends, good friends. And we tried to set up something that was really going to make us have extra financial resources. But we were not businesswomen. We were just good friends who wanted to do something to change or lives, but we were not businesswomen.

Ketiwe's statement was revealing: it signaled that she and other members of the group were aware that they had not operated the group with "good business" ethics that would have premised profit making over the ethics that bonded them together in friendship. In 2003, the group had disbanded by mutual agreement and sold most of their investment stocks and split the money evenly among all the members. The stocks that they were unable to sell for various reasons had been maintained and the group was continuing to receive dividends on those shares into the group bank account. The goal was to sell all of *Siyalinga*'s shares by the end of 2005 and then to provide final disbursement payments to members. Ketiwe's comment and other information gathered from her interview and my interviews with Lindiwe and Zanele indicated two major reasons for the collapse of *Siyalinga*. One reason relates directly to the "tragedy of *Ubuntu*" and various activities that *Siyalinga* members had engaged in earlier in their group's existence, then had ceased due to problems that arose from such activities, but ultimately returned to later in the group's life. The other reason for collapse relates to issues of management and risk taking within the group.

The first reason for *Siyalinga*'s demise surrounded the group's desire to provide financial resources to members who were experiencing various financial or family emergencies, which I had documented in my earlier research (see Greene 2002). Such action led to two difficulties, which comprised the group's inability to focus all their available resources on their investment endeavors and the development of mistrust among the members of the group. Group members desired to assist one another as the cultural logic of *Ubuntu* mandated, but over time, this assistance placed a strain on the group. They were unable to distinguish themselves as a business-oriented group rather than a social club that engaged in investments. Members of the group were caught between two paradigms, one of which mandated that they help their fellow group members who were suffering financial difficulties. The other paradigm mandated that they respond to those individuals in a dispassionate way and mandate their leaving the group if they were unable to maintain their financial commitments to the group. Ketiwe provided several examples of how the group prioritized the economic well-being of members over the need for consistent financial commitments that would sustain the economic well-being of the group. She stated:

> We knew each other, like for example, one of the people had bereavement in her family. Her mother died. And so, we all knew that her mother died. So, why we would push her to contribute that month? We understood what her problem was. And so, that happened to all of us. I remember that I had a car accident and my car was a write-off. And people understood that I had a car accident and that I would contribute when I could. We know each other, and we trusted that later on I would get out of trouble and be able to contribute. But some did not.

Ketiwe suggests that members did not operate *Siyalinga* with business ethics that would have led to more investments and to profit making for the group despite members' individual struggles. The group's expression of the cultural logic of *Ubuntu* limited the pool of funds that *Siyalinga* would have to pay on their subscriptions for their purchased stock as well as their available funds for future investment.

However, in addition to allowing members to delay their contributions to the group's investment funds for various emergences, *Siyalinga* decided early in its existence to engage in credit/moneylending practices within the group. The primary goal of such activities was to help fellow members who were struggling to make their monthly or periodic subscriptions on purchased stocks and/or their monthly savings commitment to the group. According to Ketiwe, there was a desire to "leave no one behind"; this required helping fellow members who were experiencing financial difficulties. Members also believed that engaging in such lending practices would increase the money they had for investments as members would repay their loans to the group with interest. *Siyalinga* created a joint pool of funds to which members could contribute separately from the investment pool of funds, and members who needed funds could borrow from the separate joint pool. These loan funds were to act as capital for the needy member to start a small home business, reinvest in another project, or even lend to other individuals at various rates of interest for a higher return. Members were given two months to repay the loan with interest to the group (Greene 2002:191–192).

The credit/moneylending scheme failed as some of the individuals who borrowed the money from the group's joint pool of funds often used the money to pay off debts and not as capital for an income-generating project. These members were often unable to pay the funds back to the group and still continued to have difficulty meeting their monthly contribution commitment to the group. Such activity led to tension in the group and the expulsion of two members who did not return their borrowed funds. However, when I interviewed members of *Siyalinga* in 2000, the group had recovered from the credit/moneylending experience, and members were committed to not engaging in such activities in the future. They had yet to receive any dividends from any of their investments, but they were continuing to meet monthly, make their monthly contributions, and seek out new opportunities, including the possibility of investing in their own bed-and-breakfast establishment. Members of the group were also committed to using a portion of their future dividends to provide more opportunities for women by sponsoring various educational and social development projects in some of the black township communities of Cape Town.

In 2005, when I reinterviewed Ketiwe, she informed me that despite the group's negative experience with credit/moneylending activities, *Siyalinga* had returned to the credit/moneylending practices toward the end of the group's existence and that such activity had contributed to the final disbanding of the group. These practices again were conducted to express *Ubuntu* to members who were having financial difficulty as a way to support them. However, such activities that are based on trust again brought havoc to the group, as according to Ketiwe, the members did not have the proper recording procedures to account for all the money that was being borrowed and repaid. Frustrations from engagement in the credit/moneylending activities were also attributed partly to the fact that some group members knew other members only through other people: everyone knew multiple people within the group but not everyone knew everyone well. Members of *Siyalinga* began to desire to abandon the group due to poor accounting practices and the breakdown of trust among members, as they knew that they had lost money. Some members, including Zanele, the informal chairperson/director, thought that the group was not serious about investing to make profits and acted more as a social development organization than a business organization.

Ketiwe stated that two of *Siyalinga*'s members had become frustrated with the group and left *Siyalinga* prior to its disbandment to start their own businesses, which were flourishing. One had applied for and received a grant or loan from the Department of Trade and Industry, started a cleaning company, and been able to obtain a large cleaning contract from a business. Ketiwe informed me about what the members of *Siyalinga* thought about the two women. She stated:

> They were part of us, and they never told us when they were going to start their own businesses. And we kind of felt betrayed by them because we were in the same group, and so we expected that when they got something they would tell us, and we would move together. So, they didn't. They just moved off and did their own things.

Ketiwe and the members of the group whom I interviewed still felt uncomfortable with the fact that these two members had defected from the group to form their own initiatives and attain more individual success. Yet Thornton (2005:29) argues that success entails exit, as the style of a social group may support and nurture the person but also limit achievement. The two former members of *Siyalinga* had "escaped" the group dynamic in order to engage in their own investment activities.

The second major reason for the failure of *Siyalinga* revolved around members' lack of confidence in themselves and their ability to succeed as businesswomen. They were serious about their efforts but not serious enough to fully commit their resources to their endeavors. When members, for example, were made aware of business opportunities, such as a lubrication business that they could invest in as entrepreneurs if they borrowed money from a bank, the group refused to do so. They were afraid of jeopardizing their current and future economic status as well as that of their families by engaging in such activities. Many of these members were single mothers with grown children as well as grandchildren and other dependents.

In addition to not being willing to take risks with various investments, group members informed me that no members were willing to commit to managing the group in a way that would move the group to the next level. Such a move would entail engaging in various entrepreneurial activities and further investments. Members did not believe that they had the background or time to manage the group, and no member was willing to take an official leadership position, which might then mean drawing energy and time away from her current employment position. Zanele, who agreed reluctantly to unofficially direct *Siyalinga*, admitted that she had no previous experience with investments and that she was being overstretched by her commitments to *Siyalinga* and her responsibilities in managing her NGO. Although *Siyalinga* did seek investment help from various advisers, that support was brief and only periodic. No member of the group came forward to run the group or to distinguish herself as having more skills than the other members that would enable her to run the group even though there was a member of the group, Lindiwe, who had worked in the business sector and had a law degree.

After Ketiwe initially told me about the collapse of *Siyalinga*, I thought that would be the end of the members' efforts to work as a group toward participation in BEE initiatives. However, I discovered that this was not the case and that within a few months of the collapse and disbandment of *Siyalinga*, several group members reunited to form another BWEE group called *Masibambane*, or "let us hold hands together." The members of *Masibambane* were attempting to rectify the problems that occurred in *Siyalinga* as they moved forward to focus on new investment opportunities. These problems had contributed to the fragmentation and collapse of the group in a context where *Ubuntu* was exhausted. The new group wanted to engage in practices that would aid the group in becoming more economically prosperous.

MASIBAMBANE: A CASE STUDY

Masibambane was formed in late 2003 at the request of Zanele, who had been the informal leader of *Siyalinga*. She was made aware of a BEE investment deal involving a consortium of investors in a venture connected to Women in Oil and Energy in South Africa (WOESA). WOESA was an initiative started by a group in Johannesburg to get black women involved in the diversification of ownership patterns within the energy industry of South Africa. Zanele contacted various *Siyalinga* members to see if they would be interested in forming a group to invest in the initiative. However, Zanele did not contact all the former *Siyalinga* members: she was selective in which ones she contacted. In fact, Zanele contacted only five members, whom she called her core group of friends from the group. Each of the women had known each of the other members personally over extended periods of time even before the onset of *Siyalinga*. They agreed that one of the problems of *Siyalinga* had resulted from the fact that the group consisted of individuals who were not all close friends.

Therefore, the first way that *Masibambane* was attempting to the meet the challenge of *Ubuntu* was to form a more cohesive and bonded group comprised of close friends. They also assumed that such individuals would be less likely to leave the group for individual investment opportunities and jeopardize their close relationships with other group members. As a group, they started saving money for WOESA and attending workshops about renewable energy. However, for various reasons that Zanele did not understand, the WOESA initiative did not materialize, and *Masibambane* was unable to invest in it. However, *Masibambane* did invest with other consortium groups in an environmentally safe energy product called Energreen, the name of a liquid replacement for paraffin oil/kerosene.[5] Energreen was introduced to the members of *Masibambane* by one of the initiators of the WOESA initiative.

A second way that *Masibambane* attempted to overcome the obstacles of *Ubuntu* was by changing and refining the focus of the group. Members of *Masibambane* shifted their concerns from the moral imperative of seeing the group as primarily a place of support to the pragmatic issue of the need to focus on the economic well-being of the group with regard to their investment activities. Therefore, members agreed that the group dynamics and operation of *Masibambane* should prioritize a business focus over individual members' needs that might arise. Zanele had contacted former members of *Siyalinga* who were not only her friends but who she felt would be responsive to the idea of moving the group forward into new investments and more profit-making projects. The members were thought to share similar thinking about a vision for *Masibambane*, as they had learned from their experience with *Siyalinga* that they could not engage in activities, such as credit/moneylending within the group, that would divert them from their savings and investment goals. They knew that such activities, while demonstrations of *Ubuntu*, would take some of the focus away from engaging in investment activities that could enhance the group's ability to acquire more economic benefits.

This desire to be more business oriented demonstrates another difference between *Siyalinga* and *Masibambane*. Unlike with *Siyalinga*, in *Masimbane* there was an immediate move to find an official leader who would have time to find investments. Zanele stated that in order for *Masibambane* to work, she knew that it needed to have a strong leader to push the group and run the organization. Lindiwe, the only lawyer in the group, was selected as leader by all the members of *Masibambane*. She had recently transitioned out of her job and accepted the position as director of the group. Lindiwe and the other members of the group had high expectations for the group's future.

PROBLEMS AND FRUSTRATIONS WITH *MASIBAMBANE*

Masibambane, although different from *Siyalinga*, continued to experience problems, especially with regard to the cultural logic of *Ubuntu* and various management issues. As stated above, the group did not engage in credit/moneylending practices within the group. However, when saving money together on a monthly basis became a financial difficulty for some members, the group decided to "take a break" and to restart their group savings when people had more money. The group members decided to suspend their saving as a group as a way to help one another—this expression of *Ubuntu* was in contrast to pushing each member to contribute to the group's savings for investment opportunities. At the time of my interviews with members in 2005, it had been several months since the group members had saved as a group. Ketiwe admitted that *Masibambane* had been able to invest in Energreen only when each member produced by a set deadline her portion of the group's down payment on its stock shares. Energreen was the only investment since the birth of *Masibambane*. Several members were upset and frustrated with the lack of a joint pool of funds for the group and with the fact that some members were unable to save money for future investment opportunities that might arise.

Another problem for *Masibambane*, which several members felt, involved a lack of direction and focus as well as a continued lack of desire to engage in various risk-taking activities. For example, Lindiwe, the appointed leader, had advised the group to take out a loan to provide start-up capital in order to create an office for the organization, pay her a salary, and acquire funds for new investment and entrepreneurial projects. She believed that such efforts would provide them with legitimacy as a business organization and demonstrate their commitment to the success of *Masibambane*. However, there were grave misgivings within the group about such activities, including paying Lindiwe, who at the time was otherwise unemployed. Many of the members did not believe that they could afford to maintain a paid director and refused to take out any loans for such an activity or for future investments, as they were unsure of if and how they could repay such a loan. Lindiwe stated:

> I was running the group at that time. Every one of them was working outside [in another place], and I was the one trying to drive the investments. I could not take money out of my pocket for petrol [gasoline], copies, faxes, and other business needs. I said, let me out of here. I am looking for people who are serious about making investments.

Lindiwe resigned from her post in early 2005 and distanced herself from participation in the group, although she attempted to maintain some connections to members, especially Zanele.

At the time of our interview, Lindiwe was unsure if she wanted to return to participation in *Masibambane* although she had yet to officially leave the group; she was still frustrated by the lack of drive and members' inability to take risks within the group. After Lindiwe's resignation, Zanele returned to her unofficial leadership role, but she admitted that she no longer had any time to monitor the group's affairs due to changes at the NGO where she worked. The group continued to face even more problems: they agreed to be distributors for the Energreen product, but members had been unable or unwilling to market the product, which had been delivered from the manufacturer but the majority of which was still in storage.

Among members of *Masibambane*, there was also the constraint of needing to maintain within the group the *Ubuntu*-mandated solidarity and harmony, which caused difficulties. Zanele and Lindiwe both expressed frustration at the inability or unwillingness of members to attend scheduled meetings and to arrive punctually for them. *Masibambane* had ceased to meet monthly after deciding to suspend their regular group savings activities. However, Zanele still desired to have regularly scheduled meetings and strategy sessions with members to discuss the group's future. Her extreme frustration and disappointment showed when she informed me that she had recently told members that she was considering leaving the group due to the members' continued lack of motivation to be serious about the group's work. Zanele said that some members of *Masibambane* arrived thirty to forty-five minutes late for scheduled meetings. She had told members that no excuses for tardiness were acceptable because the group is about money. She wanted group members to understand that time is money—a Western concept that she believed was not adopted by *Siyalinga*, but which had to be adopted by *Masibambane* if they were to progress as businesswomen.

However, Zanele was also quick to admit that not all members had received her comments well. Many of them had "taken it personally" and been offended by her thoughts. Zanele noted that members accused her of making her comments because she had money stashed away and did not need the group as much as they did. She explained to them that this was untrue. However, such a need to deny such independence from the group highlights the difficulty and opposition that individuals face in confronting group members about their behavior. When an individual chastised other members about their nonbusinesslike practices, it threatened the members' relationship, which members often did not want to be broken. There was still a need to raise issues of importance to the sustainability and integrity of the economic practices of the group in a way that maintained group harmony and cohesion, that is, *Ubuntu*. Zanele admitted to me that she might have to leave the group if she did not see improvements in some members' behavior because various actions and mentalities were stifling the ability of the group to progress in their economic empowerment.

CONCLUSION

As Marshall discusses in the introduction of this volume, a conscious tension between cooperation and competition often exists among individuals and in various social and economic contexts. Individuals may choose at different times and for different reasons to engage in cooperative or competitive (individualist) behavior based on their conditions and perceived needs and interests. My research of BWEE groups in South Africa demonstrates that individuals may often negotiate this tension between cooperation and competition in an economic context in which the relevance and utility of long-held and established patterns of social practice that encourage cooperative behavior are being challenged. Such challenges derive from increasingly dominant economic norms that encourage competition and the primacy of individual gain over group gain, especially if engagement in the latter compromises or constrains engagement in the former.

Maluleke (1999:13) has argued that the ethos of *Ubuntu* is not often easily reconciled to capitalism and that it may even hinder economic advancement within the capitalist system, which is based on competition and the accumulation of wealth. The various struggles of *Siyalinga* and *Masibambane* demonstrate how *Ubuntu*, which is based on demonstrations of generosity, charitableness, consideration, and social sensitivity, may create a tension for the members of BWEE groups. In the case of *Siyalinga*, some members exited, or "escaped," the group for other investment opportunities that did not have the same social stresses that their participation in *Siyalinga* manifested. As Thornton (2005:29) has argued, demonstrations of *Ubuntu* may lead to the collapse of the resources that comprise *Ubuntu*. The common resource pool of humanness became strained when multiple users continually drew from it. The continual expressions of *Ubuntu* by *Siyalinga*, such as the group's financial assistance of individuals, constrained the group's activities, incited members to "escape,"and contributed to the ultimate collapse of the group, as some members did not view the group as committed to profit making.

However, the formation of *Masibambane* by several of the former members of *Siyalinga* demonstrated that not all these individuals had given up on cooperative efforts with other individuals. They attempted to overcome the challenges of *Ubuntu* by forming a smaller, more cohesive group, by not engaging in credit/moneylending activities, and by refocusing the group to profit-making and business practices that would lead to more economic viability for the group. This refocusing is connected to the members' understanding of the neoliberal principles that have helped to broaden and encourage BEE activities in South Africa. As the South African government has moved to more neoliberal polices, so did members of *Masibambane* see the need to adopt more pragmatic business practices. Yet *Masibambane*, like *Siyalinga*, still struggled with the tension between the cultural logic of *Ubuntu* and the efforts of some members to establish a "legitimate" business group. Prioritizing *Ubuntu* meant limiting group resources by not saving on a regular basis and assisting struggling members. The group also continued to refuse to acquire loans that would provide capital for various entrepreneurial activities. In addition, the group experienced difficulties with regard to leadership and managing confrontation within the group. Such a reality frustrated some of the more "business-minded" members of the *Masibambane*.

Yet it is necessary to understand how such struggles and tensions are reflective of the larger socioeconomic and political economic context of South Africa. The South African government, as discussed above, continues to struggle with redressing the economic inequalities created by decades of apartheid against the majority of South Africa's population. The ability of initiatives such as BEE, Broad-based Black Economic Empowerment, and a neoliberal economic agenda to change the economic reality for the majority of South African citizens—not only elite members of the majority population group—is still undetermined. Both the BWEE groups and the government are coping with the growing demands and nature of capitalism.

There is also an essential gender component to the actions of *Siyalinga* and *Masibambane*, both of which were comprised solely of women. Participation in such groups was linked to members' desire to expand their savings activities and focus on their economic futures. In one view, such participation is empowering in that it provides room for some women to address their strategic interests with regard to their subordinated position to men in South African society as well as their practical interests as single mothers with household and extended family commitments (see Moser 1989; Kabeer 1994:261). As black women, not only were they engaging in formerly white-dominated investment activities, they were also doing so as women. However, in another view, the cultural logic of *Ubuntu*, which often seems to manifest itself even within these groups, acts to disempower participants as mutual obligations hamper their economic advancement. There has not been much research on black male empowerment groups, but my earlier research of rotating savings and credit associations and accumulating savings and credit associations demonstrated that male groups often did not face the same strains as those of the women's groups due to women's roles as mothers and their needs for various social networks (see Greene 2002). Therefore, while *Ubuntu* is not a cultural logic limited to women, its expressions do have a gender dynamic that should not be overlooked.

As concerns the more than a decade of democracy in South Africa, members of various BWEE groups shared with me that the high unemployment and poverty rates along with numerous social issues in South Africa demonstrate that movement toward a more equitable country has been extremely slow. They, like many other South Africans, are finding themselves losing the passion for the new democracy because it is not providing most blacks with access to a better economic life that many thought such democracy would produce. Similarly, I believe that the members of *Masibambane* are losing their hope and passion for BEE initiatives and their ability to participate in the new economic opportunities of South Africa. They are having difficulty operating in a capitalist environment that states that those who can progress economically should do so even if that means leaving others behind. Thus, the tension between the cultural logic of *Ubuntu* and the demands of a neoliberal South Africa continue to exist. However, the members of the BWEE group *Masibambane* are trying as they hold hands together.

NOTES

1. *Black* is a term used by the South African government to identify indigenous Africans, Coloureds (mixed-raced people), and Indians (Department of Trade and Industry 2004:12). Each of these groups was systematically disadvantaged to white South Africans under the apartheid system. However, my specific research focus was on BWEE groups comprised of indigenous Africans. Indigenous Africans are those individuals who are members of the South African ethnic groups (i.e., Zulu, Xhosa, Swazi, etc.) referred to as *Africans* under the Population Registration Act of 1950 in South Africa.

2. Various scholars, including Lesorogol in this volume, have challenged the utility of the "tragedy of the commons" and its unequivocal link to overexploitation with regard to common resources, especially in the context of land management. Such scholars argue that group constraints often restrain individual exploitative behavior and can result in successful common resource management. However, Thornton's (2005) comparison of the "tragedy of the commons" to the "tragedy of *Ubuntu*" is useful in demonstrating the complexities that exist with regard to the exhaustion of the social good of *Ubuntu* and the resulting exit, or "escape," of individuals from particular social contexts in South Africa due to such a reality. My research demonstrated that group attempts to limit the use of *Ubuntu* were unsustainable and often seen as detrimental to group solidarity by some members of the investment groups that I examined.

3. All the names of BWEE groups and group members are pseudonyms.

4. In 1996, the average currency exchange rate was US$1 to R4.3.

5. Paraffin oil/kerosene is linked to many fires in the informal settlements due to its flammable properties.

REFERENCES

Barben, Tanya

2006 *Umntu Ngumntu Ngabantu* (A Person Is a Person Because of Other Persons): The Ethos of the Pre-colonial Xhosa-Speaking People as Presented in Fact and Young Adult Fiction. *Quarterly Bulletin of the National Library of South Africa* 60(1&2):4–19.

Cheru, Fantu

2001 Overcoming Apartheid's Legacy: The Ascendancy of Neoliberalism in South Africa's Anti-poverty Strategy. *Third World Quarterly* 22(4):505–527.

Department of Trade and Industry

2004 South Africa's Economic Transformation: A Strategy for Broad-Based Black Economic Empowerment. South African Government. Electronic document, http://www.thedti.gov.za/bee/bee.htm, accessed March 17, 2008.

Greene, Katrina
2002 The Cultural Form of Saving as a Group: Flexible Savings Group Strategies in the New South Africa. PhD dissertation, Department of Anthropology, American University.
Hardin, Garret
1968 The Tragedy of the Commons. *Science* 162:1243–1248.
Harris, Shaun
1999 Black Chip Shares Hold Promise. *Daily Mail & Guardian* 10 September.
Kabeer, Naila.
1994 *Reversed Realities: Gender Hierarchies in Development Thought.* Verso, London.
Le Roux, J.
2000 The Concept of *Ubuntu*: Africa's Most Important Contribution to Multicultural Education? *Multicultural Teaching* 18(2):43–46.
Maluleke, T.
1999 The Misuse of *Ubuntu. Challenge* 53:12–13.
Marks, Susan
2000 *Watching the Wind: Conflict Resolution during South Africa's Transition to Democracy*. United States Institute of Peace Press, Washington, DC.
Moser, Caroline
1989 Gender Planning in the Third World: Meeting Practical and Strategic Gender Needs. *World Development* 17(11):1799–1825.
South African Government
2004 Broad-Based Black Economic Empowerment Act, 2003. *Government Gazette* 9 January. [B 27B-2003].
Sutcliffe, Jim
2006 The Black Majority Fuels South Africa's Revolution. *Financial Times* 3 May:17.
Thornton, Robert
2005 Four Principles of South African Political Culture at the Local Level. *Anthropology Southern Africa* 28(1&2):22–30.
Turner, Chris
1999 Black Economic Empowerment in South Africa and the Implication for U.S Firms. *International Market Insight (IMI)*, 25 June.
Tutu, Desmond
1994 *The Rainbow of People of God.* Transworld Publishers Ltd. (Doubleday), London.
Venter, Elza
2004 The Notion of *Ubuntu* and Communalism in African Educational Discourse. *Studies in Philosophy and Education* 23:149–160.
Williams, Gavin
2005 Black Economic Empowerment in the South African Wine Industry. *Journal of Agrarian Change* 5(4):476–504.

10

The Normative Construction of U.S. Agricultural Cooperatives, 1900–2008

Julie A. Hogeland, U. S. Department of Agriculture

This chapter explores how normative creation, conflict, and evolution shaped agricultural cooperatives' reaction to the market and to agricultural industrialization from 1900 to 2008. Little is known within new institutional economics (NIE) about how norms emerge, evolve, and stabilize. This chapter addresses that gap by analyzing how farmers' needs and cooperative experience coalesced into norms that took on a life of their own, beyond the interpretations and expectations of the people who formalized them. Such norms became a springboard for farmers to situate themselves collectively within a period marked by significant alterations in values within the food system as a whole.

Coming to terms with market failure, that is, markets less than ideally competitive in prices, service, and producer proximity (or market access) was a continuing challenge for farmers throughout the 20th century. Economist and cooperative philosopher Edwin Nourse considered turn-of-the-century agriculture to be as subservient to industrialism as the colonies once had been to England (1922a). In 1909, commercial livestock slaughter by the four largest firms—the so-called Big Four, which consisted of Swift, Wilson, Armour, and Cudahy—was 36 percent (Hogeland 1992:197). In the first half of the century, legislative challenges and structural inefficiencies weakened the market power of collusive combinations of firms known as "trusts" in industries like meatpacking. By 1971, four-firm concentration ratios bottomed out at 21 percent; according to this measure, the meatpacking industry was highly competitive.

Nevertheless, yet another phase of industry concentration would emerge later in the century based on the cumulative effect of technologies developed over several decades. These included the development of hybrid sorghum supporting cattle feeding in semiarid regions; the decentralization of packing industry from cities to rural areas (allowing more efficient single-story plant layouts); and the replacement of rail with truck transportation. The creation of boxed beef by Iowa Beef Packers (later IBP) in 1968 enabled steer and heifer slaughter to become a standard or model of low-cost competition within the food industry (Hogeland 2005). IBP's norm of "being a low-cost provider" became the capstone of agricultural industrialization and a path to the "cheap food" endorsed by agricultural policies of that era.

Boxed beef saved grocers money by eliminating the need for high-wage unionized retail butchers. With lower-wage rural labor, steer or heifer carcasses could be cut or fabricated at the plant, vacuum-packaged, and boxed into retail case-ready cuts. By 1988, four-firm concentration ratios had reached 57 percent for cattle slaughter, 70 percent for steer and heifer slaughter, and 79 percent for boxed beef production (Hogeland 1992:117). As multiple phases of production such as cattle feeding, slaughter, and boxed beef production began to be vertically integrated or coordinated under single-firm ownership, farmers became preoccupied with maintaining control over industries that seemed to be slipping out of their hands. Reallocation of control galvanized farmers more than cost reduction because they routinely reduced their standard of living to enable the overall farm enterprise to remain competitive (Nourse 1922b; Barlett 1987). Farming's high-equity, low-variable cost structure constituted farmers as a food-producing class exploited to stabilize food production (Barkley 1976:877).

The foundation for 20th-century collective marketing was established early. In 1923, California attorney Aaron Sapiro formalized the concept of "orderly marketing" through cooperatives (1993). In 1922, Nourse first hinted at the concept of cooperatives as a "competitive yardstick"; by 1945, he had fully developed the philosophy (1992). While both norms sought to make exchange more equitable for farmers, they contested over how much processing and marketing cooperatives should do.

"Orderly marketing" was based on the formative experiences of California cooperatives known today as Sunkist, Sun-Maid Raisin Growers of California, and Sunsweet. This collective marketing approach urged producers to extend the marketing season beyond a postharvest market glut through crop preservation or processing. A longer marketing season would stabilize prices. And, if the cooperative could garner a market share amounting to almost all the crop produced, it would have a strong financial foundation for intensive market development like product branding and advertising. Sapiro's ideas influenced the formation of specialty crop cooperatives such as almond cooperative Blue Diamond and cranberry cooperative Ocean Spray, among many others. Sapiro's concepts were also adopted by dairy and meatpacking cooperatives producing branded processed products.

Crops like grain and beef could not be differentiated; however, they were commodities. One bushel of No. 2 yellow corn was interchangeable with another. Intermittent talk of branding beef vaporized at the thought of the expense of market development weighed against the uncertainty of consumer acceptance. Rather, the problem facing midwestern producers was market structures defined by spatial monopolies, that is; the tendency of rural communities to contain a single firm that dominated agricultural buying or selling.

In 1945, Nourse argued that prices paid or received by farmers would improve if farmers formed a cooperative to provide an "extra bid" that could offset the market power of the (local) monopolist. The price differential (i.e., improvement) could be measured pre- and postcooperative: this was the competitive yardstick effect. Midwestern producers established grain elevators, feed mills, farm supply stores, livestock marketing cooperatives, and processing plants for dairy products, meat, fruits, and vegetables according to this philosophy. The cooperative yardstick philosophy gave producers marketing alternatives. In short, American cooperatives could compensate for market exploitation by becoming farmers' patrons—protecting them and providing support through fair prices and missing services—in return for members' production and loyalty. This exchange represented a variation on the norm of reciprocity observed by James Scott (1976) in peasant societies.

As early as 1922, Nourse saw emerging within agriculture market power so centralized and hierarchical it seemed feudal (1922b). This vivid trope implied that a dark age of feudal control could appropriate income and status from traditionally independent and entrepreneurial family farmers. This metaphor seemed appropriate to observers watching industries of small, scattered, independent producers selling through open markets become the basis for highly concentrated, integrated, and industrialized agricultural subsectors (Reimund et al. 1981:3). Industrialization disproportionately affected the small producers who represented the majority within the first subsectors to industrialize—broilers, fed cattle, and processing vegetables. Initially, these growers produced as a sideline; production was a risk-management strategy of diversifying the farm enterprise. Products were sold in local markets; producers could enter or exit production easily. Within 20 years (e.g., 1954–1974), economists observed industrialization's greater capital intensity raise productivity. Processors gained managerial and decision control through grower production contracts. Conditions of exit and entry became more difficult for growers (Reimund et al. 1981:iv).

The competitive yardstick norm became an implicit social contract between producer and cooperative. As agricultural industrialization relentlessly progressed sector by sector throughout agriculture, producers again turned to cooperatives. Loss of market access from the beef industry's transformation cast the industrialization of the pork industry into a watershed event for producers. As contract growers, hog farmers would no longer be independent entrepreneurs, their status and economic destiny dependent on their skill at managing risk; rather, they would be transformed into a modern-day equivalent of "serfs": hired hands told what to do by some distant corporate authority. Producers traditionally used cooperatives to "control their destiny." In practice, this meant using cooperatives to maintain family farming's economic viability. It seemed natural to extend cooperatives' local or regional protective role to the national level.

Experience of exploitation told farmers what it was like to exist within an emergent culture where others made the rules, where larger social forces dominated farmers' individual aspirations or preferences. The competitive yardstick norm offered producers a strategic choice of cooperatives as small rural utopias under unambiguous producer control or as expansive business enterprises potentially part of the larger economic forces hovering over farmers. These populist choices gave the competitive yardstick norm a cultural continuity with earlier farmer battles; from that perspective, the norm was reassuring and familiar. Nevertheless, the values of the competitive yardstick norm encouraged the cooperative sector to debate the question of who would control U.S. agriculture while others within agriculture were aligning with each other to realize their joint strengths (North Central Regional Extension Publication 32 1972).

Industrialization was market driven. Discovering, measuring, and responding to consumer preferences was an important feature of industrialization because it had the technological capability to engineer products to those preferences—to create lean pork or late-season blueberries, for example. Walmart's rapid growth based on "Everyday Low Prices"—the retail expression of the low-cost provider norm—was another expression of consumer sensitivity. A lens clouded by past and anticipated exploitation prevented cooperatives from seeing opportunities from industrialization. The promise of agricultural industrialization was fulfilled in the market; in the market, farmers and cooperatives found their nemesis: consumers and retailers who pressured food prices.

This chapter is a case study of how organizations adapt to inhospitable economic environments. NIE economic historian Douglass North proposes that cultural change occurs slowly and incrementally—a concept called "gradualism" —and so norms, as carriers of important cultural concepts and tensions, also change slowly (1990, 2005). North anticipates that social change will be slow and incremental in part because organizations will resist the difficulties presented by large-scale change. Nevertheless, the actual process of industrialization was rapid for broilers, fed cattle, and processing vegetables once sufficient mechanical, biological, and organizational restructuring had occurred. Economists somberly concluded that "gradual changes, however, do not create such harsh adjustment problems as those that occurred in the three subsectors under study" (Reimund et al. 1981:2).

North predicts that resistance raises costs. That is, institutions like norms have an effect on the prices individuals pay; those who perceive the rules governing exchange are fair and just will likely have lower transaction costs than those who perceive the system is unjust (North 1990:43, 76). Yet NIE also predicts that economic organizations evolve to minimize transaction costs (Eggertsson 1990:221). If they were to survive, cooperatives could not maintain a "producer oriented" culture indefinitely (Hogeland 2004). Indeed, by the end of the 20th century, many midwestern cooperatives formerly resistant to industrialization had crafted a new "value proposition" for members and customers from new crop opportunities recontextualizing the orderly marketing norm. By the beginning of the 21st century, virtually all cooperatives responding to the customer or market as a way to increase farmer returns began to identify themselves as "value-added."

This case study also offers social scientists a synopsis of the different ways norms inform social change. The transition from orderly marketing to value-added cooperative illustrates the pattern of normative evolution anticipated by North, that is, one norm emerging from or following another in an orderly progression. Like the British social structuralists, North and NIE in general are interested in how norms foster order, continuity, stability, and equilibrium conditions such as cost minimization (Hogeland 2008). Similarly, Nourse's vision of social order ascribed to farmers the role of producing crops and livestock, and to cooperatives the role of ensuring that markets remained competitive.

Identifying socially optimal structures of exchange is one goal of NIE; to this end, norms are considered coordinating mechanisms (Eggertsson 1990). Industrialization's goal of improving coordination sought to reduce conflict between the different stages of production and marketing. It also meant that "no supplier of a part of the system can make money unless all other parts of the system develop simultaneously" (Robison et al. 2002:16).

Nevertheless, the evolution of the competitive yardstick norm shows how much conflict may be an intrinsic, unavoidable aspect of profound social change. From 1945 to 1970, the competitive yardstick norm evolved from a statement on combating local market monopolies to become the intellectual foundation for widespread debate over the future structure of production agriculture (Carter and Johnston 1978). This debate intensified as industrialization made inroads in the midwestern pork industry during the 1980s. Judged by NIE standards partial to efficiency and social order, the competitive yardstick norm may appear as a maladaptive belief system that deterred cooperatives from responding to the low-cost producer norm.

Seen, rather, as a norm in competition with other norms, the evolutionary impact of the competitive yardstick norm on the cooperative sector becomes more apparent. In fact, Friedrich Hayek suggests that norms undergo a process of competitive selection (1960). In his 1945 exposition of the competitive yardstick norm, Nourse clearly regarded the Sapiro model as an inferior and competing example of collective action. Nourse also anticipated the low-cost provider norm by wondering when industrial leadership would supply their services to the public on a long-run cost basis. He believed competition from cooperatives could significantly accelerate this process (Nourse 1992:107). Nourse did not foresee how the capital-intensive concentrating and centralizing tendencies in agriculture would eventually limit the number of markets where farmer-owned cooperatives could be competitive, however. But normative conflict was clearly evident by 1972; this prompted economist Donald Paarlberg to ask whether a new and very different system of food production was necessary for increased efficiency even though family farmers had already reduced food expenditures to about 16 percent of income in an affluent nation (1973:5).

Cooperatives, as service providers, traditionally have not stressed profit maximization; indeed, some have considered "profit" a word incompatible with cooperative culture (Hogeland 2004:23). But debate over agriculture's future structure and control would reveal how much cooperatives' growth had been motivated by uniquely cooperative values. Change became inevitable when it became apparent that such values had put cooperatives out of sync with the larger economic system. Nourse's strong functionalist attempt to find a place for cooperatives in the nation's business did not recognize that industrialization was changing how firms compete. Economic theory equates (the condition of) cost minimization with profit maximization; therefore, cooperatives had to come to terms with both. The relationship between behavior and economic performance is demonstrated in the way norms attempt to resolve socially or morally complex questions, according to Nicholas Mercuro and Steven Medema (2007:322).

At the start of the 20th century, California fruit producers also experienced a problematic relationship to the market. The following section addresses how, despite these difficulties, these producers developed cooperative-based markets that anticipated the market-driven mores of the late 20th century. Following that, the competitive yardstick's normative reinforcement of a culture of market distrust and the implications for cooperative investment are explored. The chapter ends with conclusions based on cooperatives' reconciliation with the low-cost provider norm.

CONTROL THROUGH ORDERLY MARKETING

Large-scale agriculture tracing back to huge Spanish land grants allowed California to industrialize earlier some 50 years earlier than the Midwest. Hallmarks of industrialization such as a business attitude toward farming; contract production; large-scale, mechanized farming; and organization for export markets like London or Germany were evident by 1910 or 1920 (Fitzgerald 2003:15). "Chaos" is a word frequently used to describe California fruit marketing before cooperatives stabilized the marketplace (Cross 1911; Hardesty 2005). Harvey Weinstock, organizer and director of the California Fruit Union, often said that the "existing chaotic marketing of products was like placing a hundred men in a room, turning out the lights, and telling them to find the door and get out as quickly as possible" (Larsen 1958:192).

Weinstock traced the path of his fruit by train to discover "why, despite the Fruit Union's efforts to regulate shipments, fruit was rotting in San Francisco as it had rotted in Chicago before the [cooperative] marketing association was formed" (Larsen 1958:189). By tracing the route of a commodity from the shipping sheds to the final marketplace and by interviewing everyone who could offer possible reasons—pushcart operators, retailers, fruit jobbers, publicists, fruit brokers, and consumers—Weinstock displayed a systems approach of interacting with all marketing channel participants. The supply chains of the late 20th century would likewise rely on communication to improve coordination between the different stages of production and marketing.

Growers of Weinstock's era complained about their inability to affect price: they were forced to take whatever buyers offered. It was impossible to expand markets or stabilize prices when independent fruit packers restricted purchases to the amount they could profitably handle (Merritt 1924:7). Fresh fruit producers of the mid-1920s did not know how their fruit graded nor how different grades compared in market value. Shortages of market information made producers vulnerable to misleading rumors from packers intended to depress prices (Couchman 1967; Erdman 1958). Haphazard shipment by many growers and packers led to a mix of over- and undersupplied markets. When packers arbitrarily canceled contracts made early in the season, raisin growers had little legal recourse.

Formed in 1917, the California Prune and Apricot Growers Association (renamed Sunsweet in 1960) was constantly challenged by packers who feared that their fruit supply could be cut off if the association performed well. The association saw its efforts to market high-quality prune packs undone by packers who slipped in lower-quality, smaller fruit. Couchman describes the growers of 1928 as tending to mistrust any agency to which they turned over their crops, but their greater mistrust was in the packers (1967:75).

As the first state marketing director, Weinstock attempted to bring an age of collectivism to California agriculture. He used his office to organize California's producers by "publicizing as models the cooperatives formed by the raisin growers or orange growers" (Larsen 1958:192). In 1912, raisin growers formed the California Associated Raisin Company, renamed in 1925 the Sun-Maid Raisin Growers of California.

In cooperative marketing, growers pooled commodities of a similar grade and quality and received payments throughout the year as the pool was sold. The need to pool like quantities led cooperatives to initiate the development of standard grades and product brands (Wik 1958:184). With Weinstock's support, cooperative grades were documented through state certification to bring members better credit terms and prices.

Weinstock's staff attorney Aaron Sapiro drew on the collective marketing experience of prune, raisin, and citrus growers to formalize the "California Plan" of orderly marketing in 1923 (Sapiro 1993). Orderly marketing stabilized grower prices and provided market security by giving growers a home for their product. Growers raising perennial crops needed such security because they were less able to respond rapidly to fluctuating markets compared with producers of annual crops like wheat, corn, or soybeans. Sun-Maid uses raisin carryover from peak years to compensate growers when weather or other uncontrollable factors cause crop shortages.

Preservation through canning or drying made the commodity into a product that could be marketed year-round; this was the basis of orderly marketing. There were inherent limitations to the concept: nonperishable products like grain could be stored and released on the market to destabilize a cooperative (Hoffman and Libecap 1991:403). An immediate cash payment at harvest, rewarding a year's labor and investment, was irresistible to burley tobacco growers compared with pooling's partial and protracted payout schedule (Ellis 1982:109).

Sapiro's belief that production didn't count until it was sold contrasted with the more producer-oriented belief that cooperatives existed to sell whatever producers chose to grow (Larsen and Erdman 1962:255; Hogeland 2004). He may have learned sensitivity to consumer needs from the way Sun-Maid repositioned raisins from a product sold in bulk for baking to a convenient, pocket-sized snack, packaged in small red boxes called "Little Sun-Maids." Introduced in the summer of 1921, these boxes of raisins were a huge commercial success (Gary Marshburn, telephone conversation with author, July 24, 2008; Cotterill 1984). The box itself became a potent symbol; in 2005 the U.S. Department of Agriculture added a red box of dried fruit to its new food pyramid to reinforce the importance of raisins and other dried fruits within a healthy diet (Sanchez et al. 2008:364).

In developing the first pitted prune, Sunsweet saw how technology could expand the ways prunes were used as foods and as ingredients in foods. The cooperative's competitive advantage comes from the technological advantage offered by the most efficient drying and pitting systems worldwide. Sunsweet's newly developed proprietary pitter offers ingredient manufacturers and retailers a moist, attractive fruit without a doughnut hole. As cooperatives once led industry in developing fruit standards and grades, Sunsweet's goal is to edge industry into using a higher-quality product without a pit. The Sunsweet brand has become the cooperative's legacy and most valued asset because it has consistently represented fruit of the highest quality available. Sunsweet controls the world's largest supply of prunes.

Cooperative Market Dominance

California growers realized early that control over prices might be possible through gaining control over a significant proportion of their crop (Couchman 1967:31). Under the 1922 Capper-Volstead Act, agricultural producers have broad antitrust protection when they collectively market their products. Within California's microclimates, a few counties could represent almost all the growers of a particular specialty crop compared with the multistate span of midwestern grain and livestock production (Wik 1958:185). A large market share would offset the superior bargaining power of other processors, allowing cooperatives to go head-to-head with big business, as Sapiro noted in 1923:

> The egg marketing situation is today controlled by five men in Chicago—the five big packers. They use the great surplus of Midwest eggs to force down the market. Eggs are sold for future delivery just as wheat is, and the packers take a market position which makes their egg departments one of the most profitable divisions of the packing industry. In California the producers organized their own cooperative selling agency and broke the hold of the dealer. . . . They own the finest egg-packing plant in the world. . . . Their hens now lay eggs under contract, and these eggs outsell Midwest eggs constantly on the New York market, where they move at the rate of 800 carloads per year. (Prosperous Folks 1923:14)

Nevertheless, cooperatives could never attain control at the 80–95 percent commodity levels urged by Sapiro because growers were too independent (Sapiro 1993; Wik 1958). It was possible, as one speaker said, "to get one-third of the growers together in an organization; these can get another third to join; but no power outside the Almighty can draw the other one-third in" (Kraemer and Erdman 1933:120). Yet market dominance (even if imperfect) and orderly marketing still gave cooperatives the basis for significant accomplishment. In 2007, Sun-Maid represented approximately 36 percent of California's raisin growers and was the world's largest producer and processor of dried fruit.

Because overproduction is an inventory and price risk for cooperatives providing a home for the growers' product, Sapiro considered product innovation and advertising to be crucial. For that reason, Cotterill (1984) proposes that Sapiro cooperatives were driven more by innovations like contracting and product marketing than by becoming the "monopoly cooperative model" defined by Ruttan (1968:2). Industry evidence, both recent and historical, supports Cotterill's proposition. From the experience of exploitation, the forerunners of Sun-Maid saw as early as 1912 that effective collective marketing required safeguards like a "strong cooperative which would have the power to enforce crop contracts with grower-members" (Popovich 1958:13). That is, growers accepted contracting because only by banding together through a cooperative could their price exceed what they could get from the packers (Arthur Driscoll, telephone conversation with author, April 28, 2008).

THE COMPETITIVE YARDSTICK: PRODUCER PROTECTION

Systematically uniting production, processing, marketing, and distribution under the aegis of a cooperative refined the business orientation already prominent among California producers and protected them by assuring a demand for their products. To Nourse, however, cooperatives only protected producers insofar as they facilitated a market structure conducive to fair trade.

The competitive yardstick norm stated if concentrated markets failed to provide adequate prices or services for farmers, collective action could remedy the situation. Economists now regard the presence of cooperatives as evidence of market failure (Hoyt 2004). The yardstick cooperative would bring innovation to the industry, typically enhancing competition through a superior (alternative) method of distribution or processing. The cooperative's success would induce other industry entrants. As the industry became more competitive, the need for the cooperative would decline. At that point, the cooperative could either scale back operations to a "watchdog" yardstick level or terminate operations. Nourse warned that a successful cooperative could expand into a monopolist unless members checked its growth.

Rather, Nourse expected cooperatives, as the "pacesetters of competition," to define performance standards for their industries. This pacesetter role has been the most enduring, beneficial aspect of the competitive yardstick norm; as Sun-Maid stated, it forces cooperatives to continuously justify their existence (Marshburn, telephone conversation). Through this role, cooperatives establish industry "best practices" or provide industry price leadership, often with a public-good, free-rider dimension (Coffey 1992:112). Ocean Spray Cooperative has funded research investigating how cranberries reduce urinary tract infections. Sun-Maid has provided research, leadership, and education open to all raisin producers to implement dried-on-the-vine (DOV) technology. This "best practice" technology increases raisin yields per acre, lowers production costs, and, by reducing harvest labor requirements, minimizes rain damage during the drying process.

Yardstick cooperatives traditionally focus on price as a measure of comparative performance. The Raisin Bargaining Association bargains with all industry packers to establish an independent field price; this industry pricing reference establishes the commodity value for that crop year. In general, noncooperative growers who sell raisins at harvest for cash receive the field price. Sun-Maid has established a long-standing goal to return to its grower-members at least $100 per ton above the field price to reflect their equity investment in the plant processing and packing facilities, and the marketing, sales, and distribution functions that constitute Sun-Maid. In the last 20 years, Sun-Maid has exceeded the field price every year by a premium of some $100–$200 per ton. These higher grower returns are possible due to the strength of Sun-Maid's brand and its strong retail consumer business (Marshburn, telephone conversation).

The competitive yardstick norm emphasized that it was inappropriate for cooperatives to be aggressive in the marketplace. Nourse noted how growth in size and power had led some cooperators to "throw their weight around":

> Remembering flagrant abuses from which farmers suffered in the past, or chafing under a sense of present wrong, these people look to cooperatives as a power device to be used militantly to improve the farmer position. . . . This was the essence of the old Sapiro doctrine that each commodity should form its trust or domestic cartel and turn to collective bargaining with a "big stick." It was to repeat for the farmer the pattern of monopoly power first developed by tightly organized corporate business" (1992:108).

Growth, popularly known among cooperators as "growth for the sake of growth," violated Nourse's agrarian-based vision of social order because it injected the values of corporate business into cooperatives. Nourse tried to preserve cooperative integrity and "difference" against the "other," the outsider, the nonfarmer (1922b). Fearing that nonfarmer stakeholders would use cooperatives solely as yield-producing investments, he recommended that cooperatives self-protectively "rigidly exclude" investment from "outsiders" (1922b:586).

Cooperatives are presented as a rustic David confronting an armored Goliath in Nourse's explanation of the norm. David, armed simply with river stones, represented small cooperatives performing "simple local services"; the armored Goliath is encased in manufactured complexity (Nourse 1992:108). Cooperatives were "small Davids" who did "a great job breaking down the Goliaths of various market monopolies" (Nourse 1992:108). Nourse's assumption that the ideal cooperative is small and rural centered is an example of the "ideologies of scale" described by Anna Tsing (2000). His tendency to automatically associate large or expanding cooperatives with monopolistic behavior is an assumption that growth will eliminate values like fairness and egalitarianism popularly considered "the cooperative difference" (Hogeland 2006).

In contrast to Sapiro's optimistic presentation of orderly marketing where mention of competitors' marketing power occurs almost as an afterthought, the mood of the yardstick is dark, colored by the potential for cooperative betrayal. Although Goliath is a product of industrialization, his manufactured armor is nevertheless helpless against the stones that are David's rural weapons. Yet my (2007) intertextual, extended reading of the biblical text indicates that David secretly took Goliath's armor into his tent; likewise; cooperatives could be betrayed from the inside, as suggested by a *News for Farmer Cooperatives* editorial: "Over the years, farmers have seen largeness as an evil, manifest in the forces which have historically competed against them in their business. It is natural, therefore, that some farmers even today feel uncomfortable with the size of an organization they own and control" (Ingalsbe 1974:8).

Nourse's argument can be seen as an example of what Mark Purcell and J. Christopher Brown call "the local trap," that is, an assumption that "local-scale decision-making is inherently more likely to yield outcomes that are socially just or ecologically sustainable than decision-making at other scales" (2005:280). Purcell and Brown argue that scale is independent of political agendas; consequently, a larger scale is not by itself an inherent barrier to the democratic values and popular sovereignty typically associated with localization.

Producer Distrust of the Market

Cultural conflict is inherent in Americans' attitudes toward agriculture because Americans are of two minds: valuing agriculture and the family farm to the same extent as the free enterprise system and democratic choice (Tweeten 2003). The competitive yardstick norm can be regarded as an expression of this conflict because it endorses the survival of the family farm through the market choice offered by the free enterprise system. Sapiro clearly endorsed commitment to a specific cooperative; Nourse put the survival of the farm above the cooperative by suggesting that a cooperative formed by producers should be regarded, as cooperative observers often say, as "just another supplier." By requiring cooperatives to compete for business the same way as any other supplier, Nourse situated cooperatives at the same arm's-length distance from farmers as other firms. Farmers' wary relationship to the marketplace is evident from a 1923 editorial in *Successful Farming*: "Just as sure as the [meat]packers, the great bankers, the leading manufacturers or the big corporations propose something that their business experience has shown would be beneficial to . . . the farmers . . . the farmers assume an aloofness that is dramatic."

By setting the welfare of the producer above the cooperative, Nourse arguably contributed to Babcock's famous description of farmer-owned, farmer-controlled cooperatives as a "legal, practical means by which a group of self-selected, selfish capitalists seek to improve their individual economic positions in a competitive society" (Babcock 1935:153). Farmers, who considered themselves at the bottom of the economic totem pole with respect to consumers, now were sovereign, as they evaluated buyers and suppliers according to their needs and preferences, according cooperatives no special loyalty (Breimyer 1986:54).

An adversarial attitude toward further processors or processing led farmers to concentrate on production and let "marketing" end with the sale at the farm gate. At that point, cooperatives or other intermediaries would take over to perform the low-level processing functions such as the grain conditioning, grading, and sorting required by the next level of the marketing chain (Barkley 1976; Hogeland 2001:iii). Bulk buying from many producers, and commingling and blending lots for an average (No. 2) quality was also typical grain industry practice. This mass marketing strategy required end users to adopt grains to their specific requirements. The need for even these minimal services was not well understood even though cooperatives predominated in this end of the marketing channel. In 1976, Barkley commented on farmers' adversarial attitudes toward middlemen: "Farm operators, especially those in the family farm class, have continually heaped wrath on those processors . . . the wrath is surely unwarranted" (1976:814).

In 1922, Nourse suggested that the "despised middleman system" added an unnecessary layer of costs that could be eliminated if farmers controlled the (agricultural) system and operated on a strict cost-of-service-basis (1922b:590, 583). He saw middlemen and further processors adding commissions and monopoly profits to the food system through product and brand proliferation. Nourse complained, "Why this duplication of brands so indistinguishable from one another as far as their essential qualities are concerned?" (1922b:579). Since his breakfast cereal was perfectly adequate, he considered money spent on advertising other brands wasteful. His attitude that "I already know what I want, I don't need anyone to tell me" made product differentiation seem frivolous and pointless. Nourse sourly concluded, "'Salesmanship' so-called has become our god" (1922b:580). Likewise, the 1971 edition of *American Cooperation* includes the complaint that the introduction, promotion, and advertising of so-called new foods do little more than to add to the cost of food. Said the commentator, "There are very few really new products—with frozen orange juice, instant mashed potatoes, and now a new fried milk curd product being the only really new food products" (Behre 1971:248).

Farmer withdrawal from the market had become an entrenched behavioral pattern, as this 1972 *News for Farmer Cooperatives* editorial suggests:

> The degree of compatibility of cooperative concept and "contract farming" depends on the farmer redefining his operation and giving it a new perspective consistent with the developing food system. As a matter of survival, his operation needs to be viewed less as an independent family farm, isolated from the market and oppressed by stronger economic forces, and more as a production division of a cooperative enterprise complex and powerful enough to profitably do battle in the final marketplace. (Editor's Corner 1972:2)

Seeing the potential loss of income from retail markets that offered some 5,000–6,000 products, in 1972, Harvard Business School's Ray Goldberg recommended that cooperatives' business partners compensate for farmers' market isolation. Farmers' marketing ignorance resulted in too many dollars spent promoting basic agricultural products and too few on measuring the impact of advertising and research and product development, said Goldberg (1972:5).

Nevertheless, such a shift would not be easy. In a 1973 interview with *News for Cooperative Farmers*, a cooperative executive discussed joint ventures with food manufacturers. Noting the prominent firms involved in agricultural production, the executive suggested it would take "a miracle" for them to be sufficiently open to disclose critical financial details such as cost allocations and profit rates. He concluded, "The natural thought is, 'Why don't they let us alone in agriculture?'" (Ingalsbe 1973:24)

Not cooperating usually means to withdraw, according to Partha Dasgupta (2007).

COOPERATIVE RECONCILIATION WITH THE LOW-COST PRODUCER NORM: CONCLUSION

Legitimacy is essential to survival because it defines an organization's right to exist (Dowling and Pfeffer 1975:123). Norms legitimized cooperatives by defining a goal or purpose endorsed and supported by producer-members through their equity investment in the cooperative. The competitive yardstick norm directed cooperative investment toward a procompetitive effect on the market. The orderly market norm supported cooperative investment in further processing because returns from processed products were expected to exceed those from raw commodities.

To NIE, norms are culturally based traditions, conventions, or expectations that constrain property rights. This constraining role is evident from the way the competitive yardstick norm prioritized investment in the farm compared with the cooperative. In 1922, Nourse wrote, "The farmer's need of capital in his own business dictates that he go no farther afield than necessary in marketing or processing undertakings" (1922b:597). Industrialization's increased scale and global outlook brought cooperatives into competition with agribusinesses like Cargill, Continental, and Archer Daniels Midland (ADM). To compete at this level, cooperatives supplemented member equity with debt capital.

The capital requirements of cooperatives more than doubled between 1954 and 1970, and after 1962, capital was supplied by debt financing, not by members and patrons (Griffin 1973:8). In 1973, the culture established by Nourse was endorsed by Farmland Industries, then the second-largest U.S. cooperative: "The high cost of capital investment in agriculture requires that a farmer and his local cooperative use as much of their own funds as possible, on his farm and at the local grain or farm supply cooperative. That means if a regional [cooperative] can borrow money elsewhere, it should do so. Indeed, it has a responsibility to do so" (Lindsey 1973:10). To grow despite the 1970s energy crisis and inflation, large regional cooperatives incurred further debt; this was a pattern that continued throughout the 1990s (Duft 1985; Gherty 2003).

By the early 1990s, agricultural lending regulations had tightened and traditional lending resources like the Farm Credit System were no longer sufficient to supply cooperatives' capital requirements (Gherty 2003). This negative externality, or external cost, fostered a more inclusive and receptive attitude toward outside investment. In 2001, several states began creating so-called hybrid cooperatives with features of limited liability companies to facilitate outside investment. Outside equity has been instrumental in the formation of ethanol and other renewable energy cooperatives because communities want to invest in their economic future.

Eventually, the costs and consequences of extensive cooperative control—having cooperatives could "do it all," or, as Ocean Spray Cooperative would say, go from "bog to bottle"—became less important than creating value. "Succeeding today is more about getting the job done than owning the entire infrastructure," said John Johnson, CEO of CHS Inc. (Johnson 2003).

"No longer able to operate in a silo called a cooperative," Johnson initiated a meeting with Cargill in 1995 that would bring the largest U.S. cooperative into a multidimensional relationship with the agribusiness giant. Through its "Country Operations," CHS, the largest U.S. grain cooperative, competes with Cargill to purchase grain at the retail level. Through Horizon Milling, a joint venture established in 2002, CHS supplies wheat to Cargill, the nation's largest flour miller; this gives CHS a national reach in adding value to grain.

Political relations in foreign countries, fluctuating corn and oil prices, and central banking credit policies are among the unpredictable factors now exerting a decisive impact on agriculture. Situating producers in global agriculture through a well-managed cooperative has replaced 20th-century aspirations to turn back the clock on industrialization. John Campbell of Ag Processing Inc. (AGP), a regional soybean processing cooperative, has said, "We are focused on not being the biggest but being the lowest-cost producer" (Campbell 2007). Welch's president and CEO Dave Lukiewski has announced, "We're not in business just to move cases; we're here to make a profit, and we're committed to selling the right mix of products necessary for profitability" (Lukiewski 2007).

North saw norms as an attempt to solve recurring economic problems. Evidence suggests that farmers will continue to confront the concentrated markets that defined market failure for Nourse. Farmers are expected to experience a significant reduction in buyers in a wide range of markets, based on 1990s merger data from railroads, supermarket chains, and seed, equipment, and agricultural chemical providers (MacDonald 2002:177). Of particular note has been the sharp reduction in the number of different chains competing to buy produce from agricultural shippers. Fewer customers for cooperatives' products and potentially lower prices paid to growers are the implications of the 55.7 percent market share held in 2005 by the leading five U.S. grocery retailers according to Sanchez et al. (2008:366). These economists note that Walmart, essentially nonexistent in the grocery industry 15 years ago, had a 35.1 percent sales increase between 2004 and 2005. Through Walmart's mandate of "Everyday Low Prices," industrialization's cost leadership has spread to the retail sector with "overwhelming success" (Epperson and Estes 1999:39). Intensive price competition exacerbates the effect of retailer consolidation, eliminating many small farmers or forcing them to farm part-time (Fulmer 2000; Mamen 2007).

Consequently, the connection between the early 20th century and the future seems to be that farmers, through their cooperatives, will continue to encounter a high degree of buyer market power. Although market power is not market failure, the emerging retail market structure will strongly affect cooperatives' market access. Thomas Reardon predicts that suppliers will face fewer and more powerful buyers, and over the long term, as their bargaining power declines, suppliers will risk being "de-listed" by a retailer or its specialized or dedicated wholesaler (2007:29). Retail market power appears to have intensified compared with the 1970s, when control of shelf space and product exposure to the consumer was sufficient basis for cooperative observers to conclude that grocery chains represented the greatest market power within agriculture (Garoian 1972:8).

Fiercely competing for market share, chains seek strong suppliers who can, with minimal risk, assure product and offer an exciting customer mix, and do so cheaply. Suppliers can become relevant to chains, suggests Reardon, by developing procurement networks or handling processes that make international trade less challenging or costly (2007:30). Sun-Maid targets better than a 99 percent order fulfillment rate and 95 percent on-time delivery, for example (Marshburn, telephone interview). Effective global marketing is relationship based; chains need suppliers who will connect growers in one emerging market with markets in another (Reardon 2007:16). To this end, Sunsweet participates in local Chilean prune markets with advertising, industry research, and export market development. Defining food safety standards and traceability across regional and global networks is also increasingly important (Reardon 2007:21). Such tasks suggest cooperatives can make industrialization work for them by transforming the 20th-century norm of "orderly marketing" into a 21st-century norm of being a "reliable supplier."

Cooperative norms were an effort by farmers to come to terms with an economic system that contained both threat and opportunity. Nourse stressed both withdrawal (by limiting cooperative growth) and engagement ("cooperatives as pacesetters of competition"). Only when value-added potential emerged locally in grains (identity preservation) and corn (ethanol) in the late 20th century did midwestern producers (other than dairy and pork farmers) become as market driven as California specialty crop producers were some 50 years earlier. This suggests that values and norms are endogenous to the local setting.

Until that occurred, this chapter suggests that market evolution like the industrialization of agriculture was, to a notable degree, resisted by producers and their cooperatives. Such producers spent considerable effort trying to find a control that was illusory. In retrospect, Sun-Maid president Barry Kriebel said, "Nobody controls their destiny; the person who owns the store sets the rules" (Barry Kriebel, telephone conversation with author, August 2, 2007). Because new institutions or norms inevitably develop when people are dependent on forces outside their control, further normative change among cooperatives is likely.

Cooperatives needed to discipline other firms, as Nourse made clear. In turn, cooperatives needed competition from other firms to prevent them, as

Nourse said, from resting on their oars and lapsing back into the easy ways of inefficiency (1922a:86). Paradoxically, the industrialization he so feared was ultimately a conduit to contemporary retail discipline, lower prices, and improved system efficiency.

REFERENCES

Babcock, H. E.
1935 Cooperatives: The Pacesetters in Agriculture. *Journal of Farm Economics* 42:153–156.

Barlett, Peggy
1987 *American Dreams, Rural Realities*. Chapel Hill: University of North Carolina Press.

Barkley, Paul W.
1976 A Contemporary Political Economy of Family Farming. *American Journal of Agricultural Economics* 58:817–819.

Behre, Doris
1971 As Seen by the Consumer. In *American Cooperation 1971*, 246–249. Washington, DC: American Institute of Cooperation.

Breimyer, Harold F.
1986 Reflections on Cooperation and Cooperatives. *Journal of Agricultural Cooperation* 1:52–55.

Campbell, John
2007 Annual Meeting Caps Successful Year for AGP. *AGP News* 2007 (1): 1–4.

Carter, H. O., and W. E. Johnston.
1978 Some Forces Affecting the Changing Structure, Organization, and Control of American Agriculture. *American Journal of Agricultural Economics* 60:738–748.

Coffey, Joseph D.
1992 Comment: Edwin Nourse's The Place of the Cooperative in Our National Economy. *Journal of Agricultural Cooperation* 7:111–114.

Cotterill, Ronald W.
1984 The Competitive Yardstick of Cooperative Thought. In *American Cooperation 1984*, 41–53. Washington, DC: American Institute of Cooperation.

Couchman, Robert
1967 *The Sunsweet Story*. San Jose, CA: Sunsweet Growers, Inc.

Cross, Ira B.
1911 Cooperation in California. *American Economic Review* 1 (3): 535–544.

Dasgupta, Partha
2007 *Economics: A Very Short Introduction*. Oxford: Oxford University Press.

Dowling, John, and Jeffrey Pfeffer
1975 Organizational Legitimacy: Social Values and Organizational Behavior. *Pacific Sociological Review* 18 (1): 122–136.

Duft, Kenneth D.
1985 Strategies for Improving Cooperative Financial Organization and Management. In *Farmer Cooperatives for the Future: A Workshop. November 4–6, 1985, St. Louis, Missouri. North Central Regional Research Committee, NCR-140 Research on Cooperatives*, ed. Extension Committee on Organization and Policy, Agricultural Cooperative Service, U.S. Department of Agriculture. West Lafayette, IN: Purdue University.

Editor's Corner
1972 Cooperatives and Contract Farming. *News for Farmer Cooperatives* 39 (4): 2.

Eggertsson, Thrainn
1990 *Economic Behavior and Institutions*. Cambridge: Cambridge University Press.

Ellis, William E.
1982 Robert Worth Bingham and the Crisis of Cooperative Marketing in the Twenties. *Agricultural History* 56 (1): 99–116.

Epperson, J. E., and E. A. Estes
1999 Fruit and Vegetable Supply-Chain Management, Innovations and Competitiveness. *Journal of Food Distribution Research* 30 (3): 38–43.

Erdman, H. E.
1958 The Development and Significance of California Cooperatives, 1900–1915. *Agricultural History* 32 (3): 179–184.

Fitzgerald, Deborah
2003. *Every Farm a Factory*. New Haven, CT: Yale University Press.

Fulmer, Melinda
2000 Sunshine for State's Farmers. *Los Angeles Times*, January 9.

Garoian, Leon
1972 Structure and Growth—Cooperatives' Role in Our Competitive Enterprise System. *News for Farmer Cooperatives* 39 (7): 7–10.

Gherty, Jack
2003 Access to Capital Top Cooperative Issue: Ongoing Investment Is Critical to Cooperative Success. *Cooperative Partners* October/November: 31.

Goldberg, Ray A.
1972 Farmer Co-ops and Industry Profitable Partnerships. *News for Farmer Cooperatives* 39 (3): 4-8.

Griffin, Nelda
1973 Cooperatives Borrowing More of Capital Needs. *News for Farmer Cooperatives* 39 (10): 8–10.

Hardesty, Shermain
2005 The Bottom Line on the Conversion of Diamond Walnut Growers. *Agricultural and Resource Economics Update*. 8 (6): 1–4, 11.

Hayek, Friedrich A.
1972 *The Constitution of Liberty*. Chicago: University of Chicago Press.

Hoffman, Elizabeth, and Gary Libecap
1991 Institutional Choice and the Development of U.S. Agricultural Policies in the 1920s. *Journal of Economic History* 51 (2): 397–411.

Hogeland, Julie A.
1992 The Tendency toward Oligopoly in the Meat Packing Industry. PhD diss., American University.
2001 *Local Cooperatives' Role in the Identity-Preserved Grain Industry*. RBS Research Report 181. Washington, DC: U.S. Department of Agriculture, Rural Business-Cooperative Service.
2004 How Culture Drives Economic Behavior in Cooperatives. *Journal of Rural Cooperation* 32:19–36.
2005 An Application of Steindl's Theory of Concentration in the U.S. Meat Packing Industry, 1865–1988. In *Rethinking Capitalist Development: Essays on the Economics of Josef Steindl*, ed. Tracy Mott and Nina Shapiro, 36–52.New York: Routledge.
2006 The Economic Culture of U.S. Agricultural Cooperatives. *Culture & Agriculture* 28:67–79.
2007 An Interpretation of the Competitive Yardstick Model Using Critical Discourse Analysis. *Journal of Cooperatives* 20:34–48. Electronic document, www.agecon.ksu.edu/accc/ncera210/JOCArticlesV20.htm.
2008 The Role of Culture and Social Norms in Theories of Institutional Change: The Case of Agricultural Cooperatives. In *Alternative Institutional Structures*, ed. Sandra Batie and Nicholas Mercuro, 349–379. London: Routledge.

Hoyt, Ann
2004 Consumer Ownership in Capitalist Economies: Applications of Theory to Consumer Cooperation. In *Cooperatives and Local Development*, ed. Christopher D. Merrett and Norman Walzer, 265–289. Armonk, NY: M. E. Sharpe.

Ingalsbe, Gene
1973 Before Pooh-Poohing, Consider the Profit Sharing. *News for Farmer Cooperatives*. 40:24.
1974 Agway: Growth and Size Can Serve Members. *News for Farmer Cooperatives*. March. 40:8.

Johnson, John
2003 The Power of Partnership: CHS Focuses on Strategic, Economic, Marketplace Value in Forming Alliances. *Cooperative Partners*, January: 31.

Kraemer, Erich, and H. E. Erdman
1933 *History of Cooperation in the Marketing of California Fresh Deciduous Fruits*. Berkeley, CA: Agricultural Experiment Station.

Larsen, Grace
1958 A Progressive in Agriculture: Harris Weinstock. *Agricultural History* 32 (3): 187–193.

Larsen, Grace, and Henry E. Erdman
1962 Aaron Sapiro: Genius of Farm Co-operative Promotion. *Mississippi Valley Historical Review* 49 (2): 242–268.

Lindsey, Ernest T.
1973 Modern Financing for Cooperative Growth. *News for Farmer Cooperatives* 40 (1): 8–10.

Lukiewski, David
2007 Maximizing Value from Crop to Consumer. *Welch's News*, 2.

MacDonald, James M.
2002 Agribusiness Concentration, Competition and NAFTA. In *Structural Change as a Source of Trade Disputes under NAFTA*, ed. R. M. A. Loyns et al., 171–191. College Station: Texas A&M University.

Mamen, Katy
2007 Facing Goliath: Challenging the Impacts of Supermarket Consolidation on Our Local Economies, Communities and Food Security. *Policy Brief* 1 (3): 1–7 Electronic document, www.oaklandinstitute.org/pdfs/facing_goliath.pdf, accessed August 8, 2008.

Mercuro, Nicholas, and Steven G. Medema
2007. *Economics and the Law*. 2nd ed., *From Posner to Postmodernism and Beyond*. Princeton, NJ: Princeton University Press.

Merritt, Ralph P.
1924 Cooperative Marketing and the Grocer. An Address before the Thirtieth Annual Convention of the National Association of Retail Grocers at Los Angeles, California, June 18.

North Central Regional Extension Publication 32
1972 *Who Will Control U.S. Agriculture? Policies Affecting the Organizational Structure of U.S. Agriculture*. Urbana-Champaign: University of Illinois, Cooperative Extension Service, Special Publication No. 27, August.

North, Douglass C.
1990 *Institutions, Institutional Change and Economic Performance*. Cambridge: Cambridge University Press.
2005 *Understanding the Process of Economic Change*. Princeton, NJ: Princeton University Press.

Nourse, Edwin
1922a Outline for Cooperative Marketing. *Journal of Farm Economics* 4 (2): 80–91.
1922b The Economic Philosophy of Cooperation. *American Economic Review* 12:577–597.
1992 The Place of the Cooperative in Our National Economy. In *American Cooperation 1942 to 1945*, 29–33. Washington, DC: American Institute of Cooperation. Reprinted in *Journal of Agricultural Cooperation* 7 (1992): 105–111.

Paarlberg, Donald
1973 Family Farmers Can Compete. *News for Farmer Cooperatives* 40 (2): 2–5.

Popovich, George E.
1958 *History of the Sun-Maid Organization and Its Antecedents*. Based on a series of articles appearing in the Sunday Country Life section of the *Fresno Bee* beginning Sunday, February 16, 1958.

Prosperous Folks
1923 Farmers Who Help Themselves Tell How They Do It. *Farm and Fireside*. August:14.

Purcell, Mark, and J. Christopher Brown
2005 Against the Local Trap: Scale and the Study of Environment and Development. *Progress in Development Studies* 5 (4): 279–297.
Reardon, Thomas
2007 Supermarket Revolution: The Supermarket Revolution in Emerging Markets: Implications for the Produce Industry. Brief prepared for the Produce Marketing Association, December 2007. Newark, DE: Produce Marketing Association.
Reimund, Donn A., J. Rod Martin, and Charles V. Moore
1981 *Structural Change in Agriculture*. Technical Bulletin No. 1648. Washington, DC: U.S. Department of Agriculture, Economics and Statistics Service.
Robison, Lindon, A. Allan Schmid, and Peter Barry
2002 The Role of Social Capital in the Industrialization of the Food System. *Agriculture and Resource Economics Review* 31 (1): 15–24.
Ruttan, Vernon W.
1968 Bargaining Power for Farmers. Staff Paper. St. Paul: Department of Agricultural Economics, University of Minnesota.
Sanchez, Deborah S., Michael A. Boland, and Daniel Sumner
2008 Sun-Maid Growers of California. *Review of Agricultural Economics* 30 (2): 360–369.
Sapiro, Aaron
1993 True Farmer Cooperation. Reprint from *World's Work*, May 1923. Reprinted in *Journal of Agricultural Cooperation* 8 (1993): 81–93.
Scott, James C.
1976 *The Moral Economy of the Peasant*. New Haven, CT: Yale University Press.
Successful Farming. Editorial Comments.
1923 Vol. 8.
Tsing, Anna
2000 The Global Situation. *Cultural Anthropology* 15 (3): 327–360.
Tweeten, Luther
2003 *Terrorism, Radicalism, and Populism in Agriculture*. Ames: Iowa State Press.
Wik, Reynold
1958 Commentary on Dr. Erdman's Paper. *Agricultural History* 32 (3): 185–186.

IV

COOPERATION RISING

11

Creating Common Grazing Rights on Private Parcels

How New Rules Produce Incentives for Cooperative Land Management

Carolyn K. Lesorogol, Washington University

INTRODUCTION

African livestock herders depend on the natural environment to produce food, generate income, and build wealth, all of which are central to securing livelihoods of individuals and households. With limited, sporadic support from their governments and the international community, and living in fragile, semiarid environments, pastoralist communities are particularly vulnerable to environmental risk, and their very survival hinges on how they manage their resources. The ways in which land and other natural resources are managed are therefore critical determinants of the well-being of people in these societies. Most pastoralist groups, like the Samburu of northern Kenya, have historically accessed natural resources such as pasture, forest, and water through communal management systems. Unlike open access systems, communal management systems consist of local institutions that regulate access to and use of resources by delimiting the user group, establishing rules for accessing and withdrawing resources, monitoring how resources are used, and sanctioning violations of rules (Ostrom 1990). These local institutions facilitate cooperation, thus enabling pastoralists to survive in fragile environments subject to periodic crises such as drought and disease.

Such systems are not static, but rather have changed over time in response to both external and internal factors. In the Samburu case, the British colonial regime altered the pastoral system in the early 20th century through restrictions on grazing and limits on livestock holdings. Following Kenya's independence in 1963, the government instituted a process of land registration and titling that created possibilities for group and individual land tenure in some pastoral areas (Galaty 1994; Okoth-Ogendo 2000; Rutten 1992). While this led to the establishment of group ranches in most areas, another outcome of this policy was privatization of land in the early 1990s in a Samburu community, Siambu, into individual parcels of about 23 acres in size. Privatization shifts de jure control over land from the community to individual landowners, potentially undermining the former system of communal land management. Privatization also creates new possibilities for land use including enclosure, large-scale cultivation, rental, and sale of land.

My prior research in this Samburu community examined the complex effects of privatization on household well-being, individual behavior, and the authority of elders (Lesorogol 2003, 2005a, 2005b, 2008a). Recent work has revealed that in spite of the existence of individual land titles and a general recognition of individual rights to manage parcels, new rules regarding land use and management are emerging in this community. Preliminary findings indicate that these rules have the potential to reestablish communal influence over land use decisions even as these decisions remain under individual control. One of the new rules, for example, requires landowners to allow grazing on their land in order to access others' land for grazing. Conversely, individuals who fence their land or charge others to graze on it will be denied access to grazing on others' land. Such rules, if they gain wide acceptance and are effectively enforced, will enable the community to regulate individual land use decisions. This reassertion of communal power represents an intriguing case of institutional innovation that challenges standard economic thinking about the process of privatization of property rights. Additionally, these new rules create incentives for individual behavior with implications for patterns of land use and livestock movement that will affect household well-being and the local environment. This chapter presents preliminary research findings regarding the emergence and potential effects of the new land use rules, situating the discussion within the theoretical literature on institutional change, cooperation, and property rights. While several potential explanations for the rise of the new rules exist, the most likely explanation is that wealthier herders are using their bargaining power to promote these rules that they perceive as beneficial.

INSTITUTIONAL CHANGE, COOPERATION, AND PROPERTY RIGHTS

In the most general sense, social institutions such as laws, rules, norms, and conventions (much of what we think of as "culture") shape social interaction by increasing the predictability of others' behavior, thus enabling interactions and transactions—social cooperation—of all kinds (Barth 1981; North 1990;

Ostrom 2005). One only has to reflect on the challenges entailed in interpersonal interactions in a completely new setting (such as a new fieldwork location) where one does not understand the language, customs, and rules governing behavior to appreciate how critical institutions are to everyday life. They are so fundamental, in fact, that they are usually taken for granted and seem unremarkable, until they change or cease to function as expected. Several key characteristics of institutions need to be considered in analyzing how these institutions enable and require cooperation and how processes of institutional change occur. First, they are shared. Members of the relevant social group can identify and agree (at least to a significant extent) on the content of important norms, values, and rules. This does not imply that institutions are entirely functional, uncontested, or unchanging, but it does imply that there is a considerable degree of consensus—in the sense of agreement on meaning—required for an institution to exist in the first instance.

A second characteristic of institutions is that there are means of monitoring and enforcing compliance to rules among group members, ranging from mild, informal sanctions to stringent, formal ones. Three levels of enforcement are possible: first person (internal feelings of guilt or shame from violating norms, for example), second person (sanctioning someone who has wronged you), and third person (an outsider to the interaction sanctions the rule violator). Third person, or third party, enforcement of rules requires collective action among members of the relevant community and may (as in the case of formal laws) involve legal bodies such as courts. How this collective action is achieved and maintained is an important question for research on institutions (Baland, Bardhan, and Bowles 2007; Baland and Platteau 1996; Chong 1991; Henrich et al. 2006; Olson 1965).

Third, institutions tend to distribute benefits unequally among group members. For example, in the Samburu system of land management, all herders have access to pasture resources and they have obligations to help monitor and enforce rules regulating which pastures can be used at any particular time. Even this egalitarian rule of access, however, tends to benefit wealthy herders more than poor ones, since the wealthier herder requires more land on which to graze his livestock while he incurs about the same costs of monitoring and enforcement as other herders. In absolute terms, he consumes more of the common resource than poorer herders, but his contributions to common management are equivalent. While this inequity may not be noteworthy when pastures are plentiful compared to needs, it becomes more problematic as population pressure rises and available pasture reduces—this is what happened to the Samburu throughout the 20th century. The result of unequal distribution of benefits from institutional arrangements is that those who benefit most have the highest stake in maintaining the status quo while those who benefit least may seek to change the rules to their advantage if opportunities to do so arise. This characteristic creates instability in institutional arrangements as unequal benefits may generate social conflicts leading to institutional change (Ensminger and Knight 1997; Knight 1992). Institutional change may also be stimulated by external factors that alter actors' incentives to abide by extant rules (North and Thomas 1973; Ullmann-Margalit 1977) or the emergence of new attitudes and preferences (Chong 2000). As I will discuss below, both of these factors were important in the shift from communal to private land ownership among the Samburu, and they play a role in the newly emerging rules of land use.

The question of how social institutions change is here closely related to one particular class of institutions: property rights in pastoral systems. *Property rights* refers to the bundle of rights possessed by individuals or groups that determine their ability to access, use, and transfer resources to others (Gray and Kevane 1999; Meinzen-Dick et al. 1997). A system of rules and processes governs how rights are distributed within a community or society, and multiple parties may have different rights to the same resource. A case in point is women's use rights over cattle. In many pastoral systems women are allocated use rights over cattle at marriage; they milk animals, control the distribution of milk, own the hide or skin after an animal dies, and often control the use of meat from the animal. They do not, however, have the ability to transfer the animal outside the household without the husband's permission as this is a right reserved for men.[1] An important characteristic of property rights in many African pastoral systems is the communal nature of land management. Shared management of extensive, semiarid rangelands enables people and livestock to move across wide distances to access pasture, water, and other critical resources. By facilitating mobility of herds, these cooperative arrangements allow a larger number of people and livestock to utilize the patchy environments characteristic of pastoral systems as compared to settled ranching systems where large amounts of land must be kept in reserve to guard against the risk of drought (Behnke, Scoones and Kerven 1993; Sandford 1983).

Communal land ownership and management has been subject to critique, much of it based on misunderstanding the system. The "tragedy of the commons" argument popularized by Garrett Hardin (1968) posits that users of a common resource such as pasture will tend to overuse the resource since the benefits of doing so accrue to the individual user while the costs are spread across the group. This logic presumes that there are no constraints on individual users—that they are free to consume the resource indefinitely. That is indeed the case in "open access" systems but not in those that are actively managed by groups of users who do impose limits on access to and use of the resource. In spite of the flawed logic, the "tragedy of the commons" idea has been influential in both academic and policy circles, leading to calls for the privatization of communal resources in order to better specify property rights and ensure responsible management (see Platteau 1996 for an explanation and critique of this stance). The Kenyan government's policy of land adjudication in pastoral areas, developed in the 1960s and 1970s, was influenced by such arguments, leading to the establishment of group ranches and even total privatization as in Siambu (Mwangi 2007).

In the 1980s and 1990s a large body of research, much of it focused on pastoral systems, demonstrated that communities of resource users can successfully manage common resources, avoiding tragedies of overuse and degradation (Agrawal 1999; Baland and Platteau 1996; Behnke, Scoones, and Kerven 1993; Berkes 1999; McCabe 1990; Ostrom 1990; Scoones 1994). These studies show that successful management depends on cooperation and collective action by users of the resource to develop what Ostrom (1990) terms "design principles," which are rules regulating the use of the resource. Important design principles include defining the user group, creating rules of access and use of the resource, monitoring and enforcing these rules, and establishing a forum in which a broad range of resource users participate in formulating the rules themselves. These rules comprise local-level social institutions that clarify the bundle of property rights over the communal resource of land, and they emerge through social processes. To better understand why some communities are more successful than others in managing common property, scholars have investigated factors that facilitate or hinder cooperation (in rule setting, monitoring, enforcement) including group size, heterogeneity, and relations of trust (Agrawal 2003; Baland, Bardhan, and Bowles 2007; Janssen and Ostrom 2006; Ruttan 2006). In general, small, homogeneous groups with high levels of trust will be more effective in establishing and maintaining cooperation and, by extension, a system of rules around land management. Conversely, larger, more heterogeneous and less trusting groups will encounter more difficulty in doing so, and may require a stronger third party to enforce compliance. As with all institutions, cooperation can be threatened by external factors such as changing relative prices, new market opportunities, or government policies that alter the costs and benefits of cooperation. To the degree that actors respond to such incentives, they may be less willing to cooperate than previously; this has important implications for maintaining a system premised on widespread cooperation.

According to these design principles and this theory of collective action, many pastoral systems are examples of successful common property management. For example, the Samburu land management system is highly decentralized so that local groups of users (small, homogeneous groups) can decide which areas of pasture they will reserve for dry-season grazing, when and to what degree water sources will be exploited, when forest areas will be opened and closed for grazing, and so forth. The same local group is able to relatively easily monitor use patterns and sanction those who violate the agreed-on rules. All elder men (those older than about 30 years) are allowed to participate in local decision-making forums; this renders the rule-making process highly democratic (for men, at least). The continued survival of pastoralists in difficult environments over hundreds of years is a testament to their success in adapting to and managing their environment. Why, then, have some groups of pastoralists over the last few decades decided to partially or fully privatize their land resources (Galaty 1994; Mwangi 2007; Peters 1994; Rutten 1992)? The next section provides an explanation of this process for the Samburu case as background to the analysis of the resurgence of communal influence over land use.

PRIVATIZATION IN SAMBURU: THE SIAMBU CASE

In the case of Samburu, privatization emerged out of social conflict among groups with different interests and differential bargaining power. Factors both internal and external to the community contributed to the push for change. Initially, a small group of individuals sought large parcels of land for themselves, but the outcome of the conflict resulted in equal subdivision of the land among all 240 resident households. The internal factors that led to this change include a heightened awareness of inequality and a shift in the bargaining power of key social actors (see Lesorogol 2003, 2008a for details). As noted above, although Samburu have a very egalitarian rule of access to pasture, herders with more livestock tend to benefit disproportionately from access to pasture because their herds consume more of the resource while their obligations for monitoring and enforcement are similar to those of other herders. This inequity was not perceived as problematic when pastures were ample, but with growing populations and shrinking access to land due to creation of wildlife reserves, protected forests, and firmer borders with neighboring groups the differences between wealthier and poorer herders became increasingly apparent in the 1960s and 1970s. Many younger and poorer Samburu express the sentiment that private landholdings would be advantageous for them as they could exclude others from using the land and benefit more themselves, perhaps by raising fewer, more productive cattle (Lesorogol 2003:533). Some individuals were motivated to pursue privatization as a means to reduce inequities among herders by securing greater rights to land.

Another internal factor was a shift in preferences among some men who had been exposed to farming in other areas of Kenya through experiences in education, employment, and military service. These men came to associate private landownership, the norm in those areas, with greater modernity and economic opportunity. Moreover, these experiences in themselves increased the relative bargaining power of these men. Younger men in Samburu society generally have less power than elders who control access to land, livestock, political authority, and marriageable women (Spencer 1965). These young men were able to challenge the status quo of communal land management, however, through their greater understanding of government regulations regarding land adjudication and better access to government officers through knowledge of the national language and bureaucracy. Using these skills—their newly acquired bargaining power—they successfully lodged claims for private land during the adjudication of the area into a group ranch.

External factors also played a role in advancing privatization in Siambu. The government's land adjudication policy created the opportunity for challenging communal management, at least for those savvy enough to realize that there was a provision for making individual claims during the group ranch adjudication process. The local government land officers also exhibited a bias in favor of private landownership and tended to favor the individual claimants over opposition from the elders and even the local land committee (Lesorogol 2003, 2008a). Another important external factor was the increasing relative price of land in Siambu at this time. Located in the highest-elevation part of Samburu district on a broad flat plain, the area has some potential for commercial wheat production. Just as adjudication was getting under way in the early 1980s, a commercial wheat farmer approached the community offering to lease the land to grow wheat. This sudden increase in the value of land encouraged those who already wanted private parcels to seek even greater acreages while it stimulated the elders in the area to resist losing this fertile land to individual ownership. What ensued was a conflict between these two groups that lasted about five years, pitting the younger educated group against the elders who mobilized the community against the individual claimants. Ultimately, this conflict was resolved in a compromise solution brokered by the government and local leaders that granted each household in the community a parcel of privately owned land of about 23 acres, while some of the less-desirable land remained a group ranch with joint access by all community members.

AFTER PRIVATIZATION: GREATER AUTONOMY AND CONTROL OVER INDIVIDUAL PARCELS

The decision to legally privatize land in Siambu transferred authority for land use decisions from the local council of elders to individual landowners; this marked a dramatic shift considering the history of communal management there. During my early research in 2000, I expected to find a residue of resistance to privatization among members of the community who had opposed privatization. I did not. Instead, virtually all informants explained that they were very satisfied with private landownership. Interestingly, they were most positive about privatization because of the added autonomy they had over land use decisions and the inability of elders to interfere with their choices about how to use their land. They could grow crops, fence, lease, or even sell the land and there was nothing the elders could do about it, they told me. Some made comparisons with neighboring Samburu living on communal or group ranch land; in doing so, they highlighed how elders' control impeded their freedom of choice and even prevented them from developing. Elsewhere I have discussed how this rhetoric of control and autonomy has been used to reassert the leading role of the Lmasula clan, the majority in Siambu, by asserting their greater modernity (Lesorogol 2003, 2008a). Here, I want to underscore the strength of feelings about individual control over land use and opposition to control by elders within the community. Indeed, experimental games conducted in 2001 revealed a tendency to discount elders' authority (Lesorogol 2005a).

Actual land use practices in Siambu in the early 2000s were not entirely consistent with the rhetoric about modernizing pastoral production, although there were signs of change. Cultivation did increase, with about two-thirds of households engaging in some crop farming; more than half of these households began farming following privatization. Most people grew maize, beans, and potatoes for home consumption and sale on fields of one to two acres. About a third of the 100 surveyed households leased out land to the wheat farmer. Selling land was much less common. Only about 10 percent of the surveyed households had sold land, and in total land sales in the first decade following privatization comprised only about 2 percent of the total privatized area (modest compared to the rate of sales among the southern Maasai, among whom privatization has also occurred; see Galaty 1994; Mwangi 2007; Rutten 1992). Enclosing land was even less common. While fences are the quintessential marker of private property, there are only four or five individuals (out of 240) who have fenced their parcels since privatization. Even without fences, however, private rights are clearly recognized in the community. Landowners are able to sell not only their land, but also increasingly the resources on the property such as timber or even firewood (water remains a public good at present). In an interesting twist, the council of elders has begun to enforce individual land rights, penalizing herders whose livestock wander into cultivated fields and destroy crops.[2]

In the midst of these changes in land use, livestock continued to be grazed in Siambu, both on the private parcels and in Porokwai, a less-desirable area adjacent to Siambu that was declared a group ranch at the same time the private plots were demarcated. In addition, there is a government forest near Siambu and many herders took their livestock there to graze, especially in the dry season or in low-rainfall years. Herders could also take their livestock farther away for grazing, requiring them to negotiate with neighboring communities for access. While it was clear that livestock continued to graze in the privatized area of Siambu, in the early 2000s there did not appear to be any particular set of rules regulating grazing access. Rather, herders either grazed on their own land or made bilateral arrangements with others in order to bring their livestock to graze on those parcels. In the last one to two years, however, there have begun to emerge new rules that promise a greater degree of communal control over grazing access in the privatized area.

A REEMERGING COMMONS?

Two events indicated to me that new grazing rules were emerging in Siambu. The first was when one of my key informants told me that there had been some disputes in the community over public pathways. When land was divided into individual plots, public paths were demarcated between the plots. He told me that in a few cases, people had planted crops over these paths; this led to complaints to the area elders and government-appointed chief. This event, while not directly related to grazing, signaled that the elders were being called on to intervene to defend community rights to this public good. Also, since it was very unusual to hear about disputes of any kind over land, this one indicated to me that there were still some contentious issues regarding land.

The second event I heard about was disagreement over the use of wheat stubble. As noted above, many people in Siambu rent out their land for wheat farming. This land is not fenced, though there is general agreement that livestock should not graze on the wheat. The wheat farmer has used watchmen to guard the wheat, although this practice appears to be on the wane. Although there may be some problems with livestock grazing on growing wheat, it does not seem to be a significant issue. After the wheat is harvested, there is remaining stubble on the fields. The disputes revolved around the use of the stubble. According to several informants, it used to be that anyone could graze his cattle on the wheat stubble, but then in the last couple of years a few "young and clever" landowners decided to increase their profits by renting out the stubble for grazing. This way, they would earn money from wheat twice—once for the lease to the wheat farmer, and now the grazing fees charged for the stubble. Interestingly, while there was no resistance against people's leasing out their land for cultivation, leasing the wheat stubble led to considerable dissatisfaction in the community.

The argument against leasing the stubble ran something like this: these individuals were leasing out their whole parcel for stubble grazing, then taking their own livestock and grazing them on others' private parcels. Thus, they were benefiting from free access to others' land while they were reaping private rents from others' grazing on their own parcel. This was thus seen as a classic case of free riding, except that in this case the "commons" was made up of the combined private parcels of other landowners. Some elders objected to these individuals' renting out their wheat stubble. But there was a problem. The elders could not prevent them from doing so, since the individuals have the right to use their land any way they want. What the elders might have been able to do, though, was to prevent the individuals from grazing their own livestock on others' private parcels. They could use the sanction of prohibiting them from grazing on others' land unless they allowed grazing on their own parcel (i.e., give free access to the stubble rather than charge). Thus, it appears that out of this dispute over stubble emerged new rules over grazing access. Further research is required to investigate the process through which these disputes were actually transformed into a set of proposed rules and how and to what extent those rules have been adopted and are actively enforced. However, through conversations with a number of informants, it was clear to me that by 2007 there was a fairly broad recognition that such rules existed. From this preliminary research, the new rules could be stated as follows:[3]

1. **Reciprocal grazing access.** Anyone who wants to graze his livestock on others' private parcels must allow others' to graze their livestock on his parcel.

2. **Enclosure is a two-way process.** If someone fences his parcel, he may exclude others from grazing on it or charge a fee for grazing access. However, that individual cannot freely graze his livestock on others' parcels.

While the first rule stipulates something approaching free access to grazing on others' parcels, the reality seems to be that access to grazing on any particular parcel involves agreement between the owner of the parcel and the individual desiring to graze his livestock. What is significant is that these agreements should not involve exclusive grazing rights or the charging of fees. They are more akin to the kinds of negotiations pastoralists normally engage in when seeking access to grazing beyond their home area. The principle is one of reciprocity, not market exchange. That said, I also observed and heard about herders sneaking their livestock onto others' land for grazing without negotiating permission; this was a practice that appeared to be tolerated much of the time. Such sneaking might be a rule violation if the one doing the sneaking does not allow access to his land for grazing. Sneaking by those who do allow grazing on their parcels might be a strategy to reduce the transaction costs of negotiating access to daily grazing.

These rules are quite consistent with efforts to combat free riding on the commons, with the twist that the commons in this case is not legally a commons at all, because it is made up of privately owned parcels. If a landowner takes his plot out of the commons, by enclosing it or otherwise refusing others access, then he is not entitled to access the remaining commons through others' plots. Although the elders cannot prevent someone from leasing his land (either for wheat, maize, or stubble), they may be able to prevent him from grazing his livestock on others' land, but only with a high degree of cooperation among all the landowners. Since the elders do not have authority to regulate individual land use decisions, the only way these new rules can be enforced is if all landowners agree to enforce them by either individually refusing access to their land by rule violators, or by reporting violations and then imposing collective punishments on violators. Ironically, then, rules that govern this commons require all community members to take parallel, but individual, actions for effective enforcement.

INCENTIVES CREATED BY THE NEW RULES

The emergence of the new rules—assuming they can be effectively enforced—creates differential incentives for community members. Examining these incentives may provide clues about the origins of the rules as well as their likely effects. What we are considering here are the distributional implications of the new institutions—who gains and who loses under the new rules? According to institutional theory, those who perceive they will gain by new institutional arrangements are more likely to support change in that direction, while those who stand to lose will resist.[4]

The effects of the new rules are clearest for wealthier and poorer pastoralists; they create incentives for each group to engage in particular kinds of land use. Take wealthier herders with many livestock, perhaps as many as 100 cows and 200 sheep. The 23 acres they were allocated during privatization are inadequate to provide year-round grazing for all their livestock. In order to support their herd, they must have access to additional grazing beyond their own parcel. For them, maintaining reciprocity among parcels will provide access to more grazing land than they have in their single parcel, even though they will at times need to provide others access to their own land. They also have the choice to graze their livestock beyond Siambu in Porokwai, the government forest, or group ranches farther afield. These options entail additional costs, however. In the case of Porokwai, the grazing is often inferior to that in the privatized area of Siambu and there is a high level of insecurity in the area due to neighboring Pokot pastoralists who often raid Samburu herds. Grazing in Porokwai requires investment in security—older herders, possibly armed—and suffers more seasonal fluctuation than Siambu. As for the forest, grazing there is technically illegal and there is some risk of being fined by Forest Department guards. Furthermore, the forest is less-desirable grazing, especially for cattle, compared to the flat plains of Siambu. Greater herding skill is required to navigate herds through the forest. Taking livestock beyond these areas entails even higher costs: the herder must negotiate access; he must travel and live far from home for extended periods; and there need to be older boys or warriors to accompany the herds. Thus, access to grazing on the private parcels in Siambu has many advantages over these other areas. Rules that help ensure continued access to this reconstituted commons have considerable appeal to wealthier livestock owners who stand to benefit substantially from lowered costs of grazing.

What about poorer pastoralists? Individuals with few or no livestock face a very different calculus than the wealthy herders. They do not require as much land to graze their few livestock and may be able to survive most of the year on their own parcel. With a very small herd, it is even more difficult for them to move away to utilize distant pastures, however, since they will have difficulty surviving on the products of their herd. In such cases, poorer pastoralists often combine their herds with those of wealthier pastoralists, perhaps providing some labor in the form of a herder. Retaining reciprocal access to parcels has less appeal to a very poor herder because he will not make much use of others' parcels, but will be subject to others' demands for access to his land. For the poorer pastoralists, other land uses such as cultivation and leasing may be more attractive since these herders can produce food and cash on their own land even with few livestock. The new rules create an incentive for them to take their land out of the new commons, freeing them to devote it fully to other uses. Doing so, especially if they opt to fence their parcel, may make it difficult for them to rejoin the commons later, thus raising questions about what such individuals would do if they were to become better off and begin to invest in livestock and build up a herd (the ideal trajectory for a pastoralist, after all).

For both wealthier and poorer herders, the new rules create incentives to pursue particular land use options. Wealthier herders stand to benefit most from retaining reciprocal access to private parcels—the new commons—while poorer herders can benefit by enclosing their parcel and using it for farming, leasing, or grazing their own livestock. While this looks as though it might be a win-win situation, there are some unknowns worth considering. First, what will be the mix of land use practices if individuals follow these incentives? If many poorer herders take their land out of the commons, will what remains be adequate for the needs of the wealthier herders? How will these practices combine spatially? Wealthy and poor are not segregated in separate areas of Siambu, so individual decisions may result in a patchwork of open and closed parcels, possibly reducing the overall efficiency of any particular land use. Second, what are middle-wealth herders likely to do under the new rules? Their incentives are less obvious as they need grazing land but also may want to devote land to other uses for which enclosure is desirable. These questions are the subject of further research.

EXPLANATIONS FOR THE EMERGING RULES

In this final section, three possible explanations for the emergence of the new rules are considered in light of available evidence and theories of institutional change. The first candidate explanation is that the people in Siambu are reasserting communal control over their land as an act of resistance against government-imposed land reform that they never supported in the first place. This explanation has a certain appeal in its assertion of people acting to defend their way of life against a neoliberal government bent on its destruction (or at least transformation into modern, settled ranching and farming). There is indeed a history of the government's trying to change pastoralists into something else, and exhortations for them to stop wandering around with their livestock are still heard today. For their part, pastoralists have resisted such efforts. The Samburu cursed the British grazing schemes of the colonial era, and in many parts of the district that are adjudicated as group ranches, there has been no discernible change in land management practices. In Siambu, too, many community members strongly resisted privatization of land. I reject this explanation, however, for a couple of reasons. First, although many did resist privatization, in the end they overwhelmingly agreed to the compromise solution of equal subdivision of land and participated willingly in the process of land demarcation. Today, you would be hard-pressed to find someone in Siambu who wants to give up his title to land and transform the area to group ranch status.[5] You are more likely to find, as noted above, many people who think private ownership is superior to group ranch or trust land status and that it should be spread to other parts of the district. It appears unlikely, then, that the current reconstitution of the commons is an act of resistance against de jure privatization.

The second candidate explanation is that people in Siambu are reasserting communal control to combat economic distress caused by privatization. This explanation has a basis in research by ecologists and anthropologists demonstrating that extensive pastoralism is the best use of semiarid rangelands (see, for example, Behnke, Kerven, and Scoones 1993). As we have seen above, extensive pastoralism requires access to large tracts of land. Accordingly, breaking up that land into small individual parcels should undermine the basis for extensive production leading to economic decline. Indeed, there is some evidence that fencing smaller and smaller parcels will ultimately lead to an inability to support livestock herds (Boone and Hobbs 2004). The problem with this explanation is that there is no evidence of significant economic decline in Siambu following privatization. Household surveys I conducted in 2000–2001 and 2005 indicate that levels of wealth and income in Siambu are comparable to those in a similar community where privatization did not take place. The trend over time is one of relative stability with average levels of wealth increasing slightly and income remaining steady (Lesorogol 2005b, 2008b). Privatization has not caused wholesale economic collapse in part because livestock production has continued and alternative land uses have provided additional sources of food and income that may actually to some extent buffer households against periodic shocks. A growing body of research examines processes of livelihood diversification among pastoralists due to shifts in land use, increasing sedentarization, and/or new economic opportunities (see Adriansen 2006; Fratkin and Roth 2005; Little et al. 2001; McCabe 2003; Thornton et al. 2007). The effects of diversification are varied, depending on local circumstances, but in a number of cases diversification provides additional opportunities to the poor by helping to offset the loss of livestock they have experienced over the last few decades. Many Siambu residents argue that privatization has helped the poor by providing them with new sources of income from alternative land uses, such as leasing and cultivation, that were not available when land was communally managed. The current state of evidence on household well-being does not support the idea that people in Siambu are attempting to re-create the commons in order to stave off economic decline due to privatization.

The third candidate explanation is that wealthier herders in Siambu, seeking greater access to and lower costs of grazing, have supported a reconstitution of the commons because it suits their own interests. This explanation is consistent with a bargaining-power theory of institutional change that contends that social actors with greater power will be best placed to initiate and achieve changes in rules that they perceive as beneficial (Ensminger and Knight 1997; Knight 1992). Among Samburu, wealthier herders often garner more respect in the community as their wealth is taken as a signal of their success in achieving the ideals of pastoralism—a large herd, many wives, a large family, and so forth. This success should be accompanied by proper attitudes, including generosity and a sense of respect (*nkanyit*) for oneself and others (Spencer 1965). Although Samburu society is relatively egalitarian in terms of participation in public decision making, the "leaders among equals" are very often the wealthier members of the community. Whether wealthier herders still wield as much power and influence in Siambu as in other Samburu communities is a question requiring some investigation. The fact that all households in the area were allocated equal-sized parcels of land, and that land consolidation has not occurred, may to some extent balance differences in livestock wealth with equality in landownership. The 2005 household survey revealed increasing stratification in Siambu, with the wealthiest quintile experiencing large gains in per capita livestock ownership while other groups had modest gains and some suffered losses (Lesorogol 2008b). These gains may be temporary and restricted to a few individuals, so I do not want to overemphasize their significance, but it is likely that livestock wealth still translates into bargaining power in Siambu.

This explanation is consistent with the events that occurred around the wheat stubble incident, although more research is required to confirm whether it was indeed wealthier herders who supported the new rules and advocated for their adoption. In the 1970s and 1980s, wealthier herders in the area acted to ensure grazing access by sanctioning individual farmers. Currently, cultivation is accepted and even protected by the elders,[6] but perhaps wealthier herders again fear that enclosing too much land threatens their interests. At this point, I posit this explanation as a hypothesis in need of further evidence. As shown above, it is relatively clear that wealthier herders stand to benefit from the new arrangements, but this fact alone does not establish their role in proposing the new rules. It is possible that elders (in general) supported the new rules in a nostalgia for the past, or as a way to reassert their authority over land more generally, but I think these are more likely to be reasons that many of them agreed to the new rules rather than necessarily actively advocating for their adoption—a subtle but important difference. Further details about the events leading up to the formulation and agreement on the rules are needed before this explanation can be accepted or rejected.

CONCLUSION: INVESTIGATING INSTITUTIONAL INNOVATION

The emergence of new grazing rules in privatized Siambu is an intriguing case of institutional innovation. In contrast to standard economic theory suggesting that private rights are usually the most desirable and efficient, this case demonstrates the interplay of private and communal forms of management and authority. Although it is still too early to definitively explain precisely how the new rules were developed, promoted, and (at least to some degree) accepted, the history of events in Siambu and the incentives created by the new rules hint that wealthier herders probably have the most to gain from the new rules. Poorer herders may also benefit, increasing the chances that the new rules will endure as they are more likely to do so if a broad range of community members abide by them and, perhaps more importantly, participate in their enforcement. The question of enforcement is very interesting in this case because it entails collective agreement to act individually in order to sanction rule violators by denying them access to private parcels. Documenting the implementation and enforcement of the rules is another research priority likely to yield results that inform our understanding of the operation of collective action in this hybrid public-private situation.

The impact of the new rules on actual land use practice is another key area for further investigation. Much depends on the choices that landowners make in light of the rules. One possibility is a greater degree of openness of parcels, enabling easier and lower-cost access of livestock to grazing. If the rules are well enforced, then cases of sneaking livestock unauthorized onto others' land will decline. While greater openness is one possibility, another is more enclosure as individuals opt to remove their parcels from the reconstituted commons. This may benefit particular individuals, but depending on the spatial distribution of these plots, more enclosure may result in a hodgepodge of open and closed small plots that raises the costs of mobility with negative effects for wealthier herders, or indeed anyone who needs to move livestock. More enclosure of plots also implies a need for greater vigilance in ensuring that those whose plots are taken out of the commons do not free ride by sneaking their livestock onto others' land, consequently raising the cost of enforcing the rules. A bifurcation along these lines might also signal a move toward more stratification as wealthier and poorer households pursue different land uses and livelihood options with less overlap than at present. The economic and social consequences of such a change are hard to predict, but they may have significant impact on the well-being of Siambu residents.

ACKNOWLEDGMENTS

Research discussed in this chapter was supported by a National Science Foundation grant (BCS: 0456015). I would like to thank my research assistant in Kenya and the Kenyan government for granting research permission.

NOTES

1. There are some exceptions to this rule. Women have a stronger say over livestock they bring with them from their natal home and they generally have more rights over livestock they purchase with their own money. Some women's groups now engage in organized livestock trade and their right to do so and to control the proceeds is generally accepted in the community.
2. This is especially noteworthy since the elders resisted those who began farming in the area in the 1960s and 1970s. One of their methods was to force their livestock onto cultivated fields, destroying them. There was no recourse for those early farmers who were in fact being sanctioned for taking valuable pastureland out of use.
3. This is my current understanding of the rules. It's quite possible that there are nuances or even other rules that I have not yet discovered. To my knowledge, the rules are not written down anywhere.
4. Lacking more detailed information about how the rules themselves were proposed and promoted, considering the incentive effects is a way to build a hypothesis about which groups may have supported the new rules, or at least are likely to support their continuation. The hypothesis can then be assessed in further research into the origins of the rules.
5. Perhaps some of the oldest women in the area would support this position.
6. Herders whose livestock enter cultivated fields and consume crops are fined.

REFERENCES

Adriansen, H. K. 2006. Continuity and Change in Pastoral Livelihoods of Senegalese Fulani. *Agriculture and Human Values* 23:215–229.

Agrawal, A. 1999. *Greener Pastures: Politics, Markets, and Community among a Migrant Pastoral People*. Durham, NC: Duke University Press.

———. 2003. Sustainable Governance of Common Pool Resources: Contexts, Methods and Politics. *Annual Review of Anthropology* 32:243–262.

Baland, J. M., and J. P. Platteau. 1996. *Halting Degradation of Natural Resources: Is There a Role for Rural Communities?* Oxford: Clarendon.

Baland, J. M., P. Bardhan, and S. Bowles, eds. 2007. *Inequality, Cooperation, and Environmental Sustainability*. New York: Russell Sage.

Barth, F., 1981. *Process and Form in Social Life: Selected Essays of Fredrik Barth, Vol. 1*. London: Routledge and Kegan Paul.

Behnke, R., I. Scoones, and C. Kerven, eds. 1993. *Range Ecology at Disequilibrium: New Models of Natural Variability and Pastoral Adaptation in African Savannas*. London: Overseas Development Institute.

Berkes, F. 1999. *Sacred Ecology: Traditional Ecological Knowledge and Resource Management*. Philadelphia: Taylor and Francis.

Boone, R. B., and N. T. Hobbs. 2004. Lines around Fragments: Effects of Fragmentation on Large Herbivores. *African Journal of Range & Forage Science* 21:79–90.

Chong, D. 1991. *Collective Action and the Civil Rights Movement*. Chicago: University of Chicago Press.

———. 2000. *Rational Lives: Norms and Values in Politics and Society*. Chicago: University of Chicago Press.

Ensminger, J., and J. Knight. 1997. Changing Social Norms: Common Property, Bridewealth and Clan Exogamy. *Current Anthropology* 38 (1): 1–24.

Fratkin, E., and E. Roth, eds. 2005. *As Pastoralists Settle: Social, Health, and Economic Consequences of Pastoral Sedenterization in Marsabit District, Kenya*. New York and London: Kluwer Academic Publishers.

Galaty, J. G. 1994. Ha(l)ving Land in Common: The Subdivision of Maasai Group Ranches in Kenya. Special issue, *Nomadic Peoples* 34/35:109–122.

Gray, L., and M. Kevane. 1999. Diminished Access, Diverted Exclusion: Women and Land Tenure in Sub-Saharan Africa. *African Studies Review* 42 (2): 15–39.

Hardin, G. 1968. The Tragedy of the Commons. *Science* 162:1243–1248.

Henrich, J., R. McElreath, A. Barr, J. Ensminger, C. Barrett, A. Bolyanatz, J. C. Cardenas, M. Gurven, E. Gwako, N. Henrich, C. Lesorogol, F. Marlowe, D. Tracer, and J. Ziker. 2006. Costly Punishment across Human Societies. *Science* 312:1767–1770.

Janssen, M. A., and E. Ostrom. 2006. Empirically Based, Agent-Based Models. *Ecology and Society* 11:37.

Knight, J. 1992. *Institutions and Social Conflict*. Cambridge: Cambridge University Press.

Lesorogol, C. 2003. Transforming Institutions among Pastoralists: Inequality and Land Privatization. *American Anthropologist* 105 (3): 531–542.

———. 2005a. Experiments and Ethnography: Combining Methods for Better Understanding of Behavior and Change. *Current Anthropology* 46 (1): 129–136.

———. 2005b. Privatizing Pastoral Lands: Economic and Normative Outcomes in Kenya. *World Development* 33 (11): 1959–1978.

———. 2008a. *Contesting the Commons: Privatizing Pastoral Lands in Kenya*. Ann Arbor: University of Michigan Press.

———. 2008b. Land Privatization and Pastoralist Well-Being: A Longitudinal Analysis in Kenya. *Development and Change* 39 (2): 309–331.

Little, P. D., K. Smith, B. Cellarius, D. L. Coppock, and C. Barrett. 2001. Avoiding Disaster: Diversification and Risk Management among East African Herders. *Development and Change* 32:401–433.

McCabe, T. 1990. Turkana Pastoralism: A Case against the Tragedy of the Commons. *Human Ecology* 18 (1): 81–103.

———. 2003. Sustainability and Livelihood Diversification among the Maasai of Northern Tanzania. *Human Organization* 62:100–111.

Meinzen-Dick, R., L. Brown, H. Sims Feldstein, and A. R. Quisumbing. 1997. Gender, Property Rights, and Natural Resources. *World Development* 25 (8): 1303–1315.

Mwangi, E. 2007. The Puzzle of Group Ranch Subdivision in Kenya's Maasailand. *Development and Change* 38 (5): 889–910.

North, D. 1990. *Institutions, Institutional Change and Economic Performance*. Cambridge: Cambridge University Press.

North, D., and R. B. Thomas. 1973. *The Rise of the Western World: A New Economic History*. Cambridge: Cambridge University Press.

Okoth-Ogendo, H. W. O. 2000. Legislative Approaches to Customary Tenure and Tenure Reform in East Africa. In *Evolving Land Rights, Policy and Tenure in Africa*, ed. C. Toulmin and J. Quan, 123–134. London: DFID/IIED/NRI.

Olson, M. 1965. *The Logic of Collective Action: Public Goods and the Theory of Groups*. Cambridge, MA: Harvard University Press.

Ostrom, E. 1990. *Governing the Commons: The Evolution of Institutions for Collective Action*. Cambridge: Cambridge University Press.

———. 2005. *Understanding Institutional Diversity*. Princeton, NJ: Princeton University Press.

Peters, P., 1994. *Dividing the Commons: Politics, Policy and Culture in Botswana*. Charlottesville: University Press of Virginia.

Platteau, J. P. 1996. The Evolutionary Theory of Land Rights as Applied to Sub-Saharan Africa: A Critical Assessment. *Development and Change* 27:29–86.

Ruttan, L. 2006. Sociocultural Heterogeneity and the Commons. *Current Anthropology* 47 (5): 843–853.

Rutten, M. M. 1992. *Selling Wealth to Buy Poverty: The Process of the Individualization of Landownership among the Maasai Pastoralists of Kajiado District, Kenya, 1890–1990*. Nijmegen Studies in Development and Cultural Change, 10. Saarbrucken: Verlag Breitenback Publishers.

Sandford, S. 1983. *Management of Pastoral Development in the Third World*. New York: Wiley.

Scoones, I., ed. 1994. *Living with Uncertainty*. London: Intermediate Technology.

Spencer, P. 1965. *The Samburu: A Study of Gerontocracy in a Nomadic Tribe*. London: Routledge and Kegan Paul.

Thornton, P. K., R. B. Boone, K. A. Galvin, S. B. BurnSilver, M. M. Waithaka, J. Kuyiah, S. Karanja, E. Gonzalez-Estrada, and M. Herrero. 2007. Coping Strategies in Livestock-Dependent Households in East and Southern Africa: A Synthesis of Four Case Studies. *Human Ecology* 35:461–476.

Ullmann-Margalit, E. 1977. *The Emergence of Norms*. Oxford: Clarendon.

12

Cooperation and the Development of Conservation Laws

The Case of the Maine Lobster Industry

James M. Acheson, University of Maine

INTRODUCTION

One of the most important and vexing questions for social scientists is, under what circumstances do humans cooperate to devise norms and rules? Since norms are so essential to social life, one might think that social scientists would have a clear understanding about how they come into being. This is not true. Not only do different groups of social scientists have different theoretical explanations for the generation of norms and rules, but some rules are not explained by any theory in the literature. Most of the major lobster conservation laws can be explained by one well-worked-out body of knowledge or another. The V-notch practice in the Maine lobster industry is different. Although this is one of the most important lobster conservation practices, it is not explained by any well-accepted theory about how norms and institutions come into being. In this chapter, I will discuss the genesis of Maine lobster industry conservation laws and practices, with a view toward extending our understanding about cooperation and the development of norms in general.

THE MAINE LOBSTER INDUSTRY AND ITS CONSERVATION LAWS

The lobster fishery is an inshore trap fishery. It is a day fishery conducted from small boats that leave in the morning and return before dark. The vast majority of lobster boats are between 35 and 40 feet long and are operated by one- or two-man crews who fish an average of 575 wire traps. Currently there are about 6,000 lobster boats in Maine (Acheson 2003).

Lobsters grow when they molt (i.e., shed their shells), which occurs once a year in lobsters that are large enough to be caught legally. Lobster fishermen and biologists measure lobsters on the carapace—from the eye socket to the back of the body shell. It takes approximately seven years for a lobster to grow from the larval stage to 3.25 inches—the size at which they can be legally caught. Fecundity increases with size. When female lobsters first reach reproductive size (3.25 inches on the carapace), they can extrude a few hundred eggs. A single large female over five inches on the carapace can produce over 100,000 eggs. Such large lobsters have no natural enemies and can live for over 100 years.

The Maine lobster industry is one of the most successful fisheries in the world. Since the 1980s, catches have been at record-high levels despite decades of intense exploitation. Although there is no agreement on the cause of these high catches, there is a growing consensus that they are due, in large measure, to the long history of effective regulations. Most lobster laws were passed by the Maine legislature with intense lobbying pressure from the industry over the course of the past 120 years. There can be no doubt that the lobster industry has a very strong conservation ethic. However, although the vast majority of the fishermen support the conservation laws, the negotiations and strategies producing them involved some drawn-out, acrimonious disputes between industry factions that had different interests to pursue (Acheson 2003:13–19).

In this chapter, we are interested in the conservation laws passed by the Maine legislature.[1] At present, there are a number of such conservation laws, and they apply from the beach to the three-mile line, where 80 percent of the lobsters are caught:

1. It is mandatory to have a license to fish for lobsters, and to get a license one must go through an apprenticeship program.
2. It is illegal to take any female lobsters with eggs attached to their shells (i.e., "berried" or "egged" lobsters).
3. There is the "double gauge law," which is a type of "slot limit." This law makes it illegal to take lobsters that are less than 3.25 inches on the carapace, which protects the juveniles, or to take lobsters over 5 inches on the carapace, which protects the large reproductive-sized lobsters.
4. Lobsters can be caught only in traps, which is highly selective gear.
5. Trap must be equipped with an escape vent, which allows juvenile lobsters to escape, and a biodegradable panel that prevents large lobsters from being trapped for very long periods of time in a lost, or "ghost," trap.
6. In 1995, the legislature passed the Zone Management Law, which changed many aspects of lobstering. The law divides the coast into six

zones run by zone councils elected by lobster license holders. Under this law an apprenticeship program has been established for the state, and the zones have voted in different trap limits and limited entry rules.

7. The V-notch practice permits fishermen to voluntarily conserve breeding female lobsters by placing a notch in the tail. This practice is very successful and untold hundreds of thousands of reproductive-sized lobsters have been conserved in this way.

BASIC THEORY: COLLECTIVE ACTION DILEMMAS AND ESTABLISHING RULES

Rules make it possible for humans to coordinate their activities and achieve goals they could not achieve alone. But simply because rules bring about collective benefits is no guarantee that groups will develop them. The problem was framed first by Mancur Olson (1965), who pointed out that even if rules or other public goods benefit all, they will be provided only if "special incentives" exist. The essential problem, he saw, was that there is no incentive for individuals to help to produce a public good since they are going to have the benefit of it regardless of whether or not they contributed to producing it. Since it is rational for every individual to free ride on the efforts of others, the public good is not produced. Everybody has acted rationally, and yet they are all worse off than if they had cooperated. The solution is either rewards or sanctions to overcome the free-rider effect.

More recently, rational choice theorists would phrase the problem in terms of a collective action dilemma (Elster 1989:17; Taylor 1990:223). These are situations in which there is a divergence between the interests of the individual and those of the society. Most collective action dilemmas can be modeled as prisoner's dilemma games (Taylor 1990). The solution to collective action dilemmas is to establish rules constraining the behavior of individuals. In the absence of rules, rational action by the individual will bring suboptimal results or even disaster for the collectivity. In collective action dilemmas, it is not rational for individuals to cooperate, even though cooperation would bring positive results for all.

The poor results produced by "rational action" provide an incentive to get rules and norms. In collective action dilemmas, as Coleman points out (1990:251), the activities of one person produce externalities for others. That is, people are permitted to foist some of the costs of their activities on others. It is the existence of externalities that brings the demand for norms. People whose interests are being damaged by the activities of others have a strong incentive to produce rules to curb the damage, while those who stand to gain in the short run have a strong incentive to oppose such rules.

Common property resources, including marine fisheries, present a classic collective action dilemma. In the case of fisheries, it is in the self-interest of individual skippers to get as many fish as possible, even though a rule constraining exploitive effort would result in a healthier breeding stock, increased catches, lower prices for consumers, and a sustainable industry. In most fisheries, the conditions necessary for the generation of norms have been largely absent, with the result that large numbers of fish stocks are dangerously overexploited. Such failures to solve the collective action problem have been documented in great detail in the literature on fisheries and common property resources (Acheson 1989; McGoodwin 1990; Wade 1994). The lobster fishery is different in that it has repeatedly solved the collective action dilemmas it has faced. Repeatedly it has gone to the government to get formal rules, which Taylor calls a "centralized solution" (1990:225); it has also produced informal rules, a "decentralized solution."

Collective action dilemmas have received an enormous amount of attention from social scientists, primarily because they describe so many of the most vexing problems plaguing humanity. Elster and Taylor go so far as to say that "politics is the study of ways of solving collective action problems" (Taylor 1990:224).

Among rational choice theorists there is a consensus that rules to constrain individuals will improve outcomes in collective action dilemmas. However, there is little consensus on the conditions under which such rules are generated (Taylor 1990:224–225). It is clear that people will not cooperate to produce rules or other kinds of public goods if those who did not sacrifice to produce them get most of the benefits. Curbing free riding is essential. For this reason, there is a consensus that people will be able to provide themselves with rules and institutions if the group is small, people know a good deal about one another's past performances, if the game is played repeatedly, and if the rules can be enforced (Coleman 1990:254, 272; Elster 1989:41; Knight 1992:48–64, 174–178; North 1990:12, 32–36; Ostrom 1990: 71–72, 189; Taylor 1982:50–51; Wade 1994:215). In such circumstances, people know who is likely to cooperate, and can monitor behavior and sanction shirkers.

Scholars interested in the new institutionalism have evolved several different bodies of literature to understand the development of rules or norms. One group has devoted a good deal of effort to delineating the characteristics of communities that are conducive to collective action (i.e., prerequisite conditions; Ostrom 2000a, 2000b). Another group of scholars has developed a body of theory specifying the mechanisms (i.e., types of interactions) between people that give rise to rules and norms, for example, North (1990),

Sugden (1986), Lewis (1969), and Knight (1992). These interactions can be modeled as different types of games. Still another set of institutionalists has emphasized the historical aspects of developing rules (see Bates et al. 1998 and Axelrod 1986). I argue that all these perspectives are necessary if we are to understand the development of rules to manage the lobster industry.

Prerequisite Conditions Necessary to Develop Institutions

One set of scholars argues that if the resource and the people involved have the right combination of characteristics, the probability of rules' being produced by groups working independently of the government is relatively high.

The efforts of these scholars have gone into developing a number of lists of variables that the scholars argue give rise to informal, or "decentralized," institutions and rules. Elinor Ostrom, who has thought extensively about the evolution of norms and rules, recently came up with the following list of variables affecting the ability to cooperate to produce rules; among these variables are "the type of production and allocation functions; the predictability of resource flows; the relative scarcity of the good; the size of the group involved; the heterogeneity of the group; the dependence of the group on the good; common understanding of the group; the size of the total collective benefit; the marginal contribution by one person to the collective good; the size of the temptation to free ride; the loss to cooperators when others do not cooperate; have a choice of participating or not; the presence of leadership; past experience and level of social capital; the autonomy to make binding rules; and a wide diversity of rules that are used to change the structure of the situation" (Ostrom 2000b:148). Other scholars such as Wade (1994) and Baland and Platteau (1996) have developed other lists of variables, which they claim are essential to the development of norms.

While there is some overlap in the lists, many variables mentioned by one analyst do not match those of others. Agrawal (2002:64) points out that "Wade (1994), Ostrom (1990), and Baland and Platteau (1996) jointly identify 36 important conditions. On the whole there are relatively few areas of common emphasis among the analysts. If one compares across the list of conditions, interprets them carefully, and eliminates the common conditions, 24 different conditions are still to be found." Of all of the characteristics in this list, size of the group and heterogeneity are likely to be most important: they show up on virtually every theorist's list.

However, these scholars do not specify how those rules come about. As Esther Mwangi says of this school, "The issues concerning why and how institutions change are neglected while the beginning and end points in institutional evolution are overemphasized" (2001). That is the job of mechanisms theory.

Several circumstances facilitated the passage of lobster management legislation. The industry is relatively homogenous, and legislation does not benefit one group at the expense of others. Moreover, lobster fishing is highly territorial, so lobster fishermen spend their lives in a small territory, fishing with other people whom they know well. This means they are able to monitor one another, and this facilitates the enforcement of rules. The communities are very stable, and groups of fishermen have known one another for a long while; this helps them come to consensus on many issues. In short, lobstering communities have many of the characteristics that make it relatively easy to devise effective rules.

Mechanisms of Social Change: Three Theories

Another group of scholars has focused on the types of interactions (i.e., relationships between people) that are productive of rules. The most important are those proposed by (1) North and Alchian, (2) Lewis and Sugden, and (3) Knight. All these theorists assume that change stems from the rational actions of individuals, and that the development of rules or norms will give mutual benefits. However, their analyses differ greatly. Each of these theorists is assuming a different type of interaction that can be modeled by a different game (Voss 2001).

North and Alchian: Competitive Selection

North (1990) and Alchian (1950) argue that norms emerge from efforts of firms and others to negotiate contracts to facilitate exchange. When two parties can benefit from an exchange, they must agree on the terms by which that exchange will take place, including rules guaranteeing compliance. According to North (1990:86), when prices of technology, raw materials, enforcement, or production change, it sometimes becomes advantageous to negotiate new contracts. Sometimes the parties can negotiate a new contract within existing norms. In other cases, negotiating a contract may necessitate changing or ignoring more basic norms or structural principles on which the contracts depend. If, over the course of time, it is recognized that the new contract gives superior results in the form of lower transaction costs or higher profits, others will copy these contracts. Firms or organizations that do not adopt these new and efficient contractual forms will be less competitive and are more likely to be driven out of business. Over the course of time, these contracts become norms and institutions. The idea that new institutions come into being as a result of competitive selection is a theme that is first found in the work of Alchian (1950), and later echoed in the older work of North (1990).

Lewis and Sugden: The Theory of Social Conventions

According to Lewis and Sugden, the need to coordinate activities gives rise to norms, which are, in essence, social conventions. Lewis and Sugden assume that all actors have an equal amount of power and are involved in a coordination game. Under these conditions, all actors would prefer to cooperate, because cooperation gives better outcomes than any noncooperative solution. In a pure coordination game, "a coincidence of interest predominates" (Lewis 1969:14). A good example of a social convention is driving on one side of the road. Equally good results can be had from a rule specifying that everyone will drive on either the right or the left. Failure to agree on one or the other will result in bad outcomes in the form of high collision rates.

It would presumably be relatively easy for the parties to recognize what the rule should be if only one equilibrium or solution exists in the game. If two or more solutions are available, the actors might enter into an agreement to select one of them. If they cannot do this, the actors will seize on any salient information in their environment to aid in selecting one of the available solutions. Over a period of time, some of the actors focus on one solution and the others emulate them; this gradually establishes a convention (Sugden 1986:73). Once the convention is established, it will tend to be self-reinforcing, since no actor can better his own position by defecting from it (Knight 1992:99).

Knight: Conflicts over Distribution of Resources

Knight argues that norms come into being as an aftereffect of strategic conflict over assets and rewards. Knight begins with the assumption that the actors' goal is to attain a reward; rules are created to facilitate that goal. However, rules rarely distribute rewards equally—they often result in parties or groups gaining differential rewards. In some cases people are fully aware of this and consciously lobby and maneuver to create rules that will give them a distributional advantage. In other cases, rules are generated as the unplanned by-product of a struggle over rewards, or of attempts to resolve conflicts over rewards. In both cases, the actors' goal is to obtain resources; the rules that emerge facilitate this goal.

The rules are created through a process of negotiation. The parties involved have different amounts of power in the negotiations because they have different assets. The actors with more assets have a distinct advantage in the negotiations because they are in a position to accept more risk, because they have more withholding power, and because people are less willing to sanction them if they violate a norm. As a result, the rules that result from negotiation sessions are apt to favor the more powerful; the less powerful have no option but to accept those rules since they cannot do better (Knight 1992:128). If the creation of a rule is the result of a centralized, collective decision-making process, the resulting rule will reflect the asymmetries in the actors' resources. That is, we would expect those with more resources to succeed in negotiating the establishment of a rule beneficial to them.

If the norms come about via an informal, or "decentralized," process, we would expect a different sequence of events to occur. Over time, actors with more resources will be able to resolve negotiations in ways favorable to themselves. Others with similar resources will be able to do the same, establishing a pattern. As people recognize that they are dealing with someone with superior resources, they will adjust their strategies to achieve their own best outcomes. In time, they will alter their strategies to converge on a particular outcome, thus establishing a norm.

MECHANISMS THEORY AND THE PRODUCTION OF LOBSTER CONSERVATION LAWS

In the genesis of lobster legislation, history did not repeat itself. Each of the conservation laws involved different issues, different players who had different interests, and different factions.

The *prohibition against taking egged lobsters and the minimum size rule* came in the latter part of the 19th century after a 20-year battle between the lobster canners and the live-lobster industry. The canners, who wanted to be able to take any sized lobster in the warm months of the year when the canneries were operating, successfully lobbied the Maine legislature to pass a law in 1872 prohibiting taking egg-bearing females (Legislative Documents 1872), and then in 1874 a law prohibiting taking lobsters under 10.5 inches from October to April. These laws limited the live-lobster fishermen who set traps all year and permitted any size lobster to be caught in the warm months when the canneries were operating. Those in the live-lobster industry knew these laws worked to the benefit of the canners and did nothing for conservation. They wanted a law to prohibit canners from slaughtering millions of small lobster so these lobsters could grow to a size where they could be sold in the live trade. They began to lobby for such laws. Beginning in 1879, they got the legislature to pass a series of laws prohibiting taking egg-bearing and small lobsters for ever-increasing parts of the years. These laws were passed over the strong objections of the canners and lobstermen from the eastern part of the state. By 1885 the law was changed to effectively reduce the canning season to three months, and subsequent laws placed more restrictions on taking small lobsters. These laws made canning lobster so unprofitable that the last canneries left Maine in 1895.

The *double gauge law* (with a minimum size and maximum size) was passed in 1933 after a protracted battle between lobster fishermen in the western part of the state and fishermen in the east (Acheson 2003:85–87). A majority of fishermen in the western part of Maine wanted the double gauge law, which would protect the reproductive-sized lobsters (over five inches) while allowing them to sell relatively small lobsters (those over the minimum size, but under the maximum size), for which a huge market existed in southern New England and the Middle Atlantic states. Fishermen in eastern Maine wanted a large minimum size because they were convinced that a small minimum size would benefit the Canadian dealers, who they were convinced planned to flood eastern Maine with small lobsters and consequently undercut the price that Maine fishermen would receive. In the early decades of the 20th century, the eastern Maine faction managed to defeat a number of double gauge bills in the legislature.

Finally, in 1933, a special session of the legislature was called to deal with the deepening economic crisis of the Depression. One of the industries of paramount concern was the lobster industry, where a combination of low lobster prices and very low catches had driven 40 percent of the fishermen from the business. The legislature passed the double gauge law after being urged to do so by a strong coalition of fishermen from the west, who were interested in increased sales, and the commissioner and powerful legislators interested in conserving the lobster stock. After the bill was passed, a group of fishermen from eastern Maine, who were still vociferously opposed, sued to have the law repealed (Acheson 2003:88).

The *trap limit* was passed into law after another protracted distributional fight between two other industry factions (Acheson 2003:103ff). Since 1965, a large majority of people in the lobster industry had wanted a limit on the number of traps each fisherman could use to put a stop to the continual escalation in trap numbers. The argument favoring a trap limit is simple and compelling. There are a fixed number of lobsters molting into legal size each year. If everyone has 400 traps, each license holder will catch the same number of lobsters as he would catch if he had 800 traps (even though it might take a little longer), but each person will use half the amount of bait, traps, and fuel. From 1955 to 1995, 17 trap limit bills were considered in the legislature. All were defeated. The problem was that while everyone agreed that a trap limit would be desirable, there was no agreement on what the trap limit should be. Full-time fishermen wanted to be able to fish far more traps than part-time fishermen who had another job; people from different parts of the state facing different ecological conditions wanted to fish different numbers of traps, too. Moreover, many in the lobster industry believed that a trap limit would do no good unless it was coupled with a limited entry law stopping new licenses from being issued. That is, there would be no sense requiring existing fishermen to take traps out of the water if new entrants into the industry put them back in again. As a result of these disagreements, the legislature refused to pass any bill, knowing that any trap limit that was passed would displease the majority of fishermen.

By the early 1990s there had gathered a number of different forces, which would compel radical legislation in the lobster industry. The Maine Lobstermen's Association—the most powerful group representing fishermen in the western part of Maine—lobbied for a trap limit and a limited entry bill. At the same time, the commissioner was arguing for comanagement because she was convinced that several intractable problems—including a trap limit—could be solved only if fishermen on different parts of the coast were free to promulgate their own rules. Throughout this period, the federal government was pressing Maine to come into line with efforts to make uniform rules for the lobster fishery in federal waters.

The result was the 1995 passage of what is known as the Zone Management Law. This law provided an apprenticeship program, a trap tag program, and a statewide limit of 1,200 traps. It also established a comanagement system by dividing the state into six zones managed by councils elected by the fishermen themselves. These councils were empowered to propose rules on several things, including trap limits lower than the 1,200 required by the state. By 1998, all six zones had voted in limits of 800 or 600 traps. The Zone Management Law was the result of a coalition of a powerful industry faction, the commissioner, and a group of powerful legislators. The interests of these parties were aligned enough to get this law passed, and subsequently to allow the passage of trap limits.

The *escape vent* came about in the late 1970s by a different process. At that time, there was a good deal of interest in the industry and the Maine Department of Marine Resources in mandating that spaces be built into all lobster traps to allow sublegal-sized lobsters to escape from traps before being hauled up. This would reduce the amount of time it took fishermen to clean out traps. It would also reduce mortality on lobsters and the proportion of mutilated lobsters because lobsters hang onto traps and regularly have their claws pulled off when fishermen try to remove them, and they are subject to some predation from large fish after they are taken from traps and float toward the bottom.

By the mid 1970s the escape vent was an idea whose time had come. Massachusetts and Newfoundland had already established such laws. A tank experiment had already convinced the commissioner and the research staff of the Maine Department of Marine Resources that such vents worked. Moreover, many very successful fishermen had secretly equipped their traps with escape vents, which they claimed reduced the time to clean out traps and time at sea, and increased catches of legal-sized lobsters. One of these fishermen was the president of the influential Maine Lobstermen's Association, Eddie Blackmore, who became a supporter of the idea.

In 1976, an escape vent bill was introduced into the legislature by a member of the Marine Resources Committee of the legislature who had become convinced of its worth. Hearings held all over the coast revealed some strident opposition, but far more industry support. This initial bill was defeated, but a similar bill was passed the following year.

The escape vent passed quickly primarily because it was supported by all the critical players, including the commissioner of the Department of Marine Resources, legislators on the Marine Resources Committee, officers of the Maine Lobstermen's Association, and most important of all, large numbers of lobster fishermen. In this respect, the law is unique in the annals of Maine lobster legislation (Acheson 2003:90–91).

V-NOTCH PRACTICE: COOPERATION IN A PRISONER'S DILEMMA GAME

The Practice

The current V-notch law allows any fisherman who catches an egg-bearing female to cut a notch in one of the side flippers on her tail. Such V-notched lobsters may never be taken because they are considered proven breeding stock. Many lobster fishermen consider the V-notch the most important conservation measure in force today. It has tremendous support in the industry. However, it is important to realize that the V-notch practice is voluntary. The law prohibits fishermen from taking egg-bearing females, but there is no law that makes it mandatory for a notch to be cut in the tail. Large numbers of fishermen do so to preserve the breeding stock.

The practice of V-notching built on a law designed to subsidize lobster pound owners. It began slowly and gained momentum throughout the 20th century. By the World War I era, there was a general consensus that the preservation of the industry depended on protection of the breeding stock, and that additional conservation laws were needed to accomplish this task. The legislature was persuaded to pass a law to institute a program whereby egged lobsters would be purchased by the state, whose officers would punch a hole in their tails and release them (Legislative Record 1917). Only pound owners could do so (Maine Commission of Sea and Shore Fisheries 1926:16). Fishermen were forbidden to take lobsters with punched tails and they were not allowed to sell to the state wardens the egg-bearing lobsters they caught (Kelly 1990:3).

Biologist Leslie Scattergood said in an interview, "This law was passed primarily to stop pound owners from scrubbing the eggs from lobsters that had extruded eggs while they were in the pounds." (Pound owners had bought these lobsters from fishermen and felt that they had a right to sell them, even though it was illegal to do so once they had extruded eggs. The "punched-tail" law, or "seeder program," was an effort to bribe pound owners to obey the law.) By the mid-1930s, however, the "seeder program" had expanded to the point where the State of Maine was purchasing "60,000 pounds of seed lobster, from the fishermen through dealers, at market prices" (Maine Department of Sea and Shore Fisheries 1936:11). These lobsters were punched so that they could not be taken again. Most were released where the warden had purchased them, but others were used in the hatchery at Boothbay Harbor.

There were only a few changes in the laws concerning egged lobsters from 1917 to the present, and these were relatively minor. In 1948, the law was changed to state that egged lobsters would be marked by a V-shaped notch cut in the tail, rather than by a round hole punched in the tail. In addition, egged lobsters would be purchased only from people licensed by the commissioner; this was a change designed to aid enforcement efforts (Laws of Maine 1947). In 1973, the law was changed to specify that the V-notch was to be placed in the "right flipper next to the middle flipper" (Kelly 1990:4).

The big change in the V-notch practice took place on the informal level after World War II. At that time increasing numbers of lobster fishermen wanted to do something to help preserve the industry and to avoid having catches decline to the low levels that had been experienced in the late 1920s and early 1930s. Some fishermen hit on the idea of taking advantage of the law to conserve the resource by voluntarily cutting notches in the tails of the egged lobsters they had caught. Those lobsters could not be sold by any other fisherman who happened to catch that same lobster—even though no eggs were present. After all, that lobster was proven breeding stock. Eddie Blackmore, past president of the Maine Lobstermen's Association, explained the advent of the V-notch practice by describing how young returned World War II veterans were responsible for the change: "We decided that if we were going to keep it [the fishery] going, we needed to do something to replenish the supply. We knew that V-notched lobsters were protected and we decided to put more lobsters in that category. When I had an especially good day, I would notch one or two big egged females as a way of investing in the future of the industry. We didn't have to do it, but the idea caught on and a lot of people began to preserve the proven eggers in this way." Former commissioner Vinal Look pointed out, "There was never a law that stated that fishermen could not cut V-notches in the tails of egged lobsters." It became increasingly popular to do so. By the 1990s there were literally thousands of fishermen who voluntarily cut such notches in the tails of the egged females they had caught.

V-notching lobsters is especially effective when combined with the law prohibiting taking lobsters over five inches on the carapace (i.e., the oversize law). An egged female that is V-notched is likely to be preserved as long as the notch lasts, perhaps two years. By that time, a large number of those lobsters have reached the sanctuary size of five inches on the carapace and can never be taken. The combination of the V-notch and oversize law has a more positive effect on the size of the reproductive stock than either rule would have alone.

It is important to recall that the formal law states that fishermen cannot take egged lobsters or lobsters marked with a V-notch. But there is nothing in the law that states that fishermen must V-notch the egged lobsters they catch. A high percentage of fishermen do V-notch lobsters, but they do so voluntarily.

A Prisoner's Dilemma

Understanding the genesis of the V-notch is particularly difficult because the V-notch can best be considered a prisoner's dilemma game, a type of non-zero-sum game with a payoff structure that makes cooperation especially difficult. For heuristic purposes I have made up a set of payoffs that conform to the inequalities required for a prisoner's dilemma game (Table 12.1).

If both players cooperate, both get good rewards (i.e., five each). If both defect, the result is very low payoffs (two each). Unfortunately, if one defects and the other does not, the defector gets a large reward (seven) and the other gets a very low payoff (one). The very high reward for defection motivates both players to defect, with the result that they get the worst of all possible payoffs, one each. Defection dominates cooperation even though cooperation

Table 12.1. Prisoner's Dilemma

		Player 2	
		Cooperate	*Defect*
Player 1	*Cooperate*	*5,5*	*1,7*
	Defect	*7,1*	*2,2*

by both would bring higher payoffs. Defection is rational, but if both players act rationally, the result is the worst of all possible worlds for the larger society because the reproductive stock is greatly reduced. This is the problem with all collective action dilemmas (Elster 1989:17; Taylor 1990:223).

Fortunately, many fishermen V-notch lobsters despite the logic of the prisoner's dilemma in which the fishermen are caught. Why do they do this? There are three factors, I believe.

First, although the V-notch can be modeled as a prisoner's dilemma, the rewards and penalties do not give fishermen much incentive to avoid V-notching. A person who V-notches a lobster has lost only the 30 seconds it takes to cut a notch in the tail of an egg-bearing female lobster and put her back in the water. Moreover, the payoff for avoiding V-notching is not great. Even if one does not V-notch the egg-bearing female lobsters, one cannot keep those lobsters; this means that one's reward for defecting from the V-notch practice is only a very small amount of time saved.

Second, in the culture of lobster fishing, great value is placed on the V-notch. The vast majority of fishermen believe that it is effective in conserving the reproductive-sized lobsters. One fisherman once said to me, "If you do away with that law [the V-notch], you do away with the industry. It is that important." In the view of many fishermen, the V-notch practice is one of the primary reasons (the other being the oversize law) for the resulting large stock of lobsters (Acheson 2003:90, 159–164).

Recent scientific evidence reinforces the idea that the V-notch helps to conserve reproductive-sized lobsters (Acheson 2003). Studies done by university scientists (Bayer, Daniel, and Vaitones 1985), the V-notch survey run by the Maine Lobstermen's Association (Lobster Bulletin 1995:3), and the federal biologists (Lobster Technical Committee 2000:4) all have concluded that the V-notch practice is effective in maintaining the breeding stock by ensuring that a high proportion of the females that have borne eggs are returned to the water to breed again.

Third, lobster fishermen are in the business for the long run. They generally plan to earn their living from lobster fishing for years to come and they hope they children will be able to do so in the future. They are willing to sacrifice to maintain a large reproductive stock as an investment in the future of their industry.

Theoretical Considerations

The V-notch practice involves a case in which fishermen engage in cooperative behavior even when one would not predict they would do so. In the parlance of game theory, the case involves cooperation when defection is the dominant strategy. This is far from an unusual case. In the literature, there is an increasing number of cases where people are far more cooperative than would be predicted based on game theory (Baland and Platteau 1996:114; Camerer 2003; Fehr and Gachter 2000; Ostrom, Gardner, and Walker 1994). In a wonderful article, anthropologist Joseph Henrich and his colleagues state that "researchers from across the social sciences have found consistent deviations from the predictions of the canonical model of self-interest in hundreds of experiments from around the world" (Henrich et al. 2005). They go on to show that culture plays a large role in determining game strategies leading to cooperation (Henrich 2000; Henrich and Henrich 2007).

There is a considerable body of literature on the prisoner's dilemma, and some game theorists have discussed the conditions under which cooperation occurs in spite of the dominant strategy to defect (i.e., not cooperate). Some of their ideas help to illuminate why many lobster fishermen V-notch lobsters even though others are free riding on their efforts.

Three conditions can sustain cooperation in a prisoner's dilemma game. All involve adding something to the prisoner's dilemma mix to change the results.

First, the disastrous results of a one-shot prisoner's dilemma can be averted by having a rule, enforced by a third party, that effectively changes the payoffs in the prisoner's dilemma and makes defection very unattractive. This does not apply in the case of the V-notch because there are no rules mandating V-notching and thus there are no punishments for failing to V-notch.

Second is "leadership" (Dixit and Skeath 2004:359–362) that can result in public goods' being produced even if cooperation is minimal. In these cases, some people get so much from cooperation that they are willing to produce a public good even though others free ride off their efforts. This does not help to explain the V-notch program either since no group of fishermen gains more from a larger stock size than others. All gain equally.

Third and most important is repeated play, or an iterated game. If a prisoner's dilemma game is played only once, it is only rational to defect (Axelrod 1984:125). However, if the game is played a large number of times (or people interact over a long period), then defection in one period can lead to retaliation in another period, which can quickly lead to mutual defection and low payoffs far into the future (i.e., the grim strategy). Under these conditions, people may avoid defection to get the benefits of long-run mutual cooperation. Whether or not they will do so depends on the gains to be had from defection; the long-term losses that accrue when retaliation occurs; and the discount rate, which is a measure of how much people value the future.

This situation certainly helps to explain the penchant for cooperation vis-à-vis the V-notch. In the case of the lobster industry, the gains to be had from defection are very low because a person who does not V-notch is saving only a half-minute per lobster. The long-run losses from permanent mutual defection may be quite high in the form of lower lobster stocks and lower catches in the future. In addition, the discount rate is high, so lobster fishermen are in the game for the long run and they place a high value on earnings to be had in the future. Under these conditions, it is possible for cooperation to emerge. (See Axelrod [1984:12–15] and Dixit and Skeath [2004:353–355] for particularly clear explanations of how repeated play influences cooperation in a prisoner's dilemma game.)

Axelrod (1984:134–138) argues that two additional factors can induce cooperation in a prisoner's dilemma game. One of these is altruism, which involves teaching people to put the welfare of others ahead of purely selfish gain. Another is reciprocity. Sometimes there is an agreement to reciprocate others' gifts, but in some cases people offer gifts and services to elicit cooperation of other players.

Both reciprocity and altruism are involved in the V-notch practice. Fishermen are aware that if they or only a very small number of others V-notch, the practice will be ineffective. Those who do V-notch believe the practice is effective because they believe that very large numbers of others also V-notch. The fact that they catch V-notched lobsters every day reinforces that belief. What is involved here is a kind of tacit reciprocity. There is no contract or rule stating that fishermen have to V-notch, but fishermen are willing to protect reproductive-sized lobsters in exchange for others' doing the same thing. Of course, fishermen cannot observe others reciprocating and have no way to be sure that others have done so, but they V-notch regardless, trusting that others are reciprocating.

How then are we to explain the V-notch? I argue that the practice of V-notching lobsters is due to a combination of factors. It is a form of tacit reciprocity rooted in cheap altruism, a low discount rate, and a strong belief that V-notching is an effective way to ensure a large supply of lobsters for the future. Lobster fishermen, by and large, want to remain in the industry in the long run. They are willing to V-notch lobsters, even though free riders will take advantage of their efforts, because they think the practice is effective in ensuring a large stock of lobsters for the future. V-notching costs time, but not much. Their actions are altruistic, but that altruism costs them little.

Last but not least, the V-notch practice is unusual for still another reason. Many rules begin as informal norms that are then formalized into rules if they work (Knight 1992:85). The V-notch is the opposite. It is an informal practice that is built on the platform of a formal law, which makes it illegal to take V-notched lobsters. This law was designed to save lobsters that had egged out in pounds and then were bought by wardens. Fishermen take advantage of this law to save thousands of egged female lobsters they catch and want to preserve.

CONCLUSION

The development of most of the rules for the Maine lobster industry can be explained by Knight's thesis. The minimum size rules, the prohibition on taking egged lobsters, the double gauge law, and the trap limit all came to pass as a result of conflict over the distribution of resources. Sugden and Lewis's theory of *social conventions* is useful only in explaining the development of one rule, namely, the escape vent. This case can be seen as a coordination game since everyone gained from the rule. There are no instances in which lobster conservation rules were developed as a result of North's idea of *competitive selection.*

None of these theories will explain the V-notch practice. Knight's theory will not apply since the V-notch is not a rule produced by conflict between industry factions over distribution of the resource. It cannot be explained by Sugden and Lewis's theory of social conventions since the V-notch practice cannot be modeled as a coordination game. North's theory of competitive selection of contracts does not apply either since the V-notch practice did not involve new contracts' being negotiated between firms. Clearly the V-notch practice was generated by a different mechanism. I believe it can be described as a form of tacit reciprocity between fishermen who want to preserve the lobster stock in the long run, and who are operating in an environment where the costs of V-notching are low while the perceived benefits are high.

NOTE

1. Offshore, the Atlantic States Marine Fisheries Commission (ASMFC) has jurisdiction in federal waters. The federal government has passed four laws that have a great impact on the management of fisheries out to the 200 mile line: the Fisheries Conservation and Management Act of 1976, the Sustainable Fisheries Act of 1996, the Marine Mammal Act, and the Endangered Species Act. We will not be concerned with these laws since they were established by a top-down process that did not involve the lobster fishing industry in Maine.

REFERENCES

Acheson, James M. 1989. "Management of Common Property Resources." In *Economic Anthropology*, ed. Stuart Plattner, 351–78. Stanford, CA: Stanford University Press.

———. 2003. *Capturing the Commons: Devising Institutions to Manage the Maine Lobster Industry*. Hanover, NH: University Press of New England.

Agrawal, Arun. 2002. "Common Resources and Institutional Sustainability." In *The Drama of the Commons*, ed. Elinor Ostrom, Thomas Dietz, Nives Dolsak, Paul C. Stern, Susan Stonich, and Elke U. Weber, 41–85. Washington, DC: National Academy Press.

Alchian, Armen. 1950. "Uncertainty, Evolution and Economic Theory." *Journal of Political Economy* 58:2311–21.

Axelrod, Robert. 1984. *The Evolution of Cooperation*. New York: Basic Books.

———. 1986. "An Evolutionary Approach to Norms." *American Political Science Review* 80 (4): 1095–1111.

Baland, J. M., and J. P. Platteau. 1996. *Halting Degradation of Natural Resources: Is There a Role for Rural Communities?* Oxford: Clarendon.

Bates, Robert, Avner Greif, Margaret Levi, Jean-Laurent Rosenthal, and Barry Weingast. 1998. *Analytic Narratives*. Princeton, NJ: Princeton University Press.

Bayer, Robert, Peter C. Daniel, and Scott Vaitones. 1985. "Preliminary Estimate of Contributions of V-notched American Lobsters to Egg Production along Coastal Maine Based on Maine Lobsterman's Association V-notch Survey: 1981–1984." *Bulletin of the Department of Animal and Veterinary Sciences*. Orono: University of Maine Press.

Camerer, C.F. 2003. *Behavioral Game Theory: Experiments in Strategic Interaction*. Princeton, NJ: Princeton University Press.

Coleman, James. 1990. "Norm Generating Structures." In *The Limits of Rationality*, ed. Karen Cook and Margaret Levi, 250–73. Chicago: University of Chicago Press.

Dixit, Avinash, and Susan Skeath. 2004. *Games of Strategy*. 2nd ed. New York: W. W. Norton.

Elster, Jon. 1989. *The Cement of Society*. Cambridge: Cambridge University Press.

Fehr, E., and S. Gachter. 2000. "Cooperation and Punishment in Public Goods Experiments." *American Economic Review* 90 (4): 980–95.

Henrich, Joseph. 2000. "Decision Making, Cultural Transmission and Adaptation in Economic Anthropology." In *Theory in Economic Anthropology*, ed. Jean Ensminger, 251–295. Walnut Creek, CA: AltaMira.

Henrich, Joseph, Robert Boyd, Samuel Bowles, Colin Camerer, Ernst Fehr, Herbert Gintis, Richard McElreath, Michael Alvard, Abigail Barr, Jean Ensminger, Natalie Smith Henrich, Kin Hill, Francisco Gil-White, Michael Burven, Frank Marlowe, John Patton, David Tracer. 2005. "'Economic Man' in Cross-Cultural Perspective: Behavioral Experiments in Fifteen Small-Scale Societies." *Behavioral and Brain Sciences* 28:795–855.

Henrich, Joseph, and Natalie Henrich. 2007. *Why Humans Cooperate: A Cultural and Evolutionary Explanation*. New York: Oxford University Press.

Kelly, Kevin H. 1990. *A Summary of Maine Lobster Laws and Regulations: 1820–1990*. Lobster Informational Leaflet #19. Augusta: Maine Department of Marine Resources.

Knight, Jack. 1992. *Institutions and Social Conflict*. Cambridge: Cambridge University Press.

Laws of Maine. 1947. Chapter 332, *A Law to Revise the Sea and Shore Fisheries Laws*, p. 408. Augusta, ME: Office of the Secretary of State.

Legislative Record. Maine Legislature. 1917. House, March 8, 1917, p. 486.

Legislative Documents. 1872. House No. 54. *An Act to Protect the Spawn or Egg Lobsters in the Waters of Maine.*

Lewis, David. 1969. *Convention: A Philosophical Study*. Cambridge, MA: Harvard University Press.

Lobster Bulletin of the University of Maine [Orono]. 1995. "V-notching—Then, Now and Around the World." *Lobster Bulletin* 8 (2): 3.

Lobster Technical Committee. 2000. "Management Measures That Can Be Evaluated on an Area-by-Area Basis: Report to the ASMFC American Lobster Board." Washington, DC: Atlantic States Marine Fisheries Commission. Unpublished manuscript.

Maine Commission of Sea and Shore Fisheries. 1926. *Fourth Biennial Report of the Commission of Sea and Shore Fisheries of the State of Maine*. Rockland, ME.

Maine Department of Sea and Shore Fisheries. 1936. *Ninth Biennial Report of the Department of Sea and Shore Fisheries of the State of Maine*. Thomaston, ME.

McGoodwin, James R. 1990. *Crisis in the World's Fisheries: People, Problems and Policies*. Stanford, CA: Stanford University Press.

Mwangi, Esther. 2001. "Fragmenting the Commons: The Transformation of Property Rights in Kenya's Masai Land." Unpublished manuscript, Department of Political Science, Indiana University, Bloomington.

North, Douglass. 1990. *Institutions, Institutional Change and Economic Performance*. New York: Cambridge University Press.

Olson, Mancur. 1965. *The Logic of Collective Action: Public Goods and the Theory of Groups*. Cambridge, MA: Harvard University Press.

Ostrom, Elinor. 1990. *Governing the Commons: The Evolution of Institutions for Collective Action*. New York: Cambridge University Press.

———. 2000a. "Reformulating the Commons." *Swiss Political Science Review* 61 (1): 29–52.

———. 2000b. "Collective Action and the Evolution of Social Norms." *Journal of Economic Perspectives* 14 (3): 137–58.

Ostrom, Elinor, Roy Gardner, and James Walker. 1994. *Rules, Games and Common-Pool Resources*. Ann Arbor: University of Michigan Press.

Sugden, Robert. 1986. *The Economics of Rights, Cooperation and Welfare*. London: Basil Blackwell.

Taylor, Michael. 1982. *Community, Anarchy and Liberty*. New York: Cambridge University Press.

———. 1990. "Cooperation and Rationality: Notes on the Collective Action Problem and Its Solutions." In *The Limits of Rationality*, ed. Karen Cook and Margaret Levi, 222–49. Chicago: University of Chicago Press.

Thompson, Barton. 2000. "Tragically Difficult: The Obstacles to Governing the Commons." *Environmental Law* 30 (2): 241–78.

Voss, Thomas. 2001. "Game-Theoretic Perspectives on the Emergence of Social Norms." In *Social Norms*, ed. Michael Hechter and Karl-Dieter Opp, 105–36. New York: Russell Sage Foundation.

Wade, Robert. 1994. *Village Republics: Economic Conditions for Collective Action in South India*. San Francisco: ICS Press.

Index

adaptive resilience: Ghanaian market traders and, 141–42; Rio de Janeiro *catadores* and, 186–87; trader networks and, 10–11
agent-based frameworks, 152
agents, nonhuman, 166
agglutination, 69–72
agricultural commodities in Ghana. *See* Ghanaian women market traders and commodity groups
agricultural cooperatives in U.S.: competitive yardstick norm, 217–20, 224–28; hybrid, 229; industrialization and, 215–19, 221, 229, 230; low-cost producer norm, 218, 228–32; market dominance and, 223–24; norms and social change, 219; orderly marketing norm, 216–17, 221–24; profit maximization and, 220
agricultural production in Iron Age Jordan, 158
ahemma (commodity queens), 132–33, 135–38, 141
ahene (market chiefs), 135
Alchian, Armen, 264
Alexander, Richard, 33
all-in/all-out procedures, 124n9
altruism, 33–34, 274
Andean *ayni* reciprocity: overview, 55–56; class politics, contemporary implications for, 190; critique of reciprocity and, 72–75; emergence and functioning of system, 59–60; Gamarra business clusters and splintering, 65–66, 67–70, 71; gift and collective action models of reciprocity, 56–59, 73–74; logic of capital and, 66; property rights and contract enforcement, 66–67; Spanish conquest and market introduction, 60–62; Unicachi and agglutination, 70–72; urban migrants and, 62–65
animal husbandry in Iron Age Jordan, 158–60, *159*
animal husbandry in Kenya. *See* Siambu, Kenya, land privatization and communal grazing rules
animal husbandry in U.S. *See* hog contracting and moral hazard in midwestern U.S.
anonymity and strangers, 30, 67, 68–69
apartheid, 198–99
apprenticeship and mentoring, 189

archaeology in Jordan. *See* Jordan Iron Age communities
Ardren, Traci, 90
Aristotle, 48
Asantehemma (female Asante chief), 134, 135
Asantehene (male Asante chief), 132, 134, 135, 145
Asante market traders. *See* Ghanaian women market traders and commodity groups
Atlantic States Marine Fisheries Commission (ASMFC), 275n1
autonomy. *See* independence and autonomy
Axelrod, Robert, 33, 151, 164, 165, 167, 274
ayni. *See* Andean *ayni* reciprocity
Azzi, Corry, 3

Babcock, H. E., 227
Bali rice production, xix–xx
Baq'ah Valley, 161
bargaining-power theory of institutional change, 252
Barkley, Paul W., 227
Bayat, Asef, 191
bayerehemma (yam queen), 133, 134, 145
Becán, Yucatán, 86–87
Bible, 153–54, 161, 162, 163–64, 167n4
Blackmore, Eddie, 269, 270
Black Women's Economic Empowerment (BWEE) groups and *Ubuntu* in South Africa: Black Economic Empowerment policies and initiatives, 196–98; cultural logic of *Ubuntu*, 198–99; *Masibambane* case study, 206–9; research history and methods, 200–201; *Siyalinga* case study, 201–6; in socioeconomic and political economic context, 209–11; "tragedy of *Ubuntu*," 195–96, 202
Bolivia, 30
Brazilian garbage dump collectors. *See* Rio de Janeiro *catadores* (collectors)
British colonialism, 132, 239
Broad-based Black Economic Empowerment (South Africa), 197–98
Brown, J. Christopher, 226
Bulte, Erwin, 14–15
business groups in South Africa. *See* Black Women's Economic Empowerment (BWEE) groups and *Ubuntu* in South Africa
Buttel, Frederick, 120–21

Calakmul, Yucatán, 86
California Associated Raisin Company, 222. *See also* Sun-Maid Raisin Growers of California
California Plan, 222
California Prune and Apricot Growers Association, 221. *See also* Sunsweet
Campbell, John, 230
Cape Town, South Africa. *See* Black Women's Economic Empowerment (BWEE) groups and *Ubuntu* in South Africa
capitalism: agricultural cooperatives, capital requirements of, 229; hog contracting and capital vs. labor interests, 115–16; Lima migrants and capitalist vs. noncapitalist mentality, 66; shared norms as weakened by, 48–49
Capper-Volstead Act (1922, U.S.), 223
Cargill, 230
carteira assinada (Brazil), 192n2
catadores. *See* Rio de Janeiro *catadores* (collectors)
causation, 40–41
centralized authority, perspectives on, 108–9. *See also* hierarchy
centralized rule production, 263
Chac, Yucatán, 87–88
change, institutional, 241, 242, 252

child-rearing practices, cross-cultural, 32
China, xvi–xvii
CHS Inc., 229–30
Chunchucmil Maya economies: characteristics of, 82–83; conclusions, 96–97; obsidian distribution, 91–96, *92*, *95*; obsidian procurement, 84–91; quadrangles and pyramid labor, 90–91; Rathje model, 81; trade routes, *82*, 85–89; two-tiered model, 83–84, 97
Clark, John, 93
Coase, Ronald, viii
coercion, 33, 35
collective action and organization, 185–92
collective action dilemmas, 261–62
collective action model of reciprocity, 57–59, 72, 73–74
collectives, 89–90, 199. *See also* Andean *ayni* reciprocity; cooperatives
colonialism, 131–32, 239
commodity-based organizations in Ghana. *See* Ghanaian women market traders and commodity groups
common pool resources: collective action dilemma and, 262; collective action model and, 58; "tragedy of the commons" and free-rider effect, 195–96, 212n2, 242–43, 248, 261–62. *See also* prisoner's dilemma
competition: Ghanaian market traders and, 143; Jordan Iron Age communities and cooperation vs., 149–51, 166–67; in neoclassical economic theory, 3–4; out-competing vs. out-cooperating, 22–23; predatory, 8, 13–15, *14*; Rio de Janeiro *catadores* and, 191; South African BWEE groups and cooperation vs., 209–11
competitive selection, 220, 264
competitive yardstick norm, 217–20, 224–28
conflict. *See* competition; cultural conflict and competitive yardstick norm; dispute settlement
conservation laws. *See* Maine lobster industry and conservation rules
continuous flow methods, 124n9
contract negotiations leading to norms, 264. *See also* negotiation
contract operations in hog farming. *See* hog contracting and moral hazard in midwestern U.S.
cooperation, definition of, 5–6
cooperatives. *See* agricultural cooperatives in U.S.; Black Women's Economic Empowerment (BWEE) groups and *Ubuntu* in South Africa; Rio de Janeiro *catadores* (collectors)
cooperatives, hybrid, 229
coordination games, 265
Cotterill, Ronald W., 224
creativity and game theory, xviii–xx
credit: Ghanaian market traders and, 139, 140–41; Lima migrants and, 68; South African BWEE groups and, 200, 203–4, 208; U.S. agricultural cooperatives and debt financing, 229
crisis points. *See* hog contracting and moral hazard in midwestern U.S.
cross-cultural study. *See* market integration and prosocial behavior cross-cultural study
cultural conflict and competitive yardstick norm, 226–27
culturalist critiques of reciprocity, 74–75
cultural materialism, 40
culture and game theory, 273
"culture matters" school, 74–75

Dahlin, Bruce H., 90, 96
Davenport, William, xix
David and Goliath metaphor, 226
debt. *See* credit
decentralized rule production, 263, 266

defection: farmer withdrawal from market, 228; Jordan Iron Age communities and, 152, 164–65, 167; Kenyan pastoralists and, 250; Maine lobstering and, 271–74; South African *Ubuntu* and, 195–96, 199, 204–5. *See also* prisoner's dilemma
democratization and hog contracting, 120–23
Deng Xiaoping, xvi–xvii
design principles, 243
Deutsch, Morton, 34
Diamond, Jared, 149–51, 166–67
dictator games, 30, 48, 50n2, 51n7
dispute settlement: Ghanaian market traders and, 134, 137, 143, 145; lawsuits vs. internal settlement, 137; Samburu elders and, 247
distal vs. proximate cause, 40–41
distribution: of Chunchucmil obsidian, 91–96, *92*, *95*; institutions and unequal distribution, 241–42; redistribution and hierarchy, 93. *See also* reciprocity
diversification of livelihood among pastoralists, 252
Douglas, Mary, 57
Dzibilchaltún, Yucatán, 88
Dzibilnocac, Yucatán, 87

economies of scale, 138–39
Edzna, Yucatán, 87
Egypt, 154–57
Ehrenberg, Ronald, 3
El Chayal obsidian, 84–86
elites, predatory, 16–18. *See also* hierarchy
Elster, Jon, 262
encomienda system, 61
endogeneity, 40
Energreen, 206
enforcement of contracts, rules, or norms: first, second, and third person, 241; Ghanaian market traders and, 131, 136–37; Kenyan pastoralists and, 254; Lima migrants and, 67, 69
entrepreneurship: agricultural competition and, 217–18; Black Women's Economic Empowerment groups and, 205, 208; Malinowski on, 56–57; in Peru, 63–72, 75n1
equifinality, 93
escape. *See* defection
Escliar, Valeria, 191–92
ethnicity, 3, 16
evolution, hominin and human: cooperation in, 5–6; exchange networks and reciprocity, 6–7; *Homo sapiens* and Neanderthals, 14–15; *Homo* sp. and *Paranthropus*, 11–14, *12*, *14*; model for behavioral and socioeconomic evolution, 4–5; niche construction and predation pressure, 7–9; predation pressure in history of, 9–11; resiliency of cooperation and, 22
evolutionary theory, sociality in, 33
exchange networks and reciprocity, 6–7
exit from cooperation. *See* defection
exports. *See* trade

farming. *See* agricultural cooperatives in U.S.; hog contracting and moral hazard in midwestern U.S.
Farmland Industries, 229
farrow-to-finish hog production, 123n5
feedback, 13–14, *14*, 19–22
flexibility. *See* adaptive resilience
food production and practices, 10, 160, 180–85. *See also entries at* agricultural
forager societies, 5, 10
formalization of business, 67–68
fortification construction in Iron Age Jordan, 160
free-rider effect, 248, 261–62. *See also* "tragedy of the commons"

Galton's problem, 39, 50
Gamarra business clusters in Peru, 65–66, 67–70, 71
Gamble, Clive, 6
games and game theory: collective action model and, 74; coordination games, 265; culture, role of, 273; *n*-person, non-zero-sum games, xix–xx; prisoner's dilemma, ix–x, xix–xx, 33, 58; public goods games, 31; trust, conditions for, 34–35; ultimatum and dictator games, 29–30, 32, 48–50, 50n2, 51n7. *See also* market integration and prosocial behavior cross-cultural study
garbage dump workers in Brazil. *See* Rio de Janeiro *catadores* (collectors)
gender, 211
generosity, in SCCS study, *42*, 43, 47–48
Ghanaian women market traders and commodity groups: overview, 129–30; benefits of group membership, 136–39; conclusions, 142–46; flexibility, survival, and core vs. marginal members, 141–42; group structure, 131–33; information as common property, 139–41; leadership models, 134–36; loyalties, weak and strong, 133–34; research methodology, 130–31
gift model of reciprocity, 56–57, 72, 73
Golderg, Ray, 228
governance. *See* leadership
government frustration and resistance, 144–46, 251. *See also* regulation and control
gradualism, 218–19
grazing rights in Kenya. *See* Siambu, Kenya, land privatization and communal grazing rules
Growth, Employment and Redistribution Program (South Africa), 196–197

Hamilton, William, 33
Hardin, Garrett, 195, 242
Hart Keith, 175
Hayek, Friedrich, 49, 220
Hebrew Bible, 153–54, 161, 162, 163–64, 167n4
Henrich, Joseph, ix, xi, xii, 30, 32, 273
Henrich, Natalie, ix, xi, xii
hierarchy: core vs. marginal members of trade groups, 141–42; hog contracting and, 108–9; Iron Age Jordan and social hierarchies, 161–64, *163*; Kenyan pastoralists and, 252–53; nonhuman agents and, 166; personalism and, 119–20; redistribution as replication of, 93; Rio de Janeiro *catadores* and, 179, 184, 189–90, 191; two-tiered model of Maya economies, 83–84. *See also* Ghanaian women market traders and commodity groups; leadership
hinterlands, 95–96
Hobbes, Thomas, viii–ix, 58
hog contracting and moral hazard in midwestern U.S.: biological "fragility" of hogs, 110; capital vs. labor interests, 115–16; contract operations vs. simple commodity farms, 107–8; emergent-area firms and new technologies, 110–11; industrialization and, 217–18; input provisioning as crisis point, 112–13; management of crisis points, 116–17; moral hazard and crisis points, defined, 111–12; personalism and crisis points, 117–20; perspectives on, 108–9; reproduction and democratization, 120–23; residual claimancy and incentives, 114–15
hominin evolution. *See* evolution, hominin and human
Homo economicus, 72
Homo sp. *See* evolution, hominin and human
honesty, 34, 43, *44*, 109, 117
Horan, Richard D., 14–15
Horizon Milling, 230

house building in Iron Age Jordan, 154–55
houselots at Chunchucmil, 92
"hunter-gatherers." *See* forager societies

IBP, 216
identity, collective, 189
ideologies of scale, 226
ilima (communal rural farming in South Africa), 199
imports. *See* trade
Incan empire, 60. *See also* Andean *ayni* reciprocity
incentives, 114, 249–51, 261, 265
income maximization, 29, 31
independence and autonomy: land privatization, autonomy, and control in Kenya, 245–47; migrants and Lima and, 64–65, 68; Rio de Janeiro *catadores* and, 177–78, 180, 191; South African *Ubuntu* and, 199; U.S. agricultural cooperatives and, 223
industrialization: agricultural cooperative norms and, 215–19, 221, 229, 230; in hog production, 110–11
inequality, 94, 164–65, 241–42, 244. *See also* hierarchy
informal activities. *See specific cases, such as* Rio de Janeiro *catadores*
information, 139–41, 221
input provisioning, 112–13
institutional change, 241, 242, 252
institutional innovation, 253–54
interdependence, 198–99
investment groups in South Africa. *See* Black Women's Economic Empowerment (BWEE) groups and *Ubuntu* in South Africa
Iowa Beef Packers (IBP), 216
Iron Age communities. *See* Jordan Iron Age communities
Israel, ancient, 162

Japan, xv–xvi
Jardim das Flores. *See* Rio de Janeiro *catadores* (collectors)
Johnson, John, 229–30
joking, 181–82
Jordan Iron Age communities: cooperation-competition debate and, 149–51, 166–67; leadership, governance, and social hierarchy, 160–64, *163*; nonhuman agents and, 166; non-zero-sum interactions and, 151–53; production strategies, 157–60, *169*; reciprocity, defection, and time, 151–52, 164–66; settlement pattern, 153–57, *155*, *156*

Kaminaljuyú, 89
Karak Plateau, 154
Kenya. *See* Siambu, Kenya, land privatization and communal grazing rules
kinship- and community-mediated production, 75
Knight, Jack, 265–66
Kriebel, Barry, 231
kuraka (Andean village leader), 60, 61
Kusami Central Market, Ghana. *See* Ghanaian women market traders and commodity groups

labor: for Chunchucmil pyramids, 90; hog contracting and capital vs. labor interests, 115–16; mental vs. manual, 118–19; *mita* labor draft, 61–62; *mit'a* labor exchange, 60, 63–64; wage labor in Andes, 62. *See also* Andean *ayni* reciprocity; Rio de Janeiro *catadores* (collectors)
land privatization. *See* Siambu, Kenya, land privatization and communal grazing rules
Lansing, J. Stephen, xix
lawsuits vs. internal settlement, 137
leadership: in ancient Israel, 162; ceremonial functions, 138; Ghanaian market traders and, 132–39, 144–45; inequality and defections, 164–65; Jordan Iron Age communities and, 160–64; Kenyan pastoralists and,

253; patrimonial and charismatic, co-occurence of, 164; prisoner's dilemma and, 273; South African BWEE groups and, 207, 208. *See also* hierarchy
legitimacy, 228–29
lending. *See* credit
Lesorogol, Carolyn, 48
Lewis, David, 265
Lima, Peru. *See* Andean *ayni* reciprocity
listwise deletion, 39, 41
livestock grazing in Kenya. *See* Siambu, Kenya, land privatization and communal grazing rules
lobster fishing. *See* Maine lobster industry and conservation rules
the local trap, 226
Look, Vinal, 271
low-cost producer norm, 218, 228–32
loyalty, 133–34
Lukiewski, Dave, 230

Machiguenga people, 29
Maine Department of Marine Resources, 268–69
Maine lobster industry and conservation rules: conclusions, 275; conservation laws, 259–61; mechanisms theory and production of laws, 266–69; theory on rules and collective action dilemmas, 261–66; V-notch practice and prisoner's dilemma, 269–74
Maine Lobstermen's Association, 268, 269, 272
Malinowski, Bronislaw, 56–57, 74
marginal settings, 152–53, 154–57
Marine Resources Committee (Maine Legislature), 269
market dominance, 223–24
marketing: global, 231; mass marketing strategy, 227; orderly marketing norm, 216–17, 221–24
marketing cooperatives, agricultural. *See* agricultural cooperatives in U.S.
market integration and prosocial behavior cross-cultural study: overview, 29–32; conclusion, 49–50; definition of market integration, 50n1; determinants of prosocial behavior, 32–35; discussion, 47–49; econometrics issues, 39–41; estimation and results, 41–47, *44*, *45*, *46*; SCCS variables, 35–39, *36–37*, *38*
market power, 230–31
markets: Chunchucmil, 83, 94; differing practices mediated by, 72–73; introduction of, in Andes, 60–62; Smith on Leviathan and, viii–x. *See also specific cases*
Mauss, Marcel, xii, 56–57, 73, 74
Maya economies. *See* Chunchucmil Maya economies
Mead, Margaret, xi
meal sharing as cooperative practice, 182–85
mechanisms theory, 263, 266–69
mediation model of reciprocity, 75
mentoring and apprenticeship, 189
middleman system, 227–28
midwestern hog farming. *See* hog contracting and moral hazard in midwestern U.S.
migrants to Lima, 63–65
mimetic desire and crisis, 16
minorities, 3, 16
mita labor draft, 61–62
mit'a labor exchange, 60, 63–64
Moholy-Nagy, Hattula, 94
monotonic decrement, law of, 85–86
moral hazard. *See* hog contracting and moral hazard in midwestern U.S.
mortality incentives, 114, 123n7
multicollinearity, 40, 41, 43
multiple imputation, 39
Mwangi, Esther, 263

Nakahara, Japan, xv–xvi
Neanderthals, 14–15
Near Eastern Iron Age communities. *See* Jordan Iron Age communities
negotiation: in competitive selection, 264; in Ghana, 131–32, 137; Kenyan

pastoralists and, 248–49; rules created through, 265–66
neoclassical economic theory, 3–4
neoliberal analysis, 108
neo-Marxist analyses, 108–9
nepotism, 33
networks: exchange networks and reciprocity, 6–7; network-based traders (NBT), 19–22; social, 6, 183–85, 187–88, 202–3; trader networks and predation pressure, 10–11, 15–22, *17*, *20*, *21*
New Institutional Economics (NIE), viii, 215, 218–19, 229
News for Farmer Cooperatives, 226, 228
niche construction, 7–9, 11–14
Nobel Prize in Economics, vii, viii
nonhuman agents, 166
Nonzero: The Logic of Human History (Wright), 149–51
non-zero-sum interactions, xix–xx, 151–53, 164–67
norms and rules: capitalism as weakening shared norms, 48–49; competitive selection, 220, 264; competitive yardstick norm, 217–20, 224–28; factors facilitating or hindering cooperation, 244; game payoffs changed by, 273; low-cost producer norm, 218, 228–32; new institutionalist research on, 262–63; Olson on incentives and, 261; orderly marketing norm, 216–17, 221–24; prerequisite conditions for, 263–64; rational choice theory and collective action dilemmas, 261–62; of reciprocity and trust, 58–59; social change and, 219; social conventions theory, 265; social order fostered by, 219; transgression of and escape from, 199. *See also* Maine lobster industry and conservation rules; Siambu, Kenya, land privatization and communal grazing rules
North, Douglass, viii, 218–19, 230, 264
Nourse, Edwin, 215, 216, 217, 219, 220, 224–29, 227–28, 231–32

obsidian trade. *See* Chunchucmil Maya economies
Ocean Spray Cooperative, 225, 229
Ofek, Haim, 6
ôhemma (market queen), 132, 134–38
Olson, Mancur, 57, 261
O Mensajeiro da Verdade newsletter, 187
orderly marketing norm, 216–17, 221–24
organization of *catadores* labor, 185–92
Ostrom, Elinor, vii, xviii, 243, 263

Paarlberg, Donald, 220
Pakbeh Regional Economy Program, 81
paradox and game theory, xix
Paranthropus sp., 8, 9, 11–14, *12*, *14*
pastoralists in Kenya. *See* Siambu, Kenya, land privatization and communal grazing rules
patronage and Ghanaian market traders, 143
personalism, 117–20, 130, 143
Peru. *See* Andean *ayni* reciprocity
pig farming. *See* hog contracting and moral hazard in midwestern U.S.
Polanyi, Karl, 57, 59, 74
political stability and portfolio capitalists, 19–21, *20*, *21*
Porokwai, Kenya, 250
portfolio capitalists, 19–21, *20*, *21*
predatory pressure: defined, 8; in hominin evolution, 9–15, *12*, *14*; trader networks and, 10–11, 15–22, *17*, *20*, *21*; types of, 8–9
price controls, 145, 223, 225
price information, 139–40
prisoner's dilemma: altruism and, 274; Balinese rice production and, xix–xx; collective action model and, 58; conditions to sustain cooperation

in, 273–74; Jordan Iron Age communities and, 151, 167; Leviathan and, ix–x; Maine lobstering and, 271–74; reciprocity and, 33, 274; tit –for tat solution, 33, 58
privatization of land. *See* Siambu, Kenya, land privatization and communal grazing rules
production: competitive yardstick norm and producer protection, 224–26; Jordan Iron Age strategies, 157–60, *169*; in marginal environments, 152–53; nonhuman agents and, 166
profit maximization and agricultural cooperatives, 220
property rights, 66–67, 69, 242. *See also* Siambu, Kenya, land privatization and communal grazing rules
proximate vs. distal cause, 40–41
punishment, 18, 31, 34–35. *See also* enforcement of contracts, rules, or norms
Purcell, Mark, 226
Puuc hills site, Yucatán, 88

quadrangle compounds at Chunchucmil, 90–91, 96
Quirigua, Yucatán, 94

racial discrimination and church attendance, 3
Raisin Bargaining Association, 225
Ramses II, Pharaoh, 154
Rathje, William, 81
rationalism: collective action dilemmas and, 261–62; as income maximization, 29; Olson on collective action and, 57; prisoner's dilemma and, x
Reardon, Thomas, 230–31
reciprocity: altruism and indirect reciprocity, 33–34; Chunchucmil obsidian and, 94; collective action model, 57–59, 72, 73–74; critique of, 72–75; culturalist critiques of, 74–75; definitions of, 33; exchange networks and, 6–7; gift model, 56–57, 72, 73; Kenyan pastoralists and, 248; mediation model, 75; Polanyi and Sahlins on, 57; prisoner's dilemma and, 33, 274; time and, 151, 167; trader networks and, 18; trust and, 130. *See also* Andean *ayni* reciprocity; distribution
Reconstruction and Development Program (South Africa), 196
recyclers: in Buenos Aires, 191–92; South African reclaimers, 191; worldwide, 176. *See also* Rio de Janeiro *catadores* (collectors)
reducciones (forced resettlement), 61
regional associations in Peru, 64, 71
regulation and control: in Ghana, 137–38; Maine lobstering conservation laws, 259–61; predatory, 8–9; Rio de Janeiro *catadores* and, 177–78
residual claimancy, 114–15
resiliency of cooperation, evolution and, 22
retail market power, 230–31
revenue sharing in hog contracting, 114–15
rewards. *See* incentives
Rice, Prudence M., 91, 95–96
Rio de Janeiro *catadores* (collectors): overview, 175–77; collective action and organization, 185–92; food practices and production of social relations, 180–85; labor conditions on the dump, in depositories, and in cooperative, 177–80
risk management: Ghanaian market traders and, 137, 143; rules construction and, 265; South African BWEE groups and, 205; U.S. agricultural cooperatives and, 224. *See also* dispute settlement
rule of law traditions, 31
rules. *See* enforcement of contracts, rules, or norms; norms and rules

Sahlins, Marshall, 57
Samburu pastoralists. *See* Siambu, Kenya, land privatization and communal grazing rules
San Cosme settlement, Lima, 63
Sapiro, Aaron, 216, 220, 222, 223, 224
savings, 200, 207
scale: economies of, 138–39; ideologies of, 226
scapegoating of traders, 16
Scattergood, Leslie, 270
Schelling, Thomas, xviii
Scott, James, 217
self-employment and labor mobilization, 191. *See also* Rio de Janeiro *catadores* (collectors)
self-interest: argument of cooperation vs., vii–viii; Ghanaian market traders and, 129; Olson on collective action and, 57; prisoner's dilemma and, x. *See also* rationalism
Shogren, Jason F., 14–15
Siambu, Kenya, land privatization and communal grazing rules: overview, 239–40; autonomy and control after privatization, 245–47; incentives created by grazing rules, 249–51; institutional change, cooperation, and property rights, 240–44; as institutional innovation, 253–54; internal and external factors in privatization, 244–45; new grazing rules, emergence of, 247–49; possible explanations for new rules, 251–53
Sidrys, Raymond V., 86
Simmel, Georg, 48
Smith, Adam, viii, ix–x, 34
Smyth, Michael, 87
social conventions theory, 265
social hierarchies. *See* hierarchy
socialization, cross-cultural, 32
social networks: as business-oriented groups (South Africa), 202–3; Rio de Janeiro *catadores* and, 183–85, 187–88; social groups vs., 6
South Africa. *See* Black Women's Economic Empowerment (BWEE) groups and *Ubuntu* in South Africa
splintering, 67–70
Standard Cross-Cultural Sample (SCCS). *See* market integration and prosocial behavior cross-cultural study
strangers and anonymity, 30, 67, 68–69
stratification. *See* hierarchy
Successful Farming, 227
Sugden, Robert, 265
Sun-Maid Raisin Growers of California, 222, 224–25, 231
Sunsweet, 221, 223, 231

Tanzania, 30
Taylor, Michael, 262
Teotihuacán, 89, 90–91
Thornton, Robert, 195–96, 199, 212n2
Tikal, Yucatán, 86, 94
time, 151, 165–66, 167
tombs from Iron Age Jordan, 161–62
tools in hominin evolution, 7, 9–10
trade: Chunchucmil obsidian importing, 84–91; in hominin evolution, 6–7, 10; trader networks and predation pressure, 10–11, 15–22, *17*, *20*, *21*. *See also* Ghanaian women market traders and commodity groups
"tragedy of the commons," 195–96, 212n2, 242–43
"tragedy of *Ubuntu*," 195–96, 212n2
transaction cost analysis, viii, 219
transport and economies of scale, 138–39
trust and distrust: anonymity and, 67; collective action model and, 73–74; Ghanaian market traders and, 130; hog contracting and, 109, 117–18; market relationships and, 34; reciprocity and norms of, 58–59; Rio de Janeiro *catadores* and distrust, 189–90; in

SCCS study, 43, *45*, *46*, 47; size and homogeneity of groups and, 243; U.S. agricultural cooperatives and, 221
Tutu, Desmond, 198
two-tiered model of Maya economies, 83–84, 97

Ubuntu (humanness). *See* Black Women's Economic Empowerment (BWEE) groups and *Ubuntu* in South Africa
ultimatum games, 29–30, 32, 48–50
Unicachi urban investment groups, 70–72
United States. *See* agricultural cooperatives in U.S.; hog contracting and moral hazard in midwestern U.S.; Maine lobster industry and conservation rules

value-added cooperatives, 219
violence against traders, 16–17
V-notch practice in lobstering, 269–74

wage labor, 62, 178
Walmart, 218, 230
war, external, 35
Weber, Max, 66
Weinstock, Harvey, 221–22
wholesale yards in Ghana, 132, 139
Williamson, Oliver, vii
Women in Oil and Energy in South Africa (WOESA), 206
women traders in Ghana. *See* Ghanaian women market traders and commodity groups
Wright, Robert, 149–51, 166–67

yam trading in Ghana. *See* Ghanaian women market traders and commodity groups
Yaxuna, Yucatán, 88
Yucatán peninsula. *See* Chunchucmil Maya economies

Zone Management Law (Maine), 268

About the Editor and Contributors

James M. Acheson is professor of anthropology and marine sciences at the University of Maine. He has done fieldwork in the Purepecha-speaking area of Mexico and in Maine fishing communities. He is author of a number of books including *The Lobster Gangs of Maine*. He has edited volumes including *Anthropology and Institutional Economics* and *The Question of the Commons* (with Bonnie McCay). In recent years he has focused on understanding the development of institutions to manage marine fisheries using concepts from institutional economics and rational choice theory.

Matthew Bird received his PhD from the Department of Comparative Human Development at the University of Chicago and currently works as a research associate at Harvard Business School and as a research director for the Advanced Leadership Initiative at Harvard University.

His doctoral research sought to understand cultural influences on the formation of varieties of capitalist mentalities in Lima, Peru, and was based on ethnographic fieldwork and archival study. More broadly, he seeks to apply the field of cultural psychology to the study of economic behavior and is working to translate insights into action tools for policymakers, managers, and social entrepreneurs. His research has been funded by grants from the National Science Foundation, Fulbright-Hays, and the National Institute of Mental Health.

Gracia Clark has studied Kumasi Central Market in Ghana, West Africa, since 1978. Her thesis research in social anthropology at the University of Cambridge highlighted the regional dominance of this urban daily market and the relations of credit, leadership, and domestic work that kept its 20,000 traders in their stalls. She consulted for the International Labour Organization (ILO) and United Nations Development Fund for Women (UNIFEM) for several years before teaching at the University of Wisconsin, Parkside, and the University of Michigan, Ann Arbor. Subsequent fieldwork addressed development issues of food security and trade liberalization and recorded life stories from older traders. A volume of life stories titled *African Market Women* (2010) complements her 1994 book, *Onions Are My Husband*. Her current website project, Virtual Kumasi Central Market, seeks to re-create the fieldwork experience by structuring original materials interactively so that visitors' questions shape what they learn.

Bruce H. Dahlin received his PhD from Temple University in 1976 and is currently an adjunct professor with the Center for Environmental Studies at Shepherd University. His research interests include environmental archaeology, especially the relationships between climate, land use, and demography and social, political, and economic organization.

Malcolm McLaren Dow is professor emeritus of anthropology at Northwestern University. He holds a BA in mathematics (1972) and a PhD in mathematical social science (1979) from the University of California, Irvine. His interests include social network analysis, cultural ecology, demography, and the methodological/statistical problems that arise in comparative survey research. He came up with the idea of using "network autocorrelation" to characterize Galton's problem in graduate school, and over the years has published about a dozen articles on the topic. His recent collaborative work with E. Anthon Eff has led to the introduction of contemporary multiple imputation methods to handle the ubiquitous problem of missing cross-cultural data in comparative survey research, and to extensive model-checking diagnostics for the network autocorrelation effects regression model. He is currently working with Eff on extending the network autocorrelation approach to handle discrete choice dependent variables.

E. Anthon Eff is professor of economics at Middle Tennessee State University. He has a BA in anthropology from the University of Louisville (1981) and a PhD in economics from the University of Texas, Austin (1989). His interests include urban and regional economics, economic anthropology, and the history of economic thought. Since 2006, Eff has worked with Malcolm M. Dow on resolving the methodological problems that arise in cross-cultural survey research, including Galton's problem and multiple imputation of missing data.

Agustín Fuentes is currently a professor of anthropology and the director of the Institute for Scholarship in the Liberal Arts at the University of Notre Dame. His research and teaching interests include the evolution of social complexity in human and primate societies, cooperation and conflict, reproductive behavior and ecology, and issues of human-nonhuman primate interactions. His recent published work includes the books *Evolution of Human Behavior*, *Health, Risk, and Adversity* (coeditor), *Core Concepts in Biological Anthropology*, and *Primates in Perspective* (coeditor), and articles such as "The Humanity of Animals and the Animality of Humans: A View from Biological Anthropology Inspired by J. M. Coetzee's *Elizabeth Costello*" (*American Anthropologist*) and "Re-situating Anthropological Approaches to the Evolution of Human Behavior" (*Anthropology Today*). Current research projects include human-monkey interactions in Asia and Gibraltar and examining the roles of cooperation, social complexity, and niche construction in human evolution.

Katrina T. Greene is an associate professor of anthropology at Biola University. She received her PhD in anthropology from American University in 2002. Since 1997, she has conducted periodic fieldwork and research in the black African townships of Cape Town, South Africa. This includes her dissertation research (1999–2000) as a U.S. Fulbright scholar; this research examined the use and transformation of indigenous savings and credit practices among women for housing development and long-term investment projects in the new South Africa. Her current research interests focus on local forms of black economic empowerment as they relate to the gendered realities of black African women in the Cape Town townships.

Julie A. Hogeland is an agricultural economist with Rural Development, U.S. Department of Agriculture. She received an MS in agricultural economics from Michigan State University in 1977 and a PhD in economics (specializing in political economy) from American University in 1992. Her recent interests focus on cooperative norms and strategies, food safety, fruit and other specialty cooperatives, livestock and meat marketing, and identity-preserved grain marketing.

Scott R. Hutson received his PhD from the University of California, Berkeley, in 2004 and now teaches in the Department of Anthropology at the University of Kentucky. His research interests include household archaeology, settlement patterns, and social, political, and economic organization and identity. His book *Dwelling, Identity and the Maya* was recently published.

Carolyn K. Lesorogol is currently associate professor of social work and anthropology at the Brown School of Social Work, Washington University, St. Louis. Her primary research interests include processes of institutional change, particularly changing social norms related to property among pastoralists in Kenya. She has lived and worked among Samburu pastoralists in northern Kenya for more than 20 years, and her recent book, *Contesting the Commons: Privatizing Pastoral Lands in Kenya* (2008), investigates the social, political, and economic processes that led to privatization of communal land among Samburu as well as the consequences of this shift for household well-being and social relations. She has also used experimental economics games in her work to explore changes in human behavior related to institutional transformations. Her work has been funded by grants from the National Science Foundation and Fulbright-Hays, and has been published in *Science*, *Current Anthropology*, *American Anthropologist*, *Development and Change*, and *World Development*, among other journals.

Robert C. Marshall is professor of anthropology in the Department of Anthropology at Western Washington University. He has been studying Japan's worker cooperatives since 1991 and was in Japan during 2002 as a fellow of the Japan Foundation to investigate "senior cooperatives," a new consumer-worker cooperative hybrid of, by, and for the elderly in Japan. His article "The Culture of Cooperation in Three Japanese Worker Cooperatives" appeared in *Economic and Industrial Democracy*.

Daniel Mazeau is a PhD candidate in anthropology at the University at Buffalo, the State University of New York, and a principal investigator with the New York State Museum. His research interests include GIS, regional survey, and lithics.

Kathleen Millar is a doctoral candidate in the Department of Anthropology and the academic coordinator for the Center for Latin American and Caribbean Studies at Brown University. Her research focuses on the configuration of labor in the context of informal employment and its relevance to anthropological understandings of work, social class, and economies today. She recently returned from Rio de Janeiro, Brazil, where she conducted 15 months of ethnographic fieldwork on the construction of economic practices and logics among *catadores*, who earn a living by collecting recyclable material on Rio's largest garbage dump.

Rahul Oka received his PhD in archaeological anthropology from the joint program of the departments of anthropology of the University of Illinois,

Chicago, and the Field Museum (2008). He is currently assistant professor of anthropology at the University of Notre Dame and research associate at the Field Museum. His research program aims to understand the role played by regional and intercontinental commerce in shaping the rise and fall of societies and settlements. His current research is focused on understanding the role of trade and commercial networks in resource distribution in conflict zones in northern Kenya, northern Uganda, and southern Sudan. He is also codirecting archaeological research on the western coast of India and the Kenyan coast.

Benjamin W. Porter is an assistant professor of Near Eastern archaeology in the Department of Near Eastern Studies at the University of California, Berkeley. He has taught at Princeton University and the University of Pennsylvania, the latter from which he received his PhD in anthropology in 2007. He codirects the Dhiban Excavation and Development Project in Jordan and serves as an assistant editor at *Near Eastern Archaeology*. He is writing a book on ancient Near Eastern social life in marginal contexts.

Ronald Rich holds a PhD in anthropology (2003), specializing in economic anthropology, from Southern Illinois University. He specializes in economic anthropology, and currently teaches at Eastern Michigan University. Among his research and theoretical interests is the organization of inequalities in production, distribution, and consumption within industrial food systems. He has published on the ways corporate actors manipulate markets to the disadvantage of small producers and how the manufactured biology of hogs as commodities structures contract relations of inequality.